SEXUALITY AND GENDER

IN THE CLASSICAL

WORLD

INTERPRETING ANCIENT HISTORY

The books in this series contain a mixture of the most important previously published articles in ancient history and primary source material upon which the secondary literature is based. The series encourages readers to reflect upon a variety of theories and methodologies, to question the arguments made by scholars, and to begin to master the primary evidence for themselves.

PUBLISHED

Sexuality and Gender in the Classical World
Edited by Laura K. McClure

IN PREPARATION

Roman Imperialism
Edited by Craige Champion

Ancient Greek Democracy
Edited by Eric Robinson

Sexuality and Gender in the Classical World

READINGS AND SOURCES

Edited by
Laura K. McClure

14020l

Blackwell
Publishers

Editorial Offices:
108 Cowley Road, Oxford OX4 1JF, UK
  Tel: +44 (0)1865 791100
350 Main Street, Malden, MA 02148-5018, USA
  Tel: +1 781 388 8250

First published 2002 by Blackwell Publishers Ltd

Library of Congress Cataloging-in-Publication Data

Sexuality and gender in the classical world: readings and sources / edited by Laura K. McClure.
     p. cm.—(Interpreting ancient history)
   Includes bibliographical references (p.   ) and index.
   ISBN 0–631–22588–9—ISBN 0–631–22589–7
     1. Women—History—To 500.   2. Sex role—Greece—History—To 1500.
   3. Sex role—Rome—History—To 1500.   4. Sex role in literature.   5. Classical
   literature—History and criticism.   I. McClure, Laura, 1959–II. Series.

   HQ1127 .S49 2002
   305.4′09—dc21   2002001348

A catalogue record for this title is available from the British Library.

Set in 10.5/12.5 Galliard
by Kolam Information Services Private Limited, Pondicherry, India
Printed and bound in Great Britain by TJ International, Cornwall

For further information on
Blackwell Publishers visit our website:
www.blackwellpublishers.co.uk

FOR RICHARD

οὐ μὲν γὰρ τοῦ γε κρεῖσσον καὶ ἄρειον,
ἢ ὅθ' ὁμοφρονέοντε νοήμασιν οἶκον ἔχητον
ἀνὴρ ἠδὲ γυνή.

Homer, *Odyssey* 6

Contents

Illustrations

Preface

This book is designed for undergraduate students of classical humanities and their teachers. It began as a xeroxed packet of readings assigned for my course on gender and sexuality in the classical world at the University of Wisconsin–Madison. It goes without saying that my students and teaching assistants over the years have played an integral role in shaping this volume. I am particularly grateful for their enthusiasm and helpful criticism. Their input has been indispensable to the process of revising and reformulating this collection for publication. In particular, I would like to thank Rob Nelsen and Alex Pappas, my teaching assistants during fall semester, 2000, for their invaluable suggestions from the trenches.

Conversations with colleagues in my home department and elsewhere provided me with stimulating perspectives on ancient gender studies. The anonymous referees for Blackwell gave thoughtful suggestions about the book's contents, as did Ellen Green, André Lardinois, Kirk Ormand, and Maria Wyke. Departmental colleagues Carole Newlands and Victoria Pagan deserve special mention for their excellent advice on the Roman materials; in addition to strengthening the selection of essays in volume, they provided me with many hours of enjoyable reading. I am especially grateful to Carole for generously agreeing to review the Latin translations during a hectic summer. On the Greek side, thanks are due to Patricia Rosenmeyer for her thoughtful and articulate responses to the Greek translations. Any errors or infelicities that may remain are solely my own.

Lastly, thanks are owed to Al Bertrand, the commissioning editor at Blackwell, for inviting me to edit this volume and for his enduring enthusiasm about the project. Thanks also to Angela Cohen, the editorial controller at Blackwell, for her help with the production process, and to Juanita Bullough for her expert copy-editing.

L. K. M. Madison, Wisconsin

Acknowledgments

The editor and publishers gratefully acknowledge the following for permission to reprint copyright material:

Anma Company for P. Joplin, "The Voice of the Shuttle Is Ours," *Standford Literature Review* 1.1 (1984): 25–53, © 1984 by Anma Libri and Company.

The Master and Fellows of Darwin College, Cambridge, for M. I. Finley, "The Silent Women of Rome," from *Discoveries and Controversies*, pp. 129–42, © 1968 by Chatto and Windus, a division of Random House.

Oxford University Press for S. Joshel, "The Body Female and the Body Politic: Livy's Lucretia and Verginia," from A. Richlin (ed.), *Pornography and Representation in Greece and Rome*, pp. 112–30, © 1992 by Oxford University Press, Inc.

Princeton University Press for A. Richlin, "Pliny's Brassiere," from J. Hallet and M. Skinner (eds.), *Roman Sexualities*, pp. 197–220, © 1997 by Princeton University Press.

Routledge, Inc., for J. J. Winkler, "Double Consciousness in Sappho's Lyrics," from *The Constraints of Desire*, pp. 162–87 and 233–5 (notes), © 1990 by Routledge; and for H. King, "Bound to Bleed: Artemis and Greek Women," from A. Cameron and A. Kuhrt (eds.), *Reflections of Women in Antiquity*, pp. 109–27, © 1983 by Routledge. Both used by permission of the Taylor and Francis Group.

The State University of New York Press for K. J. Dover, "Classical Greek Attitudes to Sexual Behaviour," from J. Peradotto and J. P. Sullivan (eds.), *Women in the Ancient World: The Arethusa Papers*, © 1984 by the State University of New York.

Texas Tech University Press for M. Wyke, "Mistress and Metaphor in Augustan Elegy," *Helios* 16 (1989): 25–47, © 1989 by Texas Tech University Press.

The University of California Press for F. Zeitlin, "Playing the Other: Theater, Theatricality, and the Feminine in Greek Drama," *Representations* 11 (1985): 65–94, © 1985 by The Regents of the University of California.

Unless specified otherwise, all translations are the editor's own.

Editor's Introduction

> In the beginning there were three sexes, not just the two sexes, the male and the female, as at present; there was a third kind that shared the characteristics of the other two, and whose name survives, even though the thing itself has disappeared. For at that time one was androgynous in form and shared its name with both the male and the female.
>
> Plato, *Symposium*

This humorous creation myth by the comic poet Aristophanes in Plato's *Symposium* illustrates how keenly issues of gender and sexuality preoccupied classical authors and their audiences. It also suggests, if only for the sake of amusement, how such issues could be detached from the fact of biological difference even in antiquity. This book invites undergraduate students to reflect on the lives of ancient women and the social and political forces that shaped them. It also attempts to provide a sense of the evolution of gender studies within the discipline of classics and the different methodologies and approaches used by classical scholars. Finally, the volume encourages readers to consider gender and sexuality in classical antiquity as culturally determined, socially constructed categories, thereby increasing awareness of the assumptions and processes at work in the formation of modern concepts of gender.

While many excellent anthologies address the subject of women in antiquity (see References and Further Reading at the end of this introduction), most do not deal at all with constructions of sexuality and gender. This volume seeks to address this problem by including essays not only about the status and representation of women but also those concerned with sexuality and masculinity in the Greco-Roman world. Moreover, all of the essays contained in this volume, or their authors, have played a formative role in shaping the field of ancient gender studies. As discussed more fully below, research on women in antiquity has undergone several transformations since its inception as a subfield of classical studies in the early 1970s. Foucault's *History of Sexuality*, especially the two volumes that deal with classical antiquity first translated into English in 1985 and 1986, has had a major impact on how classicists view the study of women, gender, masculinity, and sexuality in the ancient world. Many of the essays contained in this volume have been in some way influenced by Foucault; while some self-consciously position themselves *against* him, others show a debt to structuralist, psychoanalytic, feminist, and anthropological theories. They cover a range of genres, including lyric and epic poetry, tragedy, philosophical prose, history, medical writings, and inscriptions.

The Study of Women in Antiquity: A Brief History

Interest in the status of women in classical antiquity extends back to the nineteeth century, when "woman" as a conceptual category, isolated from the rest of history, became the focus of scientific and positivist inquiry (Blok 1987: 2–3); not coincidentally, most of the modern academic disciplines, including classics, were delineated during this same period. Nineteenth-century positivist scholars examined not only the images of women found in poetic texts, but also studied their social position in numerous juridical, philosophical, and historical tracts from antiquity. Such thinking informed one well-known nineteenth-century German treatise on ancient women: Johann Bachofen's *MutterRecht* ("Mother Right"; an English translation of this work is given in the References) articulated stages of cultural development in which women reacted to an original communal society in which individual family ties and property rights were not sufficiently delimited. Their rebellion, Bachofen proposed, led to a new stage which recognized the primary human bond as that between mother and child; in this new development, fertility and femininity became the predominant subjects of religion until supplanted by patriarchy (Blok 1987: 29). Bachofen's views reflected a second strand of nineteenth-century thought, romantic idealism. However, just like positivism, this approach also isolated women as a separate cultural category, an idea that influenced the scholarship on women in classical antiquity until the late 1960s.

The publication of a special edition of the classics journal *Arethusa* (vol. 6, no. 1, 1973) in the early 1970s stimulated the rapid growth of the study of women in antiquity in the United States (Peradotto and Sullivan 1984).[1] The subsequent publication of Sarah Pomeroy's *Goddesses, Whores, Wives and Slaves* in 1975 had a profound and lasting impact on the study of women in antiquity both in the scholarly community and in the classroom. Pomeroy wondered "what the women were doing while men were active in all the areas traditionally emphasized by classical scholars" (Pomeroy 1975: ix). In her view, one later contested by Blok (1987), major works of ancient history simply omitted "women" as a social category. Pomeroy thus set out to recover the lives of ancient women even in the face of the acute challenges posed by the primary sources, most of which were written by men for a male audience. She observed that literary sources such as plays and epic do not bear a close correspondence to everyday life, although they may shed light on how ancient cultures conceptualized women. Rather, other types of texts, history, biography, letters, and legal works, as well as visual materials and papyri, can more accurately illuminate the daily lives of ancient women, particularly the elite. The observation that noncanonical texts may provide significant information on women in classical world is further reflected in many of the essays and sources selected for this volume.

Following the publication of Pomeroy's book, several new collections of essays devoted to the subject of women in antiquity appeared in the United States. *Reflections of Women in Antiquity*, edited by Helene Foley and published in 1981, grew out of a special issue of the journal *Women's Studies* and represented the first collection of essays on women in the ancient world to be published in a major women's studies journal. Another early anthology brought a wide range of perspectives to the study of women in the ancient world: Averil Cameron and Amelie Kuhrt's *Images of Women in Antiquity* had a comparative purpose, providing material on women from many different ancient societies, including Greece, Rome, the Near East, and historical periods, ranging from the classical world to early Christian and Jewish thought and the medieval era. In combination with the special editions of *Arethusa*, these collections facilitated the teaching of university-level courses on women in antiquity in the United States, many of which adopted the outline provided by Pomeroy in the 1973 special edition of *Arethusa*. A National Endowment for the Humanities seminar on Women in Classical Antiquity, held at Hunter College in the summer of 1983, led to the creation of "Women in Classical Antiquity: Four Curricular Modules," a pamphlet widely circulated in the United

States that also became the basis for Fantham et al.'s textbook, *Women in the Classical World* (discussed below). Finally, the publication of Mary Lefkowitz and Maureen Fant's *Women's Life in Greece and Rome* in 1982 made available a wide range of ancient sources on women, some never before published in English.

Whereas Pomeroy, as the scholars before her, concentrated on reconstructing the real-life circumstances of women's lives, other scholars considered the conceptual structures that informed the literary and mythical representation of women, and how they intersected with social and political institutions. Most of this work focused on Greek rather than Roman culture, a trend that prevailed for the next two decades. Two essays from the early 1980s on women in Athenian drama, "Conception of Women in Athenian Drama" by Helene Foley (Foley 1981: 127–68) and "Playing the Other: Theater, Theatricality, and the Feminine in Greek Drama" by Froma Zeitlin, an essay included in this volume (chapter 4), shifted the focus away from recovering women's historical reality to understanding the conceptual framework behind their literary and mythic representation and its relation to the social and ideological context of democratic Athens.

Several important literary and cultural theories brought about this shift of emphasis in classical studies. Psychoanalytic theory first made an impact on classical studies in the late 1960s. Scholars influenced by psychoanalytic thought have attempted to interpret classical mythology and literature as reflecting the psychopathology of ancient cultures. Philip Slater, in his *The Glory of Hera*, first published in 1968, considers the psychological origins of gender conflict in Greek mythology through an exploration of the Heracles myth. He claims that male anxieties in classical Athenians can be traced to the mother–son relationship: the Athenian mother, confined to the home and envious of male privilege and power, vented her negative feelings on her male children, inciting them to achieve and then punishing their successes. This ambivalence resulted in overconfident and yet insecure men who both feared and hated women and who sought to compensate for their inadequacies by a tireless quest for social status. In recent years, feminist classical scholars have taken issue with strict Freudian interpretations such as Slater's, arguing that the nineteenth-century model of nuclear family used by Freud bears little resemblance to ancient family structures. Although orthodox Freudian interpretations, especially those involving outmoded concepts such as penis envy, have fallen by the wayside, elements of psychoanalytic and post-psychoanalytic theory can still be found in feminist classical scholarship.

In contrast to the psychoanalytic approach, structuralist theory has had a more enduring legacy in the field of classics. Structuralism holds that the structure of language itself produces reality; linguistic structures, not individuals, produce and determine meaning, since people can only think by means of words. Thus individuals do not make meaning, as in the romantic humanist model, rather meaning is culturally determined. A structuralist approach, therefore, examines the symbolic structures that inform a particular culture, its mental universe or imaginary, and has a synchronic rather than diachronic focus. Jean-Pierre Vernant's *Myth and Thought among the Greeks* (published in French in 1966 and translated into English in 1983) and Pierre Vidal-Naquet's *The Black Hunter* (published in French in 1981 and translated into English in 1986) inspired a generation of classical scholars to consider ancient Greek literature and culture from this new perspective. These authors combined a structuralist viewpoint with a psychoanalytic approach as they attempted to understand not only the cognitive but also the psychological systems underlying Greek myths. Another influential work, Claude Calame's *Choruses of Young Women in Ancient Greece* (originally published in French in 1977 and translated into English in 1997), applied a structuralist approach to the study of adolescent girls in ancient Greece. Examining the "maiden songs" of the Spartan archaic poet Alcman, Calame investigated the importance of ritual choral performance for the socialization of girls in archaic Greek society.

Some scholars, especially historians of women in antiquity, have argued that the structuralist approach detaches women as subjects from their historical contexts in favor of examining "universal" thought structures and categories that presumably remain unchanged through time (Blok 1987: 40–1). Other scholars have taken issue with the structuralist tendency to rely on binary oppositions for understanding the ancient imaginary; such oppositions do not accurately reflect the actual contradictions between ideology and social practice characteristic of any society, ancient or modern (D. Cohen 1991).

The large amount of research done on women in antiquity since the 1970s has influenced how classical studies is taught in the United States and made possible the creation of the first comprehensive textbook on the subject, Fanthan et al.'s *Women in the Classical World* (1994). The book combines diachronic and synchronic approaches, collecting the most important primary sources on ancient women and placing them in their social and historical context. It shows how the study of women in antiquity has evolved from a fringe movement in the 1970s to its position within the academy, as a subject of scholarly inquiry and pedagogy.

The Study of Sexuality in the Classical World

A separate but related strand of study focuses on sexuality in classical
antiquity. In the early nineteenth century, scholars such as Friedrich-Karl
Forberg (1770–1848) compiled information about sexual behavior in the
classical world. Forberg edited a collection of obscene epigrams that
included an appendix consisting of original source material on the sexual
practices of the ancient Greeks and Romans; he catalogued, among other
things, over 90 sexual positions (Halperin, Winkler, and Zeitlin 1990:
8–9)! Forberg, however, did not discuss homosexuality, a central feature
of ancient sexual practice. Not until Paul Brandt published, under the
pseudonym Hans Licht, *Sexual Life in Ancient Greece* in 1932, did the
subjects of pederasty and male homoeroticism receive full treatment from a
classical scholar. None of these early studies of ancient sexuality fully
considered the extensive visual sources until Otto Brendel's full-length
study of erotic art in 1970. Two other works critical for the study of
sexuality in the ancient world quickly followed: Jeffrey Henderson's *Maculate Muse* (1975) provided a glossary of obscene language in Attic Old
Comedy and discussed its significance, thereby bringing to scholarly attention a wealth of material that reflected ancient views of male and female
sexuality. In 1978, Kenneth Dover published *Greek Homosexuality*, a book
that examined male homoerotic practices in art and literature, providing
valuable insights into an institution central to ancient Greek male life. Two
specifically feminist analyses of male sexuality and its consequences for
women appeared in the mid-1980s: Amy Richlin's *The Garden of Priapus*,
a study of male sexual aggression in Roman humor, and Eva Keuls's *The
Reign of the Phallus*, which examined male sexuality and female objectifi-
cation in Athenian literature.

The study of ancient sexuality and gender was powerfully affected, and
perhaps irrevocably altered, by Michel Foucault's three-volume *History of
Sexuality*. Influenced in part by Dover's research on homosexuality in
ancient Greece, the second two volumes, *The Use of Pleasure* and *The
Care of the Self*, examine noncanonical classical texts to understand not
only ancient sexual practices, but how these practices negotiated power
and constructed self-identity. Foucault distinguished "gender" as a socially constructed category separate from biological sex; in his view, a
culture constructs or produces gender difference through its various
social discourses – from the way people dress to the laws that govern
them – in order to maintain existing power structures. Gender therefore

must be understood not as an absolute category based on biological sex, but as the result of prevailing social norms and practices.

The English translation of Foucault's work in the mid-1980s inspired a number of works concerned with ancient sexuality, including Halperin's *One Hundred Years of Homosexuality*, Winkler's *The Constraints of Desire*, and the path-breaking collection of essays, *Before Sexuality*, edited by Halperin, Winkler, and Zeitlin. Published in 1990, all of these books combined Foucault's theories with varying amounts of French structuralism. In the same year, David Konstan and Martha Nussbaum edited a special issue of the women's studies journal *Differences*, entitled *Sexuality in Greek and Roman Society*.

Although Foucault's work resulted in an explosion of writings by classical scholars, he received a mixed reception from feminist scholars. Amy Richlin, whose essay appears as Chapter 8 in this volume, argues that Foucauldian analysis, and its subsequent incarnations, new historicism and cultural studies, erases women both as subjects and scholars (Richlin 1991). Foxhall, on the other hand, argues that Foucault's general analysis of power and its transmission through discursive practices provides an invaluable tool to feminist classicists and nonclassicists alike (Foxhall 1994; see also D. Cohen 1992; Skinner 1996). Moreover, classicists in general have argued that Foucault considers only those sources that suit his argument, ignoring many ancient discursive fields, such as that of the novel and other comic genres (Larmour, Miller, and Platter 1998: 25–6).

In addition to the awareness of gender and sexuality as socially constructed categories, another direct contribution of Foucault's work has been the recent scholarly fascination with the ancient body, a topic that has resulted in several anthologies (Wyke 1998; Porter 1999). These collections have expanded the already large number of books about women's bodies in ancient medical writings, including those of Aline Rouselle (1988), Lesley Dean-Jones (1994), Helen King (1998) and the numerous articles by Ann Ellis Hanson, such as "The Medical Writer's Woman" (Halperin, Winkler, and Zeitlin 1990: 309–37). Finally, some other recent anthologies address often overlooked aspects of ancient sexuality: influenced by the work of Susanne Kappeler, the essays in *Pornography and Representation in Greece and Rome* (1992), edited by Amy Richlin, apply feminist theory to Greek and Roman texts explicitly concerned with sexuality. Observing that classical scholarship, influenced by Foucault, has focused almost exclusively on Greek sexuality, editors Judy Hallett and Marilyn Skinner, in their volume *Roman Sexualities* (1997), turn their gaze to Rome.

Essays in this Volume

The essays in this volume represent a range of perspectives on women, gender, and sexuality in the ancient world. They are accessible to a general audience while at the same time challenging readers to confront problems of evidence and interpretation, new theories and methodologies, as well as their own contemporary assumptions about gender and sexuality. They also address a range of different literary genres, from ancient medical writings and inscriptions to more canonical works such as epic, lyric, elegiac, and dramatic poetry. From a pedagogical standpoint, all of the essays may be paired with a diverse array of primary sources; for example, Helen King's essay, "Bound to Bleed," responds not only to ancient Greek medical writings but also to literary accounts of Artemis such as those found in Athenian drama. Moreover, the essays represent a broad spectrum of scholarly perspectives, and somewhat trace the debates and currents of the field from the late 1960s to the late 1990s. Part I (Greece) contains four essays on Greek literature and society and Part II (Rome) includes four essays on Latin literature; Part III (Classical Tradition) concludes the volume with a consideration of the Procne and Philomela myth in both Greek and Roman sources and its relevance for feminist scholars.

An attempt has been made to include perspectives not only on ancient women, but also on men and masculinity in classical antiquity. Many of the essays that deal explicitly with women and their representation also illuminate the construction of male subjectivity. Some consider similar, issues but from different angles or periods, such as King's essay on women in Hippocrates and Richlin's on Pliny. The essays by Zeitlin and Dover both aim at elucidating a larger issue, the function of gender categories in classical Athens, although they do so by exploring the different genres of drama and oratory. Winkler and Richlin, while examining very different types of sources, both deploy a similar approach drawn from women's history that views women as agents capable of resisting male systems of control rather than victims. Both Joshel and Wyke relate the literary representation of women in Roman texts to their political environment. Unfortunately, space restrictions played a much larger role than I would have liked in formulating this volume. The focus has been restricted to literary texts, even though numerous books and articles on gender, sexuality, and the visual arts have appeared in recent years (see Kampen 1996; Stewart 1997; Koloski-Ostrow and Lyons 1997; B. Cohen 2000). These constraints also compelled me to omit many stimulating and seminal essays, some of which are included in the References and Further Reading at the end of this introduction.

To summarize the contents of the volume, it opens with an influential essay by Dover that lays out Athenian attitudes toward sexuality and serves as a good introduction to basic aspects of Athenian sexual practices and social organization. Dover discusses the seclusion and protection of reputable women, prohibitions against adultery and sexual relations outside marriage, including prostitution and homosexuality, the value placed on virginity for both males and females, and the relation of homoerotic behavior to political life and social status. Because this essay focuses mostly on fourth-century prose, including oratory and philosophy, it has been paired with an excerpt from Aristophanes' speech in Plato's *Symposium* about the origins of the two sexes.

Winkler's reading of Sappho situates a female voice in a discursive universe created and transmitted by men. He shows how Sappho's poetry appropriates traditional heroic and masculine vocabulary to articulate a private, feminine world. But in contrast to the univocal narrative of the Homeric tradition, these poems reflect multiple perspectives and shifting identifications. This "many-mindedness," Winkler suggests, reflects the difficulties encountered by women in a male-dominated culture in which they are forced to become bilingual, proficient both in the culture of the linguistic minority and in the majority language of men. This essay represents one approach to women's history that views women as agents rather than as victims, empowered by their own subculture and thus capable of resisting male control. Translations of two of Sappho's poems accompany this piece, and two passages from Homer's *Iliad* and *Odyssey* to which they are compared.

King explores the meaning of female virginity, a topic also briefly addressed by Dover, in ancient Greek thought and myth. She begins with the premise that the concept of woman for the Greeks always involved ambiguity. Focusing on a short medical treatise entitled *Peri Parthenión* (On Unmarried Girls), King draws on structuralist theory to analyze the role of the goddess Artemis in the female life cycle, especially menstruation. The treatise elucidates the importance of menstruation and pregnancy for female health: the inability to menstruate, in Hippocrates' view, induces disease and even madness. King then explores the contradictory functions of Artemis in female life: she does not bleed but governs bleeding transitions; she both binds, causing suffocation and strangulation, and releases, thereby facilitating childbirth. These two contrary motions provide a conceptual framework for understanding the meanings of female transitions in ancient Greek culture. A translation of the Hippocratic treatise and a passage from Euripides' *Hippolytus* concerning virginity conclude the chapter.

While King focuses primarily on fifth-century medical writing, Zeitlin provides another perspective on the male representation of women in a different but contemporary literary genre, that of Athenian tragedy. Influenced by social anthropology and structuralist and psychoanalytic theory, Zeitlin analyzes how tragedy constructs and deconstructs categories of masculine and feminine. She argues for tragedy as a feminizing genre that functions as an "initiatory process" with the ultimate purpose of strengthening male civic identity. Athenian tragedy thus exploits the female as an Other through which the male spectator comes to understand himself. In the theater of Dionysus, female characters serve as a vehicle for exploring the "male project of selfhood." Passages that illustrate some of Zeitlin's discussion follow the essay, including Deianira's speech announcing her intention to restore her husband's love by means of magic and Heracles' final condemnation of her in Sophocles' *Women of Trachis*, and the metatheatrical scene of cross-dressing in Euripides' *Bacchae*.

Like the Dover essay in Part I, Finley's piece offers a general introduction to the study of women – although not sexual behaviour – in Roman society. The essay emphasizes the problems facing social historians who attempt to study Roman women, since they appear only in male authors predisposed to the "salacious and scandalous." Finley traces the problem to the Roman practice of denying women social subjectivity: they lacked individual names in the proper sense and their virtues – beauty, evenness of temperament, chastity, and childbearing – served to reinforce the male-governed *familia*. Only religion provided an outlet for Roman women's energies and talents. The essay has been paired with a range of Roman funerary inscriptions for departed wives and daughters that highlight the traditional female virtues and even praise some non-traditional ones.

Observing that Livy's history of Rome is full of raped, dead, or absent women, such as Tarpeia and the Sabines, Joshel examines the role played by violence against women in Roman myths of foundation. She focuses on Lucretia, a virtuous wife raped by an arrogant king, who commits suicide to protect her reputation and to provide a public lesson about female chastity, and on Verginia, a daughter killed by her father to defend her from the threat of rape. Joshel seeks to understand why each of these stories precedes or catalyzes a revolutionary moment in the political prehistory of Rome. Influenced by Theweleit's *Male Fantasies* (see *Works Cited* in Chapter 7), an account of masculinist ideology in Nazi Germany, she juxtaposes images of violence against women in Rome, Nazi Germany, and the contemporary United States to interrogate representations of gender in the formation and destruction of empires. The women in these texts therefore comment not only on the status of women in Roman society, but also on the Roman construction of manhood. A translation of Livy's account of Lucretia from *The Founding of Rome* accompanies the essay.

Wyke addresses more fully the question of the relation between literary representation and social reality raised earlier by Finley in connection with Roman women. Her essay also fruitfully engages with the issue of compromised masculinity raised by Zeitlin, albeit from the angle of the mistress, or *puella domina*, of Latin love elegy. Focusing on the figure of Cynthia in Propertius, Wyke attempts to "read through" the poems to a living woman as a means of elucidating the difficulties of relating women in texts to women in society. She argues that Cynthia's representation is inextricably bound to issues of poetic practice: although realistically drawn, Cynthia as mistress is a poetic fiction that conforms to the requirements of the elegiac genre, related not to the life of the poet, but to the "grammar" of his poetry. At the same time, Wyke shows how this literary construction engages with contemporary political discourses on women in the early Empire. The essay is paired with translations of Propertius 1.8a-b and 2.5 as well as a passage from Cicero's *Pro Caelio* on another notorious mistress, Clodia, the real-life lover of the poet Catullus.

Richlin's analysis of Pliny the Elder's treatise on the curative and harmful powers of the products of the female body in his encyclopedic *Natural History*, especially breast milk and menstrual fluid, concludes the Roman section. This essay examines some rather obscure material, "a little-known wilderness" that could be characterized as folk medicine, to understand Roman ideas about female sexuality; in doing so, it engages directly with work on women in the Greek medical writers, such as that of King. Pliny's text considers the mundane aspects of female life, including menstruation, fertility, contraception, abortion, aphrodisiacs, pregnancy, childbirth, and infant care, topics of little interest to the Roman poets. She shows how Pliny's discussion attributes a dangerous power to the female body and its reproductive capacity that reveals how deeply ambivalent the Romans felt about women. Richlin argues that Pliny can serve as starting point for two different approaches to women's history, one that views women as the victims of male oppression, the other that sees them as agents able to subvert the male system. In the former view, Pliny reinforces ideas about Roman society as an oppressive patriarchy; in the latter, he shows the fundamental power this society attributed to women and their bodies. The essay concludes with a translation of the relevant passage from Pliny's *Natural History*.

In the final essay, Joplin examines the myth of Philomela, a woman raped and then brutally silenced by her sister's husband, and its meanings for feminist scholars. The tragic poet Sophocles coined the phrase, "the voice of the shuttle," to refer to the tapestry that Philomela wove to tell her story. Joplin critiques the appropriation of this phrase by a male scholar to celebrate male literary creation rather than "the violated woman's emergence from silence." By beginning with this critique, Joplin shows the reader how traditional critics reinforce the cultural assumptions of the texts they interpret. Approaching Ovid's version of the myth from a structuralist perspective, she demonstrates how such classical myths, even violent ones, may empower feminist critics. For example, the Philomela myth posits woman as an agent who shapes her own destiny, as an artist and creator, while the successful weaving stratagem shows the ultimate failure of male domination. Readings that resist traditional interpretations may therefore rescue classical sources for feminist scholars and writers. The essay concludes with a selection from Ovid's *Metamorphoses* that tells the story of Tereus, Procne, and Philomela.

NOTE

1   According to Hawley and Levick 1995: 13, the first international conference on women in the ancient world was not held in the UK until 1993.

REFERENCES AND FURTHER READING

Archer, L., Fischler, S., and M. Wyke (eds.). 1994. *Women in Ancient Societies: "An Illusion in the Night."* New York and London.
Bachofen, J. J. 1967. *Myth, Religion, and Mother Right.* Tr. R. Manheim. Princeton, NJ.
Blok, J. 1987. "Sexual Asymmetry: A Historiographical Essay." In J. Blok and P. Mason (eds.), *Sexual Asymmetry: Studies in Ancient Society*, 1–57. Amsterdam.
Brendel, O. 1970. "The Scope and Temperament of Erotic Art in the Graeco-Roman World." In T. Bowie et al. (eds.), *Studies in Erotic Art*, 3–107. New York.
Calame, C. 1997. *Choruses of Young Women in Ancient Greece: Their Morphology, Religious Role and Sexual Functions.* Lanham, MD.
Cameron, A. and A. Kuhrt (eds.). 1993. *Images of Women in Antiquity.* 2nd ed. Detroit, MI.

Clark, G. 1993. *Women in Late Antiquity: Pagan and Christian Lifestyles.* Oxford.

Cohen, B. 2000. *Not the Classical Ideal: Athens and the Construction of the Other in Greek Art.* Leiden.

Cohen, D. 1991. *Law, Sexuality, and Society: The Enforcement of Morals in Classical Athens.* Cambridge.

——. 1992. "Review Article: Sex, Gender and Sexuality in Ancient Greece." *Classical Philology* 87: 145–67.

—— and R. Saller. 1994. "Foucault on Sexuality in Greco-Roman Antiquity." In J. Goldstein (ed.), *Foucault and the Writing of History,* 35–59. Oxford.

Dean-Jones, L. 1994. *Women's Bodies in Classical Greek Science.* Oxford.

Dover, K. J. 1989. *Greek Homosexuality: Updated and with a New Postscript.* Cambridge, MA.

Fantham, E. 1986. "Women in Antiquity: A Selective (and Subjective) Survey 1979–84." *Echos du Monde Classique/Classical Views* 30, n. s. 51: 1–24.

——, Foley, H., Kampen, N., Pomeroy, S., and H. Shapiro (eds). 1994. *Women in the Classical World.* New York.

Foley, H. P. (ed.). 1981. *Reflections of Women in Antiquity.* New York, London, and Paris.

——. 1981. "Conception of Women in Athenian Drama." In H. P. Foley (ed.), *Reflections of Women in Antiquity,* 127–68. New York, London, and Paris.

Foucault, M. 1988. *The Use of Pleasure: The History of Sexuality Vol. 2.* Trans. R. Hurley. New York.

——. 1988. *The Care of the Self: The History of Sexuality Vol. 3.* Trans. R. Hurley. New York.

Foxhall, L. 1994. "Pandora Unbound: A Feminist Critique of Foucault's *History of Sexuality.*" In A. Cornwall and N. Lindisfarne, *Dislocating Masculinity: Comparative Ethnographies,* 133–46. New York and London.

Garrison, D. 2000. *Sexual Culture in Ancient Greece.* Norman, OK.

Hallett, J. and M. Skinner (eds.). 1997. *Roman Sexualities.* Princeton, NJ.

Halperin, D. 1990. *One Hundred Years of Homosexuality.* New York and London.

——, Winkler, J. J., and F. Zeitlin (eds.), 1990. *Before Sexuality: The Construction of Erotic Experience in the Ancient Greek World.* Princeton, NJ.

Hanson, A. E. 1990. "The Medical Writer's Woman. In D. Halperin, J. J. Winkler, and F. Zeitlin (eds.), *Before Sexuality: The Construction of Erotic Experience in the Ancient Greek World,* 309–38. Princeton, NJ.

Hawley, R. and B. Levick (eds.). 1995. *Women in Antiquity: New Assessments.* New York and London.

Henderson, Jeffrey. [1975] 1991. *The Maculate Muse: Obscene Language in Attic Comedy.* 2nd ed. Oxford.

Henderson, John. 1989. "Satire Writes Woman: Gendersong." *Proceedings of the Cambridge Philological Society* 215: 50–80.

Kampen, N. 1996. *Sexuality in Ancient Art.* Cambridge.

Kappeler, S. 1986. *The Pornography of Representation*. Minneapolis, MN and Cambridge.

Keuls, E. 1985. *The Reign of the Phallus*. New York.

King, H. 1998. *Hippocrates' Woman*. New York and London.

Koloski-Ostrow, A. and C. Lyons (eds.). 1997. *Naked Truths: Women, Sexuality, and Gender in Classical Art and Archaeology*. New York and London.

Konstan, D. and M. Nussbaum (eds.). 1990. *Sexuality in Greek and Roman Society*. Special issue of *Differences* 2.1.

Larmour, D., Miller, P. A., and C. Platter (eds.). 1998. *Rethinking Sexuality: Foucault and Classical Antiquity*. Princeton, NJ.

Lefkowitz, M. and M. B. Fant (eds.). 1992. *Women's Life in Greece and Rome: A Source Book in Translation*. 2nd ed. Baltimore, MD.

Licht, H. 1932. *Sexual Life in Ancient Greece*. New York.

McAuslan, I. and P. Walcot (eds.). 1996. *Women in Antiquity*. Oxford.

Peradotto, J. and J. P. Sullivan (eds.). 1984. *Women in the Ancient World: The Arethusa Papers*. Buffalo, NY.

Pomeroy, S. 1975. *Goddesses, Whores, Wives and Slaves*. New York.

——. 1991. "The Study of Women in Antiquity: Past, Present, and Future." *American Journal of Philology* 112: 263–8.

——. 1991. *Women's History and Ancient History*. Chapel Hill, NC.

Porter, J. (ed.). 1999. *Constructions of the Classical Body*. Ann Arbor, MI.

Rabinowitz, N. and A. Richlin (eds.). 1993. *Feminist Theory and the Classics*. New York and London.

Richlin, A. 1983. *The Garden of Priapus: Sexuality and Aggression in Roman Humor*. New Haven , CT and Oxford.

——. 1991. "Zeus and Metis: Foucault, Feminism, Classics." *Helios* 18: 160–79.

——. (ed.). 1992. *Pornography and Representation in Greece and Rome*. New York and Oxford.

Rousselle, A. 1988. *Porneia: On Desire and the Body in Antiquity*. Trans. F. Pheasant. Oxford.

Rowlandson, J. 1998. *Women and Society in Greek and Roman Egypt*. Cambridge.

Scott, J. 1986. "Gender: A Useful Category of Historical Analysis." *American History Review* 91: 1053–75.

Skinner, M. (ed.). 1986. *Rescuing Creusa: New Methodological Approaches to Women in Antiquity*. Special Issue of *Helios* 13.2. Lubbock, TX.

——. 1987. "Classical Studies, Patriarchy and Feminism: The View from 1986." *Women's International Studies Forum* 10.2: 181–6.

——. 1993. "*Ego Mulier*: The Construction of Male Sexuality in Catullus." *Helios* 20: 107–30.

——. 1996. "Zeus and Leda: The Sexuality Wars in Contemporary Classical Scholarship." *Thamyris* 3: 103–23.

Slater, P. 1992. *The Glory of Hera: Greek Mythology and the Greek Family*. Princeton, NJ.

Stewart, A. 1997. *Art, Desire and the Body in Ancient Greece*. Cambridge.

Vernant, J. -P. 1983. *Myth and Thought among the Greeks.* Boston and London.

Vidal-Naquet, P. 1986. *The Black Hunter: Forms of Thought and Forms of Society in the Greek World.* Trans. A. Szegedy-Maszak. Baltimore, MD.

Winkler, J. 1990. *The Constraints of Desire: The Anthropology of Sex and Gender in Ancient Greece.* New York and London.

Wyke, M. (ed.). 1998. *Parchments of Gender: Deciphering the Body in Antiquity.* Oxford.

PART I
GREECE

Figure 1 *Zeus and Ganymede.* Attic red figure kylix, c.455 BCE. Museo Archeologico Nazionale, Ferrara, 9351 Zeus, indicated by the thunderbolt at left, abducts the beautiful youth, Ganymede. As a lover's gift, the cock at right signifies an amorous context. Zeus later made Ganymede immortal and appointed him cup-bearer of the gods.

1
CLASSICAL GREEK
ATTITUDES TO SEXUAL
BEHAVIOUR

K. J. Dover

1. Words and Assumptions

The Greeks regarded sexual enjoyment as the area of life in which the goddess Aphrodite was interested, as Ares was interested in war and other deities in other activities. Sexual intercourse was *aphrodisia*, 'the things of Aphrodite.' Sexual desire could be denoted by general words for 'desire,' but the obsessive desire for a particular person was *eros*, 'love' in the sense which it has in our expressions 'be in love with . . .' (*eran*) and 'fall in love with . . .' (*erasthenai*). Eros, like all powerful emotional forces, but more consistently than most, was personified and deified; treated by some early poets as a cosmic force older than Aphrodite, occasionally (though not often) alleged to be her son, he was most commonly thought of as her minister or agent, to the extent that she could, when she wished (as in Euripides' *Hippolytus*), cause X to fall in love with Y.

At some time in the latter part of the fifth century Prodicus defined eros as 'desire doubled'; eros doubled, he said, was madness.[1] Both philosophical and unphilosophical Greeks treated sexual desire as a response to the stimulus of visual beauty, which is reasonable enough; rather more surprisingly, they also treated eros as a strong response to great visual beauty, a response which may be intensified by admirable or lovable qualities in the desired person but is not in the first instance evoked by those qualities. Plato finds it philosophically necessary in *Phaedrus* and *Symposium* to treat eros as a response to beauty; but even

Plato shows his awareness elsewhere (*Rep.* 474bE) that superior visual stimuli from Z do not necessarily make X fall out of love with Y.[2]

Eros generates *philia*, 'love'; the same word can denote milder degrees of affection, just as 'my *philoi*' can mean my friends or my inner-most family circle, according to context. For the important question 'Do you love me?' the verb used is *philein*, whether the question is put by a youth to a girl as their kissing becomes more passionate[3] or by a father to his son as an anxious preliminary to a test of filial obedience.[4]

2.   Inhibition

Our own culture has its myths about the remote past, and one myth that dies hard is that the 'invention' of sexual guilt, shame and fear by the Christians destroyed a golden age of free, fearless, pagan sexuality. That most pagans were in many ways less inhibited than most Christians is undeniable. Not only had they a goddess specially concerned with sexual pleasure; their other deities were portrayed in legend as enjoying fornication, adultery and sodomy. A pillar surmounted by the head of Hermes and adorned with an erect penis stood at every Athenian front-door; great models of the erect penis were borne in procession at festivals of Dionysus, and it too was personified as the tirelessly lascivious Phales.[5] The vase-painters often depicted sexual intercourse, sometimes masturbation (male or female) and fellatio, and in respect of any kind of sexual behaviour Aristophanic comedy appears to have had total license of word and act. A century ago there was a tendency to explain Aristophanic obscenity by positing a kind of dispensation for festive occasions which were once fertility-rituals, but this has no relevance to the vase-painters, nor, indeed, to the iambic poets of the archaic period, Archilochus and Hipponax, in whom no vestige of inhibition is apparent.

There is, however, another side of the coin. Sexual intercourse was not permitted in the temples or sanctuaries of deities (not even of deities whose sexual enthusiasm was conspicuous in mythology), and regulations prescribing chastity or formal purification after intercourse played a part in many Greek cults. Homeric epic, for all its unquestioning acceptance of fornication as one of the good things of life, is circumspect in vocabulary, and more than once denotes the male genitals by *aidos*, 'shame,' 'disgrace.' Serious poetry in the early classical poetry was often direct in what it said, but preserved a certain level of dignity in the ways of saying it; even when Pindar states the parentage of Castor in terms of Tyndareus' ejaculation into Leda, his style has the highest poetic credentials.[6] Poets (notably

Homer) sometimes describe interesting and agreeable activities – cooking, mixing wine, stabbing an enemy through a chink in his armour – in meticulous detail, but nowhere is there a comparable description of the mechanisms of sexual activity. Prose literature, even on medical subjects, is euphemistic ('be with . . . ' is a common way of saying 'have sexual intercourse with . . . '), and can degenerate into coyness, as when 'we all know what' is substituted for 'the genitals' in a list of the bodily organs which convey pleasurable sensations.[7] The fourth-century orators show some skill in insinuating allegations of sexual misconduct and simultaneously suggesting that both the speaker's sense of propriety and the jury's would be outraged by a plain statement of the facts; when a coarse word is unavoidable, they make a show of reluctance to utter it.[8] By the late fourth century, the obscene words which had been so lavishly used by Aristophanes and his contemporaries had been almost entirely excluded from comedy; Aristotle, commenting on this, calls the old style *aiskhrologia*, 'speaking what is shameful (disgraceful, ugly).'[9]

Linguistic inhibition, then, was observably strengthened in the course of the classical period; and at least in some art-forms, inhibition extended also to content. These are data which do not fit the popular concept of a guilt-free or shame-free sexual morality, and require explanation. Why so many human cultures use derogatory words as synonyms of 'sexual' and reproach sexual prowess while praising prowess in (e.g.) swimming and riding, is a question which would take us to a remote level of speculation. Why the Greeks did so is a question which can at least be related intelligibly to the structure of Greek society and to Greek moral schemata which have no special bearing on sex.

3.   Segregation and Adultery

As far as was practicable (cf. § 7), Greek girls were segregated from boys and brought up at home in ignorance of the world outside the home; one speaker in court seeks to impress the jury with the respectability of his family by saying that his sister and nieces are 'so well brought up that they are embarrassed in the presence even of a man who is a member of the family.'[10] Married young, perhaps at fourteen[11] (and perhaps to a man twenty years or more her senior), a girl exchanged confinement in her father's house for confinement in her husband's. When he was invited out, his children might be invited with him, but not his wife;[12] and when he had friends in, she did not join the company. Shopping seems to have been a man's job, to judge from references in comedy,[13] and slaves could be sent on other errands outside the house. Upholders of the proprieties pronounced the front door to be the boundaries of a good woman's territory.[14]

Consider now the situation of an adolescent boy growing up in such a society. Every obstacle is put in the way of his speaking to the girl next door; it may not be easy for him even to get a glimpse of her. Festivals, sacrifices and funerals, for which women and girls did come out in public, provided the occasion for seeing and being seen. They could hardly afford more than that, for there were too many people about, but from such an occasion (both in real life and in fiction) an intrigue could be set on foot, with a female slave of respectable age as the indispensable go-between.[15]

In a society which practices segregation of the sexes, it is likely that boys and girls should devote a good deal of time and ingenuity to defeating society, and many slaves may have co-operated with enthusiasm. But Greek laws were not lenient towards adultery, and *moikheia*, for which we have no suitable translation except 'adultery,' denoted not only the seduction of another man's wife, but also the seduction of his widowed mother, unmarried daughter, sister, niece, or any other woman whose legal guardian he was.[16] The adulterer could be prosecuted by the offended father, husband or guardian; alternatively, if caught in the act, he could be killed, maltreated, or imprisoned by force until he purchased his freedom by paying heavy compensation. A certain tendency to regard women as irresponsible and ever ready to yield to sexual temptation (see § 5) relieved a cuckolded husband of a sense of shame or inadequacy and made him willing to seek the co-operation of his friends in apprehending an adulterer,[17] just as he would seek their co-operation to defend himself against fraud, encroachment, breach of contract, or any other threat to his property. The adulterer was open to reproach in the same way, and to the same extent, as any other violator of the laws protecting the individual citizen against arbitrary treatment by other citizens. To seduce a woman of citizen status was more culpable than to rape her, not only because rape was presumed to be unpremeditated but because seduction involved the capture of her affection and loyalty;[18] it was the degree of offense against the man to whom she belonged, not her own feelings, which mattered.

It naturally follows from the state of the law and from the attitudes and values implied by segregation that an adolescent boy who showed an exceptional enthusiasm for the opposite sex could be regarded as a potential adulterer and his propensity discouraged just as one would discourage theft, lies and trickery, while an adolescent boy who blushed at the mere idea of proximity to a woman was praised as *sophron*, 'right-minded,' i.e. unlikely to do anything without reflecting first whether it might incur punishment, disapproval, dishonour or other undesirable consequences.

4.   Commercial Sex

Greek society was a slave-owning society, and a female slave was not in a position to refuse the sexual demands of her owner or of anyone else to whom he granted the temporary use of her. Large cities, notably Athens, also had a big population of resident aliens, and these included women who made a living as prostitutes, on short-term relations with a succession of clients, or as *hetairai*, who endeavoured to establish long-term relations with wealthy and agreeable men. Both aliens and citizens could own brothels and stock them with slave-prostitutes. Slave-girls and alien girls who took part in men's parties as dancers or musicians could also be mauled and importuned in a manner which might cost a man his life if he attempted it with a woman of citizen status. In an instructive scene at the close of Aristophanes' *Thesmophoriazusae* (1160–1231) Euripides, disguised as an old woman, distracts the attention of a policeman with the help of a pretty dancing-girl; for a drachma, the policeman is allowed to have intercourse with the girl, but it is the 'old woman,' not the girl, who strikes the bargain, exactly as if it were a matter of paying rent for use of an inanimate object.

It was therefore easy enough to purchase sexual satisfaction, and the richer a man was the better provision he could make for himself. But money spent on sex was money not spent on other things, and there seems to have been substantial agreement on what were proper or improper items of expenditure. Throughout the work of the Attic orators, who offer us by far the best evidence on the moral standards which it was prudent to uphold in addressing large juries composed of ordinary citizens, it is regarded as virtuous to impoverish oneself by gifts and loans to friends in misfortune (for their daughters' dowries, their fathers' funerals, and the like), by ransoming Athenian citizens taken prisoner in war, and by paying out more than the required minimum in the performance of public duties (the upkeep of a warship, for example, or the dressing and training of a chorus at a festival). This kind of expenditure was boasted about and treated as a claim on the gratitude of the community.[19] On the other hand, to 'devour an inheritance' by expenditure on one's own consumption was treated as disgraceful.[20] Hence gluttony, drunkenness and purchased sexual relations were classified together as 'shameful pleasures'; Demosthenes[21] castigates one of his fellow-ambassadors for 'going round buying prostitutes and fish' with the money he had corruptly received. When a young man fell in love, he might well fall in love with a hetaira or a slave, since his chances of falling in love with a girl of citizen status were so restricted, and to secure the object of his love he would need to purchase or ransom her. A close association between eros and extravagance therefore tends to be assumed, especially in comedy; a character in Menander[22] says, 'No one is so parsimonious as not to make some sacrifice of his property to Eros.' More than three centuries earlier, Archilochus[23] put the matter in characteristically violent form when he spoke of wealth accumulated by long labour 'pouring down into a whore's guts.' A fourth-century litigant[24] venomously asserts that his adversary, whose tastes were predominantly homosexual, has 'buggered away all his estate.'

We have here another reason for the discouragement and disapproval of sexual enthusiasm in the adolescent; it was seen as presenting a threat that the family's wealth would be dissipated in ways other than those which earned honour and respect from the community. The idea that one has a right to spend one's own money as one wishes (or a right to do anything which detracts from one's health and physical fitness) is not Greek, and would have seemed absurd to a Greek. He had only the rights which the law of his city explicitly gave him; no right was inalienable, and no claim superior to the city's.

5. Resistance

Living in a fragmented and predatory world, the inhabitants of a Greek city-state, who could never afford to take the survival of their community completely for granted, attached great importance to the qualities required of a soldier: not only to strength and speed, in which men are normally superior to women, but also to the endurance of hunger, thirst, pain, fatigue, discomfort and disagreeably hot or cold weather. The ability to resist and master the body's demands for nourishment and rest was normally regarded as belonging to the same moral category as the ability to resist sexual desire. Xenophon describes the chastity of King Agesilaus together with his physical toughness,[25] and elsewhere[26] summarises 'lack of self-control' as the inability to hold out against 'hunger, thirst, sexual desire and long hours without sleep.' The reasons for this association are manifold: the treatment of sex – a treatment virtually inevitable in a slave-owning society – as a commodity, and therefore as something which the toughest and most frugal men will be able to cut down to a minimum; the need for a soldier to resist the blandishments of comfort (for if he does not resist, the enemy who does will win), to sacrifice himself as an individual entirely, to accept pain and death as the price to be paid for the attainment of a goal which is not easily quantified, the honour of victory; and the inveterate Greek tendency to conceive of strong desires and emotional states as forces which assail the soul from the outside. To resist is manly and 'free'; to be distracted by immediate pleasure from the pursuit of honour through toil and suffering is to be a 'slave' to the forces which 'defeat' and 'worst' one's own personality.

Here is a third reason for praise of chastity in the young, the encouragement of the capacity to resist, to go without, to become the sort of man on whom the community depends for its defence. If the segregation and legal and administrative subordination of women received their original impetus from the fragmentation of the early Greek world into small, continuously warring states, they also gave an impetus to the formation of certain beliefs about women which served as a rationalization of segregation and no doubt affected behaviour to the extent that people tend to behave in the ways expected of them. Just as it was thought masculine to resist and endure, it was thought femine to yield to fear, desire and impulse. 'Now you must be a *man*,' says Demeas to himself as he tries to make up his mind to get rid of his concubine,[27] 'Forget your desire, fall out of love.' Women in comedy are notoriously unable to keep off the bottle, and in tragedy women are regarded as naturally more prone than men to panic, uncontrollable grief, jealousy and spite. It seems to have been believed not only that women enjoyed sexual intercourse more intensely than men,[28] but also that experience of intercourse put the woman more under the man's power than it put him under hers,[29] and that if not segregated and guarded women would be insatiably promiscuous.

6. Homosexuality

It was taken for granted in the Classical period that a man was sexually attracted by a good-looking younger male,[30] and no Greek who said that he was 'in love' would have taken it amiss if his hearers assumed without further enquiry that he was in love with a boy and that he desired more than anything to ejaculate in or on the boy's body. I put the matter in these coarse and clinical terms to preclude any misapprehension arising from modern application of the expression 'Platonic love' or from Greek euphemism (see below). Xenophon[31] portrays the Syracusan tyrant Hiero as declaring that he wants from the youth Dailochus, with whom he is in love, 'what, perhaps, the nature of man compels us to want from the beautiful.' Aphrodite, despite her femininity, is not hostile to homosexual desire, and homosexual intercourse is denoted by the same term, *aphrodisia*, as heterosexual intercourse.[32] Vase-painting was noticeably affected by the homosexual ethos; painters sometimes depicted a naked woman with a male waist and hips, as if a woman's body was nothing but a young man's body plus breasts and minus external genitals,[33] and in many of their pictures of heterosexual intercourse from the rear position the penis appears (whatever the painter's intention) to be penetrating the anus, not the vagina.[34]

Why homosexuality – or, to speak more precisely, 'pseudo-homosexuality,'[35] since the Greeks saw nothing surprising in the co-existence of desire for boys and desire for girls in the same person-obtained so firm and widespread a hold on Greek society, is a difficult and speculative question.[36] Segregation alone cannot be the answer, for comparable segregation has failed to engender a comparable degree of homosexuality in other cultures. Why the Greeks of the Classical period accepted homosexual desire as natural and normal is a much easier question: they did so because previous generations had accepted it, and segregation of the sexes in adolescence fortified and sustained the acceptance and the practice.

Money may have enabled the adolescent boy to have plenty of sexual intercourse with girls of alien or servile status, but it could not give him the satisfaction which can be pursued by his counterpart in a society which does not own slaves: the satisfaction of being welcomed *for his own sake* by a sexual partner of equal status. This is what the Greek boy was offered by homosexual relations. He was probably accustomed (as often happens with boys who do not have the company of girls) to a good deal of homosexual play at the time of puberty, and he never heard from his elders the suggestion that one was destined to become *either* 'a homosexual' *or* 'a heterosexual.'[37] As he grew older, he could seek among his juniors a partner of citizen status, who could certainly not be forced and who might be totally resistant to even the most disguised kind of purchase. If he was to succeed in seducing this boy (or if later, as a mature man, he was to seduce a youth), he could do so only by *earning* hero-worship.[38]

This is why, when Greek writers 'idealize' eros and treat the physical act as the 'lowest' ingredient in a rich and complex relationship which comprises mutual devotion, reciprocal sacrifice, emulation, and the awakening of sensibility, imagination and intellect, they look not to what most of us understand by sexual love but to the desire of an older for a younger male and the admiration felt by the younger for the older. It is noticeable also that in art and literature inhibitions operate in much the same way as in the romantic treatment of heterosexual love in our own tradition. When physical gratification is directly referred to, the younger partner is said to 'grant favours' or 'render services'; but a great deal is written about homosexual eros from which the innocent reader would not easily gather that any physical contact at all was involved. Aeschines, who follows Aeschylus and Classical sentiment generally in treating the relation between Achilles and Patroclus in the *Iliad* as homoerotic, commends Homer for leaving it to 'the educated among his hearers' to perceive the nature of the relation from the extravagant grief expressed by Achilles at the death of Patroclus.[39] The vase-painters very frequently depict the giving of presents by men to boys and the 'courting' of boys (a mild term for an approach which includes putting a hand on the boy's genitals), but their pursuit of the subject to the stage of erection, let alone penetration, in a variety of positions, is commonplace.[40]

We also observe in the field of homosexual relations the operation of the 'dual standard of morality' which so often characterizes societies in which segregation of the sexes is minimal.[41] If a Greek admitted that he was in love with a boy, he could expect sympathy and encouragement from his friends, and if it was known that he had attained his goal, envy and admiration. The boy, on the other hand, was praised if he retained his chastity, and he could expect strong disapproval if he was thought in any way to have taken the initiative in attracting a lover. The probable implication is that neither partner would actually say anything about the physical aspect of their relationship to anyone else,[42] nor would they expect any question about it to be put to them or any allusion to it made in their presence.

7.   Class and Status

Once we have accepted the universality of homosexual relations in Greek society as a fact, it surprises us to learn that if a man had at any time in his life prostituted himself to another man for money he was debarred from exercising his political rights.[43] If he was an alien, he had no political rights to exercise, and was in no way penalized for living as a male prostitute, so long as he paid the prostitution tax levied upon males and females alike.[44] It was therefore not the physical act *per se* which incurred penalty, but the incorporation of the act in a certain deliberately chosen role which could only be fully defined with reference to the nationality and status of the participants.

This datum illustrates an attitude which was fundamental to Greek society. They tended to believe that one's moral character is formed in the main by the circumstances in which one lives: the wealthy man is tempted to arrogance and oppression, the poor man to robbery and fraud, the slave to cowardice and petty greed. A citizen compelled by great and sudden economic misfortune to do work of a kind normally done by slaves was shamed because his assumption of a role which so closely resembled a slave's role altered his relationship to his fellow-citizens.[45] Since prostitutes were usually slaves or aliens, to play the role of a prostitute was, as it were, to remove oneself from the citizen-body, and the formal exclusion of a male prostitute from the rights of a citizen was a penalty for disloyalty to the community in his choice of role.

Prostitution is not easily defined – submission in gratitude for gifts, services or help is not so different in kind from submission in return for an agreed fee[46] – nor was it easily proved in a Greek city, unless people were willing (as they were not)[47] to come forward and testify that they had helped to cause a citizen's son to incur the penalty of disenfranchisement. A boy involved in a homosexual relationship absolutely untainted by mercenary considerations could still be called a prostitute by his family's enemies, just as the term can be recklessly applied today by unfriendly neighbours or indignant parents to a girl who sleeps with a lover. He could also be called effeminate; not always rightly, since athletic success seems to have been a powerful stimulus to his potential lovers, but it is possible (and the visual arts do not help us much here) that positively feminine charac-teristics in the appearance, movements and manner of boys and youths played a larger part in the ordinary run of homosexual activity than the idealization and romanticisation of the subject in literature indicates. There were certainly circumstances in which homosexuality could be treated as a substitute for heterosexuality; a comic poet[48] says of the Greeks who besieged Troy for ten years, 'they never saw a hetaira ... and ended up with arseholes wider than the gates of Troy.' The homosexual courting scene which becomes so common in vase-paintings of the sixth century B.C. – the man touching the face and genitals of the boy, the boy indig-nantly grasping the man's wrists to push them away – first appears in the seventh century as a youth courting a woman.[49] A sixth-century vase in which all of a group of men except one are penetrating women shows the odd man out grasping his erect penis and approaching, with a gesture of entreaty, a youth – who starts to run away.[50] In so far as the 'passive partner' in a homosexual act takes on himself the role of a woman, he was open to the suspicion, like the male prostitute, that he abjured his prescribed role as a future soldier and defender of the community.

The comic poets, like the orators, ridicule individuals for effeminacy, for participation in homosexual activity, or for both together; at the same time, the sturdy, wilful, roguish characters whom we meet in Aristophanes are not averse to handling and penetrating good-looking boys when the opportunity presents itself,[51] as a supplement to their busy and enjoyable heterosexual programmes. They represent a social class which, though in the main solidly prosperous, is below the level of most of the people we meet in reading Plato, and there is one obvious factor which we should expect to determine different sexual attitudes in different classes. The thoroughgoing segregation of women of citizen status was possible only in households which owned enough slaves and could afford to confine its womenfolk to a leisure enlivened only by the exercise of domestic crafts such as weaving and spinning. This degree of segregation was simply not possible in poorer families; the women who sold bread and vegetables in the market – Athenian women,[52] not resident aliens – were not segregated, and there must have been plenty of women in the demes of the Attic countryside who took a hand in work on the land and drove animals to market. No doubt convention required that they should protect each other's virtue by staying in pairs or groups as much as they could, but clearly the generalizations which I formulated in § 3 on the subject of segregation and the obstacles to love-affairs between citizens' sons and citizens' daughters lose their validity as one goes down the social scale. Where there are love-affairs, both boys and girls can have decided views – not enforceable *de jure*, but very important *de facto* – on whom they wish to marry. The girl in Aristophanes' *Ecclesiazusae* who waits impatiently for her young man's arrival while her mother is out may be much nearer the norm of Athenian life than those cloistered ladies who were 'embarrassed by the presence even of a male relative.' It would not be discordant with modern experience to believe that speakers in an Athenian law-court professed, and were careful to attribute to the jury, standards of propriety higher than the average member of the jury actually set himself.

8. Philosophers and Others

Much Classical Greek philosophy is characterized by contempt for sexual intercourse, which the author of the Seventh Letter of Plato,[53] offended at the traditional association of sex with a deity, calls 'the slavish and ugly pleasure wrongly called *aphrodisios*.' Xenophon's Socrates, although disposed to think it a gift of beneficent providence that humans, unlike other mammals, can enjoy sex all the year round,[54] is wary of troubling

the soul over what he regards as the minimum needs of the body.[55]
Virtue reproached Vice, in Prodicus' allegory of the choice of Herakles,[56]
for 'forcing sexual activity before [a man] has a need of it.' Antisthenes
boasted[57] of having intercourse only with the most readily available
woman (and the least desired by other men) 'when my body needs it.'
One logical outcome of this attitude to sex is exemplified by Diogenes the
Cynic, who was alleged to have masturbated in public when his penis
erected itself,[58] as if he were scratching a mosquito-bite.[59] Another
outcome was the doctrine (influential in Christianity, but not of Christian
origin)[60] that a wise and virtuous man will not have intercourse except for
the purpose of procreating legitimate offspring, a doctrine which necessarily proscribes much heterosexual and all homosexual activity.

Although philosophical preoccupation with the contrast between 'body'
and 'soul' had much to do with these developments, we can discern, as the
ground from which these philosophical plants sprouted, Greek admiration
for invulnerability, hostility towards the diversion of resources to the
pursuit of pleasure, and disbelief in the possibility that dissimilar ways of
feeling and behaving can be synthesised in the same person without
detracting from his attainment of the virtues expected of a selfless defender
of his city. It is also clear that the refusal of Greek law and society to treat a
woman as a responsible person, while on the one hand it encouraged a
complacent acceptance of prostitution and concubinage, on the other
hand led to the classification of sexual activity as a male indulgence which
could be reduced to a minimum by those who were not self-indulgent.[61]

Comedy presents a different picture. The speech put into the mouth of
Aristophanes in Plato's *Symposium* differs from the speeches of the other
characters in that work by treating eros as the individual's passionate
search for the 'other half' of himself (or of herself). This view of eros is
firmly rejected by Plato,[62] who presumably chose Aristophanes as its
proponent because it seemed to him the view which one would expect
of a comic poet; and it may have seemed so to him because comedy
looked at sexual behaviour through the eyes of the lower middle class
(cf. § 7). Certainly in comedy of the late fourth century we find much
which accords with Plato's Aristophanes, notably the remorse of a sensi-
tive young man who realizes that he has adopted a 'dual standard' in
condemning his wife and excusing himself.[63] But we have to consider also
Aristophanes' *Lysistrata*, produced in 411. There is much fantasy and
inconsequentiality in the play, more, indeed, than is commonly observed
– and the fact that citizens denied intercourse by their wives are apparently unable to turn their attention to slaves, prostitutes or boys, or even
to masturbation,[64] may be no more than inconsequentiality; Aristophanic

comedy easily ignores all those aspects of reality which would be inconvenient for the development of the comic plot. Yet when every allowance is made for that important comic convention, the central idea of the play, that a sex-strike by citizens' wives against their husbands can be imagined as having so devastating an effect, implies that the marital relationship was much more important in people's actual lives than we would have inferred simply from our knowledge of the law and our acquaintance with litigation about property and inheritance; more important, too, than could ever be inferred from a comprehensive survey of the varieties of sexual experience and attitude which were possible for the Greeks.

NOTES

1   Prodicus fr. B7 (Diels-Kranz).
2   See for more detailed discussion my article, "Aristophanes' Speech in Plato's *Symposium*," *Journal of Hellenic Studies* lvi (1966), 41 ff., especially 48 f.
3   Xenophon, *Symposium* 9.6.
4   Aristophanes, *Clouds* 82.
5   Aristophanes, *Acharnians* 259–279.
6   Pindar, *Nemean Odes* 10.80–82.
7   Xenophon, *Hiero* 1.4.
8   E.g. Aeschines i 52.
9   Aristotle, *Nicomachean Ethics* 1128^a 22–25.
10 Lysias iii 6.
11 E.g. Xenophon, *Oeconomicus* 7.5.
12 Isaeus iii 14 (general statement); Aristophanes, *Birds* 130–132 bears it out.
13 E.g. Aristophanes, *Ecclesiazusae* 818–822, *Wasps* 788–790.
14 E.g. Menander fr. 592, Euripides fr. 521.
15 E.g. Lysias i 8 (an adulterer's designs on a married woman), Theocritus 2.70–103.
16 The law is cited and discussed by Demosthenes xxiii 53–55. Cf. A. R. W. Harrison, *The Law of Athens*, i (Oxford, 1968), 32–38.
17 The speaker of Lysias i regards his wife and children as "shamed" by the adulterer but himself as "wronged." However, an alternative view seems to be expressed in Callias fr. 1, "Profit is better than shame; off with the adulterer to the inner room!"
18 Lysias i 32 f.
19 E.g. Lysias xix 9 f., "My father, throughout his life, spent more on the city than on himself and his family. . . ."
20 E.g. Aeschines i 42, on Timarchus' "devouring of his considerable estate . . . because he is a slave to the most shameful pleasures."

21 Demosthenes xix 229.
22 Menander fr. 198.
23 Archilochus fr. 118 (Tarditi) = 142 (Bergk).
24 Isaeus x 25.
25 Xenophon, *Agesilaus* 5.
26 Xenophon, *Memorabilia* iv 5.9.
27 Menander, *Samia* (Austin) 349 f.
28 Hesiod fr. 275 (Merkelbach and West).
29 Cf. Euripides, *Troades* 665 f., *Medea* 569–575, fr. 323.
30 I have discussed the evidence more fully in "Eros and Nomos," *Bulletin of the Institute of Classical Studies* x (1964), 31–42.
31 Xenophon, *Hiero* 1.33.
32 E.g. Xenophon, *Oeconomicus* 12.14, *Symposium* 8.21.
33 E.g. J. D. Beazley, *Greek Vases in Poland* (Oxford, 1928), pl. 19.1, *Corpus Vasorum Antiquorum*, Italy VIII, III Ic 1.38.
34 E.g. B. Graef and E. Langlotz, *Die antiken Vasen von der Akropolis zu Athen* i (Berlin, 1925), pl. 85 (no. 1639), 90 (no. 1913).
35 Cf. G. Devereux, "Greek Pseudo-Homosexuality and the 'Greek Miracle,'" *Symbolae Osloenses* xlii (1967), 69–92.
36 The Greeks never suggested that it originated among "decadent Asiatics"; Herodotus i 135 regards the Persians as having learned pederasty from the Greeks.
37 That is not to say that no one was exclusively or predominantly homosexual; Pausanias and Agathon maintained a relationship that sounds rather like a homosexual "marriage" (Plato, *Symposium* 193B).
38 E.g. [Xenophon], *Cynegeticus* 12.20 on the efforts of the lover to excel when the eyes of his boy are on him.
39 Aeschines i 142.
40 *Corpus Vasorum Antiquorum*, Italy III, III He 50.13 (two youths), Italy XL, III I 3.2 (group of youths); H. Licht, *Sittengeschichte Griechenlands*, iii (Dresden and Zürich, 1928), figg. 192, 199 (boys).
41 See, especially Plato, *Symposium* 182A–183D.
42 No doubt an ungentlemanly lover would boast of success, as suggested by Plato, *Phaedrus* 232A.
43 Aeschines i *passim*.
44 Aeschines i 119 f.
45 Cf. the embarrassment of the speaker of Demosthenes lvii 44 f. on the "servile and humble" function to which his mother had been compelled by poverty (she was a wet-nurse).
46 Cf. Aristophanes, *Wealth* (= "*Plutus*") 153–159.
47 Cf. Aeschines i 45 f., on the difficulty of getting Timarchus' lover (or client) Misgolas to give evidence.
48 Eubulus fr. 120.

49 K. Schefold, *Myth and Legend in Early Greek Art* (English tr. London, 1966), pl. 27b.

50 *Corpus Vasorum Antiquorum*, Germany XXXI, III Hd 143 f.

51 Aristophanes, *Birds* 136–143, *Knights* 1384–1387, *Wasps* 578.

52 The bread-woman of Aristophanes, *Wasps* 1388–1414 is plainly of citizen status.

53 335B; whether the author is Plato or not, does not matter in the present context.

54 Xenophon, *Memorabilia* i 4.12.

55 Ibid., i 3.14.

56 Ibid., ii 1.30.

57 Xenophon, *Symposium* 4.38.

58 Plutarch, *De Stoicorum Repugnantiis* 1044B.

59 Socrates was said to have compared Critias' eros for Euthydemus to the desire of a pig to rub its itching back against a rock (Xenophon, *Memorabilia* i 2.30). Democritus fr. B 127 (Diels-Kranz) is evidence for high valuation of scratching rather than low valuation of sex.

60 Musonius Rufus (p. 63.17 ff., Hense) can hardly be supposed to exhibit Christian influence.

61 Modern Christian critics of the "permissive society" sometimes speak as if they really believed (and maybe they do) that an extra-marital sexual relationship with a person of the opposite sex is the same sort of experience as sinking one's teeth into a tender steak.

62 Plato, *Symposium* 205DE, 212C, *Laws* 731D–732B.

63 Charisius in Menander, *Epitrepontes* 588–612 (Körte).

64 However inadequate a substitute for sexual intercourse masturbation may be, it is Aristophanes himself, by representing the Athenians and Spartans as creeping around in an unremitting state of erection, who forces us to ask, "Why don't they masturbate?" Cf. also Eubulus fr. 120 on the Greeks at Troy: "they masturbated for ten years...."

Source

Plato (c. 429–347 BCE) uses the dramatic setting of the symposium, an all-male aristocratic drinking party, to set forth a debate about erôs ("love"). The participants include contemporary historical persons such as the tragic poet Agathon, the comic poet Aristophanes, and the philosopher Socrates. In this passage, Aristophanes, who had to forfeit his first attempt at speaking because of an onset of hiccups, resumes his speech with a humorous account of the mythological origins of the sexes.

Aristophanes' Speech from Plato, *Symposium* 189d7–192a1

In the beginning there were three sexes, not just the two sexes, the male and the female, as at present; there was a third kind that shared the characteristics of the other two, and whose name survives, even though the thing itself has disappeared. For at that time one was androgynous in form and shared its name with both the male and the female. Today it no longer exists except as a term of abuse. Back then the form of each human being was rounded, with back and sides forming a circle. Each had four hands and an equal number of legs, and two faces, identical in every way, upon on a circular neck. There was one head common to both faces, which were turned in opposite directions. Each creature also had four ears and two sets of genitals, and all the other corresponding parts one might imagine. Each walked upright as today, in whichever direction was desired. And whenever one launched itself into a quick run, pushing off from the ground with all eight limbs, it spun swiftly in a circle, like a tumbler who executes cartwheels and returns to an upright position.

The reason for these three sexes was that the male sprang from the sun and the female from the earth, while the androgyne evolved from the moon, because the moon shares both male and female natures. They inherited their circular shape and their manner of movement from their parents. Their strength and power made them terrible, while their arrogance led them to challenge the gods. What Homer says about the twin giants Ephialtes and Otus and their attempt to climb up to Heaven in order to attack the gods is also said about these [three sexes].

So Zeus and the other gods deliberated about what they ought to do with them, and they were puzzled. They did not want to kill them outright with lightning, as they had destroyed the race of the giants, because the honors and sacrifices from humans would then disappear. Nor did they want them to go on behaving wantonly. At last, after lengthy reflection, Zeus said,

> I think I have found a way to stop human beings from their licentiousness and to make them weaker. I will cut each of them in two, thus they will be both weaker and at the same time more useful to us by becoming more numerous. They will walk upright on two legs. And if they continue to behave wantonly and if they refuse to stay quiet, I will cut them in two again so that they will hop along on one foot.

After he said this, he cut human beings in two, just as one slices apples for preserving, or [hard-boiled] eggs with a hair. And as he cut each one, he called upon the god Apollo to turn the face around and the remaining half of the neck toward the cut side, so that the human being, by looking upon his own division, might be more well-behaved. He also ordered him to heal the wounds. So Apollo turned around the faces and, gathering together the skin – like the drawstring of a purse – onto what is now called the belly, making one mouth, he fastened it tight in the middle of the belly, a spot they now call the navel. And he smoothed out the other numerous wrinkles and put the chest together with a tool of the kind used by shoemakers to smooth out wrinkled leather on the last. But he left a few wrinkles around the belly itself and the navel as a reminder of their ancient suffering.

When their original form was cut in two, each half, in longing for its other part, would come to it. And then, throwing their arms around one another and embracing, they longed to join their natures together. But they began to die of hunger and inactivity, because they refused to do anything apart. Whenever one of the halves died, the other was left behind, and the abandoned part sought and embraced another half, whether it happened to be from the female whole – and we now call that half a "woman" – or from the male. And in this way they perished. Meanwhile Zeus, taking pity upon them, devised another plan, and moved their private parts to the front. For until then they had these, too, on the outside, and they conceived and reproduced not with each other, but with the earth, like grasshoppers. So he brought these organs around to their front, and in doing so caused them to reproduce with one another, the male in combination with the female. He did this for the following reasons: if a man should embrace and have intercourse with a woman, he would engender and create offspring; while if a male should have intercourse with a male, he would at any rate have the satisfaction of intercourse, take a rest from desire, and turn himself toward work and focus on the other parts of life. So desire for one another is innately human from as long ago as that; it unites our ancient suffering, attempting to make one thing from two and to heal our human nature.

Therefore each of us is like part of an interlocking puzzle that needs to be matched with another piece, inasmuch as we have been cut just like flatfish, into two parts from one. We each eternally seek our missing piece. All the men who have been severed from the mixed sex, that which used to be called the androgyne, are lovers of women, and many of these become adulterers. Similarly, women in this category become promiscuous lovers of men and adulteresses. All the women who have been severed from the female sex pay no attention at all to men, but rather are attracted to women; those who prefer only women belong to this category. Men severed from the male sex pursue men, and as long as they are boys – since they are slices of the male – they love men and take pleasure in embracing and reclining with men. These are the best of boys and youths, for they have the most manly nature.

Figure 2 *Sappho and Alcaeus.* Detail. Attic red figure kalathos, attributed to the Brygos Painter, c.470 BCE. Staatliches Antikensammlungen und Glyptothek, Munich, 2416. Sappho stands next to her contemporary, the lyric poet Alcaeus, also from the island of Lesbos.

2
DOUBLE CONSCIOUSNESS IN SAPPHO'S LYRICS

J. J. Winkler

Monique Wittig and Sande Zeig in their *Lesbian Peoples: Material for a Dictionary*[1] devote a full page to Sappho. The page is blank. Their silence is one quite appropriate response to Sappho's lyrics, particularly refreshing in comparison to the relentless trivialization, the homophobic anxieties and the sheer misogyny that have infected so many ancient and modern responses to her work.[2] As Mary Barnard (34) puts it:

> I wanted to hear
> Sappho's laughter
> and the speech of
> her stringed shell.
>
> What I heard was
> whiskered mumble-
> ment of grammarians:
>
> Greek pterodactyls
> and Victorian dodos.

The very eminent classical scholars from F. G. Welcker to Denys Page who have assembled and sifted through so much of what can or might be known of Sappho, and whose work is indispensable to us, had their own matrices of understanding, their own concerns and commitments, which were, I should think, no more and no less time-bound and culture-specific than are ours.[3] But I doubt that those scholars would have understood our matrices (feminist, anthropological, pro-lesbian), given that their expertise was in such things as ancient metrics ("pterodactyls") rather than in ancient mores, whereas we are able in some good measure to understand theirs. This is an example of what I will refer to below as double consciousness, a kind of cultural bilingualism on our part, for we must be aware of and fluent in using two systems of understanding. Because Lobel and Page assumed the validity of Victorian no-no's, they were (it now seems to us) deaf to much of what Sappho was saying, tone-deaf to her deeper melodies. The forms of both worship and anxiety that have surrounded Sappho in the ancient and modern records require some analysis.[4] Part of the explanation is the fact that her poetry is continuously focused on women and sexuality, subjects which provoke many readers to excess.[5]

But the centering on women and sexuality is not quite enough to explain the mutilated and violent discourse which keeps cropping up around her. After all Anakreon speaks of the same subjects. A deeper explanation refers to the *subject* more than the object of her lyrics – the fact that it is a *woman* speaking about women and sexuality. To some audiences this would have been a double violation of the ancient rules which dictated that a proper woman was to be silent in the public world (defined as men's sphere) and that a proper woman accepted the administration and definition of her sexuality by her father and her husband.

I will set aside for the present the question of how women at various times and places actually conducted their lives in terms of private and public activity, appearance, and authority. If we were in a position to know more of the actual texture of ancient women's lives and not merely the maxims and rules uttered by men, we could fairly expect to find that many women abided by these social rules or were forced to, and that they sometimes enforced obedience on other women; but, since all social codes can be manipulated and subverted as well as obeyed, we would also expect to find that many women had effective strategies of resistance and false compliance by which they attained a working degree of freedom for their lives.[6] Leaving aside all these questions, however, I simply begin my analysis with the fact that there was available a common understanding that proper women ought to be publicly submissive to male definitions, and that a very great pressure of propriety could at any time be invoked to shame a woman who acted on her own sexuality.

This is at least the public ethic and the male norm. It cannot have been entirely absent from the society of Lesbos in Sappho's time. Unfortunately, our knowledge of that period and place is limited to a few general facts and rumors – a culture of some luxury, at least for the wealthy; aristocratic families fighting each other for power; the typical sixth-century emergence of tyrannies (Myrsilos) and mediating law-givers (Pittakos). Sappho's kin were clearly active in this elite feuding since she was banished with them from Lesbos to Sicily around the turn of the century. Lacking a reasonably dense texture of social information, . . . and given the fragmentary state of her literary remains (in contrast to *Daphnis and Chloe* and the *Odyssey*), [other] kinds of anthropological investigation . . . become much more difficult.

What I want to recover in this chapter are the traces of Sappho's consciousness in the face of these masculine norms of behavior, her attitude to the public ethic and her allusions to private reality. This is becoming a familiar topic and problem in feminist anthropology: Do women see things in the same way as men? How can gender-specific differences of cultural attitude be discerned when one group is muted? Does their silence give consent? Or have we merely not found the right questions to ask and ways of asking them? My way of "reading what is there"[7] focuses on the politics of space – the role of women as excluded from public male domains and enclosed in private female areas – and on Sappho's consciousness[8] of this ideology. My analysis avowedly begins with an interest in sexual politics – the relations of power between women and men as two groups in the same society. In some sense the choice of a method will predetermine the kind and range of results which may emerge: a photo-camera will not record sounds, a non-political observer will not notice facts of political significance. Thus my readings of Sappho are in principle not meant to displace other readings but to add to the store of perceptions of "what is there."

There are various "publics and privates" which might be contrasted. What I have in mind here by "public" is quite specifically the recitation of Homer at civic festivals considered as an expression of common cultural traditions. Samuel Butler notwithstanding, Homer and the singers of his tradition were certainly men and the homeric epics as we have them cannot readily be conceived as women's songs. Women are integral to the social and poetic structure of both *Iliad* and *Odyssey*, and the *notion* of a woman's consciousness is particularly vital to the *Odyssey*. . . But Nausikaa and Penelope live in a male-prominent world, coping with problems of honor and enclosure which were differentially assigned to women, and their "subjectivity" in the epic must ultimately be analyzed as an expression of a male consciousness. Insofar as Homer presents a set of conventional social and literary formulas, he inescapably embodies and represents the definition of public culture as male territory.[9]

Archaic lyric, such as that composed by Sappho, was also not composed for private reading but for performance to an audience (Merkelbach

1957; Russo 1973–4). Sappho often seems to be searching her soul in a very intimate way but this intimacy is in some measure formulaic (Lanata) and is certainly shared with some group of listeners. And yet, maintaining this thesis of the public character of lyric, we can still propose three senses in which such song may be "private": first, composed in the person of a woman (whose consciousness was socially defined as outside the public world of men); second, shared only with women (that is, other "private" persons: "and now I shall sing this beautiful song to delight the women who are my companions," frag. 160 L-P,[10]); and third, sung on informal occasions, what we would simply call poetry readings, rather than on specific ceremonial occasions such as sacrifice, festival, leave-taking, or initiation.[11] The lyric tradition, as Nagy argues, may be older than the epic, and if older perhaps equally honored as an achievement of beauty in its own right.

The view of lyric as a subordinate element in celebrations and formal occasions is no more compelling than the view, which I prefer, of song as honored and celebrated at least sometimes in itself. Therefore I doubt that Sappho always needed a sacrifice or dance or wedding *for which* to compose a song; the institution of lyric composition was strong enough to occasion her songs *as songs*. Certainly Sappho speaks of goddesses and religious festivities, but it is by no means certain that her own poems are either for a cult-performance or that her circle of women friends (*hetairai*) is identical in extension with the celebrants in a festival she mentions.[12] It is possible that neither of these latter two senses of "private" were historically valid for Sappho's performances. Yet her lyrics, as compositions which had some publicity, bear some quality of being in principle from another world than Homer's, not just from a different tradition, and they embody a consciousness both of her "private," woman-centered world and the other, "public" world. This chapter is an experiment in using these categories to unfold some aspects of Sappho's many-sided meaning.

Poem 1: Many-mindedness and Magic

One of the passages in Sappho which has been best illuminated in recent criticism is her first (and now only) complete poem, *poikilophron athanat' Aphrodita*. The reason for thinking that it stood first in a collection of her works is that Hephaistion, writing a treatise on meters in the second century C.E., took it as his paradigm of what was by then called the Sapphic stanza. The very notion, however, of a first poem in a first book hardly makes sense in Sappho's world, where the text seems to have circulated at first as a script and score for professional and amateur performers. Then we have to allow for some three to four hundred years in which single songs, groups of songs, various collections which interested performers made for their own use were in circulation before the scholar-librarians at Alexandria assembled, sorted, and compared the many variant versions to produce a canonical corpus of Sappho's lyrics in eight or nine books.

There were in fact at least two editions produced at the Alexandrian library, one by Aristophanes (who seems to have invented the convention that there were exactly nine great lyric poets of early Greece; Pfeiffer 205) and one by his pupil and successor Aristarchos.[13] Two of her fragments survive in written copies which may actually pre-date those standard editions: one scrawled on a shard and one on papyrus, both of the third century B.C.E. (fragments 2 and 98). The survival of poem 1 is due to the fact that Dionysios of Halikarnassos, writing a treatise on style, chose it for quotation as an example of perfect smoothness. This is sheer good luck for us; he might have quoted Simonides.

In the handing on of the text from one scribe or performer to another until it reaches our modern editors, who fiddle with it some more before handing it over to us, further uncertainties are introduced. The works of Dionysios and Hephaistion were themselves copied many times over before they reached us. The sort of problem which infects even canonical book texts is illustrated by the first word in Sappho's poem 1. Some manuscripts of Dionysios and some of Hephaistion write *poikilothron'*, which all modern editors prefer, and other manuscripts have *poikilophron* (Neuberger-Donath), for which a strong and interesting argument may be made. *Poikilophron* means "having a mind (*-phron*) which is *poikilos*," a notion usually translated by words like "dappled," "variegated," "changeful," "complex." It designates the quality of having many internal contrasts, whether perceived by the eye or by the mind. An embroidered robe is *poikilos*, Odysseus' crafty mind is *poikilos*.

I call attention to this not only as a lesson in the almost immeasurable distance, with all its stages of loss and distortion, which separates Sappho and her whole world from us but also because poem 1 is an astonishing example of *many-mindedness* (for want of a more elegant term). Other Greek lyric poets sing marvelous poems of hate and sorrow and personal ecstacy which is somehow never very far from regret and chagrin, but they do so from a single perspective, elaborating the mind and feelings of a single persona in a fixed situation. Sappho's poem 1, however, contains several personal perspectives, whose multiple relations to each other set up a field of voices and evaluations. This field-effect makes the rest of Greek lyric appear, by contrast, relatively single-minded, or as we can now say, not-*poikilos*. The field in poem 1 includes at least three Sapphos, two Aphrodites, an unnamed girlfriend (representative of many), and (in virtue of echoing and parody effects) several homeric characters as well.

Let us consider the last first. Several analyses have developed the idea that Sappho is speaking in an imagined scene which represents that of Diomedes on the battlefield in *Iliad* 5 (Cameron 1949; Page 1955: 7; Svenbro; Stanley; Rissman). Sappho uses a traditional prayer formula, of which Diomedes' appeal to Athena at *Iliad* 5. 115–7 is an example ("Hear me, Atrytone, child of aegis-bearing Zeus; if ever you stood beside my father supporting his cause in bitter battle, now again support me, Athena"), and she models Aphrodite's descent to earth in a chariot on the descent of Athena and Hera (5. 719–72), who are coming to help the wounded Diomedes (5.781). Sappho asks Aphrodite to be her ally, literally her companion in battle, *summachos*.

> Intricate, undying Aphrodite, snare-weaver, child of Zeus, I pray thee,
> do not tame my spirit, great lady, with pain and sorrow. But come to me
> now if ever before you heard my voice from afar and leaving your father's
> house, yoked golden chariot and came. Beautiful sparrows swiftly
>   brought you
> to the murky ground with a quick flutter of wings from the sky's height
> through clean air. They were quick in coming. You, blessed goddess,
> a smile on your divine face, asked what did I suffer, this time again,
> and why did I call, this time again, and what did I in my frenzied heart
> most want to happen. Whom am I to persuade, this time again . . .
> to lead to your affection? Who, O Sappho, does you wrong? For one who
>   flees will
> soon pursue, one who rejects gifts will soon be making offers, and one
>   who
> does not love will soon be loving, even against her will. Come to me
>   even now
> release me from these mean anxieties, and do what my heart wants done,
> you yourself be my ally.[14]

About the Greek text we should first note that even this one integral poem has a nick on its surface. At the beginning of its fifteenth line (line 19 in the quatrain arrangement adopted in many editions), the manuscripts of Dionysios give a garbled reading and the papyrus copy (P. Oxy. 2288), which is from the second century C.E., although it gives a slightly more intelligible run of letters is still not entirely clear. Second, about pronunciation we have, I think, to confess that the music of a pitch-accent language is not easily appreciated by speakers of a stress-accent language, and further that there are deep uncertainties not only about the placement of the pitch in Aeolic Greek but about fundamental principles concerning their vowels and consonants. The ancient Greek grammarians tell us that Aeolic Greek was psilotic (that is, it did not use initial h), that its accent was everywhere recessive (did not fall on the final syllable of a word), that it used -sd-for-ds- and br-for initial -r-. But as Hooker has emphasized, this information is very dubious, in some cases being contradicted by inscriptions found on Lesbos, in others applying at most to orthography rather than to actual pronunciation, and in any case of questionable relevance to the state of verbal performance and the art of singing many centuries before the grammarians.

Just as we can demonstrate that virtually all biographical information recorded by the Peripatetic and Alexandrian scholars is based on inferences from the poems themselves, and are frequently mistaken inferences, because they had nothing but the texts themselves to work with, so the grammarians' dogmas are not based on any privileged access to the seventh century B.C.E. and in certain respects we actually know more than they did.

But with that very skeptical prelude, I invite you now to read aloud what was one of the most beautiful compositions in all of archaic Greek verse:

poikilophron âthanat' Aphroditâ
pai Dios doloploke, lissomai se,
mê m' asaisi mêd' oniaisi damna, potnia, thûmon.

alla tuid' elth', ai pota kâterôta
tâs emâs audâs aïoisa pêloi
eklues, patros de domon lipoisa chrûsion êlthes,
arm' upasdeuxaisa; kaloi de s' âgon
ôkees strouthoi peri gâs melainâs
pukna dinnentes pter' ap' ôranôitheros dia messô,

aipsa d' exîkonto; su d', ô makaira,
meidiaisais' âthanatôi prosôpôi
êre' otti dêute pepontha kôtti dêute kalêmmi

kôtti moi malista thelô genesthai
mainolai thûmôi. "Tina dêute peithô
aps s'agên es san philotâta? Tis s', ô Psapph', adikêei?
kai gar ai pheugei, tacheôs diôxei;

ai de dôra mê deket', alla dôsei;
ai de mê philei, tacheôs philêsei kouk etheloisa.

elthe moi kai nûn, chalepân de lûson
ek merimnân, ossa de moi telessai
thûmos îmerrei, teleson; su d' autâ summachos esso.

One way of interpreting the correspondences which have been noticed is to say that Sappho presents herself as a kind of Diomedes on the field of love, that she is articulating her own experience in traditional (male) terms and showing that women too have manly excellence (*aretê*; Bolling 1958, Marry). But this view that the poem is mainly about *erôs* and *aretê* and uses Diomedes merely as a background model, falls short.[15] Sappho's use of homeric passages is a way of allowing us, even encouraging us, to approach her consciousness as a woman and poet reading Homer. The homeric hero is not just a starting point for Sappho's discourse about her own love, rather Diomedes as he exists in the *Iliad* is central to what Sappho is saying about the *distance* between Homer's world and her own. A woman listening to the *Iliad* must cross over a gap which separates her experience from the subject of the poem, a gap which does not exist in quite the same way for male listeners. How can Sappho murmur along with the rhapsode the speeches of Diomedes, uttering and impersonating his appeal for help? Sappho's answer to this aesthetic problem is that she can only do so by substituting her concerns for those of the hero while maintaining the same structure of plight / prayer / intervention. Poem 1 says, among other things, "This is how I, a woman and poet, become able to appreciate a typical scene from the *Iliad*."

Though the Diomedeia is a typical passage, Sappho's choice of it is not random, for it is a kind of test case for the issue of women's consciousness of themselves as participants without a poetic voice of their own at the public recitations of traditional Greek heroism. In *Iliad* 5, between Diomedes' appeal to the goddess and the descent of Athena and Hera, Aphrodite herself is driven from the battlefield after Diomedes stabs her in the hand. Homer identifies Aphrodite as a "feminine" goddess, weak, *analkis*, unsuited to take part in male warfare (331, 428). Her appropriate sphere, says Diomedes exulting in his victory over her, is to seduce weak women (*analkides*, 348–9). By implication, if "feminine" women (and all mortal women are "feminine" by definition and prescription) try to participate in men's affairs – warfare or war poetry – they will, like Aphrodite, be driven out at spear point.

Poem 1 employs not only a metaphorical use of the *Iliad* (transferring the language for the experience of soldiers to the experience of women in love) and a familiarization of the alien poem (so that it now makes better sense to women readers), but a *multiple identification* with its characters.

Sappho is acting out the parts both of Diomedes and of Aphrodite as they are characterized in *Iliad* 5. Aphrodite, like Sappho, suffers pain (*odunêisi*, 354), and is consoled by a powerful goddess who asks "Who has done this to you?" (373). Aphrodite borrows Ares' chariot to escape from the battle and ride to heaven (358–67), the reverse of her action in Sappho's poem (Benedetto, who refers to the poem as "Aphrodite's revenge"). Sappho therefore is in a sense presenting herself both as a desperate Diomedes needing the help of a goddess (Athena/Aphrodite) and as a wounded and expelled female (Aphrodite/Sappho) seeking a goddess' consolation (Dione/Aphrodite).

This multiple identification with several actors in an Iliadic scene represents on another level an admired feature of Sappho's poetics – her adoption of multiple points of view in a single poem. This is especially noteworthy in poem 1 where she sketches a scene of encounter between a victim and a controlling deity. The intensification of both pathos and mastery in the encounter is due largely to the ironic *double consciousness* of the poet-Sappho speaking in turn the parts of suffering "Sappho" and impassive goddess. Consider the cast of characters in poem 1, each different and each regarding the others with a look of mingled admiration and distrust. There is first the speaker in need, whose name we learn in line 15 is Psappo.[16] She is praying for help to Aphrodite, who is therefore the implied fictional audience of the entire poem and is to be imagined listening to all its words. Part of what Aphrodite hears is a narrative account of how she herself on a previous occasion mounted her sparrow-drawn chariot and drove down the sky and answered Sappho's prayers with a series of questions. This past-Aphrodite is not at all the same as the present-Aphrodite: the past-Aphrodite is an active character in the praying-Sappho's narrative, while the present-Aphrodite says nothing, does nothing, only listens – and presumably smiles.

One might wonder at the lengthy elaboration of the chariot-narrative, full of circumstantial detail, but I think the point is to create a slow build-up from distance to nearness, the goddess coming gradually closer to the speaker, taking her time (poetically, in the movement of the verse, even though she twice says it was a quick journey). As Aphrodite comes physically closer, she also becomes more vivid. First, her words are reported in indirect speech, and then she breaks into direct speech, so that Sappho the singer, impersonating Sappho in needful prayer, now suddenly is speaking in the voice of Aphrodite herself, so that the word "you," which from the beginning has been directed to Aphrodite, in line 15 now refers to Sappho. Fictional speaker and fictional audience change places, or rather the present-Aphrodite now hears from the mouth of praying Sappho the words which the past-Aphrodite spoke to the past-Sappho. The slow approach to this direct speech, starting far away (*pêloî*) in heaven, makes Aphrodite's words a kind of epiphany, a reported epiphany in a prayer asking for a repetition of the same.

For Sappho is once again tied up in a state of anxious desire. The three times repeated word for this is *dêute*, which is a contraction of *aute*, "again," and *dê*, an intensifying particle, something like "indeed," which gives a flavor to "again" which we might read as quizzical or ironic or pretended disappointment. Since the past-Aphrodite says "once again" to the past-Sappho, we are led to think of yet another Sappho, the one who got into the same fix before. The doubling of Aphrodite (present and past) and the tripling of Sappho (present, past, and . . . pluperfect) leads like the mirrors in a fun house to receding vistas of endlessly repeated intercessions, promises, and love affairs.

The appearance of an infinite regress, however, is framed and bounded by another Sappho. The person who we must think of as designing the whole is functionally and indeed practically quite different from any of the Sapphos in the poem. The author-performer who impersonates a character-in-need is not at the moment, at least *qua* performer, in need. In fact my primary impression of poem 1 is one of exquisite control, which puts Sappho-the-poet in a role analogous to Aphrodite's as the smiling, tolerant, ever helpful ally of her own *thumos*, "spirit." The guileful weaver, the many-minded one who performs intricate shifts of perspective, is fictionally Aphrodite but poetically Sappho herself.

The sounds of the first line are worth a close inspection, for they contain a meaning which is quite untranslatable. With the reading *poikilophron*, "many-minded," aided by the compound *âthanat'*, "not-mortal," it might be possible to hear in the very name of Aphrodite a playful etymology: the negative prefix *a-* plus the root *phro-* would yield "no-minded." Certainly the verbal field of the poem, with all its references to guile and to Sappho going out of her mind, encourages the possibility. Note too how the sounds of *poikilophron* and *doloploke* are recycled: *poikilo-* and *-ploke* have just the same consonants.

Such attention to micro-accuracies is typical of much Greek verse, and for Sappho we have at least one other case of etymologizing a divine name in a novel way. Fragment 104a reads "Hesperos, bringing together everything which shining Dawn scattered, you bring the sheep, you bring the goat, you bring the child to its mother" (or possibly, "you bring the child away from its mother"). The two syllables of the Greek root meaning Evening Star, *(H)es-per*, are echoed in the word "you bring," *pher-eis*, three times repeated. J. S. Clay, who pointed this out (a scholiast on Euripides' *Orestes* had noticed it too), takes it as a revaluation of Hesiod's characterization of Dawn as the one who scatters the family and sends people to work.[17] This is a good example of how closely textured and in-wrought Sappho's verse can be, and what a high standard of complexity and intention we are justified in applying.

But if such weaving and complexity give *poikilophron* a good claim to being the first word of Sappho's poem 1, there are also attractive reasons on the side of *poikilothron'*, which is most often taken to mean "sitting on an elaborately wrought throne." Although there certainly were, as Page (1955: 5) catalogues, elaborately wrought thrones, the interesting side of this compound word is not *thronos* meaning "throne" but a much rarer root, *throna*, found once in Homer, once in Theokritos, and several times in the Alexandrian poets Nikandros and Lykophron (Lawler; Bolling 1958; Putnam; see also Bonner). In the later poets it refers to some kind of magic drugs. Theokritos' young woman in Idyll 2 is trying to perform a ceremony which will enchant her lover and bring him back to her. She tells her servant to smear the drugs, *throna*, on the threshold of Delphis' house and say "I am sprinkling the bones of Delphis." "Sprinkle" is the standard translation of the verb *passô*, but homeric physicians also "sprinkle" drugs (*pharmaka*) onto wounds, so possibly the verb can include the more general action of applying or putting on.[18]

The homeric occurrence of the word is highly suggestive. Andromache is sitting at her loom, soon to hear the news of her husband Hektor's death. "She was weaving loom-cloth in a corner of the high house, a red double cloak, and she was sprinkling variegated *throna* on it" (*Iliad* 22.440–1): *en de throna poikil' epasse*. The conjunction of *throna* and *poikila* here might well tempt us to wonder whether Sappho actually did sing *poikilothron'*, and if so what would it mean. The usual interpretation of *throna* in *Iliad* 22 is "embroidered flowers." "Embroidered flowers" is surely too diminished a translation of the *throna* which Andromache is "sprinkling" onto her cloth. Instead I would sketch the semantic field of *throna* as somehow including both drugs and weaving.

I have already noted that "sprinkle" (*passô*) is what one does with *throna*, whether they are put on wounds or on loom-cloth. For further connections between drugs and weaving, I would cite the figure of Helen the weaver, who not only weaves (literally, "sprinkles") the story of the *Iliad* into her loom-cloth (3.125–8) but when she is home with Menelaos sits near him with a basket of wool and a spindle and when the war-tales they tell make everyone melancholy she puts drugs (*pharmaka*) into the wine-bowl and has it served around (*Odyssey* 4.120–35, 219–33).

   Another locus for the conjunction of weaving and drugs is the *kestos*, the girdle, of Aphrodite, which too is described as *poikilos* and contains worked into it the powers to charm and enchant (*Iliad* 14.214–21). Helen's drugs and Aphrodite's charmed girdle are powerful magic, using the world loosely to designate many forms of alternate, unofficial therapy. Since women did sing while spending long hours at the loom (so Kirke at *Odyssey* 10.221–2), I can readily imagine that some of those chants would wish good things onto the cloth and even that filaments of lucky plants and patterns of luck-bringing design would be woven into the best fabric.

   In 1979 a new papyrus fragment of a Greek magical handbook was published which is very important for the fragmentary and suppressed history of that subject (Brashear; Maltomini; Obbink; Janko). Since most of the surviving collections of spells exist in copies made in the second to fourth centuries C.E., it is easy enough for traditional historians to dismiss all that as a late and alien intrusion into the sanctuary of rational Greek culture. But the new papyrus belongs to the late first century B.C.E. and confirms what is likely enough on other grounds – that the writing down of magic has a history comparable to other kinds of writing. Magical spells to produce love or cure a headache (both contained in the new papyrus) are like collections of natural marvels and folktales, the sort of cultural product which has a long and detailed oral history but which no one thought to write down until the changed social conditions of the Alexandrian and Roman empires. Certainly in the one area of magic which does have a continuous textual history from the sixth century B.C.E. to the sixth century C.E. – viz., curses written on lead and buried, sometimes with tortured dolls, in graves of the untimely dead – we can assert with confidence that the practice itself is ancient and uninterrupted.

   For students of Sappho the fascinating feature of the new magical papyrus is that its language has some resemblance to that of poem 1. It involves an enchanted apple which is to be thrown in the direction of the intended love-object. The throwing of apples as a token of erotic interest is a quite widespread custom in Greek communities.[19] The incantation is a hexameter prayer to Aphrodite, asking her to "perfect this perfect song," or "fulfill a song of fulfillment," using the same word which Sappho repeats in her last stanza, "accomplish what my heart desires to accomplish." This is fairly standard in the language of prayer and request (*Iliad* 14.195–6). Standard too is the address to a great goddess as *potnia thea*, "lady goddess," found both in poem 1 and in the magical papyrus, but in the fragmentary magical text it is found next to the word *apothanô*, "I may die," which is found several times in Sappho (fragment 94: "I wish without guile to die;" fragment 31: "I seem to be little short of dying"). Closer still are the words *katatrechô, autos de me pheugei*, "I am running after, but he is fleeing from me" (column 2, line 12). Other magical papyri contain calls for assistance in terms as immediate and direct as Sappho's to Aphrodite to come and stand beside her in battle as a fellow-fighter: e.g., "Come and stand beside me for this project and work with me" (PGM XII.95). All of this may mean no more than that the magical papyrus shows the influence of Sappho, but the magical associations of *throna* (if that is the right reading) might explain why the later enchanter would naturally be drawn to echoing Sappho poem 1.

Poised between two possibilities – the many-mindedness of *poikilo-phron*, the magic of *poikilothron'* – I can see no way to decide that one must be right and the other wrong. Better to allow both to be heard and to appreciate how Sappho in poem 1 may be alluding to a goddess' magic and certainly is demonstrating her many-mindedness. Such multiple self-mirroring in the face of another, along with the alternation of viewpoints so that we in turn sympathize with and stand apart from each of the poem's five characters, is an achievement which reaches out into a different dimension, compared with the other Greek poets of the seventh and sixth centuries B.C.E. This complexity of understanding, which generates a field of personal perspectives, each regarding the other as alike but different, shows how comparable lyrics by poets of her time are quite truly and profoundly solo performances.

Such many-mindedness is intrinsic to the situation of Greek women understanding men's culture, as it is to any silenced group within a culture which acknowledges its presence but not its authentic voice. This leads to an interesting reversal of the standard (and oppressive) stricture on women's literature that it represents only a small and limited area of the larger world.[20] Such a view portrays women's consciousness according to the *social* contrast of public/private, as if women's literature occupied but a small circle somewhere inside the larger circle of men's literature, just as women are restricted to a domestic enclosure. But insofar as men's public culture is truly public, displayed as the governing norm of social interaction "in the streets," it is accessible to women as well as to men. Because men define and exhibit their language and manners as *the* culture and segregate women's language and manners as a subculture, inaccessible to and protected from extra-familial men, women are in the position of knowing two cultures where men know only one.

From the point of view of *consciousness* (rather than physical space) we must diagram the circle of women's literature as a larger one which includes men's literature as one phase or compartment of women's cultural knowledge. Women in a male-prominent society are thus like a linguistic minority in a culture whose public actions are all conducted in the majority language. To participate even passively in the public arena the minority must be bilingual; the majority feels no such need to learn the minority's language. Sappho's consciousness therefore is necessarily a double consciousness, her participation in the public literary tradition always contains an inevitable alienation.

Poem 1 contains a statement of how important it is to have a double consciousness. Aphrodite reminds "Sappho" of the ebb and flow of conflicting emotions, of sorrow succeeded by joy, of apprehensiveness followed by relief, of loss turning into victory. The goddess' reminder not to be singlemindedly absorbed in one moment of experience can be related to the pattern of the *Iliad* in general, where the tides of battle flow back and forth, flight alternating with pursuit. This is well illustrated in *Iliad* 5, which is also the homeric locus for the specific form of alternation in fortunes which consists of wounding and miraculous healing. Two gods (Aphrodite and Ares) and one hero (Aineias) are injured and saved.

Recuperative alternation is the theme of poem 1, as it is of *Iliad* 5. But because of Sappho's "private" point of view and double consciousness it becomes not only the theme but the *process* of the poem, in the following sense: Sappho appropriates an alien text, the very one which states the exclusion of "weak" women from men's territory; she implicitly reveals the inadequacy of that denigration; and she restores the fullness of Homer's text by isolating and alienating its deliberate exclusion of the feminine and the erotic.

For when we have absorbed Sappho's complex re-impersonation of the homeric roles (male and female) and learned to see what was marginal as encompassing, we notice that there is a strain of anxious self-alienation in Diomedes' expulsion of Aphrodite. The overriding need of a battling warrior is to be strong and unyielding; hence the ever-present temptation (which is also a desire) is to be weak. This is most fully expressed at *Iliad* 22.111–30, where Hektor views laying down his weapons to parley with Achilles as effeminate and erotic. Diomedes' hostility to Aphrodite (= the effeminate and erotic) is a kind of scapegoating, his affirmation of an ideal of masculine strength against his *own* possible "weakness." For, in other contexts outside the press of battle, the homeric heroes have intense emotional lives and their vulnerability there is much like Sappho's: they are as deeply committed to friendship networks as Sappho ("He gave the horses to Deipylos, his dear comrade, whom he valued more than all his other age-mates," 325–6); they give and receive gifts as Sappho does; they wrong each other and re-establish friendships with as much feeling as Sappho and her beloved. In a "Sapphic" reading, the emotional isolation of the Iliadic heroes from their domestic happiness stands out more strongly ("no longer will his children run up to his lap and say 'Papa,'" 408). We can reverse the thesis that Sappho uses Homer to heroize her world and say that insofar as her poems are a reading of Homer (and so lead us back to read Homer again) they set up a feminine perspective on male activity which shows more clearly the inner structure and motivation of the exclusion of the feminine from male arenas.

I return to the image of the double circle – Sappho's consciousness is a larger circle enclosing the smaller one of Homer. Reading the *Iliad* is for her an experience of double consciousness. The movement thus created is threefold: by temporarily restricting herself to that smaller circle she can understand full well what Homer is saying; when she brings *her* total experience to bear she sees the limitation of his world; by offering her version of this experience in a poem she shows the strengths of her world, the apparent incompleteness of Homer's, and casts new illumination on some of the marginal and easily overlooked aspects of Homer. This threefold movement of appropriation from the "enemy," exposure of his weakness and recognition of his worth is like the actions of homeric heroes who vanquish, despoil and sometimes forgive. Underlying the relations of Sappho's persona to the characters of Diomedes and Aphrodite are the relations of Sappho the author to Homer, a struggle of reader and text (audience and tradition), of woman listening and man reciting.

Poem 16: What Men Desire

A sense of what we now call the sexual politics of literature seems nearly explicit in poem 16:

> Some assert that a troup of horsemen, some of foot-soldiers, some that a fleet of ships is the most beautiful thing on the dark earth; but I assert that it is whatever anyone desires. It is quite simple to make this intelligible to all, for she who was far and away preeminent in beauty of all humanity – Helen – abandoning her husband, the ..., went sailing to Troy and took no thought for child or dear parents, but beguiled ... herself ..., for ... lightly ... reminds me now of
> Anaktoria
> absent: whose lovely step and shining glance of face I would prefer to see than Lydians' chariots and fighting men in arms ... cannot be ... human ... to wish to share ... unexpectedly.

[This is a poem of eight stanzas, of which the first, second, third and fifth are almost intact, the rest lost or very fragmentary.]

It is easy to read this as a comment on the system of values in heroic poetry. Against the panoply of men's opinions on beauty (all of which focus on military organizations, regimented masses of anonymous fighters), Sappho sets herself – "but I" – and a very abstract proposition about desire. The stanza first opposes one woman to a mass of men and then transcends that opposition when Sappho announces that "the most beautiful" is "whatever you or I or anyone may long for." This amounts to a reinterpretation of the kind of meaning the previous claims had, rather than a mere contest of claimants for supremacy in a category whose meaning is agreed upon (Wills, duBois 1978). According to Sappho, what men mean when they claim that a troup of cavalrymen is very beautiful is that they intensely desire such a troup. Sappho speaks as a woman opponent entering the lists with men, but her proposition is not that men value military forces whereas she values desire, but rather that all valuation is an act of desire. Men are perhaps unwilling to see their values as erotic in nature, their ambitions for victory and strength as a kind of choice. But it is clear enough to Sappho that men are in love with masculinity and that epic poets are in love with military prowess.

Continuing the experiment of reading this poem as about poetry, we might next try to identify Helen as the Iliadic character. But Homer's Helen cursed herself for abandoning her husband and coming to Troy; Sappho's Helen, on the contrary, is held up as proof that it is right to desire one thing above all others, and to follow the beauty perceived no matter where it leads. There is a charming parody of logical argumentation in these stanzas; the underlying, real argument I would reconstruct as follows, speaking for the moment in Sappho's voice. "Male poets have talked of military beauty in positive terms, but of women's beauty (especially Helen's) as baneful and destructive. They will probably never see the lineaments of their own desires as I do, but let me try to use some of their testimony against them, at least to expose the paradoxes of their own system. I shall select the woman whom men both desire and despise in the highest degree. What they have damned her for was, in one light, an act of the highest courage and commitment, and *their own poetry* at one point makes grudging admission that she surpasses all the moral censures leveled against her – the Teichoskopia [Survey from the Wall, *Iliad* 3.121–244]. Helen's abandonment of her husband and child and parents is mentioned there (139, 174), and by a divine manipulation she feels a change of heart, now desiring her former husband and city and parents (139) and calling herself a bitch (180). But these are the poet's sentiments, not hers; he makes her a puppet of his feeling, not a woman with a mind of her own. The real Helen was powerful enough to leave a husband, parents and child whom she valued less than the one she fell in love with. (I needn't and won't mention her lover's name: the person – male or female – is not relevant to my argument.) Indeed she was so powerful that she *beguiled Troy itself* at that moment when, in the midst of its worst suffering, the senior counselors watched her walk along the city wall and said, in their chirpy old men's voices, 'There is no blame for Trojans or armored Achaians to suffer pains so long a time for such a woman' (156–7)."

So far I have been speaking Sappho's mind as I see it behind this poem. There is an interesting problem in lines 12ff., where most modern editors of Sappho's text have filled the gaps with anti-Helen sentiments, on the order of "but (Aphrodite) beguiled her . . . , for (women are easily manipulated,) light(-minded . . .)." We do not know what is missing, but it is more consistent with Sappho's perspective, as I read it, to keep the subject of *paragag'*, "beguiled," the same as in the preceding clause – Helen. "Helen beguiled . . . itself (or, herself)," some feminine noun, such as "city" (*polis*), "blame" (*nemesis*), or the like. What is easily manipulated and light-minded (*kouphôs*) are the senior staff of Troy, who astonishingly dismiss years of suffering as they breathe a romantic sigh when Helen passes.

Poem 31: Sappho Reading the Odyssey

Perhaps Sappho's most impressive fragment is poem 31:

> That one seems to me to be like the gods, the man whosoever sits facing you and listens nearby to your sweet speech and desirable laughter – which surely terrifies the heart in my chest; for as I look briefly at you, so can I no longer speak at all, my tongue is silent, broken, a silken fire suddenly has spread beneath my skin, with my eyes I see nothing, my hearing hums, a cold sweat grips me, a trembling seizes me entire, more pale than grass am I, I seem to myself to be little short of dead. But everything is to be endured, since even a pauper. . . .

The first stanza is a *makarismos*, a traditional formula of praise and well-wishing, "happy the man who . . . ," and is often used to celebrate the prospect of a happy marriage (Snell; Koniaris; Saake 17–38). For instance, "That man is far and away blessed beyond all others who plies you with dowry and leads you to his house; for I have never seen with my eyes a mortal person like you, neither man nor woman. A holy dread grips me as I gaze at you" (*Odyssey* 6.158–61). In fact this passage from Odysseus' speech to Nausikaa is so close in structure (*makarismos* followed by a statement of deep personal dread) to poem 31 that I should like to try the experiment of reading the beginning of Sappho's poem as a re-creation of that scene from the *Odyssey.*

If Sappho is speaking to a young woman ("you") as Nausikaa, with herself in the role of an Odysseus, then there are only two persons present in the imagined scene (Del Grande). This is certainly true to the emotional charge of the poem, in which the power and tension flow between Sappho and the woman she sees and speaks to, between "you" and "I." The essential statement of the poem is, like the speech of Odysseus to Nausikaa, a lauding of the addressee and an abasement of the speaker which together have the effect of establishing a working relationship between two people of real power. The rhetoric of praise and of submission are necessary because the poet and the shipwrecked man are in fact very threatening. Most readers feel the paradox of poem 31's eloquent statement of speechlessness, its powerful declaration of helplessness; as in poem 1, the poet is masterfully in control of herself as victim. The underlying relation of power then is the opposite of its superficial form: the addressee is of a delicacy and fragility which would be shattered by the powerful presence of the poet unless she makes elaborate obeisance, designed to disarm and, by a careful planting of hints, to seduce.

The anonymous "that man whosoever" (*kênos ônêr ottis* in Sappho, *keinos hos ke* in Homer) is a rhetorical cliché, not an actor in the imagined scene. Interpretations which *focus* on "that someone (male)" as a bridegroom (or suitor or friend) who is actually present and occupying the attention of the addressee miss the strategy of persuasion which informs the poem and in doing so reveal their own androcentric premises. In depicting "the man" as a concrete person central to the scene and godlike in power, such interpretations misread a figure of speech as a literal statement and thus add the weight of their own pro-male values to Sappho's woman-centered consciousness. "That man" in poem 31 is like the military armament in poem 16, an introductory set-up to be dismissed. We do not imagine that the speaker of poem 16 is actually watching a fleet or infantry; no more need we think that Sappho is watching a man sitting next to her beloved. To whom, in that case, would Sappho be addressing herself? Such a reading makes poem 31 a modern lyric of totally internal speech, rather than a rhetorically structured public utterance which imitates other well-known occasions for public speaking (prayer, supplication, exhortation, congratulation).

My reading of poem 31 explains why "that man" has assumed a grotesque prominence in discussions of it. Androcentric habits of thought are part of the reason, but even more important is Sappho's intention to hint obliquely at the notion of a bridegroom just as Odysseus does to Nausikaa. Odysseus the stranger designs his speech to the princess around the roles which she and her family will find acceptable – helpless suppliant, valorous adventurer, and potential husband (Austin 1975: 191–200). The ordinary protocols of marital brokerage in ancient society are a system of discreet offers and counter-offers which must maintain at all times the possibility for saving face, for declining with honor and respect to all parties. Odysseus' speech to Nausikaa contains these delicate approaches to the offer of marriage which every reader would appreciate, just as Alkinoos understands Nausikaa's thoughts of marriage in her request to go wash her brothers' dancing clothes: "So she spoke, for she modestly avoided mentioning the word 'marriage' in the presence of her father; but he understood her perfectly" (*Odyssey* 6.66f.). Such skill at innuendo and respectful obliquity is one of the ordinary-language bases for the refined art of lyric speech. Sappho's hint that "someone" enjoys a certain happiness is, like Odysseus' identical statement, a polite self-reference and an invitation to take the next step. Sappho plays with the role of Odysseus as suitor extraordinary, an unheard of stranger who might fulfill Nausikaa's dreams of marriage contrary to all the ordinary expectations of her society. She plays too with the humble formalities of self-denigration and obeisance, all an expansion of *sebas m'echei eisoroôsa*, "holy dread grips me as I gaze on you" (*Odyssey* 6.161).

"That man is equal to the gods": this phrase has another meaning too. Sappho as reader of the *Odyssey* participates by turn in all the characters; this alternation of attention is the ordinary experience of every reader of the epic and is the basis for Sappho's multiple identification with both Aphrodite and Diomedes in *Iliad* 5. In reading *Odyssey* 6 Sappho takes on the roles of both Odysseus and Nausikaa, as well as standing outside them both. I suggest that "that man is equal to the gods," among its many meanings, is a reformulation of Homer's description of the sea-beaten Odysseus whom Athena transforms into a god-like man: *nun de theoisin eoike toi ouranon eurun echousin*, "but now he is like the gods who control the expanse of heaven" (6.243). This is Nausikaa's comment to her maids as she watches Odysseus sit on the shore after emerging from his bath, and she goes on to wish that her husband might be such.[21] The

point of view from which Sappho speaks as one struck to the heart is that
of a mortal visited by divine power and beauty, and this is located in the
Odyssey in the personae of Odysseus (struck by Nausikaa, or so he says), of
Nausikaa (impressed by Odysseus), and of the homeric audience, for
Sappho speaks not only as the strange suitor and the beautiful princess
but as the *Odyssey* reader who watches "that man" (Odysseus) face to face
with the gently laughing girl.[22]

In performing this experiment of reading Sappho's poems as expressing, in part, her thoughts while reading Homer, her consciousness of
men's public world, I think of her being naturally drawn to the character
of Nausikaa, whose romantic anticipation (6.27) and delicate sensitivity
to the unattainability of the powerful stranger (244f., 276–84) are among
the most successful presentations of a woman's mind in male Greek
literature.[23] Sappho sees herself both as Odysseus admiring the nymph-
like maiden and as Nausikaa cherishing her own complex emotions. The
moment of their separation has what is in hindsight, by the normal
process of re-reading literature in the light of its own reformulations, a
"Sapphic" touch: *mnêsêi emei'*, "Farewell, guest, and when you are in
your homeland remember me who saved you – you owe me this" (*Odyssey*
8.461–2). These are at home as Sappho's words in poem 94.6–8: "And I
made this reply to her, 'Farewell on your journey, and remember me, for
you know how I stood by you'" (Schadewaldt 1936: 367).

Gardens of Nymphs

The idyllic beauty of Phaiakia is luxuriously expressed in the rich garden
of Alkinoos, whose continuously fertile fruits and blossoms are like the
gardens which Sappho describes (esp. poems 2, 81b, 94, 96), and it
reminds us of Demetrios' words, "Virtually the whole of Sappho's poetry
deals with nymphs' gardens, wedding songs, eroticism." The other side
of the public/private contrast in Sappho is a design hidden in the lush
foliage and flower cups of these gardens. There are two sides to double
consciousness: Sappho both re-enacts scenes from public culture infused
with her private perspective as the enclosed woman and she speaks
publicly of the most private, woman-centered experiences from which
men are strictly excluded. They are not equal projects, the latter is much
more delicate and risky. The very formulation of women-only secrets,
female *arrhêta*, runs the risk not only of impropriety (unveiling the bride)
but of betrayal by misstatement. Hence the hesitation in Sappho's most
explicit delineation of double consciousness: *ouk oid' otti theô, dicha moi ta*

noêmmata, "I am not sure what to set down, my thoughts are double," could mean "I am not sure which things to set down and which to keep among ourselves, my mind is divided" (51).

Among the thoughts which Sappho has woven into her poetry, in a way which both conceals and reveals without betraying, are sexual images. These are in part private to women, whose awareness of their own bodies is not shared with men, and in part publicly shared, especially in wedding songs and rites, which are a rich store of symbolic images bespeaking sexuality (Bourdieu 1979: 105; Abbott chap. 11). The ordinary ancient concern with fertility, health, and bodily function generated a large family of natural metaphors for human sexuality and, conversely, sexual metaphors for plants and body parts. A high degree of personal modesty and decorum is in no way compromised by a daily language which names the world according to genital analogies or by marriage customs whose function is to encourage fertility and harmony in a cooperative sexual relationship.

The three words which I will use to illustrate this are *numphê, pteruges,* and *mêlon*. The evidence for their usage will be drawn from various centuries and kinds of writing up to a thousand years after Sappho; but the terms in each case seem to be of a semi-technical and traditional nature rather than neologisms. They constitute the scattered fragments of a locally variegated, tenacious symbolic system which was operative in Sappho's time and which is still recognizable in modern Greece.

Numphê has many meanings: at the center of this extended family are "clitoris" and "bride." *Numphê* names a young woman at the moment of her transition from maiden (*parthenos*) to wife (or "woman," *gunê*); the underlying idea is that just as the house encloses the wife and as veil and carriage keep the bride apart from the wedding celebrants, so the woman herself encloses a sexual secret.[24] "The outer part of the female genital system which is visible has the name 'wings' (*pteruges*), which are, so to speak, the lips of the womb. They are thick and fleshy, stretching away on the lower side to either thigh, as it were parting from each other, and on the upper side terminating in what is called the *numphê*. This is the starting point (*archê*) of the wings (labia), by nature a little fleshy thing and somewhat muscular (or, mouse-like)" (Soranos *Gynaecology* 1.18).

The same technical use of *numphê* to mean clitoris is found in other medical writers[25] and lexicographers,[26] and by a natural extension is applied to many analogous phenomena: the hollow between lip and chin (Rufus *Onom.* 42, Pollux 2.90, Hesychios), a depression on the shoulder of horses (*Hippiatr.* 26), a mollusc (Speusippos ap. Athen. 3.105B), a niche (Kallixinos 2 = Müller *FHG* 3, p. 55), an opening rosebud,[27] the point of a plow (Pollux 1.25.2; Proklos *ad* Hesiod *Erga* 425) – this last an interesting reversal based on the image of the plowshare penetrating the earth.

The relation of *numphê*, clitoris, to *pteruges*, wings/labia, is shown by the name of a kind of bracken, the *numphaia pteris*, "nymph's-wing," also known as *thelupteris*, "female wing," by the name of the loose lapels on a seductively opening gown (Pollux 755, 62, 66 = Aristophanes frag. 325 OCT), and by the use of *numphê* as the name for bees in the larva stage just when they begin to open up and sprout wings (Aristotle *Hist. Anim.* 551.[b] 2–4; Photios *Lexikon s.v. numphai*; Pliny *Nat. Hist.* 11.48).

This family of images extends broadly across many levels of Greek culture and serves to reconstruct for us one important aspect of the meaning of "bride," *numphê* as the ancients felt it.[28] Hence the virtual identity of Demetrios' three terms for Sappho's poetry: nymphs' gardens, wedding songs, eroticism. Several of Sappho's surviving fragments and poems make sense as a woman-centered celebration and revision of this public but discreet vocabulary for women's sexuality.

The consciousness of these poems ranges over a wide field of attitudes. The first, in fragment 105a, can be seen as Sappho's version of male genital joking,[29] but when applied to the *numphê* Sappho's female ribaldry is pointedly different in tone:

> Like the sweet-apple [*glukumêlon*] ripening to red on the topmost branch,
> on the very tip of the topmost branch, and the apple-pickers have
>   overlooked it –
> no, they haven't overlooked it but they could not reach it.

Mêlon, conventionally translated "apple," is really a general word for fleshy fruit – apricots, peaches, apples, citron, quinces, pomegranates. In wedding customs it probably most often means quinces and pomegranates, but for convenience sake I will abide by the traditional translation "apple." Like *numphê* and *pteruges, mêlon* has a wider extension of meanings, and from this we can rediscover why "apples" were a prominent symbol in courtship and marriage rites.[30] *Mêlon* signifies various "clitoral" objects: the seed vessel of the rose (Theophrastos *Hist. Plant.* 6.6.6), the tonsil or uvula,[31] a bulge or sty on the lower eyelid (Hesychios *s.v. kula*), and a swelling on the cornea (Alexander Tralles *peri ophthalmôn*, ed. Puschmann, p. 152). The sensitivity of these objects to pressure is one of the bases for the analogy; I will quote just the last one. "And what is called a *mêlon* is a form of fleshy bump (*staphulôma*, grape-like or uvular swelling), big enough to raise the eyelids, and when it is rubbed it bothers the entire lid-surface."

Fragment 105a, spoken of a bride in the course of a wedding song, is a sexual image. We can gather this sense not only from the general erotic meaning of "apples" but from the location of the solitary apple high up on the bare branches of a tree,[32] and from its sweetness and color. The verb *ereuthô*, "grow red," and its cognates are used of blood or other red liquid appearing on the surface of an object which is painted or stained or when the skin suffuses with blood (Hippokrates *Epid.* 2.3.1, *Morb. Sacr.* 15, *Morb.* 4.38 of a blush).

The vocabulary and phrasing of this fragment reveal much more than a sexual metaphor, however; they contain a delicate and reverential attitude to the elusive presence-and-absence of women in the world of men. Demetrios elsewhere (148) speaks of the graceful naivete of Sappho's self-correction, as if it were no more than a charming touch of folk speech when twice in these lines she changes her mind, varying a statement she has already made. But self-correction is Sappho's playful format for saying much more than her simile would otherwise mean. The words are inadequate – how can I say? – not inadequate, but they encircle an area of meaning for which there have not been faithful words in the phallocentric tradition. The real secret of this simile is not the image of the bride's "private" parts but of women's sexuality and consciousness in general, which men do not know as women know. Sappho knows this secret in herself and in other women whom she loves, and she celebrates it in her poetry. Where men's paraphernalia are awkwardly flaunted (bumping into the lintel, frag. 111, inconveniently large like a rustic's feet, frag. 110), women's are protected and secure. The amazing feature of these lines is that the apple is not "ripe for plucking" but unattainable, as if even after marriage the *numphê* would remain secure from the husband's appropriation.[33]

Revision of myth is combined with a sexual image in fragment 166: *phaisi dé pota Lêdan uakinthôi pepukadmenon / éurên ôion,* "They do say that once upon a time Leda found an egg hidden in the hyacinth." As the traditional denigration of Helen was revised in poem 16, so the traditional story of Helen's mother is told anew. Leda was not the victim of Zeus' rape who afterwards laid Helen in an egg, rather she discovered a mysterious egg hidden inside the frilly blossoms of a hyacinth stem, or (better) in a bed of hyacinths when she parted the petals and looked under the leaves. The egg discovered there is

(1)   a clitoris hidden under labia
(2)   the supremely beautiful woman, a tiny Helen, and
(3)   a story, object, and person hidden from male culture.[34]

The metaphor of feeling one's way through the undergrowth until one discovers a special object of desire is contained in the word *maiomai*, "I feel for," "I search out by feeling." It is used of Odysseus feeling the flesh of Polyphemos' stomach for a vital spot to thrust in his sword (*Od.* 9.302), of animals searching through dense thickets for warm hiding places (Hesiod *Erga* 529–33), of enemy soldiers searching through the luxurious thicket for the hidden Odysseus (*Od.* 14.356), of Demeter searching high and low for her daughter (*Hom. Hymn* 2.44), of people searching for Poseidon's lover Pelops (Pindar *Ol.* 1.46). The contexts of this verb are not just similar by accident: *maiomai* means more than "search for," it means "ferret out," especially in dense thickets where an animal or person might be lurking.

In view of the consistency of connotations for this verb there is no reason to posit a shifted usage in Sappho 36, as the lexicon of Liddell, Scott and Jones does. As those lexicographers read it, Sappho's words *kai pothêô kai maomai* are redundant – "I desire you and I desire you." Rather they mean "I desire and I search out." I would like to include the physical sense of feeling carefully for hidden things or hiding places.[35] In the poetic verb *maiomai* there is a physical dimension to the expression of mutual passion and exploration. Desire and touching occur together as two aspects of the same experience: touching is touching-with-desire, desire is desire-with-touching.

The same dictionary which decrees a special meaning for *maiomai* when Sappho uses it invents an Aeolic word *matêmi* (B) = *pateô*, "I walk," to reduce the erotic meaning of a Lesbian fragment of uncertain authorship, Incert. 16: "The women of Krete once danced thus – rhythmically with soft feet around the desirable altar, exploring the tender, pliant flower of the lawn." *Matêmi* is a recognized Aeolic equivalent of *mateuô*, akin to *maiomai*. The meanings "ferret out," "search through undergrowth," "beat the thickets looking for game," "feel carefully" seem to me quite in place. Appealing to a long tradition, Sappho (whom I take to be the author) remarks that the sexual dancing of women, the sensuous circling of moving hands and feet around the erotic altar and combing through the tender valleys, is not only current practice but was known long ago in Krete.

I have been able to find no *simple* sexual imagery in Sappho's poems. For her the sexual is always something else as well. Her sacred landscape of the body is at the same time a statement about a more complete consciousness, whether of myth, poetry, ritual, or personal relationships. In the following fragment, 94, which contains a fairly explicit sexual statement in line 23 (West 322), we find Sappho correcting her friend's view of their relation.

...Without guile I wish to die. She left me weeping copiously and said, "Alas, what fearful things we have undergone, Sappho; truly I leave you against my will." But I replied to her, "Farewell, be happy as you go and remember me, for you know how we have stood by you. Perhaps you don't – so I will remind you...and we have undergone beautiful things. With many garlands of violets and roses...together, and...you put around yourself, at my side, and flowers wreathed around your soft neck with rising fragrance, and...you stroked the oil distilled from royal cherry blossoms and on tender bedding you reached the end of longing...of soft...and there was no...nor sacred...from which we held back, nor grove...sound....

As usual the full situation is unclear, but we can make out a contrast of Sappho's view with her friend's. The departing woman says *deina peponthamen*, "fearful things we have suffered," and Sappho corrects her, *kal'epaschomen*, "beautiful things we continuously experienced." Her reminder of these beautiful experiences (which Page 1955: 83 calls a "list of girlish pleasures") is a loving progression of intimacy, moving in space – down along the body – and in time – to increasing sexual closeness: from flowers wreathed on the head to flowers wound around the neck to stroking the body with oil to soft bed-clothes and the full satisfaction of desire. I would like to read the meager fragments of the succeeding stanza as a further physical landscape: we explored every sacred place of the body. To paraphrase the argument, "When she said we had endured an awful experience, the ending of our love together, I corrected her and said it was a beautiful experience, an undying memory of sensual happiness that knew no limit, luxurious and fully sexual. Her focus on the termination was misplaced; I told her to think instead of our mutual pleasure which itself had no term, no stopping-point, no unexplored grove."

Poem 2 uses sacral language to describe a paradisal place (Turyn) which Aphrodite visits:

Hither to me from Krete, unto this holy temple, a place where there is a lovely grove of apples and an altar where the incense burns, and here is water which ripples cold through apple branches, and all the place is shadowed with roses, and as the leaves quiver a profound quiet ensues. And here is a meadow where horses graze, spring flowers bloom, the honeyed whisper of winds.... This is the very place where you, Kypris..., drawing into golden cups the nectar gorgeously blended for our celebration, then pour it forth.

The grove, Page comments, is "lovely," a word used "elsewhere in the Lesbians only of *personal* charm" (1955: 36). But this place is, among other things, a personal place, an extended and multi-perspectived metaphor for women's sexuality. Virtually every word suggests a sensuous ecstasy in the service of Kyprian Aphrodite (apples, roses, quivering followed by repose, meadow for grazing, spring flowers, honey, nectar flowing). Inasmuch as the language is both religious and erotic, I would say that Sappho is not describing a public ceremony for its own sake but is providing a way to experience such ceremonies, to infuse the celebrants' participation with memories of lesbian sexuality. The twin beauties of burning incense on an altar and of burning sexual passion can be held together in the mind, so that the experience of either is the richer. The accumulation of topographic and sensuous detail leads us to think of the interconnection of all the parts of the body in a long and diffuse act of love, rather than the genital-centered and more relentlessly goal-oriented pattern of love-making which men have been known to employ.

I have tried to sketch two areas of Sappho's consciousness as she has registered it in her poetry: her reaction to Homer, emblematic of the male-centered world of public Greek culture, and her complex sexual relations with women in a world apart from men. Sappho seems always to speak in many voices – her friends', Homer's, Aphrodite's – conscious of more than a single perspective and ready to detect the fuller truth of many-sided desire. But she speaks as a woman to women: her eroticism is both subjectively and objectively woman-centered. Too often modern critics have tried to restrict Sappho's *erôs* to the strait-jacket of spiritual friendship.

A good deal of the sexual richness which I detect in Sappho's lyrics is compatible with interpretations such as those of Lasserre and Hallett 1979,[36] but what requires explanation is their insistent denial that the emotional lesbianism of Sappho's work has any physical component. We must distinguish between the physical component as a putative fact about Sappho in her own life and as a meaning central to her poems. Obviously Sappho as poet is not an historian documenting her own life but rather a creative participant in the erotic-lyric tradition.[37] My argument has been that this tradition includes pervasive allusions to physical *erôs* and that in Sappho's poems both subject and object of shared physical love are women. We now call this lesbian.[38] To admit that Sappho's discourse is lesbian but insist that she herself was not seems quixotic. Would anyone take such pains to insist that Anakreon in real life might not have felt any physical attraction to either youths or women?

It seems clear to me that Sappho's consciousness included a personal and subjective commitment to the holy, physical contemplation of the body of Woman, as metaphor and reality, in all parts of life. Reading her poems in this way is a challenge to think both in and out of our time, both in and out of a phallocentric framework, a reading which can enhance our own sense of this womanly beauty *as subject and as object* by helping us to un-learn our denials of it.

NOTES

1 English translation of *Brouillon pour un dictionnaire des amantes* (New York 1976). There are some uncritical myths in Wittig's own account of Sappho in her essay "Paradigm," in Stambolian and Marks 1979.

2 Lefkowitz 1973 and Hallett 1979 analyze the bias and distortions found in critical comments, ancient and modern, on Sappho.

3 Calder analyzes Welcker's treatise "Sappho Liberated from a Prevalent Prejudice" (1816), suggesting that Welcker's determination to prove that Sappho was not a lesbian can be traced to his idealization of the mother figures in his life (155–6).

4 This has now been done for the French tradition by DeJean.

5 My statement that this is Sappho's central topic throughout her nine books is based not merely on the few fragments (obviously), but on the ancient testimonies, especially those of Demetrios, who provided the original title of this essay ("... nymphs' gardens, wedding songs, eroticism – in short the whole of Sappho's poetry") and Himerios ("Sappho dedicated all of her poetry to Aphrodite and the Erotes, making the beauty and charms of a maiden the occasion for her melodies"). These and the other testimonia are collected in Gallavotti and Campbell.

6 There was also the category of heroic, exceptional woman, e.g. Herodotos' version of Artemisia, who is used to "prove the rule" every time he mentions her (7.99, 8.68, 8.87f., 8.101), and the stories collected by Plutarch *de virtutibus mulierum*. The stated purpose of this collection is to show that *aretê*, "virtue" or "excellence," is the same in men and women, but the stories actually show only that some women in times of crisis have stepped out of their regular anonymity and performed male roles when men were not available (Schaps 1982).

7 "A feminist theory of poetry would begin to take into account the context in history of these poems and their political connections and implications. It would deal with the fact that women's poetry conveys...a special kind of consciousness.... Concentrating on consciousness and the politics of women's poetry, such a theory would evolve new ways of reading what is there" (Bernikow 10–1).

8 Consciousness of course is not a solid object which can be discovered intact like an easter egg lying somewhere in the garden (as in the Sapphic fragment 166 Leda is said to have found an egg hidden under the hyacinths). Sappho's lyrics are many-layered constructions of melodic words, images, ideas, and arguments in a formulaic system of sharable points of view (personas). I take it for granted that the usual distinctions between "the real Sappho" as author and speaker(s) of the poems will apply when I speak here of Sappho's consciousness.

9 In this territory and at these recitations women are present – Homer is not a forbidden text to women, not an arcane *arrhêton* of the male mysteries. In the *Odyssey* (1.325–9) Penelope hears and reacts to the epic poetry of a bard singing in her home, but her objections to his theme, the homecoming from Troy, are silenced by Telemakhos. Arete's decision to give more gifts to Odysseus (*Od.* 11.335–41) after he has sung of the women he saw in the Underworld may be an implicit sign of her approval of his poetry. Helen in *Iliad* 6 delights in the fact that she is a theme of epic poetry (357–8) and weaves the stories of the battles fought for her into her web (125–8).

10 The text of Sappho used here is that of Edgar Lobel and D. Page (abbreviated L-P), *Poetarum Lesbiorum Fragmenta* (Oxford 1955).

11 Homer seems to include this possibility in the range of performing *klea andrôn* ["deeds of men"] when he presents Achilles singing to his own *thumos* ["spirit"], while Patroklos sits in silence, not listening as an audience but waiting for Achilles to stop (*Il.* 9. 186–91).

12 Sappho is only one individual, and may have been untypical in her power to achieve a literary life and renown. Claims that society in her time and place allowed greater scope for women in general to attain a measure of public esteem are based almost entirely on Sappho's poems (including probably Plutarch *Lykourgos* 18.4, *Theseus* 19.3, Philostratos *Life of Apollonios* 1.30). The invention of early women poets is taken to extremes by Tatian in his *adversus Graecos* and by Ptolemy Chennos (Chapter Five, p. 143–4).

13 The evidence is found in Hephaistion *peri sêmêiôn* 138, quoted by Hooker 1977: 11.

14 Translations of Sappho in this chapter are my own; ellipses indicate that the Greek is incomplete.

15 As Boedeker shows for fragment 95: "a consciously 'anti-heroic' persona, specifically perhaps an anti-Odysseus.... The poem becomes a new personal statement of values, a denial and reshaping of epic-heroic ideals" (52).

16 We may take it as another measure of our distance from her that the pep and bite of the consonants in "Psappo," with all the p's sounded, have evaporated into the tired fizz of "Saffo."

17 Hesiod *Works and Days* 578–81. Clay suggests that the interpretation "but you bring the child *away* from its mother" could fit into a wedding song.

18 That would solve the problem felt at Theokritos 2.61, where editors emend *passô* to *massô*.

19   "The classic custom of wooing a damsel by throwing an apple into her lap still exists, though it is condemned by public opinion as improper, and is strongly resented by the maid's kinsfolk as an impertinence" (Abbott 147–8). Other literature is cited in n. 30 below.

20   E.g. J.B. Bury, "...while Sappho confined her muse within a narrower circle of feminine interests" (*Cambridge Ancient History* IV, 1953, 494f.) and similarly Werner Jaeger, *Paideia* (English translation, B. Blackwell, Oxford 1965) vol. 1, p. 132.

21   The comparison to gods runs throughout the Phaiakian scenes: Nausikaa (16, 105–9), her maids (18), the Phaiakians (241), Nausikaa's brothers, *athanatois enalinkioi* (7.5).

22   One could also experiment with reading the speaker's symptoms (fever, chill, dizziness) as the result of an erotic spell.... The deadening of the speaker's tongue (so beautifully contradicted, of course, by the eloquence and precision of the poet herself) is a typical affliction brought on by a *katadesmos*.

23   Apollonios of Rhodes' Medea is conscious of love in terms drawn from Sappho (Privitera), and note especially the characteristic presentation of Medea's mental after-images and imaginings (3.453–58, 811–6, 948–55), which is the technique of Sappho 1, 16, and 96.

24   "One of the men in Chios, apparently a prominent figure of some sort, was taking a wife and, as the bride was being conducted to his home in a chariot, Hippoklos the king, a close friend of the bridegroom, mingling with the rest during the drinking and laughter, jumped up into the chariot, not intending any insult but merely being playful according to the common custom. The friends of the groom killed him" Plutarch *mul. virt.* 244E.

25   Rufinus ap. Oribasios 3.391.1, Galen 2.370E, Aetios 16.103–4 (clitoridectomy), Paulus Aigin. 6.70 (clitoridectomy for lesbians).

26   Photios *Lexikon* s.v.; Pollux 2.174, with the anagram *skairon sarkion*, "throbbing little piece of flesh."

27   Photios *Lexikon*. s.v. *numphai*: "And they call the middle part of the female genitals the *numphê*; also the barely opened buds of roses are *numphai*; and newly-wed maidens are *numphai*." The equation of flowers and female genitals is ancient (Krinagoras *Anth. Pal.* 6.345, Achilles Tatius 2.1) and modern (art: Lippard, Dodson, Chicago 1975, 1979; poetry: Lorde, "Love Poem" in Bulkin and Larkin). Sappho appears to have made the equation of bride and roses explicit, according to Wirth.
      I would not reject the suggestion that Sappho's feelings for Kleis, as imagined in fragment 132, were given a consciously lesbian coloring: "I have a beautiful child, her shape is like that of golden *flowers*, beloved Kleis; in her place I would not...all Lydia nor lovely...." Indeed, taking it a step further, this "child" (*pais*) may be simply another metaphor for clitoris (*Kleis/kleitoris*). The biographical tradition which regards Kleis as the name of Sappho's daughter and mother may be (as so often) based on

nothing more than a fact-hungry reading of her poems. (The same name occurs at frag. 98b1.) On flowers and fruit see Stehle 1977.

28 For the connection of Nymphs to marriage and birth see Ballentine.

29 In her fragments 110 and 111: Kirk 1963, Killeen; fragment 121 may be "una variazione scherzosa nel nota fr. 105," Lanata 66.

30 Foster, McCartney, Trumpf 1960, Lugauer, Littlewood, Kakridis; P. Oxy. 2637, frag. 25.6; Abbott 147f., 170, 177.

31 Rufus *Onom.* 64; Galen *de usu partium* 15.3: "The part called *numpha* gives the same sort of protection to the uteri that the uvula gives to the pharynx, for it covers the orifice of their neck by coming down into the female pudendum and keeps it from being chilled." Sappho's fragment 42, on the warmth afforded by enfolding wings (*ptera*), may be read of labia as well as of birds.

32 "In other parts (of Macedonia) . . ., especially among the Wallachs, a pole with an apple on top and a white kerchief streaming from it . . . is carried by a kilted youth in front of the wedding procession" (Abbott 172).

33 This sense of *numphé* gives further meaning to a fragment of Praxilla, 754 in Page 1962. "Looking in beautifully through the windows, your head that of a maiden, but you are a *numphé* underneath," *ô dia tôn thuridôn kalon emblepoisa / parthene tan kephalan ta d'enerthe numpha.* Praxilla is, according to Aly's fine interpretation (RE 22 [1954] 176), addressing the moon shining through her windows (cp. Page 1962: 747, *selênaiês te prosôpon*); its mystery and elusive attraction are expressed by the image of a woman with a youthful, innocent face and a look that bespeaks deeper experience and knowledge. The physical comparison is to a woman whose face alone is visible: wrapped up under all those clothes, says Praxilla, is the body of a sexually mature woman. Page at the opposite extreme envisions a woman peeping into the windows of houses in order to attract other women's husbands (*quae more meretricio vagabunda per fenestras intueri soles, scilicet ut virum foras unde unde elicias,* Page 1962: 754 app. crit.). This level of significance may also be relevant to Page 1962: 286 (Ibykos) and 929 e-g (anonymous).

34 The verb *pukazô* refers not to just any kind of "hiding" but to covering an object with clothes, flower garlands, or hair, either as an adornment or for protection. "Thick" flowers (*huakinthon / puknon kai malakon*) cover the earth to cushion the love-making of Zeus and Hera (*Iliad* 14.347–50).

35 Fragment 48 may be read in a similar sense: *élthes kai m' epothêsas egô de s' emaioman / on d' ephlexas eman phrena kaiomenan pothôi,* "You came and you desired me; I searched you carefully; you stirred the fires of my feeling, smoldering with desire." *ephlexas* is Wesseling's conjecture for *phulaxas; m'epothêsas* is my conjecture for *epoêsas.* I would support this conjecture by reference back to fragment 36, which joins *poth/* and *mai/,* and by the symmetry achieved: you desired me – I felt you – you stirred me – I desired you, which we might call Sapphic reciprocity. Cf. Lanata 79.

36 "Sarebbe augurabile che nelle allusioni all'amore saffico cadesse in disuso la sgradita definizione di 'turpe amore' inventata da un moralismo se non altro anacronistico," Gentili 1966: 48 n.55. Stehle 1979 is excellent.

37 Late Greek rhetoric maintains the tradition of praising a public official at a ceremonial event by a declaration of love. Himerios (48) and Themistios (13) tell their audiences that the honored official is their *erómenos*, boyfriend.

38 "Women who love women, who choose women to nurture and support and create a living environment in which to work creatively and independently, are lesbians" (Cook 738).

REFERENCES

Abbott, G. F. 1903. *Macedonian Folklore*. Cambridge.

Austin, N. 1975. *Archery at the Dark of the Moon*. Berkeley, CA.

Ballentine, F. G. 1904. "Some Phases of the Cult of the Nymphs." *Harvard Studies in Classical Philology* 15: 97–110.

Barnard, M. 1980. "Static." *Woman Poet, I: The West*, 34. Reno, NV.

Bernikow, L. 1974. *The World Split Open*. New York.

Boedeker, D. D. 1979. "Sappho and Acheron." In G. W. Bowersock, W. Burkert, and M. Putnam (eds.), *Arktouros: Hellenic Studies presented to Bernard W. M. Knox on the Occasion of his 65th birthday*, 40–52. New York.

Bolling, G. 1958. "POIKILOS and THRONA." *American Journal of Philology* 79: 275–82.

———. 1959. "Restoration of Sappho, 98a 1–7." *American Journal of Philology* 80: 276–87.

Bonner, C. 1949. "KESTOS IMAS and the Saltire of Aphrodite." *American Journal of Philology* 70: 1–6.

Bourdieu, P. 1979. *Algeria 1960*. Cambridge.

Brashear, W. 1979. "Ein Berliner Zauberpapyrus." *Zeitschrift für Papyrologie und Epigraphik* 33: 261–78.

Bulkin, E. and J. Larkin (eds.), 1975. *Amazon Poetry*. New York.

Calder, W. M. 1988. "F. G. Welcker's *Sapphobild* and its Reception in Wilamowitz." In W. M. Calder et al. (eds.), *Friedrich Gottlieb Welcker, Werk und Wirkung*, 131–56. Stuttgart.

Cameron, A. 1949. "Sappho's Prayer to Aphrodite." *Harvard Theological Review* 32: 1–17.

Campbell, D. A. 1982. *Greek Lyric. I. Sappho, Alcaeus*. Cambridge, MA.

Chicago, J. 1975. *Through the Flower*. Garden City, NY.

———. 1979. *The Dinner Party*. Garden City, NY.

Clay, J. S. 1980. "Sappho's Hesperus and Hesiod's Dawn." *Philologus* 124: 302–5.

Cook, B. W. 1979. "'Women Alone Stir my Imagination': Lesbianism and the Cultural Tradition." *Signs* 4: 718–39.

DeJean, J. 1989. *Fictions of Sappho, 1546–1937.* Chicago.

Dodson, B. n.d. *Liberating Masturbation.* B. Dodson, Box 1933, New York, NY 10001.

duBois, P. 1978. "Sappho and Helen." *Arethusa* 11: 88–99.

Foster, B. O. 1899. "Notes on the Symbolism of the Apple in Classical Antiquity." *Harvard Studies in Classical Philology* 10: 39–55.

Gallavotti, C. 1947. *Saffo e Alceo: Testimonianze e frammenti.* Naples.

Gentili, B. 1966. "La veneranda Saffo." *Quaderni Urbinati di Cultura Classica* 2: 37–62.

Hallett, J. P. 1979. "Sappho and her Social Context." *Signs* 4: 447–64.

Hooker, J. T. 1977. *The Language and Text of the Lesbian Poets.* Innsbruck.

Janko, R. 1988. "Berlin Magical Papyrus 21243: A Conjecture." *Zeitschrift für Papyrologie und Epigraphik* 72: 293.

Kakridis, Ph. I. 1972. "Une Pomme mordue." *Hellenica* 25: 189–92.

Killeen, J. F. 1973. "Sappho Fr. 111." *Classical Quarterly* 23: 197.

Kirk, G. S. 1963. "A Fragment of Sappho Reinterpreted." *Classical Quarterly* 13: 51–2.

Koniaris, G. 1968. "On Sappho fr. 31 (L–P)." *Philologus* 112: 173–86.

Lanata, C. 1966. "Sul linguaggio amoroso di Saffo." *Quaderni Urbinati di Cultura Classica* 2: 63–79.

Lasserre, F. 1974. "Ornements érotiques dans la poésie lyrique archaïque." In J. L. Heller (ed.), *Serta Turyniana*, 5–33. Urbana, IL.

Lawler, L. B. 1948. "On Certain Homeric Epithets." *Philological Quarterly* 27: 80–4.

Lefkowitz, M. R. 1973. "Critical Stereotypes and the Poetry of Sappho." *Greek, Roman and Byzantine Studies* 14: 113–23.

Liddell, H. G., Scott, R., and H. S. Jones. 1968. *A Greek–English Lexicon* (with Supplement). Oxford.

Lippard, L. 1977. "Quite Contrary: Body, Nature, Ritual in Women's Art." *Chrysalis* 2: 30–47.

Littlewood, A. R. 1968. "The Symbolism of the Apple in Greek and Roman Literature." *Harvard Studies in Classical Philology* 72: 147–81.

Lobel, E. and D. Page. 1955. *Poetarum Lesbiorum Fragmenta.* Oxford.

Lugauer, M. 1967. "Untersuchungen zur Symbolik des Apfels in der Antike." Unpublished dissertation. Erlangen-Nürnburg.

Maltomini, F. 1988. "P. Berol. 21243 (Formulario Magico): Due Nuove Letture." *Zeitschrift für Papyrologie und Epigraphik* 74: 247–8.

Marry, J. D. 1979. "Sappho and the Heroic Ideal." *Arethusa* 12: 271–92.

McCartney, E. S. 1925. "How the Apple Became the Token of Love." *Transactions of the American Philological Association* 56: 70–81.

Merkelbach, R. 1957. "Sappho und ihr Kreis." *Philologus* 101: 1–29.

Nagy, G. 1974. *Comparative Studies in Greek and Indic Meter.* Cambridge, MA.

Neuberger-Donath, R. 1969. "Sappho Fr. 1.1: POIKILOTHRON' oder POI-
KILOPHRON." *Wiener Studien* 82: 15–17.

Obbink, D. n.d. "Apples and Eros: Hesiod frag. 72–75 M.-W." Unpublished
paper.

Page, D. 1955. *Sappho and Alcaeus.* Oxford.

———. (ed.). 1962. *Poetae Melici Graeci.* Oxford.

Pfeiffer, R. 1968. *History of Classical Scholarship – From the Beginning to the End
of the Hellenistic Age.* Oxford.

Privitera, G. A. 1969. "Ambiguità antitesi analogia nel fr. 31 L–P di Saffo."
Quaderni Urbinati di Cultura Classica 8: 37–80.

Putnam, M. 1960/1. "Throna and Sappho 1.1." *Classical Journal* 56: 79–83.

Rissman, L. 1983. *Love as War: Homeric Allusion in the Poetry of Sappho.*
Königstein.

Russo, J. 1973–4. "Reading the Greek Lyric Poets (Monodists)." *Arion* 1:
707–30.

Saake, H. 1971. *Zur Kunst Sapphos.* Munich.

Snell, B. 1931. "Sapphos Gedicht *phainetai moi kênos.*" *Hermes* 66: 71–90.

Stambolian, G. and E. Marks (eds.). 1979. *Homosexualities and French Literature.* Ithaca, NY and London.

Stanley, K. 1976. "The Role of Aphrodite in Sappho Fr. 1." *Greek, Roman and
Byzantine Studies* 17: 305–21.

Stehle, E. 1977. "Retreat from the Male: Catullus 62 and Sappho's Erotic
Flowers." *Ramus* 6: 83–102.

———. 1979. "Romantic Sensuality, Poetic Sense: A Response to Hallett on
Sappho." *Signs* 4: 464–71.

Svenbro, J. 1975. "Sappho and Diomedes." *Museum Philologum Londoniense* 1:
37–49.

Trumpf, J. 1960. "Kydonische Apfel." *Hermes* 88: 14–22.

Turyn, A. 1942. "The Sapphic Ostracon." *Transactions of the American Philological Association* 73: 308–18.

West, M. L. 1970. "Burning Sappho." *Maia* 22: 307–30.

Wills, G. 1967. "The Sapphic 'Umwertung aller Werte.'" *American Journal of
Philology* 88: 434–42.

Wirth, P. 1963. "Neue Spuren eines Sapphobruchstücks." *Hermes* 91: 115–17.

Sources

Sappho

Born on the island of Lesbos in the second half of the seventh century BCE, Sappho originally composed nine books of poetry; only one complete poem (Sappho 1) and several substantial fragments survive. Although many of the poems concern the love between women, little is known about her personal life or about her relationship to the companions mentioned in her poems.

Sappho 1

O deathless Aphrodite on your patterned throne,
wile-weaving daughter of Zeus, I beg you,
do not overwhelm my heart,
O mistress, with suffering and sorrows,

but come here, if also before perceiving my voice
you listened from afar and came,
yoking your car
and leaving the golden house

of your father. Beautiful, swift sparrows
drew you over the dark earth
whirring their dense wings
through the middle of the shimmering air.

Swiftly you arrived, and you, O blessed goddess,
with a smile on your deathless face
asked, what again I suffered,
why again I called,

and what did I most wish to happen
in my maddened heart. "Whom now shall I persuade
to lead you back into her love? Who, O Sappho,
has hurt you?"

For if she flees, soon she will pursue,
if she refuses your gifts, soon she will give,
if she does not love, soon she will love,
even against her will.

Come to me even now, and release me from bitter
anguish. Accomplish all that my heart longs
to accomplish, and you yourself
be my ally!

Sappho 31

Equal to the gods seems that man to me,
who sits opposite you
and nearby listens to your sweet voice
and amorous laughter.

Then the heart within my breast trembles,
for when I look at you, even for a moment,
it is no longer possible
for me to speak;

my tongue has snapped into silence,
straight away a delicate fire runs under my skin.
there is no sight in my eyes,
my ears ring,

a cold sweat flows over my body
and trembling seizes all of me —
for I am greener than grass
and I seem close to death. . . .

Homer

In this passage from Homer's *Iliad* (c. 750 BCE), a poem about the escalating conflict between Agamemnon and Achilles in the final year of the Trojan war, the Greek hero Diomedes confronts a foe on the battlefield and prays to Athena, goddess of military strategy, for help. She promises to aid him, and even encourages him to wound Aphrodite, a goddess who belongs more to the bedroom than to the battlefield!

Homer, *Iliad* 5.114–32

Next Diomedes skilled at the war cry spoke,
"Hear me, child of aegis-bearing Zeus, Atrytone,
if ever before you stood with kindly thoughts near my father
in hostile battle, now in turn be kind to me, Athena.
Grant that going into the onslaught of the spear, I kill this man,
who struck me by surprise and then vaunted, saying
that I would no longer look upon the light of the sun!"
So he spoke in prayer. And Pallas Athena heard him,
and she made his limbs light again, both his feet and his arms above.
Standing near him she uttered winged words:
"Diomedes, dare now to enter into battle with the Trojans.
For the strength of your father has come into your chest,
unshakeable, such as the horseman, the shield-brandisher Tydeus had.
I have taken the mist away from your eyes, which was there before,
so that you may easily recognize god and mortal.
Therefore, if a god comes forward and makes trial of you,
do not battle directly with the rest of the immortal gods,
but only if the daughter of Zeus, Aphrodite,
goes into battle; her you may wound with the piercing bronze."

Homer, *Odyssey* 6.139–85

Only the daughter of Alcinous remained. For Athena
put courage into her chest, and took the fear from her limbs.
She faced him and held her ground. Odysseus debated
whether to supplicate the fair-faced girl, clasping her knees,
or whether to stay where he was and beg her with gentle, persuasive words
to show him the city and to give him clothing.

The latter plan seemed best to him as he pondered:
to stay where he was and beg her with gentle, persuasive words,
so that the maiden would not become angry at him for clasping her knees.
Then straightaway he spoke in gentle, persuasive tones:
"I am clasping your knees in supplication, lady. But tell me,
are you a goddess or a mortal woman?
If you are a goddess and have as your home broad heaven,
you resemble most of all Artemis, daughter of mighty Zeus,
in your features, stature and form.
But if you are one of the mortals who live on earth,
three times blessed are your father and your queenly mother,
three times blessed are your brothers. Their heart
always grows warm with pleasure at the thought of you,
when they see their fair flower taking her place in the dance.
But that man is most blessed above all others in his heart
who leads you to his house, winning you with his bride gifts.
For never have I laid eyes on such a creature,
neither a man nor a woman. Awe overwhelms me as I gaze!
Once in Delos I saw such a thing alongside the altar of Apollo,
a sapling of young palm shooting up. I went there once,
and a great army followed me on that journey
which caused great suffering for me.
And just as I marveled in my heart at that tree, looking for a long time,
since such a trunk had never before sprung from the earth,
so now I admire you, lady, and I marvel, and I am terribly afraid
to clasp your knees. And yet hard sorrow comes upon me.
Yesterday, after twenty days on the wine-dark sea, I escaped.
Until then the waves and sweeping storms carried me
from the island of Ogygia. Now a god has cast me ashore here,
until I suffer some further evil. For I do not think my troubles
will cease; before then the gods will accomplish many things.
But take pity on me, lady. After suffering many evils,
I have come first to you, nor do I know any of the other
mortals who inhabit this city and land.
Show me your city, give me a scrap to wear,
if indeed you brought a covering for your laundry when you came here.
And may the gods grant all that you desire in your heart,
a husband and a home, and may they bless you with like-mindedness.
For there is nothing better or more excellent
than when two people manage a household with a united mind,
the husband and wife together. They are a great grief to their foes,
a joy to their friends, but they know it best themselves."

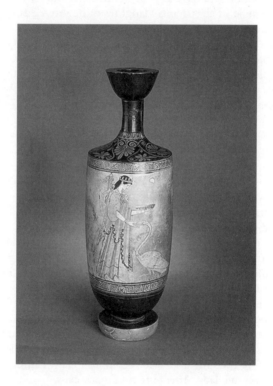

Figure 3 *Artemis and Swan.* White ground lekythos, attributed to the
Pan painter, c.490 BCE. State Hermitage Museum, St. Petersburg, inv.
no. B 670. Wearing a deerskin and carrying a quiver, Artemis propitiates
a wild swan, the animal form adopted by Zeus when he appeared to her
mother.

3

BOUND TO BLEED: ARTEMIS AND GREEK WOMEN

H. King

In Edwin Ardener's influential paper 'Belief and the problem of women' (1975), the 'problem', that of finding out how women see the world of which they are a part when our only informants are men, is shown to be twofold. There is a 'technical' problem: women are less likely to 'speak', to act as our sources. There is also an 'analytical', or conceptual, dimension for, even when our informants are women, the model of the world and of their place in it which they give may be less acceptable to the observer than the neat, bounded categories given by the male informant (1975, pp. 1–3).

A particular form of technical/conceptual division can be applied to ancient Greek source material. The problem of Greek women is usually presented as a technical problem; that is, as something originating in the sources. In the words of Vatin: 'It is in the deeds, the words and the laws of men that we must look for the traces [of Greek women]' (1970, pp. 2–3: my translation). The evidence available to us was mostly written by Greek men; although this statement itself tells us something about Greek women it also acts as a screen to distance us from them. In addition, the sources are preselected so that, where comparative material raises interesting questions, the type of evidence required to answer them may simply be unavailable.

The often conflicting images of women which emerge from the evidence similarly tend to be seen in terms of the technical problems of the sources. Shaw's article on women in fifth-century Athenian drama (1975) criticises a very simple example of this approach, the division of the evidence into two main classes; firstly legal and historical material, in which women are 'defined as near slaves, or as perpetual minors' (p. 255), and secondly literature and the visual arts, in which women seem to have a prominent role. Either category of evidence can be discarded by those working on the period; law as only theory, drama as mere fantasy. A more sophisticated and inclusive division of the source material, as concerned with 'social organisation', 'popular morality' or 'myth', appears in Just's article (1975).

The 'problem' of Greek women, then, is firstly that we have no direct means of access to them; we only have sources written by men. Secondly, however, even these sources give us the contrast between the strong, dominant women of tragedy and the almost invisible women of the Funeral Speech of Thucydides, in which Pericles says that 'the greatest glory of a woman is to be least talked about by men' (2.46). Both Shaw and Just claim that there is a coherent model of Greek women beneath these different images given in the evidence, but I would suggest that they are mistaken in giving so much weight to the problems of the sources. The discovery that different types of evidence give different, even contradictory, presentations of women is not a problem, but a solution, and it should be acknowledged rather than being concealed by the division of that evidence into categories such as 'law', 'custom' and 'myth' (as in Gould, 1980) based on our own society's criteria of rationality.

It is important to realise here that, even outside the Greek context, the concept of 'woman' has inherent potential for ambiguity. 'Woman' can be opposed to 'man', as female to male, or subsumed under the category 'man' so that humanity is set up against 'gods' or 'beasts' (cf. Hastrup, 1978, p. 54): 'woman' is thus both excluded and included, alien and familiar. For the Greeks woman is a necessary evil, a *kalon kakon* (Hesiod, *Theogony* 585); an evil because she is undisciplined and licentious, lacking the self-control of which men are capable, yet necessary to society as constructed by men, in order to reproduce it.[1]

In social terms, women can be put under the control of men, being assigned a specific space within male culture and society where they can give birth, weave and cook, while being excluded from economic and political spheres. The Greek word for woman, *gynē*, is also the word for 'wife', and it was as a wife and mother that woman was most fully brought into male culture. Her domestication could be so complete that she would express and enforce the male model of society, including the reasons for her own entry into it (Redfield, 1977, p. 149); yet even here the risk that she would run wild remained.

In the words of Sarah B. Pomeroy's title, women were 'Goddesses, Whores, Wives and Slaves' (1975): in conceptual terms these four identities are all strands which can be taken out of the basic, ambiguous term 'woman', but such a separation can never be complete because the sub-categories have a tendency to drift back towards their original unity.[2] The goddesses of the Greek pantheon include Hera the wife, Demeter the mother, and Artemis as the woman who rejects both marriage and motherhood; all women are potential whores, if they are allowed to surrender to their uncontrolled desires; all women are slaves to their emotions, of which only man can be a master.

In this paper I intend to look at another way in which the range of meanings of 'woman' was separated out in Greek thought. As the positive values of 'woman' tended to be centred on the concept of the reproducer, the *gynē*, so the negative values shifted to the unmarried girl. The focus of this paper is therefore not on the technical problems of the sources, but on the conceptual framework within which they were produced, the ideas about 'woman' which governed the perception of the female life-cycle; in particular, on the entry into what was culturally established as the category of the mature woman, the *gynē*.

From Parthenos to Gynē

All women start their lives conceptually 'outside' male society, but most are taken 'inside' through the process of maturation. Children, for the Greeks, are by nature wild (Plato, *Timaeus*, 44a–b; *Laws* II, 653d–e, 666a–e); in particular, the *parthenos*, 'childless, unmarried, yet of the age for marriage',[3] is untamed (*admēs*) and must be domesticated before it is even possible for a man to carry on a conversation with her (Xenophon, *Oeconomicus*, 7. 10: use of *tithaseuein*). A girl's upbringing is represented as the 'taming' or 'breaking in' of a filly, and marriage is the end of this process: marriage also opens the process of submission to the yoke of Aphrodite.[4]

There are a number of biologically and socially defined points at which the transition from *parthenos* to *gynē* can be situated, the most obvious being menarche, defloration, marriage and the first parturition. In connection with the choice[5] of one or more of these as involving a significant change of status the factor of control is particularly relevant. Menarche is a transition which neither men nor women can control (although Soranus, *Gynaecology* 1. 25, gives exercises to encourage it). Marriage, in Greek society, is under male control, being arranged between *oikos* heads.

Defloration is more ambiguous, covering a spectrum ranging from male control (rape) to female control (seduction). The first parturition may appear as an entirely female event, but there is scope for male control;[6] men are necessary not only for conception (although see Detienne, 1976) but also to bring on labour by having intercourse with their wives (Aristotle, *Historia Animalium*, 584a 30–1) and as doctors to speed up labour with appropriate drugs (e.g. PG, 1. 34).[7] There is in addition the possibility that a registration or initiation procedure linked to age may be used, although this does not seem to have been the case with Greek women.[8]

In a society in which women are valued above all for their reproductive capacities, it is to be expected that a biological event or series of events will be used to form the entry to the category 'mature woman': in a society in which woman can also be seen as the 'Other' (Arthur, 1976, p. 390; Padel, [1983]) to be brought under male control, it is to be expected that the cultural ideal will be one of a close connection between the male-controlled social event, marriage, and the less controllable physical changes in a woman's life. Ideally, therefore, menarche confirmed that a girl was 'ripe' for marriage (on ripeness see for example Pausanias 2. 33. 2 and *Greek Anthology* (hereafter *Anth. Pal.*), VII.600) and defloration (Soranus, *Gyn*, I.33.4, 33.6): she would be deflowered by her husband on her wedding night (the 'first yoke of Aphrodite' in *Anth. Pal.*, IX.245): she would begin bearing children as soon as possible. The temporal gap between *parthenos* and *gynē* would be short; the Greek process of becoming married, extending from betrothal to the birth of the first child, would cover it (Vernant, 1974) and the term *nymphē* would be applied to those in the 'latent period' stretching from marriageable to married (Schmitt, 1977, p. 1068; see also Chantraine, 1946–7, pp. 228–9 on *nymphē/gynē* overlap).

In practice, however, there are many reasons why a girl may be trapped between categories so that she becomes anomalous, not really a *parthenos* but not fully a *gynē*. Social and biological status may not coincide: menarche may not have occurred, although in all other respects (age, vocal changes, breast development – see Aristotle, *Hist. Anim.*, 581a 31–b 24) she is ripe for marriage (Soranus, *Gyn*. 1.29.6); she may be pregnant but unmarried (Coronis in Pindar, *Third Pythian* 34, is a *parthenos* although she carries Apollo's child); she may have difficulty conceiving; or she may not want to marry.

In view of Greek ideas about the two sides of 'woman' – the outsider, product of a separate act of creation (see Loraux, 1978), who must nevertheless be brought into society to reproduce it – gynaecological texts are a particularly appropriate field of study. Their concern is with woman as reproducer, yet the very autonomy of the study of female diseases reflects the separation of woman from the superior, complete[9] human form, man.

In the Hippocratic medical texts female functions such as menstruation and childbirth are regarded as pathological (cf. Ehrenreich and English, 1979, p. 99 on nineteenth-century medical theory) and hence require treatment: yet they are also natural, for it is wrong for a woman to develop masculine characteristics (as in Ep. VI, 8.32) and they can, as *katharsis*, have a healing effect (Burkert, 1977, p. 133, n. 31; Manuli, 1980, pp. 401–2). To circumvent this problem of women's physical processes as both negative and positive – itself a result of wider views of 'woman' – the texts establish physical 'norms'. Thus the normal blood loss during menstruation is set at about a pint over two or three days; any more or less is pathological and needs therapy (PG 1. 6; *Aphorisms* 5. 57 (*L* IV 552)). A further distinction is drawn between the 'womb-woman' and those 'outside the logic of generation' (*ek tōn tokōn*, PG 2. 127; see Manuli, 1980, pp. 398–9). The female object of the text is split, and the non-reproductive are exhorted to reproduce. Young girls are advised to marry, widows that 'it is best to become pregnant' (e.g. NW 3: PG 2. 127, 131, 135, 162).

The Peri Partheniōn

Text

The *Peri Partheniōn* is one of a series of gynaecological treatises in the Hippocratic corpus; it probably dates to the fifth or fourth century BC and, as a practical handbook for doctors, it may have been modified many times before reaching the form in which it survives (Lloyd, 1975, pp. 180ff.). The title is usually translated 'On the diseases of young girls' or 'On the diseases of virgins'; here the Greek term will be retained because, although virginity and youth were aspects of the ideal *parthenos*, there is no current English equivalent. The main focus of the semantic field covered by *parthenos* is not 'virgin' but 'unmarried' (see Loraux, 1981, p. 241, n. 183); the idea of youth is present but, if suitably qualified, the term can be applied to older unmarried women (e.g. 'older *parthenoi*' in PG 2. 127). Soranus clearly applies it to girls before menarche (*Gyn* 1.29.6).

This short fragment, on one set of problems preventing the *parthenos* to *gynē* transition, opens with a statement on the origins and nature of the *tekhnē* (profession, trade) of medicine and a reference to the symptoms of the 'sacred disease', epilepsy. Such symptoms, the writer explains, may result in suicide by hanging. This is more common in women than in men, and most common among *parthenoi* who, despite being 'ripe for marriage', remain unmarried.

Such *parthenoi* risk illness at menarche[10] when blood flows to the womb as if it were going to pass out of the body. In the *parthenos* who does not marry at the proper time the blood cannot flow out because 'the orifice of exit' is not open. The blood instead moves to the heart and diaphragm, where its effect is described as producing similar sensations to those felt in the feet after sitting still for a long time. However, when the heart and diaphragm are involved there is great danger, since the veins which return the blood are not straight, so that the return is delayed, and the area itself is a vital one. The *parthenos* therefore exhibits a number of symptoms; for instance, she is delirious, she fears the darkness, and she has visions which seem to compel her to jump, to throw herself down wells and to strangle herself. In the absence of visions she shows an erotic fascination with death (*eraō*: she welcomes death as a lover). The text ends:

> When her[11] senses return, the *gynaikes* dedicate many objects to Artemis, above all, the most splendid of their garments. They are ordered to do this by diviners (*manteis*) who thoroughly deceive them. But she is relieved of this complaint when nothing prevents the flow of menstrual blood. I order (*keleuō*) *parthenoi* to marry as quickly as possible if they suffer like this. For if they become pregnant, they become healthy. If not, then at puberty or a little later she will suffer from this or from some other disease. Among married *gynaikes*, the sterile suffer most from these conditions. (My translation).

The interpretation of this text is made more difficult by the apparently indiscriminate shifts between singular and plural. I would suggest that the plural forms should always be taken as '*gynaikes*'; thus we have, 'For if *gynaikes* become pregnant, they become healthy', another example of the common idea that the role of the *gynē* is to reproduce. Where the singular appears, we can read '*parthenos*'; for example, 'at puberty or a little later' covers the ideal age range for this term. This leaves as problematic only the first line of this section. Who are the *gynaikes* who are told by the diviners to dedicate their garments to Artemis? Are they perhaps close female kin of the afflicted *parthenos* offering their garments for her recovery?

There is, however, another possibility. No change of subject may be intended in this sentence (see, e.g. Fasbender, 1897, p. 229): the *parthe-*

noi, through their recovery, have become *gynaikes*. Menarche, the 'flow of menstrual blood' mentioned here, is thus the cause of the 'return of the senses' which is otherwise unexplained either by the ritual actions which precede it or by the social cure which follows it. In this text the *parthenos* to *gynē* transition would therefore seem to be centred on menarche, while still extending across marriage and into childbirth. It is with this interpretation that the remainder of the present paper is concerned. The doctor sees menarche in physiological terms, as due to the removal of something preventing the flow. Hence the recommendation of marriage, which may be related to the theory that childbirth widens the veins and so eases menstruation (PG 1. 1; Fasbender, 1897, p. 224) or to the idea that the menstrual flow is blocked by the hymen (Fasbender, 1897, p. 79). The diviners, in ordering dedications to Artemis after menarche,[12] make reference to the role played by this goddess at other stages of female maturation.

Context: medicine

Many features mentioned in the *Peri Partheniōn* find parallels in other gynaecological texts. These include delayed menarche causing mental disturbances (SF 34), the close of the 'orifice of exit' preventing normal menstruation (PG 3. 213, 228), terror (PG 2. 182), the desire for death (*thanein eratai*, PG 2. 177), the use of *keleuō* by the doctor (PG 3. 220), the sudden and unexplained return of reason (SF 34) and the advice to *parthenoi* to marry (PG 2. 127).

Other aspects of the text can be located within wider themes. The condemnation of 'deceit' in others who claim they can treat the disease is part of the attempt to establish medicine as a specific *tekhnē*, and it is found in *On the Sacred Disease* as well as in *Articulations*, 42–44, where the writer condemns those who use the spectacular therapy of succussion on a ladder (illustrated in *L* IV 187) merely to impress the crowds, but does not reject the technique altogether. Direct competition seems to have been the norm in Greek medicine, sometimes between doctors and *manteis* but often between those claiming to be of the same *tekhnē* (Lloyd, 1979, p. 39 and n. 152). Each individual had to persuade his patient that, of all the available therapies, his was the best (Lloyd, 1979, pp. 89 ff.), and to this is related the emphatic use of the first person in these texts: 'But *I* say…' (e.g. SacDis 1, PP, PG 1. 1, 43). This suggests that the condemnation of dedications to Artemis should be taken not as a simple opposition between 'scientific' and 'religious' healers but as the product of a period in which competition for the existing clientele was intense, and in which it was necessary not only to offer a convincing explanation of one's own therapy but also to denigrate the work of all others working in the same field.

Another theme to which the *Peri Partheniōn* relates is that of abnormal blood loss in menstruation, mentioned briefly above. Excessive loss is always bad: if it is due to the nature of the woman (*physis*) then she must be sterile, but if it is the result of disease (*pathēma*) it may respond to treatment (PG 3. 213). Total absence of menstruation, a common symptom in the gynaecological texts, is always bad and often fatal (as in PG 2. 133 and Ep. VI 8.32). Its origin is usually either movement of the womb to another part of the body (e.g. PG 2. 128, 129, 133) or, as in the *Peri Partheniōn*, closure of 'the orifice' (*to stoma* – cervix? vaginal orifice? – in PG 2. 156, 157, 162–4; 3. 213, 228).

Movement of the womb is one component of the complex of symptoms which Littré (see Note 7) takes as constituting 'hysteria'; others include sudden loss of voice, coldness, grinding the teeth and *pnix*, or suffocation. The attempt to impose the category of 'hysteria' on these texts may be misguided: the concomitant symptoms vary in different cases, so that while the womb may move but a characteristic symptom be absent (no *pnix* in PG 2. 127), many of the symptoms may be present but the cause is something other than uterine movement (red flux, a visible cause, in PG 2. 110). An analysis of the sections which Littré describes as 'hysteria' shows that he is classifying together groups of symptoms which the Hippocratic writers separate in terms of cause and remedy (Bourgey, 1953, pp. 149–52; Littré's section headings are also criticised by Rousselle, 1980, p. 1090).

Littré also distinguishes between 'hysteria' and 'displacement' (e.g. VIII 275, 327, 389), an opposition not found in the texts. When Littré was writing, the cause of 'hysteria' was disputed: some doctors believed that there was an organic cause, others that there was none (Merskey, 1979, p. 12 ff.). Since Freud, psychological explanations have been favoured. Littré's position in this debate is clear: the hysteria/displacement opposition corresponds not to psychological/physiological but rather to imaginary/real. In this it recalls the current usage of 'hysterical' as a pejorative term: 'She's just hysterical' is used to mean, 'There's nothing really wrong with her'. For Littré, too, the 'hysterical' woman is ill for no organic reason, and this judgement is repeated in more recent work on these texts (e.g. Simon, 1978, p. 242); yet in *Peri Gynaikeiōn*, *hysterikē pnix* has no such derogatory sense, for there *is* a physical cause, namely the tendency of the womb to run wild within the body if it is not allowed to conceive (e.g. Plato, *Timaeus* 91; the most detailed ancient description of 'hysteria' is Soranus, *Gyn* 3.26–9).

This judgement of the ancient sources occurs also in the labels 'psychic' and 'psychosomatic' which can imply 'imaginary'. Summarising the section in which he discusses the texts on women's diseases, Laín Entralgo says: 'In all these clinical and therapeutic descriptions the predominantly psychic state of the symptomatic picture is quite obvious.' Earlier in the same section he describes the *parthenoi* as 'certain ill – perhaps hysterical, to judge by what is said of them – women' (1970, 168; 158).

Such a 'diagnostic approach', which attempts to diagnose disease across two and a half millennia and through a text of this kind, is deeply unconvincing and takes us away from the text and the cultural values which it carries. Perhaps there were real girls, seen by the author, who exhibited symptoms for which there was no organic cause; perhaps these were the result of mental stress or perhaps the girls sought attention by a convincing deception:[13] perhaps there were real girls suffering from hormonal or glandular disturbances which could cause the same symptoms: or perhaps the text embodies a 'terrorismo igienico' (Manuli, 1980, p. 404) in order to scare women into acting as society dictated, marrying and giving birth at the age seen as appropriate. We simply cannot say. I intend here to concentrate instead on the internal logic of the representation and on other texts which show similar operations of thought, believing that at this level the question of the referent behind the text is of only secondary importance and also that a reading which emphasises what is specific to the text contributes more than one dominated by the principle of generalisation.

Two aspects of the *Peri Partheniōn* appear to be unique in the gynaecological corpus: firstly the outline of an alternative approach to difficulties at menarche, through the cult of Artemis, and secondly the use of the verb (*ap*)*ankhō* for the symptom of feeling strangled and for the girls' desire to strangle themselves. This may seem to link the text to the symptom of *pnix*, suffocation, found in many sections of the *Peri Gynaikeiōn* (e.g. 1. 7, 32, 55: 2. 116, 123–8, etc.), often in connection with menstrual retention. Later lexicographers and medical writers equate the two verbs (e.g. *ankhomenos* = *pnigomenos*, Galen 19.69 (ed. Kuhn): the Suda s.v. *apankhonisai* : *pnixai*), thus strengthening this suggestion, but a glance at their cognates shows that whereas *ankhō* suggests the pressure on the throat of strangulation or hanging, *pnigō* evokes suffocation through stifling heat (e.g. *pnigeus*, oven; *pnigos*, heat). *Pnix* is particularly common when the womb moves; remembering the womb/oven analogy

(Aristophanes, *Peace* 891: cf. Herodotus 5. 92 on Periander), *pnix* is a very appropriate symptom in such cases.

Context: myth

I would suggest that the use of (*ap*)*ankhō* in the *Peri Partheniōn*, which leads the writer into the subject of *parthenoi*, should be understood not as a sub-category of *pnix* but as an expression of the role of Artemis at transitions in a woman's life which involve bloodshed. While the doctor and the *manteis* disagree about the treatment which is best, they not only agree about the end in sight – the transformation of the *parthenos* into a reproductive *gynē* – but make reference to the same cultural tradition concerning *parthenoi*, strangulation and bleeding.

Plutarch describes a condition which is supposed to have afflicted the *parthenoi* of Miletus: it was manifested in a desire for death (*epithymia thanatou*) which made them hang themselves. As in the *Peri Partheniōn* the verb used is (*ap*)*ankhō* and the text contains both 'medical' and 'divine' explanations of the condition (*Moralia* 249 B–D).[14]

To discover why *parthenoi* have what almost amounts to an 'elective affinity' with hanging and strangulation (cf. the myths listed by Brelich, 1969, pp. 443–4, n. 2), it is necessary to glance at other stories which involve this form of death, and in particular to look at a tradition associated with the goddess Artemis who has been granted eternal *partheneia* by her father Zeus (Callimachus, *Hymn to Artemis*, 5 ff.).

Artemis strangled. Pausanias (8.23.6–7) tells a curious story about the origin of the epithet Apankhomene, the Strangled Lady, held by Artemis at Kaphyae in Arkadia. Once some children tied a rope around her image during a game, and playfully said that Artemis was being strangled. For this apparent sacrilege their elders stoned them to death. The *gynaikes* of Kaphyae were then struck with a disease, and as a result their babies were still-born. The priestess of Apollo was consulted and ordered that the children should be buried and should receive annual sacrifices, because they had been put to death wrongly. From then on, Artemis was called Apankhomene.

The *aition* reflects the role of the goddess in children's lives. As Kourotrophos she protects their upbringing and leads them to adulthood, receiving dedications of childhood toys (references in Van Straten, 1981, p. 90, n. 126). Another aspect of the story is the pattern by which an error is made, the guilty are struck by disease, and equilibrium restored after the Pythia gives advice. This is very common in myths of Artemis (see Calame, 1977, p. 281). Here, however, one other point should be drawn out of the text; that it is correct to call Artemis 'Strangled'. The children were right to give her this title, and their innocent game revealed the truth.

Assuming that the origin of such legends is the misunderstanding of ritual, scholars have suggested that Apankhomene arises from the practice of hanging images of vegetation deities on trees (e.g. Farnell, 1896, p. 428; Nilsson, 1967, p. 487). This misses the pertinence of the epithet to Artemis. It should be noted that the punishment in this text is not merely a disease, but is an interruption of the normal reproduction of the city through its *gynaikes*. Artemis, who herself never gives birth, can give or withhold a successful labour;[15] here she chooses to prevent birth because the Kaphyan women will not call her 'Strangled'.

Why should Artemis be 'Strangled'? Strangulation, for the Greeks, meant shedding no blood. In the field of sacrifice, for example, the Scythians were supposed to strangle their beasts; 'normal' Greek sacrifice of animals shed blood and so ensured communication between men and gods (Herodotus 4. 60; see Hartog, 1980, pp. 191–4). As a form of human death, strangulation or hanging evoked horror (see for example Phaedra in Euripides, *Hippolytus* 778, 802 and Hartog, 1980, pp. 195, n. 4) but as a means of suicide it can again be related to shedding no blood. To avoid the bloodshed of rape or unwanted defloration a bloodless suicide is appropriate. The Chorus in Aeschylus's *Suppliants* threaten to hang themselves (465) rather than sleeping with men whom they hate (788) and the Caryatides actually use this mode of suicide because they fear rape (see Calame, 1977, p. 270). The action of Phaedra is not merely a negative gesture performed from fear that Hippolytus will tell Theseus the truth (as in Diodorus Siculus 4.62); it is a positive action, for by choosing this death she inserts herself into an established tradition and thus strengthens her false claim that Hippolytus has raped her.

Strangulation can therefore be culturally opposed to unwanted sex; the avoidance of the latter may be appropriately achieved through the former, although it may be carried out after the event. In the *Peri Partheniōn* the afflicted *parthenoi* avoid not only the bloodshed of defloration but also that of menarche which ideally precedes it.[16] Defloration may be feared if the *parthenos* is not 'ripe':[17] these *parthenoi*, despite being 'ripe for marriage', are represented as fearing both menarche and marriage, preferring death.

Herodotus (4. 180) tells of a Libyan festival of Athena in which the most beautiful *parthenos* is dressed in a Corinthian helmet and Greek panoply and driven along the shores of a lake in a chariot. After this, the other *parthenoi* are divided into two groups and fight with stones and sticks. Those who die of their wounds are called '*pseudoparthenoi*'; that is, 'they distinguish the true from the false by metaphor: the true virgin is inviolate or unwounded, hence the survivors are true virgins' (Benardete, 1969, p. 125). The real *parthenos* does not bleed; the eternal *parthenos* Artemis does not shed her own blood in the hunt, in sex or in childbirth. Artemis Apankhomene can therefore be seen as expressing her *partheneia*, and the strangulation symptoms and chosen mode of death in the *Peri Partheniōn* as an identification with her as 'Strangled'.

Artemis does not bleed, but she does shed the blood of others, both as huntress and as director of the process by which a *parthenos* becomes a *gynē*. The 'true' *parthenoi* in Herodotus's story similarly shed the blood of others.[18] Those in the *Peri Partheniōn* are on the contrary 'ripe for marriage', ready to bleed and thus to enter the gradual transition which will make them *gynaikes*. The *gynē* is the opposite pole to the *parthenos*; she should bleed, in menstruation, defloration and childbirth, as part of her role of reproducing society – and the Hippocratic writers supply theories to support this idea – but she should not shed blood. Only a man may shed blood in war and sacrifice (see for examples Detienne, 1979, pp. 187–9); the *gynē* is explicitly compared to the sacrificed beast which bleeds (Aristotle, *Hist. Anim.* 581b 1–2; *PG* 1. 6, 72).

Becoming a *gynē* involves a series of bleedings, each of which must take place at the proper time. Artemis, associated with the correct time for delivery (contrast Hera in *Iliad* 19. 114–7) and death (Callimachus *H. Art.* 131–2, 126: cf. *Anth. Pal.* VII 228), is naturally also associated with this process.

Pausanias's story reflects Artemis as both the goddess who sheds no blood and the goddess who makes others bleed. The Kaphyan *gynaikes* only accept the second aspect: by denying that Artemis is strangled they claim her as a *gynē* like themselves. The children instead recognise the first aspect. The references to strangulation in the *Peri Partheniōn* show *parthenoi* clinging to the first when it is time for them to accept the second: in dedicating garments to Artemis they finally acknowledge her role in initiating the transition which takes them further towards being full *gynaikes*.

Parallel to the bleeding/strangulation opposition in stories of *parthenoi* and Artemis is the releasing/binding relationship. Artemis is Lysizōnos, releaser of the girdle: she is also Lygodesma, bound with the *agnos castus*.

Artemis releaser. The use of the *zōnē* or girdle in female clothing reflects the stages of a Greek woman's life. The first girdle is put on at puberty and later dedicated to Artemis as part of the marriage process; a special girdle, tied with a ritual knot, is worn on the wedding night and untied by the spouse; a married woman unties her girdle in labour. There is evidence to suggest that loosening the hair and garments is a necessary precaution in dangerous situations and when performing magical acts (listed in Heckenbach, 1911, pp. 78 ff.), but I believe that the association between Artemis and the *zōnē*, worn throughout the *parthenos* to *gynē* transition, deserves to be seen not as one of many examples of the release of all knots at times of transition but as a far more specific reference to the powers of Artemis.

As protector of childbirth, Eileithyia, Artemis is invoked by women calling on her, often as Lysizōnos, in labour (e.g. Theocritus 17.60–1, Euripides, *Hipp.* 166–9) and after childbirth the girdle may be dedicated to her (e.g. *Anth. Pal.* VI 200, 202, 272).

Birth is not, however, the only time when Artemis releases. The phrase *luein tēn zōnēn*, to release the girdle, is used not only in labour (Soranus, *Gyn.* 2.6.1) but also for defloration (*Anth. Pal.* VII 164, 324; Euripides, *Alcestis* 177; Kaibel, 319.3, 684.3: see Daremberg, 1887, p. 142, and Farnell, 1896, p. 444) and the epithet Lysizōnos evokes the presence of Artemis on both occasions. She releases the blood from those who are 'strangled' in the *Peri Parthenōn*, and she performs a similar action at the transitions of defloration and parturition, where she 'releases' the *parthenos* to cross the threshold of bleeding into a fuller expression of the status of *gynē*.

The girdle is released at these times of bloodshed: it can also be tied as a noose when *parthenoi* commit suicide. Kylon's daughter Myro, 'loosing her girdle and making a noose of it', should be seen in this context: she is 'a *parthenos* ripe for marriage' but instead of her spouse releasing her girdle before defloration she must release it herself so that it may be tied as the instrument of her death (Plutarch, *Moralia*, 253Cff.). Marriage and death – more specifically, sexual bloodshed and hanging – are inverted, and from this the story derives its pathos.

There remains one other transitional bleeding which should be considered here. The birth of the first child is particularly important in making the woman into a true *gynē* (Schmitt, 1977, p. 1064, cf. Lysias 1.6: on the ancient Near East see Cassin 1982, pp. 252–5) and this is completed by the first lochia, the discharge from the uterus after childbirth. Among the epithets referring to her role in childbirth, Artemis is called Lochia (e.g. Euripides, *Suppliants* 958; *Iphigenia in Tauris* 1097: *SEG* III 400.9). When a woman dies in our just after childbirth she remains 'not fully a *gynē*' (Kaibel, 505.4), perhaps because she has not experienced the lochia.

Medical texts regard their absence as a threat to future fertility or to life itself (PG 1. 29, 40, 41): in either case the woman would not reach the full status of *gynē*.

In the Hippocratic texts the lochia are analogous to menarche; both are normally 'like the flow of blood from a sacrificed beast' (PG 1.6/ 1. 72 and 2. 113, NC 18 (*L* VII 502): Fasbender, 1897, p. 181 and n. 2, p. 225 n. 4) and the symptoms of lochial displacement are explicitly (PG 1. 41) compared to those caused by displacement of menstrual blood in the *Peri Partheniōn*. The lochial bleeding is most difficult after the first parturition (PG 1. 72, NC 18). Menarche and first lochia thus seem to complement each other, forming the opening and the completion of the transformation of *parthenos* to *gynē*. At each of them Artemis is involved. As Apankhomene she expresses the ideal of the *parthenos* who does not bleed; but she is the goddess of transition, and assists other women to cross the boundaries which she rejects. Thus as Lochia and Eileithyia she assists in childbirth, although she has not given birth; as Lysizōnos she 'releases the girdle' both in defloration and in labour.

Chaste herb, virgin goddess. Another epithet of Artemis acts to combine the 'strangled' *parthenos* who sheds none of her own blood with the goddess who makes other women cross boundaries of bleeding. This is Lygodesma, meaning bound with the plant called lygos or agnos castus, the use of which in the ancient world ranged from wickerwork and perfume-making to medicinal and ritual purposes. Pausanias (3.16.11), who gives the epithet as an alternative title of Artemis Orthia, explains it by a story that the cult image was found in a thicket of this plant which made it stand upright (*orthos*).

The most important work to date on this epithet is that of Meuli (summary 1975, 1043–7) which places it in the context of other 'gefesselte Götter', thus grouping deities by a shared feature. Here I prefer to focus instead on the links between different attributes of one deity, an approach which I believe is equally valid and which, by showing the axes on which epithets intersect, shows how it can 'make sense' that Lygodesma, Apankhomene and Lysizōnos 'are' all Artemis.[19]

No detailed study of the connection between Artemis and the agnos exists.[20] Recent work by Detienne concerns its use in a festival of Demeter, the Thesmophoria, where its apparently opposed associations with fertility and with chastity seem to be related to the image of the ideal *gynē*, fruitful but faithful (Detienne, 1972, pp. 153–4; 1976, pp. 79–80; 1977, p. 130, n. 197; 1979, pp. 213–4).

Calame has nevertheless isolated three possible connections between agnos and Artemis (1977, pp. 285–9). Firstly, Artemis is associated with the plant world; not just with wild trees, as Farnell supposed (1896, p. 429), but also with cultivated trees. Near the sanctuary of Artemis Kalliste in Arkadia were many trees, *akarpa* and *hēmera* (Pausanias 8.35.8): in human terms, both *parthenoi* who bear no fruit, and tamed *gynaikes*, are protected by Artemis. Secondly, plant and goddess are associated with wet and marshy areas (Daremberg, 1892, p. 135; Farnell, 1896, pp. 427–8; Motte, 1973, p. 93ff; Calame, 1977, p. 262). This in turn links both to women, usually seen as 'wetter' than men (e.g. NC 15).

Finally, and most importantly, Calame looks at the medical qualities of the agnos. It reduces sexual desire but encourages menstruation and lactation;[21] in the Hippocratic texts, which Calame does not use, these opposite qualities are brought out clearly. The final section of *Peri Gynaikeiōn* 1 (74–109) is devoted to recipes considered therapeutic in various gynaecological disorders; the wide range of ingredients includes the agnos, used as an astringent in a severe flux (2. 192), to encourage conception (1. 75), to bring on birth in an unusually long labour (1. 77) and to expel the afterbirth (1. 78). The last two uses, where the agnos expels, are supported by other texts which say that it drives away snakes and acts as an abortive; the first two show that it may cause retention.

Calame (p. 289) goes on to suggest that when young boys were beaten at the altar of Orthia the intention was to stimulate the forces of growth; he suggests that girls were consecrated to Artemis at menarche, hence for them Lygodesma implied the stimulation of the menses. Such a conjecture, while consonant with the suggestions I have made above, concentrates on only one side of the agnos, thus detracting from the dual mode of operation of plant and goddess. The agnos as repressive astringent corresponds to the strangled *parthenos* Artemis and to the *parthenos* whose *stoma* is closed so that her menses cannot flow out: the agnos which promotes menstruation to the Artemis of the *Peri Partheniōn* and to Artemis who releases. The epithet Lygodesma makes explicit the parallel between the agnos in the plant code and Artemis in the schema of deities concerned with women.

The analogy can be taken further. The strength and flexibility of the agnos/lygos make it ideal for use in bonds, thongs and ropes, but these uses also recall the role of the girdle in a woman's life. Artemis is both bound with the lygos and releaser of the girdle, spanning the two temporal aspects of 'woman': strangled, non-bleeding *parthenos* and released, bleeding *gynē*. Yet although she is concerned with the transition between them, she herself stays firmly on one side. She who sheds the blood of others is 'strangled': she who releases others is 'bound'.

Conclusion

The Greeks saw 'woman' as a contrast between the undisciplined threat to social order and the controlled, reproductive *gynē*. The presentation of female maturation as a movement from the first form to the second expresses the hope that women can safely be incorporated into society in order to reproduce it. The Hippocratic texts try to define what is normal for a woman, but their focus on the reproductive woman is achieved through the creation of categories which fall short of this ideal and through admitting that a supposedly 'tamed' woman may suddenly be afflicted by a disease which prevents normal childbirth. By presenting cures for such disorders they make the non-reproductive groups temporary phenomena; just as the *parthenos* will in time become a *gynē*.

The *Peri Parthenión* expresses the fear that some *parthenoi* may not enter the category of *gynē*, identifying instead with an image of Artemis found in a number of stories concerning binding and releasing, strangling and bleeding. The doctor recommends marriage, accusing of deceit those who recommend dedications to Artemis after menarche; he emphasises the difference between the two sets of advice because he wants to prove the superiority of his own cure. The *parthenos* who chooses not to be a *gynē* and the man who can never be a *gynē* are however united in their wish to initiate the sequence of bleedings which will bring the *parthenos* to full maturity. The male doctor, even while trying to show that his cure is different, uses vocabulary which inserts the text into a tradition of stories about *parthenoi*: if the *parthenos* followed his advice and married, she would merely substitute another form of bloodshed and other dedications to Artemis at various stages of the process.

This overlap between cures reflects the wider problem of overlap between the two forms of woman. The *parthenos*, supposedly ignorant of 'the works of golden Aphrodite' (Hesiod, *Works and Days*, 521), whispers about love (Hesiod, *Theogony*, 205) and is highly attractive to men (Aeschylus, *Suppliants*. 1003–5; Aristotle, *Hist. Anim.*, 581b 11–21; Loraux, 1978, p. 50; Calame, 1977, pp. 189 and 256). It is logically difficult to make the *parthenos* wholly asexual, because every *parthenos* is a potential *gynē*. Similarly, every *gynē* was once a *parthenos* and even as a *gynē* may be struck by a disease which will prevent her from giving birth. The two terms thus drift back towards their original fusion in the ambiguous concept 'woman'. Artemis is the exception to the rule that all *parthenoi* are potential *gynaikes*; the true *parthenos*, she throws into greater relief the nature of her opposite pole, the true *gynē*, yet it is nevertheless the eternal *parthenos* who presides over the creation of new *gynaikes*.

ADDENDUM

Since 'Bound to Bleed', awareness of the medical texts of the Hippocratic corpus as a source for images of women has grown, in line with a wider interest in the history of the body and of sexuality. There are important sections on women and medicine in Geoffrey Lloyd's *Science, Folklore and Ideology* (Cambridge, 1983), while among the recent publications of Ann Ellis Hanson must be mentioned 'Continuity and change: three case studies in Hippocratic gynecological therapy and theory', in *Women's History and Ancient History*, ed. S. Pomeroy (Chapel Hill, 1991) and 'The medical writers' woman', in *Before Sexuality*, ed. D.M. Halperin, J.J. Winkler and F.I. Zeitlin (Princeton, NJ, 1990). On menstruation in particular, see Lesley Dean-Jones, 'Menstrual bleeding according to the Hippocratics and Aristotle', *Transactions of the American Philological Association* 119 (1989), 177–92; in relation to the hazards of the transformation from *parthenos* to *gynē*, see my own 'The daughter of Leonides: reading the Hippocratic corpus', in *History as Text*, ed. Averil Cameron (London, 1989), 13–32. The cultural representations of virginity have been discussed by Giulia Sissa, *Greek Virginity* (Cambridge, Mass., 1990) and the significance of hanging in relation to female death by Nicole Loraux, *Tragic Ways of Killing a Woman* (Cambridge, Mass., 1987). The companion piece to 'Bound to Bleed' is my article 'Sacrificial blood: the role of the *amnion* in Hippocratic gynecology', *Helios*, 13/2 (1987), and also in *Rescuing Creusa*, ed. M. Skinner (Lubbock, Texas, 1987), 117–26.

NOTES

1   Undisciplined and licentious: Detienne (1972), p. 128; Redfield (1977), pp. 148–9 on Spartan women. Self-control: Just (1975), pp. 164–5 and see Manuli (1980), p. 402. On the *kalon kakon*, Loraux (1978), pp. 43ff.

2   The model which I am using, of a separation followed by a process of 'drift'
     back towards the original fusion of the terms, owes much to the work of
     Pucci (1977); see for example p. 132 and pp. 32–3 on the re-merging of
     polarised terms in Hesiod. See pp. 92–3; an absolute dichotomy between
     two temporal aspects of 'woman' cannot be maintained because each pole of
     the precariously established opposition in fact evokes and depends for its
     meaning on the other. Compare Pucci pp. 32–3: 'underneath these polar-
     isations the *logos* undoes that fabric'.

3   Epitaph of Philostrata, Kaibel (1878), p. 463.

4   *Parthenos* as filly: Aristophanes, *Lysistrata* 1308; Euripides, *Hippolytus* 546–
     7; Merkelbach and West (1967), p. 59.4; Vernant (1979–80), p. 456.
     Taming/yoking metaphors: Calame (1977), pp. 411–20, pp. 330–3.

5   On choices in locating age-sex category transitions, Linton (1942), p. 591.

6   Grave monuments show both; only women on the *lekythos* of Pheidestrate
     (Conze, 1893, p. 308), some men on that of Theophante (*op. cit.* 309) and
     on the 'Stele of Plangon' (Johansen, 1951, p. 51).

7   In citing Hippocratic texts I am using the edition of E. Littré (Paris, 1839–
     61, 10 vols: reprinted Hakkert, Amsterdam). *L* followed by a Roman
     numeral refers to that volume of Littré. I also use the following abbrevi-
     ations: PP = *Peri Partheniōn*, *L* VIII 466–471; PG = *Peri Gynaikeiōn*, *L*
     VIII 10–463; SF = Superfetation, *L* VIII 476–509; NW = On the nature of
     the woman, *L* VII 312–431; NC = On the nature of the child, *L* VII 486–
     538; Ep VI = Epidemics VI, *L* V 266–357; Sac Dis = On the Sacred
     Disease, *L* VI 352–397; *Articulations* can be found in *L* IV 78–327.
     Other ancient sources are given in full at their first citation and thereafter
     abbreviated.

8   The Attic Apatouria was related to marriage, not to age; a girl was admitted
     through her relationship to her spouse, not in her own right (Schmitt, 1977,
     pp. 1059–60). The stages in a girl's life given in Aristophanes, *Lysistrata*
     641–7 have been much discussed since Brelich's attempt to extract from
     them a series of fixed age-grades (1969, pp. 229ff.); for a pertinent reminder
     that these lines can best be understood in the context of the play rather than
     as 'information' intended to instruct posterity on age categories, see Loraux
     (1981), pp. 174ff.

9   On woman as the incomplete form, see Aristotle, *de generatione animalium*
     737a, and Clark (1975), p. 210; also Manuli (1980), p. 393, and Carlier
     (1980–1), p. 28. Greek medicine, like our own, did not have a branch to
     study 'the diseases of men'; maleness was the norm, and women were the
     deviant forms.

10   While *ta epiphainomena prōta* (PG 1. 41; also in Soranus, *Gyn.* 1.17.2,
     1.33.6) clearly means menarche, *hama te kathodō tōn epimēniōn*, used
     here, may mean 'at the descent of [every] menstrual flow'. Two consider-
     ations point towards the reading adopted here. Firstly, the phrase is followed
     by 'suffering disorders to which she was previously [*proteron*] not exposed';

as Geoffrey Lloyd has pointed out to me, *proteron* suggests that this is the first menstruation. Secondly, PG 1.41, which specifies menarche, appears to be paraphrasing PP. I see no grounds for Lefkowitz's translation, '*After* the first menstrual period' (1981, 14).

11 Cf. the use of *anthrōpos* for 'woman patient' in PG 2. 230 (*L* VIII 444).

12 Dedication of garments to Artemis is particularly associated with Artemis Brauronia in Attika: Van Straten (1981), p. 99, n. 170–1, for references.

13 Cf. Ehrenreich and English (1979), pp. 124–6. Hysteria as a strategy for gaining attention, Lewis (1971), especially Ch. 3.

14 Diepgen (1937), p. 194, notes the similarity between PP and *Mor* 249B-D.

15 Artemis preventing childbirth as a punishment: Callimachus, *H. Art.* 122 ff. and Cahen (1930), p. 123.

16 Defloration *before* menarche: Rousselle (1980), pp. 1104–5.

17 *Anth. Pal.* IX 245 claims that fear of the wedding night is 'a common fear among *parthenoi*'.

18 Cf. the analysis of the Herodotus story in Vernant (1968), pp. 15–16, where *parthenos* = true warrior.

19 Cf. Burkert (1977), p. 192: 'The great goddess of Ephesos, the cruel Laphria and the goddess for whom girls dance at Brauron are obviously different but are nevertheless called "Artemis"' (my translation). I am interested here in the links between epithets which meant that the Greeks could regard supposedly 'different' deities as 'being' Artemis in some way.

20 Farnell (1896), p. 429 and Daremberg (1892), p. 136, make only brief mention of the epithet. Nilsson (1967), p. 487, links it to Apankhomene; scholars from Fehrle (1910), pp. 142–8, to Meuli (1975), p. 1043, have tried to privilege one of the poles with which the plant is associated above the other.

21 The main sources for this section are Pliny, *Natural History* 13.14 and 24.59–62; Dioscorides, *Materia Medica* 1.103 (ed. Wellmann); Galen 9 p. 810 (ed. Kuhn); Eustathius, *in Od.* 9. 453, *ad Il.* 11.106; Aelian, *de natura animalium* 9.26; Etymologicon Magnum *sv agnos, moskoisi lygoisin*.

REFERENCES

Ardener, E. A. 1975. "Belief and the Problem of Women." In S. Ardener (ed.), *Perceiving Women*, 1–17. London.

Arthur, M. B. 1976. "Review Essay: Classics." *Signs* 2: 382–403.

Benardete, S. 1969. *Herodotean Inquiries.* The Hague.

Bourgey, L. 1953. *Observation et expérience chez les médécins de la collection hippocratique.* Paris.

Brelich, A. 1969. *Paides e Parthenoi.* Rome.

Burkert, W. 1977. *Griechische Religion der archaischen und klassischen Epoche.* Stuttgart.

Cahen, E. 1930. *Les Hymnes de Callimaque.* Paris.

Calame, C. 1977. *Les choeurs de jeunes filles en Grèce archaïque,* Part 1. Rome.

Carlier, J. 1980–1. "Les Amazones font la guerre et l'amour." *L'Ethnographie* 76: 11–33.

Cassin, E. 1982. "Le Proche-Orient ancien: virginité et strategie du sexe." In Tordjinian (ed.), *La première fois ou le roman de la virginité perdue,* 241–58. Paris.

Chantraine, P. 1946–7. "Les Noms du mari et de la femme, du père et de la mère en grec." *Revue des etudes grecques* 59–60: 219–50.

Clark, S. R. L. 1975. *Aristotle's Man.* Oxford.

Conze, A. 1893–1922. *Die attischen Grabreliefs.* Berlin.

Daremberg, C. and E. Saglio. 1877–1919. *Dictionnaire des antiquités.* Paris.

Detienne, M. 1972. *Les Jardins d'Adonis.* Paris.

——. 1976. "Protagenie de femme, ou comment engendrer seule." *Traverses* 5–6: 75–81.

——. 1977. *Dionysos mis à mort.* Paris.

——. 1979. "Violentes 'eugénies'." In M. Detienne and J.-P. Vernant, *La cuisine du sacrifice en pays grec.* Paris.

Diepgen, P. 1937. *Die Frauenheilkunde der alten Welt.* Munich (W. Stoekel (ed.), *Handbuch der Gynäkologie* XII/1).

Ehrenreich, B. and D. English.1979. *For Her Own Good.* London.

Farnell, L. R. 1896–1909. *Cults of the Greek States.* 5 vols. Oxford.

Fasbender, H. 1897. *Entwicklungslehre, Geburtshülfe und Gynäkologie in den hippokratischen Schriften.* Stuttgart.

Fehrle, E. 1910. *Die kultische Keuschheit im Altertum. Religionsgeschichtliche Versuche und Vorarbeiten 6.6.* Giessen.

Gould, J. P. 1980. "Law, Custom and Myth: Aspects of the Social Position of Women in Classical Athens." *Journal of the Historical Society* 100: 38–59.

Hartog, F. 1980. *Le Miroir d'Hérodote.* Paris.

Hastrup, I. 1978. "The Semantics of Biology: Virginity." In S. Ardener (ed.), *Defining Females,* 49–65. London.

Heckenbach, J. 1911. *De nuditate sacra sacrisque vinculis.* Giessen.

Johansen, K. F. 1951. *Attic Grave-reliefs.* Copenhagen.

Just, R. 1975. "Conceptions of Women in Classical Athens." *Journal of the Anthropological Society of Oxford* 6.3: 153–70.

Kaibel, G. (ed.). 1878. *Epigrammata Graeca.* Berlin.

Laín Entralgo, P. 1970. *The Therapy of the Word in Classical Antiquity.* New Haven, CT.

Lefkowitz, M. 1981. *Heroines and Hysterics.* London.

Lewis, I. M. 1971. *Ecstatic Religion.* Harmondsworth.

Linton, R. 1942. "Age and Sex Categories." *American Sociological Review* 7: 589–602.

Littré, E. 1839–61. *Oeuvres complètes d'Hippocrate*. Paris.

Lloyd, G. E. R. 1975. "The Hippocratic Question." *Classical Quarterly* 25: 171–92.

——. 1979. *Magic, Reason and Experience*. Cambridge.

Loraux, N. 1978. "Sur la race des femmes et quelques-unes de ses tribus." *Arethusa* 11: 43–87.

——. 1981. "Le lit, la guerre." *L'Homme* 21: 37–67.

Manuli, P. 1980. "Fisiologia e Patologia del Femminile negli Scritti Ippocratici dell' Antica Ginecologia Greca." In M. D. Grmek (ed.), *Hippocratica. Actes du Colloque hippocratique de Paris*. September 4–9, 1978, 393–408. Paris.

Merkelbach, R. and M. L. West. 1967. *Fragmenta Hesiodea*. Oxford.

Merskey, H. 1979. *The Analysis of Hysteria*. London.

Meuli, K. 1975. *Gesammelte Schriften II*. Basle.

Motte, A. 1973. *Prairies et jardins de la Grèce antique*. Brussels.

Nilsson, M. 1961–7. *Geschichte der griechischen Religion*. 2 vols. Munich (I. von Müller (ed.), *Handbuch der Altertumswissenschaft* II, 1–2).

Padel, R. 1983. "Women: Model for Possession by Greek Daemons." In A. Cameron and A. Kuhrt (eds.), *Images of Women in Antiquity*, 3–19. London. (2nd ed. 1993, Detroit, MI).

Pomeroy, S. 1975. *Goddesses, Whores, Wives and Slaves*. New York.

Pucci, P. 1977. *Hesiod and the Language of Poetry*. Baltimore, MD.

Redfield, J. 1977. "The Women of Sparta." *Classical Journal* 73: 141–61.

Rousselle, A. 1980. "Observation féminine et idéologie masculin: le corps de la femme d'après les médécins grecs." *Annales ESC* 35: 1089–115.

Schmitt, P. 1977. "Athene Apatouria et la ceinture." *Annales ESC* 32: 1059–73.

Shaw, M. 1975. "The Female Intruder: Women in Fifth-Century Drama." *Classical Philology* 70: 255–66.

Simon, B. 1978. *Mind and Madness in Ancient Greece*. Ithaca, NY.

Van Straten, F. T. 1981. "Gifts for the Gods." In H. Versnel (ed.), *Faith, Hope and Worship*, 65–151. Leiden.

Vatin, C. 1970. *Recherches sur le mariage et la condition de la femme mariée à l' époque hellénistique*. Paris.

Vernant, J.-P. 1968. Introduction to *Problèmes de la guerre en Grèce ancienne*. Paris.

——. 1974. "Le mariage." In *Mythe et société en Grèce ancienne*, 57–81. Paris [*Myth and Society in Ancient Greece*, trans. J. Lloyd, Oxford, 1980].

—— 1979–80. Cours. *Annuaire du Collège de France*, 435–66.

Sources

Hippocrates

This text belongs to a large group of medical writings referred to as the Hippocratic corpus. Although named after the famous physician, Hippocrates, who lived during the second half of the fifth century BCE, this body of writings is not the work of a single man but the product of a group of writers who shared similar views about illness and the human body. The corpus contains extensive writings about women's bodies, most of which have not yet been translated into English.

The translation refers to the text of E. Littré (ed.), *Oeuvres Complètes d'Hippocrate* (Amsterdam, 1962).

Hippocrates, *On Unmarried Girls*

From visions of this sort, many people have choked to death, more women than men. For the female nature is slighter and not as spirited as the male. But girls who remain unmarried at the appropriate time for marriage experience such visions more around the time of their first monthly cycle, although previously they did not suffer any ill effects. For at this time, the blood collects in the uterus so that it might flow out. Yet whenever the passage is not fully open, and more blood flows in because of the nourishment of the body and its growth, then the blood, not being able to flow out because of its mass, surges into the heart and the diaphragm.

Whenever these parts become full of blood, the heart grows sluggish. This sluggishness causes numbness, which in turn brings about madness. In the same way, numbness results when someone has been sitting for a long time, because the blood that has been squeezed out of the hips and thighs flows into the calves and feet. This numbness renders the feet incapable of walking, until the blood returns to its place. It returns most quickly when the person stands in cold water and bathes the part above the ankles. The numbness therefore is easily managed, for the blood flows back quickly on account of the straightness of the veins, and this part of the body is not very vulnerable.

But it flows more slowly around the heart and lungs. The veins there are crooked and the site plays a critical role both in delirium and madness. Whenever these parts fill with blood, shivering accompanied by fever arises. They call this "erratic fevers." When this happens, violent inflammation drives the girl mad. Because of the putrefaction she has murderous thoughts, and because of the darkness she becomes fearful and afraid. The pressure on their hearts makes the girls long to hang themselves, and the spirit, wayward and anguished because of the bad condition of the blood, attracts trouble.

Sometimes the girl says frightful things; the visions order her to leap up and to throw herself into a well and drown herself, as if these actions were better for her and had an entirely useful purpose. In the absence of these visions, a certain pleasure causes the girl to love death as if it were something good. When the girl returns to her senses, women dedicate many objects to Artemis: above all, the most costly of their garments. They are ordered to do this by diviners, but they are deceived.

There is relief from this complaint if nothing hinders the flow of menstrual blood. I recommend that unmarried girls who suffer from this malady marry men as soon as possible. For if they become pregnant, they become healthy. If not, then at puberty or a little while later she will succumb to this or some other disease. Among married women, the childless suffer most from these conditions.

Euripides

Produced in 428 BCE by Euripides (born c. 480 BCE), the youngest of the three major tragic poets of the classical period, *Hippolytus* tells the story of a wife desperate to suppress her illicit love for her stepson. The chaste Hippolytus offends Aphrodite, goddess of female sexuality, by refusing to worship her, shunning marriage and women out of devotion for his special patron, the virginal goddess Artemis. Although Hippolytus enters the stage singing a pious song in her honor, the exchange that follows portends his ultimate demise at the hands of Aphrodite.

Euripides, *Hippolytus* 59–105

HIPPOLYTUS:
> Follow me, companions, follow me,
> singing of the daughter of Zeus, the heavenly one,
> Artemis, in whose care we are.

HIPPOLYTUS AND COMPANIONS:
        Lady, Lady most reverend,
        sprung from Zeus,
        hail, hail to you, O Artemis,
        daughter of Leto and Zeus,
        fairest by far of the maidens,
        you who dwell in the great sky
        in the house of your noble father,
        in Zeus' dwelling rich in gold.
        Hail to you, O fairest
        fairest of all in Olympus.

HIPPOLYTUS:
        For you, mistress, I bring this woven garland
        woven from a pure meadow,
        where neither the shepherd dares to graze his beasts
        nor the blade of iron yet has come. A pure meadow
        where only the bee passes through in the spring,
        and Virtue tends it with her river waters.
        Those who have not been taught self-control,
        but who possess it always in their natures toward all things–
        they alone may pick the flowers, not the wicked.
        Please accept, dear mistress, this crown
        for your golden hair from my pious hand.
        For I alone among mortals have the privilege
        of your companionship and conversation,
        hearing only your voice, but not seeing your face.
        May I reach the end of life just as I began it.

COMPANION: King – for one ought to call only the gods "master"–
would you care to receive some good advice from me?

HIPPOLYTUS: Of course, or else I would not appear very wise.

COMPANION: Well, do you know the custom that is established among men?

HIPPOLYTUS: I am not sure I do. Which one are you asking me about?

COMPANION: The one that decrees you should hate that which is haughty and
hateful to all.

HIPPOLYTUS: Certainly. What haughty person does not annoy?

COMPANION: And there is charm in those who like to converse?

HIPPOLYTUS: Yes, charm indeed, and profit too, for little trouble.

COMPANION: Now do you suppose this same thing holds among the gods?

HIPPOLYTUS: If indeed we mortals follow the customs of the gods.

COMPANION: Then how is it that you do not acknowledge a haughty goddess?

HIPPOLYTUS: What goddess? Careful, lest your tongue commit some slip.

COMPANION: The goddess here, Cypris, who stands near your gate.

HIPPOLYTUS: Since I am pure, I greet her from afar.

COMPANION: Yet she is haughty and distinguished among mortals.

HIPPOLYTUS: I like no deity whose worship is at night.

COMPANION: One must respect the powers of the gods, my son.

HIPPOLYTUS: Each has his preferences, in gods and men alike.

COMPANION: I wish you good fortune – and the good sense you need!

Figure 4 *Heracles and Deianeira with Poisoned Robe.* Attic red figure pelike in the manner of the Washing Painter, c.440–30 BCE. British Museum, London, E370. The painter has rendered the myth's critical moment, when Deianeira proffers the fatal garment to her husband.

4

PLAYING THE OTHER:
THEATER, THEATRICALITY,
AND THE FEMININE IN
GREEK DRAMA

F. I. Zeitlin

For a specimen of sheer theatrical power, it would be difficult to match the climactic scene of Euripides' *Bacchae* (788–861) where Pentheus at last comes under the spell of his adversary, the god Dionysus, and acknowledges his secret desire to spy upon the women of Thebes who have left the city to go as maenads to the mountain. His violent antagonism toward the women who, in abandoning their homes, children, and domestic tasks, have challenged the civic, masculine authority of the king gives way to a sudden softening of will – a yielding to the cunning wiles of the god disguised on stage as the Asiatic stranger, the leader of his own troops of maenads. This first surrender is followed by another. Giving up now his original intention to marshal his forces for an open combat of men against women, Pentheus gives up his stubborn claim to an unequivocal masculine identity. To see what the women are doing without himself being seen, Pentheus must trade his hoplite military tactics for an undercover operation that involves adopting a devious stratagem and assuming a remarkable disguise. He must let the god take him inside the palace and dress him as a woman in a flowing wig and headdress, a long pleated robe and belt, to which he adds the typical insignia of the maenads – the dappled fawnskin and ritual thyrsus. When the god completes this elaborate toilette, Pentheus will also resemble Dionysus himself, whose effeminate appearance the king had earlier mocked.[1] But as much as they might seem doublets of one another, the power relations between them have been decisively reversed. Now Dionysus will turn Pentheus from the one who acts to the one who is acted upon, from the one who would inflict pain and suffering, even death, on the other, to the one who will undergo those experiences himself. For now, however, the preliminary sign of Pentheus' total defeat, first at the hands of Dionysus and then at the hands of the women, is given to us on stage in the visual feminization of Pentheus when he is induced against all inhibitions of shame to adopt the costume and gestures of the woman.

But if feminization is the emblem of Pentheus' defeat, Dionysus' effeminacy is a sign of his hidden power. Here are two males, cousins in fact through their genealogical ties, both engaged in a masculine contest for supremacy. One, however, gains mastery by manipulating a feminized identity and the other is vanquished when he finally succumbs to it. What we might perceive in their ensemble at the moment when the two males appear together on stage in similar dress is an instructive spectacle of the inclusive functions of the feminine in the drama – one on the side of femininity as power and the other on the side of femininity as weakness.

Pentheus, first ashamed of wearing women's clothing, and terrified that he make a ridiculous spectacle of himself for all the city to see, now has a fleeting intimation of the new force he has acquired, exulting in the surge of unnatural physical strength that suffuses him and dreaming of uprooting mountains with his bare hands. But under the god's gentle prodding, he just as eagerly abandons his desire for violence to acquiesce with pleasure in the contrary tactics of hiding and deception that will confront the women on their own terms (953–56). The moment of triumph and confidence, however, is brief. We know already in advance what the fate of Pentheus will be once the feminized god Dionysus, who plays *his* role to perfection, delivers over his disguised victim, his man clumsily concealed in women's dress, to the "real" women who will tear the imposter apart in a terrible ritual *sparagmos*, while the god reverts to his function of divine spectator at the drama he himself has arranged on stage.

I have chosen to begin with the robing of Pentheus, for beyond its dramatic impact within the context of the play, the mechanics of this scene also suggests in its details a wider and more emblematic set of significations. These refer both to the conditions of Dionysiac ritual itself as a deadly version of initiation into the mysteries of the god's worship and to the conditions of the theater of Dionysus and the accepted terms of its artistic representations.[2] For the first, Pentheus must be dressed as a woman for consecration to the god as the surrogate beast-victim he will become in the ritual on the mountain; for the second, the costuming of Pentheus reminds us that the theater requires mimetic disguise by which it creates and maintains its status as dramatic festival.[3] Thus through this scene we arrive at the dynamic basis of Greek drama, catching a momentary glimpse of the secrets of its ritual prehistory as it merges with and is imitated by the techniques of the theater. In particular, the fact that Pentheus dons a feminine costume and rehearses in it before our eyes exposes perhaps one of the most marked features of Greek theatrical mimesis, namely that men are the only actors in this civic theater; in order to represent women on stage, men must *always* put on a feminine costume and mask.[4] What this means is that it is not a woman who speaks or acts for herself and in herself on stage; it is always a man who impersonates her.[5]

Still further, if we also consider that in order to direct the proceedings of the drama, to manipulate its theatrical effects, contrive its plots, set its stage, and control its mimetic play of illusion and reality, Dionysus, the god of the theater, must also take on womanish traits, then perhaps we may venture yet further: can there be some intrinsic connections linking the phenomenon of Athenian tragedy, invented and developed in a historical context as a civic art form, and what the society culturally defines as feminine in its sex/gender system?[6]

There is nothing new in stressing the associations of Dionysus and the feminine for the Greek theater. After all, madness, the irrational, and the emotional aspects of life are associated in the culture more with women than with men. The boundaries of women's bodies are perceived as more fluid, more permeable, more open to affect and entry from the outside, less easily controlled by intellectual and rational means. This perceived physical and cultural instability renders them weaker than men; it is also all the more a source of disturbing power over them, as reflected in the fact that in the divine world it is feminine agents, for the most part, who, in addition to Dionysus, inflict men with madness – whether Hera, Aphrodite, the Erinyes, or even Athena as in Sophocles' *Ajax*.

On the other hand, we might want to view the androgyny of Dionysus, already in Aeschylus called a *gunnis* (womanish man) and *pseudanor* (counterfeit man, frag. 61 Nauck, 2nd ed.), as a true mixture of masculine and feminine. This mixture, it can be argued, is one of the emblems of his paradoxical role as disrupter of the normal social categories; in his own person he attests to the *coincidentia oppositorum* that challenges the hierarchies and rules of the public masculine world, reintroducing into it confusions, conflicts, tensions, and ambiguities, insisting always on the more complex nature of life than masculine aspirations would allow.[7] Such a view would stress male and female aspects alike; it would regard the god as embodying a dynamic process or as configuring in his person an alternate mode of reality. Convincing as this view may be, it runs the risk of underrating the fact that it is precisely Dionysus' identification with the feminine that gives him and his theater their power.

Along the same lines, in the quest for equivalence between the genders, one could remark, not without justice, that although all the actors are male in tragedy, we find that within the plays feminized males are countered by masculinized women: for example, Aeschylus' Clytemnestra of the "man-counseling mind" (*Agamemnon*), Euripides' Medea, and, of course, the maenadic Agave herself, who in the *Bacchae* boasts of her warrior prowess over the body of Pentheus, as yet unrecognized as the son whom she has killed. This notion of a balanced, symmetrical inversion finds support in Greek festivals outside Athens where men and women change their costumes for a day, each imitating the appearance and behavior of the other.[8] Better yet, there is evidence that in initiation rites at puberty or sometimes in nuptial arrangements, young men and women in their own spheres temporarily adopt the dress and behavior of the other sex.[9] Such reversals are usually explained according to a ritual logic that insists that each gender must for the last time, as it were, act the part of the other before assuming the unequivocal masculine and feminine identities that cultural ideology requires.[10]

As a theoretical concept, this proposition makes eminent sense. On the level of practice, however, these symmetries are often more apparent than real; the notion conforms better with our habits of binary thinking than with recorded evidence as these rites are far better and more numerously attested for men than for women, not least because their performance, aimed at creating men for the city, is of greater concern to the culture at large.

Second, and more to the point, critics treat inversion of roles as a sufficient explanation in itself, that is, a temporary reversal before its decisive correction. They do not extend their analysis to consider what the various aspects of the actual experience might imply for achieving male identity. What more specifically might these actions and attitudes teach him? How might the processes of imitating the feminine prepare him for access to adult status, other than to teach him the behaviors he must later scrupulously avoid? Unless there were something to learn and something necessary to repeat, we would not need the genre of tragedy at all to call these different roles into question and, most of all, to challenge the masculine civic and rational view of the universe.

Finally, the pairing of feminized men and masculinized women, a useful notion in many respects, runs the risk of assuming mutually inverted categories without looking to the internal dynamics of tragic conventions that shape and predict the conditions of this exchange. Even more, such a concept tends to reduce the scope of the feminine in the drama. It is too limited to encompass her double dimensions – a model of both weakness and strength, endowed with traits and capacities that have negative and positive implications for self and society.

Thus my emphasis falls not upon the equal interchange or reversal of male and female roles but upon the predominance of the feminine in the theater, a phenomenon that used to (and may still) puzzle some commentators, who perceived a serious discrepancy between the muteness of women in Athenian social and political life and their expressive claims to be heard and seen on stage.[11] And my focus on imbalances rather than on equivalences between the genders is aimed here not so much at the content and themes of the various dramas in their political and social dimensions but on the implications of theater and theatricality as these are integrally related to and reflective of the thematic preoccupations of drama. If tragedy can be viewed as a species of recurrent masculine initiations, for adults as well as for the young,[12] and if drama, more broadly, is designed as an education for its male citizens in the democratic city, then the aspects of the play world I wish to bring into sharper relief may well merit the speculations I am about to offer on theater, representation, plot and action, experience and identity – all linked in some radical way with the feminine.

From the outset, it is essential to understand that in Greek theater, as in fact in Shakespearean theater, the self that is really at stake is to be identified with the male, while the woman is assigned the role of the radical other.[13] It seems unfair perhaps that, given the numbers and importance of female protagonists in Greek tragedy (by contrast, it should be said, to the case of Shakespeare),[14] theoretical critics from Aristotle on never consider anyone but the male hero as the central feature of the genre; they devote their attention to outlining *his* traits, configurations, and dilemmas. Yet despite Clytemnestra, Antigone, Phaedra, Medea, and many others, it must be acknowledged that this critical blindness is also insight. Even when female characters struggle with the conflicts generated by the particularities of their subordinate social position, their demands for identity and self-esteem are nevertheless designed primarily for exploring the male project of selfhood in the larger world as these impinge upon men's claims to knowledge, power, freedom, and self-sufficiency – not for some greater entitlement or privilege, as some have thought, that the female might gain for herself, not even for revising notions of what femininity might be or mean. Women as individuals or chorus may give their names as titles to plays; female characters may occupy the center stage and leave a far more indelible emotional impression on their spectators than their male counterparts (as Antigone, for example, over Creon). But *functionally* women are never an end in themselves, and nothing changes for them once they have lived out their drama on stage. Rather, they play the roles of catalysts, agents, instruments, blockers, spoilers, destroyers, and sometimes helpers or saviors for the male characters. When elaborately represented, they may serve as anti-models as well as hidden models for that masculine self, as we will see, and, concomitantly, their experience of suffering or their acts that lead them to disaster regularly occur before and precipitate those of men.[15]

An excellent case in point is Sophocles' *Trachiniae*, a play that will serve us well throughout this essay. Although the distress and despair of Deianeira, the innocent, virtuous wife, commands our attention for most of the play, and although she loses none of our sympathy when unwittingly destroying her husband Heracles for love of him, we come to realize that her entire experience, her actions and reactions, are in truth a route for achieving another goal, the real *telos* or end of the drama. She is the agent designated to fulfill the deceptive, riddling oracles which predict the tragic destiny of Heracles rather than a well-earned respite from his labors here on earth. She kills herself offstage in remorse, but his are the sufferings we witness publicly on stage, and it is he who, in his first and last appearance before us, provides the climax and resolution of the drama.

Moreover, if we consider more generally that the tragic universe is one that the specifically male self (actor and/or spectator) must discover for himself as other than he originally imagined it to be, then the example of Deianeira is particularly instructive for articulating the complex position occupied by that feminine other. For in the course of the action, Deianeira indeed does come to that discovery for herself, realizing too late that she had been duped. The love charm the centaur had bequeathed to her was in fact a deadly poison, whose fiery potential had been concealed within the recesses of the house until exposed to the warming heat of the sun. But her education into the treacherous opacity of the tragic world holds no interest for Heracles, preoccupied as he is with unraveling the riddle of his own story. The ensemble of her life and death seems to have nothing to teach Heracles that he can acknowledge openly on his death-bed, and, even more telling, neither will he allow it to have meaning for their son Hyllus when he prescribes for the boy's future in terms that define him only as his father's son.

Medea in Euripides' play comes closest to the demand for an equivalence of that feminine self to the male, preferring, as she says, to stand three times in the van of battle than to bear one child (*Medea* 250–51). Yet although she has a defined geographical destination to which she will go once she leaves Corinth in exile, having obtained in advance from its king the promise of sanctuary in Athens, her spectacular departure from the city on the dragon chariot of her immortal ancestor, the Sun, suggests that there can be no place for her in the social structure down here on earth. A woman who insists on the binding nature of the compact she made on her own with a man, who defends her right to honor and self-esteem in terms suspiciously resembling those of the male heroic code, and finally who would reverse the cultural flow in founding a new genre of poetry that celebrates now the exploits of women rather than those of men (as the chorus sings, 410–45) is meant not for human but superhuman status.[16] Accordingly, it is only logical that she disappear once the drama is over – upward and out of sight. Yet even in this revolutionary play the typology still holds. Medea's formal function in the plot is to punish Jason for breaking his sacred oath to her, through an exacting retribution of tragic justice, and she is the typical and appropriate agent, even if embodied in exotic form, for accomplishing that crucial end.

Let us return now to the central topic – to identify those features that are most particular to drama, serving to differentiate it from all other art forms that precede it: narrative (epic), choral lyric and dance, solo songs, and perhaps even stylized exchanges of dialogue. Though profoundly indebted, to be sure, to ritual representations and reenactments, to ritual costumes and masks, drama develops along the deeper lines of character and plot and establishes its own conventions and entitlements in the more secular sphere.[17]

At the risk of drastic (I repeat, drastic) oversimplification, I propose four principal elements as indispensable traits of the theatrical experience, all interlinked in various ways with one another and to the sum total of the tragic spectacle. And I will assume another more dangerous risk by boldly proposing in advance that each of these traits can find not its only, to be sure, but its more radical cultural referent in the traits and aspects that the society most associates with the feminine domain.

First, the representation of the body itself on stage as such – its somatic dimensions and the sense of its physical reality. Second, the arrangement of architectural space on stage that continually suggests a relational tension between inside and outside. Third, the plot itself, that is, the strategies by which theater best represents a tragic story on stage and contrives to bring that story through often surprising means to the conclusion that the terms of its myth demand. In this sense, plot as shape of the story often coincides in fact, as we will see, with the other connotation of plot as intrigue and deception. And finally, the most extensive category – the condition of theatrical mimetism itself, limited in this discussion to the question of role playing and disguise – or more generally, the representation of a self as other than it seems or knows itself to be, a self with inner and outer dimensions.

The Body

The emphasis in theater must inevitably fall upon the body – the performing body of the actor as it embodies its role, figures its actions, and is shown to us in stylized poses, gestures, and attitudes. We see this body before us in the *theatron*, the viewing place, in rest and in movement. We observe how it occupies different areas at different times on stage, how it makes its entrances and exits, how it is situated at times alone or, more often, in relation with others. This performing body engages at every moment its sensory faculties – to hear, see, touch, and move; above all, it is the actor as body or body as actor who projects the human voice in all its inflections.

Theater has been defined as "the adventure of the human body,"[18] but for Greek tragedy it would be more accurate to call it "the misadventure of the human body." What interests the audience most in the somatics of the stage is the body in an unnatural state of *pathos* (suffering) – when it falls farthest from its ideal of strength and integrity. We notice it most when it is reduced to a helpless or passive condition – seated, bound, or constrained in some other way; when it is in the grip of madness or disease, undergoing intermittent and spasmodic pain, alternating between spells of dangerous calm before the stormy symptoms assail the body again. Tragedy insists most often on exhibiting this body, even typically bringing back corpses killed offstage so as to expose them to public view. When characters are still alive, some demand us to witness the spectacle of their suffering so we may pity them. Others call for a covering to hide their shame or wish to be hidden inside the house – or in some supernatural way to vanish from the eyes of the beholders. More to the point, it is at those moments when the male finds himself in a condition of weakness that he too becomes acutely aware that he has a body – and then perceives himself, at the limits of pain, to be most like a woman.

Heracles, at the end of Sophocles' *Trachiniae*, when his flesh is being devoured by the poison of the fateful robe, appeals to his son: "Pity me, / for

I seem pitiful to many others, crying / and sobbing like a girl, and no one could ever say / that he had seen this man act like that before. / Always without a groan I followed a painful course. / Now in my misery I am discovered a woman" (*Trachiniae* 1070–75; cf. Euripides *Heracles* 1353–56). Sophocles' Ajax, in despair after the madness that the goddess Athena had sent upon him has abated and determined now to die a manly death that will restore his heroic image to himself, considers the temptation to yield through pity to his wife's entreaties. If he tempers his will, his tongue that is hard and firm like a sword, he has blunted its sharp edge; he has in effect feminized it, as he says (*ethelunthēn*, for the sake of a woman [*Ajax* 650–52]). A warrior man often likens himself to a sword; his mind is obdurate, his will and words are whetted like iron (cf. Aeschylus *Seven Against Thebes* 529–30, 715). His is the instrument of power that wounds others, while his body remains impenetrable to outside forces. Ajax will harden his will; he will have his heroic death by the sword of iron. But how? By burying that sword in the earth and falling upon it, breaking through the flesh of his side (*pleuran diarrexanta*, 834). As he violates the boundaries of his body, he also violates tragic convention by staging his death as a public act. Yet paradoxically, there is yet another anomaly in the method he chooses. Suicide is a solution in tragedy normally reserved only for women – and what we are given to witness is this convention borrowed for a man's version of its. A heroic death then in the woman's way, a whetted will penetrated by a whetted weapon, befitting (as we will discuss further in another context) the curious ambiguities of this most masculine hero.[19]

My last example here is Hippolytus in Euripides' play. Refusing eros, refusing the touch, even the sight of a woman, he is brought back on stage in mortal agony after his horses had stampeded in fright before the apparition of the bull from the sea. Then he cries out that pains dart through his head and spasms leap up in his brain, while his desire is now all for a sword to cleave himself in two and "put his life at last to bed" (*Hippolytus* 1351–52, 1371–77). His symptoms are those of a woman, racked with the pain of childbirth or the torment of sexual desire.[20] We remember then Phaedra's last words, which prophesied that he would "share in her disease" (*Hippolytus* 730–31) – the deadly pangs of unrequited eros that earlier had reduced her to a sick and suffering body. Yet in that first scene, when no one on stage yet knows the cause of her malady, the chorus speaks in generic terms about the body of a woman. They call it a *dustropos harmonia*, an ill-tuned harmony; it suffers the misery of helplessness (*amechania*), and is open to the breeze that darts through the womb in pregnancy as well as to the torments of eros.[21] This body is permanently at odds with itself, subject to a congenital dissonance between inside and outside. Woman can never forget her body, as she experiences its inward pain, nor is she permitted to ignore the fact of its outward appearance in that finely tuned consciousness she acquires with respect to how she might seem to the eyes of others. Bodiliness is what most defines her in the cultural system that associates her with physical processes of birth and death and stresses the material dimensions of her existence, as exemplified, above all, in Hesiod's canonical myth of how the first woman, Pandora, was created.[22] Men have bodies, to be sure, but in the gender system the role of representing the corporeal side of life in its helplessness and submission to constraints is primarily assigned to women.

Thus, it is women who most often tend the bodies of others, washing the surface of the body or laying it out for its funeral. Theirs is the task to supply the clothing that covers the body, and they have a storehouse of robes that may encircle the male victim in its textured folds. When men suffer or die in the theatrical space, it is the female who most typically is the cause. She seems to know, whether consciously or not, how vulnerable, how open – how mortal, in fact – is the human body. These figures may be goddesses like Aphrodite and Hera or, above all, the Erinyes, avenging ministers of retributive justice. But these are also women like Clytemnestra, Deianeira, Hecuba, and, of course, Agave, the mother of Pentheus.[23]

On the other hand, dressed as a woman, Pentheus makes the first discovery of his corporeal self. Before this he defends himself militantly against any touch of the other. But now he allows Dionysus to make contact with his body and, in a grotesque parody of female coquetry, is eager for the god to adjust the fine details of his costume and to arrange the stray locks of hair peeping out from beneath its snood (*Bacchae* 925–38). With this laying on of hands, Dionysus breaches that physical integrity so dear to the male and prepares Pentheus for the terrible sequel, when the voyeur, coming to see as a spectator what he imagines are the women's illicit physical contacts with others, is himself exposed to view, *his* body becoming instead the focus of their ministering hands. Then they indeed touch his body, and in the strength induced by their maenadic state easily tear it apart in the literal act of *sparagmos*.

In this primitive regression, women undo the body; its structures cannot hold, its limbs are unbound, and the masculine self, originally so intent on opposing himself to anything feminine, is fragmented and flies apart. Female violence may be viewed through the lens of role reversal, but in the Greek imagination the maenadic woman is regularly endowed with this power, especially over the masculine body, and is the model herself for the male who, when he too is seized like Euripides' Heracles in the grip of this madness, can only be described as "playing the Bacchant" and imitating the part of the woman.[24]

Theatrical Space

Second is the space itself on stage in the Greek theater, where the human actors situate themselves and the theatrical action takes place before the spectator. By convention this space is constructed as an outside in front of a façade of a building, most often a house or palace, and there is a door that leads to an inside that is hidden from view. What happens inside must always in some way be brought outside – for example, through use of the wheeled platform called the *ekkyklema*, most often used to display the corpses of those bodies who have met their fatal doom within the house – visual proof of the violence that must also by convention take place offstage. But the very business of entrances and exits, of comings and goings through the door of the house, continually establishes a symbolic dialectic between public and private, seen and unseen, open and secret, even known and unknown.[25]

In this simple mapping of spatial relations, the stage conventions not only chart the bounded areas of social relations between the genders, which assign men to the outside and women to the inside, but they also suggest an analogy to the tragic world itself, which in the course of its plot and actions inevitably reveals its hidden and unknown dimensions.[26]

Earlier I defined the tragic universe as one that is other than the self originally imagined it to be. Going one step further, we may add that tragedy is the epistemological form par excellence. What it does best through the resources of the theater is to chart a path from ignorance to knowledge, deception to revelation, misunderstanding to recognition. The characters act out and live through the consequences of having clung to a partial single view of the world and themselves.[27] In the process, in the conflicts and tensions that mark the relations between the opposing characters, all come in some way to experience the complexities of the world – its multiple dimensions, its deceptions and illusions. Inside and outside organize the dramatic action of the drama, and they refer not only to the shifting planes of reality (the known and the unknown) but to the tragic self – both mind and body – and find their material referent in the house and the façade it presents to the outside world.

The house, let us now observe, is the property of the male and his family line. The *oikos* is the visual symbol of paternal heredity that entitles sons to succeed their fathers as proprietor of its wealth and movable goods and as ruler over its inhabitants. As the male in tragedy is often conflated with king, the house extends further as a locus of masculine power to include the sign of sovereignty over the city as a whole, and the solidity of its architectural structure symbolically guarantees the enduring stability of the social order. Yet the house, as we know, is more primarily the proper domain of the woman, to which the social rules of the culture assign her, while its men go forth into the outside world to pursue manly accomplishments in war and politics.

Thus, in conflicts between house and city or between domestic and political concerns that are the recurrent preoccupations of tragic plots, the woman, whether wife or daughter, is shown as best representing the positive values and structures of the house, and she typically defends its interests in response to some masculine violation of its integrity. As a result, however, of the stand she takes, the woman also represents a subversive threat to male authority as an adversary in a power struggle for control that resonates throughout the entire social and political system, raising the terrifying specter of rule by women. Here we might note how strongly alien is the presence of this feminine other who, in asserting legitimate values most associated with her social role, is also perceived as illegitimately asserting the rights reserved for the masculine project of self. She never achieves these in any permanent way. But in the contest over rights to control domestic space that the stage conventions exploit, it is the woman and not the man who, by reason of her close identification with the house as her intimate scene, consistently rules the relations between inside and outside and shows herself as standing on the threshold betwixt and between.

Men find out in tragedy that they are likely to enter that interior domain mostly to their peril, whether Agamemnon as he walks upon the crimson carpets his wife has spread to lead him to his death at her hands within the house, or Hippolytus confronted inside with the nurse's revelation to him of Phaedra's guilty secret that is the beginning of his doom, or Polymestor in Euripides' *Hecuba* whom the Trojan queen lures into the tent to take a woman's revenge on the perfidious Thracian king who has killed her child.

As a general principle, the absent hero returns to his house either never to enter through its doors again, as for the extreme case of Heracles in the *Trachiniae*, or to meet with his own destruction within, as in the cases cited above, or finally, like the Heracles in Euripides' play, to go mad once inside the house, slaying his wife and children and literally insuring the fall of the house by toppling its columns. On the other hand, if the male would successfully penetrate the interior of the house and reclaim it for his own, he typically requires feminine assistance, best exemplified in the fact that, as we will discuss further in a different context, all the extant versions of Orestes' story insist upon pairing him with his sister, Electra.

Men imagine they can control that interior space by attempting to control the women within it, and they object, often violently as Pentheus does in the *Bacchae*, when in the most dramatic reversal they leave the stifling environment of the house to venture forth to the open (although equally uncivic world) of forest and mountains. But the king's authority lapses on all fronts. He is unable to bring back his Theban women from the mountains to put them in their rightful place, ultimately going out to meet them on their new terrain with the results we already know. But he fails too on domestic territory when he would lock up the other maenads (and their leader Dionysus) and imprison them within the house. Literally binding them with fetters, he discovers all too soon the futility of applying coercive force as they easily – magically – loosen themselves from his restraints, while his larger demands for mastery over the house literally collapse when Dionysus sends the earthquake to shake the *oikos* to its very foundations.

The situation of Pentheus leads to a further point. The king erects barriers around himself (and his psyche) against the invasion of Dionysus even as he struggles to maintain the integrity of the house and the walled city of Thebes.[28] If tragedy, as I have suggested, is the epistemological genre par excellence, which continually calls into question what we know and how we think we know it, it does so often by confronting the assumptions of rational thought with those psychological necessities that may not be denied.

The master example of Pentheus therefore gives another turn to the dialectic of inside and outside that focuses on the woman and the house as containers for the emotional energies of the self and the society. The house has its many kinds of secrets that men do not know, and the challenge to male authority over it therefore takes place on several levels – the social, cognitive, and psychological. If men enter this domain, assuming their legitimate rights to its custody, only to meet with a welcome they had not foreseen, at the same time they also inevitably fail to lock up, to repress those powerful forces hidden in the recesses of the house. Quite the contrary – tragic process, for the most part, conveyed through the catalyzing person and actions of the feminine, puts insistent pressure on the façade of the masculine self in order to bring outside that which resides unacknowledged and unrecognized within. Here in the *Bacchae*, where the inversion of roles is expressly posed in spatial terms that send the women outside and situate the man within, the stage conventions are used to their best effect as Pentheus leaves the interior space now for the last time – for his liberation and for his destruction – dressed, as we might now expect, like a woman.

The Plot

Third, the plot itself – that which brings about the recognition, the *anagnorisis* – the plot whose process Aristotle describes as a combination of *desis*, binding, and *lusis*, unbinding, dénouement, and which in its complex form he calls by the corresponding Greek term, a *sumploke*, an interweaving as that which describes the fabric, the texture of the play (*Poetics* 1455b).

At a higher level, these terms are even more suggestive as they might remind us how the tragic world works its ruinous effects through modes of entrapment and entanglement that causes its characters first to stumble through ignorance and error and then to fall. In the elaborate tragic game, the metaphoric patterns of binding and unbinding continually operate in a reciprocal tension as signs of constraint and necessity, on the one hand, and of dissolution and death, on the other, defining the parameters between which characters are caught in the "double bind."[29]

In the cognitive psychology of tragic man, inner choice and external necessity (or *ethos*, character, and *daimon*, divine power) finally converge to sanction whatever form of tragic justice the plot demands for its satisfying fulfillment. Thus the "nature of tragic action appears to be defined by the simultaneous presence of a 'self' and something greater at work that is divine."[30] In this sense, the gods finally may be said to direct the energy of the action and to be understood retrospectively as supporting and advancing the outcome of the myth.

Gods sometimes appear on stage (and I have already remarked how frequently these figures are goddesses), although most often they operate from afar as inhabiting that other unknown dimension of existence which mortals may only grasp dimly and, of course, too late. But it is remarkable how often that energy is channeled through the feminine other, who serves as their instrument even when she acts or seems to act on her own terrain and for her own reasons and even when she acts out of ignorance or of only partial knowledge of the tragic world she inhabits. Thus women frequently control the plot and the activity of plotting and manipulate the duplicities and illusions of the tragic world.

On the one hand, women's exclusion from the central area of masculine public life seems to be matched by their special access to those powers beyond men's control, to those outside forces that make sudden forays into human lives, unsettling all their typical assumptions. On the other hand, that same exclusion which relegates them to the inside as mistresses of the interior space equips them for deviousness and duplicity, gives them a talent, or at least a reputation, for weaving wiles and fabricating plots, marks of their double consciousness with regard to the world of men.

Tragedy is the art form, above all, that makes the most of what is called discrepant awareness – what one character knows and the other doesn't or what none of the characters know but that the audience does. Thus it is that irony is tragedy's characteristic trope, that several levels of meaning operate at the same time. Characters speak without knowing what they say, and misreading is the typical and predictable response to the various cues that others give.

This pervasive irony may manifest itself in many ways, and it owes its effectiveness to a strong conviction about the ambiguous, even opaque nature of verbal communication that is reflected in the belief in oracles. These riddling, divine utterances invite interpretation and/or evasion and, at the same time, suggest, when the outcome proves disastrous, how misguided and ignorant these human attempts may be. Apollo and his oracle often serve as a primary source, as Oedipus, his most famous client, confirms. But other factors make for dramatic irony, particularly in connection with the deceptive powers of the feminine and the special verbal skills that accompany these.

Clytemnestra in Aeschylus' *Agamemnon* is the most powerful paradigm of the woman who plots, who through the riddling doubleness of the language to which she resorts builds the play to its climax in the murder of her husband within the house where she entangles him in the nets of the robe, and only Cassandra, another woman of second sight, perceives but cannot convey what lies behind the guileful persuasion. The case of Phaedra, the virtuous wife in Euripides' *Hippolytus*, is also instructive. Caught in the conflict between desire and honor and determined to preserve her integrity at any cost. Theseus' queen, despite herself or rather in defense of that apparently indefensible feminine self, fabricates the lying message that will implicate Hippolytus as the cause of her death and lead to his literal entanglement in the reins of his own chariot.

The pattern holds too even at the other end of the dramatic spectrum where in the late romantic plays of Euripides, which shift to exotic locales, the feminine other takes on a different configuration as the remote object of a mythic quest. Now men are sent forth, albeit unknowing, in search of the absent, forgotten woman who longs to return to the home and loved ones she has lost; in the process of rescuing the feminine, they find out they have redeemed and refound a version of male heroic identity. But still it is the woman who plots and now openly devises a plan on stage before us – this time for the best of reasons – her own rescue and that of her menfolk, as does Iphigenia in the *Iphigenia in Tauris* or Helen in the play of the same name. The men here are only adjuncts of the women; they offer prior schemes of their own but inevitably yield to and cooperate in the woman's superior plans that all involve elaborate dramas of deception.

If we take a rapid inventory of the plot as intrigue in the extant plays of the tragic corpus, some interesting principles emerge.[31] First, it is the women whose plots are more generally successful.[32] If men succeed, however, it is precisely because they have allied themselves with women – for example, in the Euripidean plays just cited, and more broadly in the various treatments of the Orestes story where Orestes succeeds in avenging his father through the murder of his mother because he has joined forces with his sister, Electra. Thus the recognition between them must necessarily precede the *praxis* of vengeance. In the *Choephoroi* of Aeschylus (the second play of the *Oresteia*), for example, it is only after the long interchange between himself, Electra, and the female chorus of libation bearers that Orestes is able at last to interpret the dream of Clytemnestra, and thus, psychologically equipped, is ready to assume a stranger's disguise that will gain him successful entry into the feminine domain of the house.[33]

Second, whereas deceit and intrigue are condemned in woman, they are also seen as natural to her sphere of operations and the dictates of her nature.[34] For the male, however, resort to *dolos*, trickery, is what most undermines masculine integrity and puts him under the gravest of suspicions. These are best mitigated when the one to be deceived is a cruel, barbarian king of another land (as in the late Euripidean plays) whose adversary status comes closer to the role of melodramatic villain.[35] The case of Orestes at home in Argos is even more informative in this regard. His success, it is true, depends on reunion with his sister, but his resort to trickery and disguise (*dolos, mechane*) entails a further risk to his masculine stature, no matter how urgent and obligatory is his task of vengeance. Appeal to the authority of Apollo the god is therefore needed to justify this mode of action. The god (in both Aeschylus and Sophocles) must explicitly decree a retribution that exactly matches the original crime: as she (Clytemnestra) killed, so must she be killed in turn – by guile (Aeschylus *Choephoroi* 556–59; Sophocles *Electra* 32–37).

Sophocles' *Trachiniae*, that schematic model of gender relations, again supplies an excellent version of the norm. Heracles too practices deception, first to conquer the girl Iole, the current object of his erotic desire and the immediate cause of all his woe, and then to introduce her secretly into the house. But in his case, deception returns quite literally (and most dramatically) against him. His deception, revealed by others to his wife, activates the Centaur's ruse, plotted long ago as the deadly poison entrusted as a secret love charm to Deianeira's safekeeping inside the house. The point is that innocent as Deianeira may be of conscious intent to harm her husband, she still easily proves a better and more successful plotter than he. Masculine guile is repaid in full – even when retaliation does not openly bear the name of revenge.

If this Heracles conforms so well to the normative pattern, Ajax, that other great hero, does not. His is a curious case, but one whose anomaly might just prove the point. At the crucial moment of Sophocles' play, having determined to die an honorable death, he delivers a deceptive speech that suggests he has changed his mind and has learned to bend with the vicissitudes of time and change. With this speech he puts off those who would guard him and leaves himself alone to stage that elaborate suicide to which I have earlier referred. Critics have energetically contested the status of this speech as truth or lie. For while the outcome of the plot tells us that Ajax has not undergone any fundamental conversion of spirit, he also seems to have arrived at the kind of tragic knowledge we recognize as intrinsically true to the genre.

How then can we read the enigma of this speech? Better still, how can we read Ajax, the traditional epic hero, who would resort to a deceptive plot that goes against the grain of strict masculine values in which Ajax puts too much store? This is the man, after all, we might note with respect to spatial relations, who could not endure, as the oracle riddlingly suggests for his salvation, to remain *inside* the tent even for the space of one single day. But it is precisely the ambiguities of this hero who in his madness has not acted the part of the hero and precisely the question of dishonor converted finally to honor that account for the interesting ambiguities of his subsequent actions, which rewrite the theatrical conventions associated with gender. Thus the deceptive speech makes sense as a feminine strategy enlisted in the service of restoring an unequivocal manliness that he can only achieve, as I suggested before, by dying the manly death – heroically and publicly on stage – yet in the woman's way.

Now when other male characters, those not designated as tragic figures in the dramatic action, seek to deceive, their devices flounder, and men as these are dismissed out of hand.[36] Agamemnon, so easily duped by his wife in Aeschylus' play, miserably fails, for his part, when in Euripides' *Iphigenia in Aulis* he and Menelaus plot to bring Iphigenia as a sacrifice for the expedition to Troy under the pretext of a marriage with Achilles. Clytemnestra finds them out – by a fortuitous accident – and the sacrifice only takes place through Iphigenia's voluntary and open choice of the role assigned to her by her father and the myth. Most telling of all perhaps, Odysseus, the master plotter on his own epic territory (and a familiar trickster figure in the plots of mischievous satyr plays), only sees his plans go awry on the tragic stage – for example, in Sophocles' *Philoctetes* when Neoptolemus, son of Achilles, rejects finally the man and his plans, he of whom his father had said in the *Iliad*, "I hate like the gates of Hades a man who hides one thing in his heart and speaks another" (9.312–13).

The *Bacchae* finally, as we might expect, furnishes the most remarkable example of the uses of plotting and exposes the conventions of its theatrical deployment as the pivotal point around which the entire play revolves and the peripeteia depends. All the operative terms come into play – secrecy, guilefulness, entrapment, and femininity – as Dionysus and Pentheus engage in their power struggle for control over the other, the city, the women, and ultimately, over the outcome of the plot itself. Pentheus aligns himself, of course, with physical force as the masculine means to victory, trying and failing to bind his adversary (and his follow-ers), and ready to dress as a soldier and deploy an army for a military battle against the women. What Dionysus does is to retaliate against threats of force at this critical moment with a devious plot – to entice Pentheus to go alone to the mountains in secrecy.

What this means is that he persuades Pentheus to trade his ready reliance on physical combat for that other, diametrically opposite mode of action – resort to a cunning plot of self-concealment. In other words, Dionysus' strategy for victory over his opponent is first to lure him into embracing the same kind of strategy. They are co-conspirators now, plotting together but for ultimately divergent results, as for one the intrigue will succeed in every respect and for the other it will disastrously fail.

But the first conquest of Pentheus already lies in the fact that he agrees to shift his tactics from open force to the secret deception of hiding, and the second, which follows upon the first, is the change in dress from male to female that, as Dionysus argues, is essential for the success of the project. These two steps, however, imply one another – it is the woman who has recourse to devious plotting, the very charges Pentheus has laid against both Dionysus and the maenads (e.g., 475, 487, 805–6), and the costume Pentheus dons therefore matches and visually represents the feminine nature of the strategy he has already chosen. But in the ways of women Pentheus is only an imposter, easily betrayed by the other superior plotter, and hence the scheme he contrives and carries out can only recoil against him for his own doom.

Mimesis

I come now very briefly to my fourth and most inclusive element – that of mimesis itself, the art of imitation through which characters are rendered lifelike and plot and action offer an adequate representation of reality. Yet mimesis also focuses attention on the status of theater as illusion, disguise, double dealing, and pretense. There is a serious and wonderful paradox here. For while theater resorts continually to artifice, as it must, to techniques of make-believe that can only resemble the real, it can also better represent the larger world outside as it more nearly is, subject to the deceptions, the gaps in knowledge, the tangled necessities, and all the tensions and conflicts of a complex existence.

Role playing is what actors must literally do in the theater as they don their costumes and masks to impersonate an other – whether king or servant, mortal or god, Greek or barbarian, man or woman. But the reverse side of the coin is to be dubbed an actor, a *hypokrites*, who is only playing a role, offering only a *persona* (a *prosopon*) to the other that does not match what lies behind the mask.

Recognition, *anagnorisis* of persons whose identities were unknown or mistaken is, of course, a typical and even focal device of tragic action. But this kind of recognition is the overtly theatrical event that condenses the epistemological bias of the entire phenomenon of drama. Thus recognition extends along a far wider spectrum, embracing the world, the other, and the self. The problem of accurately reading the other is a continuing, obsessive concern in Greek tragedy that increases in urgency as the genre displays a greater self-consciousness with regard to its own theatrical resources. But recognition of the unknown self, as for Oedipus, or of the hidden self, as for Pentheus or even for Deianeira, is perhaps the most elusive but also the most psychologically significant result on the tragic stage, suggesting what the invention of theater for and in the city might imply about an emerging image of the private individual and the growing pains of masculine identity.[37]

This double dimension of role playing is a feature that Greek society would perceive as not exclusively but yet fundamentally feminine.[38] Woman is the mimetic creature par excellence, ever since Hesiod's Zeus created her as an imitation with the aid of the other artisan gods and adorned her with a deceptive allure.[39] Woman is perennially under suspicion as the one who acts a part – that of the virtuous wife – but hides other thoughts and feelings, dangerous to men, within herself and the house. "Counterfeit evil" is the charge that Hippolytus is not alone in bringing against the *genos*, the race of women, for she has the best capacity, by her nature and origin, to say one thing and hide another in her heart, to sow the doubt in her husband's mind, to cite perhaps the radical cause, that the child she bears may be his but again may not be.[40]

Woman speaks on the tragic stage, transgressing the social rules if she speaks on her own behalf. In this role, her speech and action involve her in the ensemble of tragic experience and thereby earn her the right to tragic suffering. But by virtue of the conflicts generated by her social position and ambiguously defined between inside and outside, interior self and exterior identity, the woman is already more of a "character" than the man, who is far more limited as an actor to his public social and political roles. Woman comes equipped with a "natural" awareness of those very complexities men would resist, if they could. Situated in her more restrictive and sedentary position in the world, she is permitted, she is asked, we might say, to reflect more deeply, like Phaedra, on the paradoxes of herself. Through these she can arrive better at the paradoxes of the world that she, much better than men, seems to know is subject to irreconcilable conflict, subject as well to time, flux, and change (the very themes I might add of Ajax's great deceptive speech). Hence the final paradox may be that theater uses the feminine for the purposes of imagining a fuller model for the masculine self, and "playing the other" opens that self to those often banned emotions of fear and pity.

Woman may be thought to speak double, and sometimes she does. But she also sees double; the culture has taught her that too, and it is perhaps not an accident that only when Pentheus dresses as a woman does he see double for the first time – two suns, two Thebes. This is a symptom of madness, to be sure, attributed by the ancient commentators to inebriation, but madness is the emblem of the feminine, and seeing double is also the emblem of a double consciousness that a man acquires by dressing like a woman and entering into the theatrical illusion. The very fact of that dressing up already demonstrates the premise in unequivocal and theatrical terms.

The feminine is a tragic figure on the stage; she is also the mistress of mimesis, the heart and soul of the theater. The feminine instructs the other through her own example – that is, in her own name and under her own experience – but also through her ability to teach the other to impersonate her – whether Pentheus or Dionysus.

This brief discussion can suggest only in outline how closely the tragic genre in its theatrical form, representation, and content is linked to Greek notions of gender, and how for the most part man is undone (or at times redeemed) by feminine forces or himself undergoes some species of "feminine" experience. On the simplest level, this experience involves a shift at the crucial moment of the peripeteia from active to passive, from mastery over the self and others to surrender. Sometimes there is madness, always suffering and pathos, which lead in turn to expressions of lamentation and pity from the chorus and/or the characters. In a more complex view, tragedy, understood as the worship of Dionysus, expands an awareness of the world and the self through the drama of "playing the other" whose mythic and cultic affinities with the god logically connects the god of women to the lord of the theater.

If drama, however, tests masculine values only to find that these alone are inadequate to the complexity of the new situation, it also, as Linda Bamber remarks, "does not dismiss them" but rather most often shows that manliness and self-assertion need no longer compete with pity and even forgiveness.[41] Moreover, the male characters whose sufferings are the most stringent and reductive of self are also allowed to discover the internal strength for transcending them.[42] In the end, tragedy arrives at closures that generally reassert male, often paternal, structures of authority, but before that the work of the drama is to open up the masculine view of the universe. It typically does so, as we have seen, through energizing the theatrical resources of the female and concomitantly enervating the male as the price of initiating actor and spectator into new and unsettling modes of feeling, seeing, and knowing.

We can trace the persistence of this "initiatory" process from the work of the first tragic poet to the third.[43] History has cunningly arranged it that Euripides' last play, the *Bacchae*, should also refer back to the archaic scenario that underlies the ritual conditions of the theater.[44] Yet viewed in its metatheatrical aspects, the *Bacchae* also makes claims to be considered in a diachronic perspective as a belated examplar of the genre that by now has developed a keen awareness of its own properties and conventions. As a result, the play is in a position to exemplify and reflect back what was always implicit in the theater, and at the same time, by the very admission of that theatrical awareness, to transform its object of reflection and reorient it in new and different directions.

If my basic hypothesis is valid, then the distinctive features of Euripidean theater (which are more obvious, in fact, in plays other than the *Bacchae*) may well lend support to what I have been suggesting about the intimate relations between the feminine and the theater. Thus I see all the following traits of Euripidean drama as various and interlocking functions of one another, starting with Euripides' greater interest in and skill at subtly portraying the psychology of female characters, and continuing to his general emphasis on interior states of mind as well as on the private emotional life of the individual, most often located in the feminine situation. We may add to these his particular fondness for plots of complex intrigue (usually suggested by women) that use *dolos, apatē, technē*, and *mechanē*, which with their resort to disguise and role playing are an explicit sign of an enhanced theatricality. Finally, we may include more generally Euripides' thematic concern with metaphysical questions of reality and illusion in the world.

The *Helen* is the most splendid example, as it is a drama that allows itself the fullest play with the resources of theater and uses these to direct the most elaborate inquiry into the complexities of being and seeming and the paradoxical crossings of illusion and reality.[45] The source of the confusion is the ontological status of the feminine itself. There are two Helens, the real, chaste version who was left in Egypt and never went to Troy, and the more traditional adulterous wife whom Menelaus thinks he has recovered at Troy but is really a phantom, an *eidolon*, impersonating Helen's true self. I alluded earlier to the symbolic implications we might infer from Pentheus dressing as a woman and seeing double for the first time. Here in the *Helen*, where double vision rules the play in every respect, the woman is both a character who to her irremediable sorrow learns first hand about the most fundamental problems of the self's identity and, at the same time, serves as an objective referent through which the man must question all his previous perceptions of the world. What is more, the essential strategy for insuring the success of the intrigue she invents for their rescue requires that he too adopt a disguise and pretend to be another than himself, allowing her to recount the most dangerous fiction that the real Menelaus has died.

The uses of the play, to be sure, have their deadly serious side for all concerned, and the unhappy residue of spoiled lives persists behind the successful outcome of the play. But for love of this woman, whether in her imagined or real *persona*, the man willingly enters into the theatrical game and shows a capacity now to act a part and enter into a stage illusion. The *Helen* is a rare play that pushes its original improbable (and theatrical) premises as far as they can go, but the uxorious Menelaus is also a novelty, and the erotic element already diverts the play away from the more typical tragic mode to that of romance. In this new kind of play world Euripides invents, the uses to which he puts the feminine and the theater may be seen as the logical result of the premises of tragedy. On the other hand, by disclosing those premises too well, he also alters them and subverts the genre that was so firmly bound up with the context of the masculine civic world.

Thus, in this sense, Euripides may be said to have "feminized" tragedy and, like his Dionysus in the *Bacchae*, to have laid himself open to the scorn that accrues to those men who consort with women. Aristophanic comedy, which loves to lampoon Euripides and all his new-fangled ideas, continually presses the scandal of his erotic dramas, especially those that let women speak more boldly (and hence more shamefully) upon the stage until Aristophanes, in his own late play, the *Frogs*, evaluates on a full-fledged scale the development of the tragic genre by staging an open contest between the old poet, Aeschylus, and the new, Euripides (755–1853).

At stake is the choice of which poet Dionysus should bring back from the underworld to the city and theater of Athens. Which one is more worthy to save the city, which seems to link its loss of political potency to the absence of a fertile, potent poet in the tragic theater? Broadly stated, the contest develops into one between masculine and feminine sides, with Aeschylus espousing a manly, virile art that exhorts its citizens to military valor and Euripides representing a feminine, slender Muse who is weaker and more insubstantial, leaning toward the sensual and the pathetic. Not surprisingly, when these two are tested in the scales, Aeschylean tragedy outweighs the Euripidean by its superior mass and weight. Dionysus therefore abandons his original desire for Euripides, to whose seductive allure he had earlier succumbed, in favor of resurrecting the heroic warrior energies of the earlier poet and, by extension, of the past.[46] Aristophanes not untypically assumes that when things go badly for men and masculine interests the cause lies in a decay of moral and aesthetic values that slides easily into hints of effeminacy and all that that implies.

In any case, the solution of the *Frogs* in bringing back the archaic spirit of Aeschylus as a solution to the city's problems is also a formal, generic one. It is predicated on the controlling convention of Old Comedy that fulfills its festive function of social renewal by consistently choosing the idealized past over the distressing, chaotic present, even as it prefers to rejuvenate the old (father) rather than, as in New Comedy, to promote the young (son). Moreover, the comic poet paints with a broad, satirical brush, and whatever the justice or truth of the cause he thinks he is advancing (and *his* play, of course, is what he imagines will save the city), he has the generic right to misrepresent, and how he does it here affects Aeschylus even more perhaps than Euripides.

Leaving aside the fact that Euripides too has his military and patriotic plays, Aristophanes would have us believe that the essence of the *Seven Against Thebes*, that drama "full of Ares" invoked to support Aeschylus' case, was some conventional treatment of military prowess. It was rather a tragedy concerning the sons of Oedipus and the dangers they posed to the safety of the city by their resort to armed combat in the style of the old heroic duel, while the function of the avenging Erinys returning to fulfill the father's curse conforms precisely, even schematically, to the rules of the feminine in the theater as I have earlier outlined them.

Nevertheless, Aristophanes is a witness we cannot afford to ignore. He speaks about the theater from within the theater. Skewed as his caricature of Euripides (and his drama) may be, his strategy of clustering the poet's theatrical, psychological, and noetic innovations around a particular affinity for the feminine is valuable testimony to a popular contemporary perception of Euripidean theater, even if it is bought at the price of suppressing the continuities with earlier drama.

Along the same lines, we may even be able to swallow Aristophanes' parting shot that implies Euripides' loss of the tragic art is due to "sitting at the feet of Socrates" (1491–95), another favorite target for comic misrepresentation. Yet however justified Aristophanic comedy may be to single out both Euripides and Socrates as spokesmen for the new intellectual trends that confuse and unsettle the older, simpler (hence more manly) values of the city, philosophy would never consort with tragedy, which it comes to see as its implacable rival in laying claim to teach the truth, impart knowledge, improve its fellow citizens, and without doubt – to save the city.

Socrates, as Plato in the next generation has him argue, makes no distinction whatsoever among any of the tragic poets when he comes to discuss the theatrical arts. Indeed, he founds his critique of drama on Homer, whom he characterizes as the first teacher and guide of tragedy.[47] That same Aeschylean play is invoked again when Socrates' interlocutor in the *Republic* first quotes a famous verse from it in a proper context only at the next moment to turn around the meaning of the lines that follow it so as to apply it to the unjust man rather than to the just.[48] The argument in Plato between tragedy and philosophy is well known, and it is not my intention to air all the old questions or to solve the old dilemmas. But I want to suggest that Plato, standing outside the drama, can be called in as a last witness to support my claims about the intrinsic links between femininity and theater, viewed now from a wholly negative perspective. Plato's insistence on banishing tragedy from his ideal state and his consistent distaste throughout his career for the tragic poets, whom he sometimes associates quite closely with sophists and rhetoricians, are based, to be sure, on a number of complex and disparate factors. But in addition to the explicitly philosophical issues, I want to argue that Plato's position on theater can also be illuminated by considering its relation to his notions of gender and his attitudes toward the feminine.[49]

Strange as it may seem, Plato's aim is not all that remote from what Aristophanes wants in the *Frogs*. The project is more far-reaching, to be sure, in every respect, and the means are those which will forever change the shape of Western thought. But, like Aristophanes, Plato is concerned with restoring men and their morals in the city, and, like the comic poet, he insists on the relevance of aesthetic style and form. Briefly put, for the purposes of this discussion, Plato's larger concerns may also be translated into his general desire to remake man in a masculine society and through philosophical training to purify and enhance the traditional heroic notion of manliness (*andreia*) in a new, revised version in which courage, vigilance, and strength may be better utilized for the improvement of self and society.

Certainly, Plato comes closest to codifying under the name of philosophy the dream of the Greek male for a world that is constituted as his alone, where he might give birth to himself and aspire finally to an immortality he has always craved. In tragedy, this desire leads to disaster, most often, as we have seen, through the resistance of the gods – and of the women. Philosophy, on the other hand, offers the promise of success in this endeavor, providing one follows the blueprints that are carefully designed to retrain the masculine self.

It may be objected that Plato breaks with the old stereotypes of gender when he insists that women may be just like men with the exception of a natural inferiority in physical strength, which does not disqualify them from participating as guardians (and even warriors) in his vision of the ideal city in the *Republic*. This is a revolutionary proposal whose significance we ought not minimize.[50] But we should note that this reevaluation of women does not really upgrade the feminine in its differences from the masculine. Quite the contrary – Plato defuses the power and specificity of the feminine when he would abolish the family and the domestic sphere in which that influence operated. If he includes the participation of certain women who may prove to possess masculine abilities, it is precisely because in the *Republic* he believes that they may be successfully taught to imitate the masculine model. Even here, the principle of equality falters when Plato would reward with special breeding privileges men who have distinguished themselves in battle but does not suggest granting the same opportunities to their female counterparts. This may or may not be a trivial slip. What is striking, however, is that elsewhere femininity plays for Plato throughout his work its usual role of negative foil to the masculine as it heads the long list of undesirable models for men that descends to the servile, the buffoonish, the bestial, and the non-human (*Republic* 3.395d–396b).

Plato's attack on tragedy and its traditional repertory operates on several fronts: he objects to the deceptiveness of theatricality as a misleading and deficient imitation of reality, deplores the often unworthy quality of what or who is being imitated, and insists upon the damaging effects such imitations are liable to produce on the actors and spectators in the theater.[51]

For the first case, I would not go so far as to claim that Plato explicitly refers the art of making illusions to the feminine per se, even if women, like children, are most susceptible to its charms (e.g., *Laws* 658d, 817c) and most likely, in fact, to tell those lying stories about the gods to their young (*Republic* 377c). But Plato's interest never focuses for long on women as such but rather on the inferior type of man, who deceptively passes off appearances for truth and who appeals to the inferior parts of the self (and the citizenry) that will yield to the emotions and pleasures (not lessons) of make-believe. Thus, although he confirms the conventional dictum that woman is inclined by nature to be secretive (*lathraioteron*) and crafty (*epiklopoteron*) because of her intrinsic weakness (*to asthenes*) – and concomitantly, her natural potential for virtue is inferior to a man's (*Laws* 781a–b) – Plato hardly sees her (or her representation) as a powerful acting force in the world of men.[52]

But by a whole series of innuendos and juxtapositions, poets (and artists) are enrolled in the ranks of male trickster figures who fall furthest from the ideal of manliness and seek only to cajole, seduce, and pander to the tastes of their audience. Imitators (artists and musicians) and poets and their entourage of actors, dancers, and producers join the multitude of callings that are signs of the luxury that corrupts the primitive city, and these directly precede those "makers of all sorts of goods, especially those that have to do with women's adornment"; the sequence then continues with those servants like "beauty-shop ladies, barbers, cooks, and confectioners" (*Republic* 373b–c).

Once assimilated to the larger category of sophists, dramatic art, reduced finally to prose rhetoric on a par with oratory, shares in the same field of reference that likens their false imitations of justice to those activities practiced by and for women: cookery (especially confectionery), which "puts on the mask of medicine and pretends to know what foods are best for the body" (*Gorgias* 464c–d), and beauty-culture, "the counterfeit to physical training...a mischievous, swinddling, base, servile trade, which creates an illusion by the use of artificial adjuncts and make-up and depilatories and costume" (*Gorgias* 465b–c). All these arts traffic in deceptive appearances, and their effect on others is to pander to appetites and pleasurable gratification.

The *Gorgias* stresses a certain sensual, effeminate pleasure. But the *Republic*, in which Plato specifically addresses the emotional power of the tragic, emphasizes the experience of pain and suffering, and evaluates its effects on those who act in and attend the tragic spectacles. Here the association with the feminine is clear and explicit, reiterated each time Plato returns to the topic: when heroes are shown to weep and lament their misfortunes, they are not only endorsing a false theology about the justice of the gods but are weakening themselves and others by their indulgence in womanish grief (*Republic* 387e–388a, 605d–e). Such a man does not remain steadfast to himself, exercising self-control and rationally pondering the events that have happened to him. Rather he gives way to cowardice, terror, and a host of conflicting, changeful emotions that ill suit the model of a brave and noble manliness that the state (and the soul) requires. Worst of all, he entices the spectators into the pleasures of vicariously identifying with his pitiable state, and ends by setting them the example they unfortunately will learn to imitate for themselves.[53]

For Plato, who so often strives to efface or remove all mixture, confusion, and changeability, his theory of drama is simple because, stripped down to essences, his categories are also simple. The mobility of temporary reversals and dialectical play with opposites already introduces a cognitive complexity that is the sign itself of a dangerous indeterminacy; it undermines the principle of like to like that regulates his thought and is designed, by its literalness, to reinforce a simple stability. At the most inclusive level is the dictum that no man can play more than one part, in life or in the theater (e.g., *Republic* 3.394e–395b).

The other is always weaker and inferior to the self, whose idealization requires that, once perfectly established, it cannot change and still be itself. As such, that lack of strength (attributable to the lack of mastery by the rational faculty and hence equatable finally to a lack of wisdom) can be most easily codified according to the conventional terms of the society under the name of the feminine other, to include the cognate negative traits of cowardice, fearfulness, and emotional lability. Hence, in Plato's reductive view of drama and of gender, playing the other is a species of wrongful imitation that threatens to infect reality and degrade the aspiring, virile self. It is therefore forbidden, above all, "for a man, being a man – in training, in fact to become a good/brave man," to imitate a woman in any way whatsoever: "whether old or young, whether railing against her husband, or boasting of a happiness which she imagines can rival the gods, or overwhelmed with grief and misfortune; much less a woman in love, or sick, or in labor" (*Republic* 3.395d–e). Men are neither permitted to impersonate a woman nor to show themselves in a male *persona* as undergoing the experiences of a woman, precisely the routes I have proposed as leading to masculine initiation into the lessons (and benefits) of the tragic world.

Limited as his discussion of theater may be, Plato, as a spectator who fails to come under the spell of tragic mimesis (or who perhaps once did and was cured), nonetheless darkly confirms the inextricable relationship between theater and the feminine. Tragedy cannot control the ambiguities of role playing, as most particularly when the male actor is called upon to represent the woman who is not under control either because she is actively unruly or because she succumbs to the pressures of her body. More generally, tragedy by its very nature and intention can make no solid provision for controlling the ambiguities of a world view that theater is expressly designed to represent. Thus Plato, from his point of view, is entitled to deny to "the solemn and marvelous *poiesis* of tragedy" the very task we might agree it is well equipped to accomplish, namely that of imparting "beneficial if unpleasing truths," and to claim instead that it gives its uncritical and vulgar audience what it desires to see and hear (*Gorgias* 502b).

Plato goes still further into the matter of gender and drama in the playful contest he stages between theater and philosophy in the *Symposium*, where the party to celebrate the recent victory of the tragic poet, Agathon, at the City Dionysia ends with the crowning of Socrates instead of Agathon. In mounting his own rival drama to explore the subject of eros, Plato excludes the presence of the feminine at the banquet but subtly and significantly uses the categories of effeminacy and femininity to enhance the philosophical position that is meant to include and supersede the appeal of the theater.

The *Symposium* is one of Plato's most artful and complex dialogues and deserves, of course, much fuller discussion.[54] It is established early on that love of women is an inferior sort of eros (181a–d). This is not the crucial point. But we may note in our context the persuasive if unfair value of using Agathon as the representative of all tragic art. Agathon speaks last, just before Socrates, and in his flowery speech on eros, which parodies perhaps the very play that earned him the tragic victory (*anthos*

= flower), he demonstrates the soft and effeminate nature for which he was known and which Aristophanes wickedly lampoons in his comedies (e.g., *Thesmophoriazousae*).[55] Although Aristophanes in the *Symposium* is made at the end to fall asleep before Agathon, thus establishing his rank in the hierarchy that leads from comedy to tragedy and then to philosophy, the comic poet is represented as a far more robust character than the tragic poet, and his contribution to the theme of eros is more memorable and more substantial.[56] The contrast, to be sure, is even more striking between the lovelorn Agathon and Socrates, whose physical endurance and resistance to pederastic temptation attest to the remarkable self-control of this soldier/philosopher/lover/hero.

On the other side, however, philosophy appropriates for its own use the one kind of feminine authority that the culture acknowledges as legitimate when Socrates names the prophetic priestess, Diotima, as the source of his initiation long ago into the sacred mysteries of Eros and as the original author of the inspiring discourse on eros he now is about to deliver. The feminine retains here her more instinctive alliance with the erotic as well as her mysterious connection with that other world and its secrets whose power we have come to recognize when manifested in the theater. And the woman, armed with the prestige of her sacred vocation, is called upon to instruct men as to how they might transcend feminine influence and, through the sublimations of pederastic love, even give birth to themselves.

In Plato's counter-drama the female as benevolent priestess has no cause of her own to protect and no conflictual interests to distract her. She is then free to lend whole-hearted support to the cause of men and to transmit to them a wisdom without tragic pain that may become entirely theirs. She imparts a myth about the genealogy of Eros that makes the erotic principle a male child and explains his nature by assigning potency and presence to his father, Poros (Ways and Means), and a famished emptiness to his mother, Penia (Poverty), who deceitfully (and characteristically) tricks the one who is endowed to consort with the one who is not.

In suborning theater as well as the feminine, Plato's drama puts the former to sleep in the presence of the wakeful philosopher and transfers feminine oracular power to Socrates – the midwife – who also incorporates the Dionysiac into his satyr-like image of Silenus. In the process Plato obviates the tragic necessity that requires the feminine presence upon the stage and whose complicated and essential functions in the theater of Dionysus we have followed throughout the course of this essay.

NOTES

1 E.g., *Bacchae* 451–59; Dionysus is called *thelymorphos*, 351 (cf. Pentheus' description as *gynaikomorphos* [his costume as imitating a woman's, *gynaiko-mimoi;* 981]).

2 For the fullest account of this hypothesis, see Richard Seaford, "Dionysiac Drama and Dionysiac Mysteries," *Classical Quarterly* 31 (1981): 252–75.

3 For the metatheatrical aspects of this scene in particular (and the play as a whole), see Helene Foley, "The Masque of Dionysus," *Transactions of the American Philological Association* 110 (1981): 107–33; and Charles Segal, *Dionysiac Poetics and Euripides' Bacchae* (Princeton, 1982), 215–71.

4 See further F. I. Zeitlin, "Travesties of Gender and Genre in Aristophanes' *Thesmophoriazousae*," in *Reflections of Women in Antiquity*, ed. Helene P. Foley (New York and London, 1981), 169–217 (a shorter version appears in *Critical Inquiry* 8 [1981]: 301–28, and is collected in *Writing and Difference*, ed. E. Abel [Chicago, 1982], 131–58).

5 It should be noted that, unlike other public Dionysiac festivals in Attica (and elsewhere) where both men and women participate, the City Dionysia seems to belong to men only (with the sole exception of a girl assigned to carry the ritual basket in the preliminary procession).

6 The question I raise here about the development of drama in Athens and its political and social motivations is obviously too complex for this limited discussion. I would suggest merely that the historical conditions of drama, interestingly enough, coincide with a period that sharply polarizes definitions and distinctions of masculine and feminine roles. Drama, like the woman, we might say, is useful for its society, and at the same time potentially subversive and destructive. It is also worth remarking that as theater reaches its full flowering in the fifth century, the iconography of Dionysus undergoes a shift in the vase paintings from a masculine, bearded figure to one, more youthful, who displays effeminate and more androgynous features.

7 For the bisexual consciousness of Dionysus, see especially James Hillman, *The Myth of Analysis* (Evanston, Ill., 1972), 258–66. For the more general paradoxes of Dionysus' role, see the synthesis of Segal, *Dionysiac Poetics*, 10–19.

8 These festivals are occasions for riotous carnival (e.g., the Cretan Ekdysia, the Argive Hybristika). Dionysiac merriment also lends itself to such behavior, at least as Philostratus, a late source, describes a painting of a Dionysiac revel: "Dionysus is accompanied by a numerous train in which girls mingle with men, for the revel (*komos*) allows women to act the part of men, and men to put on women's clothing and play the woman" (*Imagines* 1.2).

9 On the various forms of transvestism in Greek rite and myth, see Marie Delcourt, *Hermaphrodite: Myths and Rites of the Bisexual Figure in Classical Antiquity*, trans. J. Nicholson (London, 1956), 1–16; Clara Gallini, "Il travestismo rituale di Penteo," *Studi e materiali per la storia delle religioni*

34 (1968): 211–18, esp. 215, n. 6; and Walter Burkert, *Structure and History in Greek Mythology and Ritual* (Berkeley, 1979), 29–30.

10 "For both sexes the initiation through which a young man or woman is confirmed in his or her specific nature may entail, through a ritual exchange of clothing, temporary participation in the nature of the opposite sex whose complement he or she will become by being separated from it" (Jean-Pierre Vernant, "City-State Warfare," in *Myth and Society in Ancient Greece*, trans. J. Lloyd [Sussex, 1980], 24). Cf. also Henri Jeanmaire, *Couroi et Courètes* (Lille, 1939), 153, 321. See further Pierre Vidal-Naquet, "The Black Hunter and the Origin of the Athenian Ephebeia" and "Recipes for Greek Adolescence," in R. L. Gordon, ed., *Myth, Religion, and Society* (Cambridge, 1981), 147–85. I borrow his term, "law of symmetrical inversion."

11 The best recent discussion of the question is Helene P. Foley, "The Conception of Women in Athenian Drama," in *Reflections of Women in Antiquity*, 127–68, who offers a judicious and nuanced analysis that, however, leans too far perhaps in seeking a matched symmetry and reciprocity between masculine and feminine roles.

12 On tragedy as initiation, related both to the mysteries and to puberty rites, see the discussion of Seaford, "Dionysiac Drama" (drawing upon the early pioneering work of George Thomson, *Aeschylus and Athens*, 2nd ed. [London, 1946]). For aspects of puberty ritual reflected imaginatively in the various dramas see, for Aeschylus' *Oresteia*, Pierre Vidal-Naquet, "Hunting and Sacrifice in Aeschylus' *Oresteia*," in Jean-Pierre Vernant and Pierre Vidal-Naquet, *Tragedy and Myth in Ancient Greece*, trans. J. Lloyd (Sussex, 1981), 150, and F. I. Zeitlin, "The Dynamics of Misogyny: Myth and Mythmaking in the *Oresteia*," *Arethusa* 11 (1978): 149–84 (now in *Women and the Ancient World: The Arethusa Papers*, ed. John Peradotto and J. P. Sullivan [Albany, 1984]); for Sophocles' *Philoctetes*, Pierre Vidal-Naquet, "Sophocles' *Philoctetes* and the Ephebeia," in *Tragedy and Myth*, 175–99; for Euripides' *Hippolytus*, see especially Charles Segal, "Pentheus and Hippolytus on the Couch and on the Grid: Psychoanalytic and Structuralist Readings of Greek Tragedy," *Classical World* 72 (1978–79): 129–48, and F. I. Zeitlin, "The Power of Aphrodite: Eros and the Boundaries of the Self in Euripides' *Hippolytus*," in *Directions in Euripidean Criticism*, ed. Peter Burian (Durham, N. C., 1985), 52–111, 187–206; and for the *Bacchae*, in addition to Seaford, see Segal, *Dionysiac Poetics*, chap. 6, "Arms and the Man: Sex Roles and Rites of Passage," 158–214. Also relevant to these speculations is Louis Montrose, "The Purpose of Playing: Reflections on a Shakespearean Anthropology," *Helios* [n.s.] 7.2 (1980): 51–74, who discusses the public functions of Shakespearean theater as a secularized means of confronting the transitions of life that had earlier been framed in the milieu of Catholic ritual.

13 I am indebted here to the stimulating discussion of Linda Bamber, *Comic Women, Tragic Men: A Study of Gender and Genre in Shakespeare*

(Stanford,1982), as much for its provocative arguments as for its use in confronting some fundamental differences between the feminine in Greek and Elizabethan tragedy. There are other "others," to be sure, on the Athenian stage (e.g., barbarians, servants, enemy antagonists, and even gods), but the dialectic of self and other is consistently and insistently predicated on the distinctions between masculine and feminine, far more even than in Shakespeare. Even the plays with more strictly military and political themes (excepting only Sophocles' *Philoctetes*) arrange their plots around critical confrontations between masculine and feminine.

14 No Shakespearean tragedy has a woman as its main character, although sometimes she shares double billing – Juliet, Cleopatra. By contrast, in extant Greek drama women often lend their individual names or collective functions to the titles (Antigone, Electra, Medea; Choephoroi, Trachiniae, Bacchae, etc.). Moreover, women play far more extensive roles in Greek tragedy, which increase in subtlety and variety as the genre develops.

15 The functional argument is even more obviously true in the case of those plays which I will not discuss in this essay, in which the plot revolves around the demand made upon an army for a virgin sacrifice (such as Iphigenia and Polyxena) and where female heroic nobility in dying is used most often to offer an ironic counterpoint to masculine *Realpolitik*.

16 See especially B. M. W. Knox, "The *Medea* of Euripides," *Yale Classical Studies* 25 (1977): 198–225, for the discussion of Medea's "imitation" of male heroic traits.

17 It should be stressed that I equate drama here with serious drama rather than with comic types such as satyr play and comedy itself, whose primitive elements may well have preceded the growth of the strange mutant that is tragedy. For even if we renounce any hopes of reconstructing a plausible story of origins, there seems no doubt that the tragic play is the first to achieve the status of art and that the other forms only follow subsequently in its wake and under its influence. To speak of theater then is to speak first of tragedy.

18 Y. Belaval, "Ouverture sur le spectacle," in *Histoire des spectacles*, ed. R. Queneau (Paris, 1965), 3–16, esp. 8.

19 I have profited from the discussion in the unpublished paper of Nicole Loraux, "Ways of Killing Women in Greek Tragedy," who views Ajax' suicide as an unequivocal warrior's death. It is true, of course, that the sword is a man's weapon and that if women resort to it, it is they who are violating the rules of gender. Yet it is also true that Ajax' death, by whatever means and in whatever mood, is still a suicide, an act the culture regards in itself as inherently shameful and therefore imagined far more as a feminine solution.

20 On the general question of the female body as the model of male suffering, see the superb study of Nicole Loraux, "Le Lit, la guerre," *L'Homme* 21 (1981): 36–67. For these symptoms in the *Hippolytus*, see respectively

Loraux, "Le Lit," 58–59, and Charles Segal, "The Tragedy of the *Hippolytus:* The Waters of Ocean and the Untouched Meadow," *Harvard Studies in Classical Philology* 70 (1965): 117–69, esp. 122.

21 See the discussion of this remarkable passage and its key function in the play in Zeitlin, "The Power of Aphrodite," 68–74.

22 On Pandora in the Hesiodic text, see especially the fine analyses by Jean-Pierre Vernant, "The Myth of Prometheus in Hesiod," in *Myth and Society*, 168–85; and Nicole Loraux, "Sur la race des femmes et quelques-unes de ses tribus," *Arethusa* 11 (1978): 43–88 (collected in her *Les Enfants d'Athéna: Idées athéniennes sur la citoyenneté et la division des sexes* [Paris, 1981], 75–117).

23 It is worth noting too that the details of the sacrifice of the virgin's body holds particular fascination for the messenger speeches of the relevant tragedies.

24 See further Ruth Padel, "Women: Model for Possession by Greek Daemons," in *Images of Women in Antiquity*, ed. Averil Cameron and Amélie Kuhrt (London, 1983), 3–19. It is remarkable that in Euripides' *Heracles*, where the great Heracles goes mad and kills his wife and children, the chorus in response compares him only with women: the Danaids (who slew their husbands on their wedding night) and Procne (who slew her child in revenge for her husband's rape and mutilation of her sister, Philomela; *Heracles* 1016–27).

25 On the uses of these stage conventions and their relations of the inside/outside, see especially A. M. Dale, "Seen and Unseen on the Greek Stage," in *Collected Papers* (Cambridge, 1969), 119–29; the discussion of Padel, "Women"; and Zeitlin, "The Power of Aphrodite," 74–79.

26 The *locus classicus* is Xenophon's *Oeconomicus*. The best discussion is Jean-Pierre Vernant, "Hestia-Hermès: Sur l'expression religieuse de l'espace et du mouvement chez les Grecs," in *Mythe et pensée chez les Grecs* (Paris, 1965), 6–27.

27 See, for example, the incisive remarks of Jean-Pierre Vernant, "Tensions and Ambiguities in Greek Tragedy," in Vernant and Vidal-Naquet, *Myth and Tragedy*, 6–27. This epistemological emphasis therefore both exploits and is conditioned by the special capacity of theater to represent and embody the interaction between other points of view, attitudes, gestures, and language.

28 On the symbolic value of the house, see J. Wohlberg, "The Palace-Hero Equation in Euripides," *Acta Antiqua Academiae Scientiarum Hungaricae* 16 (1968): 149–55; and the much fuller discussion in Segal, *Dionysiac Poetics*, 86–94 and passim.

29 For fuller discussion of these terms and their relation to the structures and structuring capacities of plots, see Zeitlin, "The Power of Aphrodite," 58–64.

30 Jean-Pierre Vernant, "Intimations of the Will in Greek Tragedy," in *Myth and Society*, 51. His is the most nuanced discussion of this double determination that is often misnamed as a conflict between fate and free will.

31 For discussions of intrigue plots in general, see especially Friedrich Solmsen, "Zur Gestaltung des Intriguenmotivs in den Tragödien des Sophokles und Euripides," *Philologus* 84 (1932): 1–17; and Hans Strohm, "Trug und Taüschung in der euripideischen Dramatik," *Würzburger Jahrbücher für die Altertumswissenschaft* 4 (1949/50): 140–56, collected in *Euripides*, ed. E. Schwinge, Wege der Forschung, no. 89 (Darmstadt, 1968) as 326–44 and 345–72, respectively. See now also the wider-ranging discussion of Frances Muecke, " 'I Know You – By Your Rags': Costume and Disguise in Fifth-Century Drama," *Antichthon* 16 (1982): 17–34.

32 The *Ion* of Euripides, a play in many ways a precursor of New Comedy, foils the woman's plot against her unrecognized son (not without some fancy help from the gods) so as to bring about the joyful reunion. The play, I might add, is careful not to credit the woman Creusa as the one who first initiates the intrigue.

33 Euripides' *Electra* is still more complex, as the play separates the two acts of vengeance against Clytemnestra and her lover, Aegisthus. The old servant suggests the plot against Aegisthus (to take place outside far away from the house), while Electra contrives the elaborate and doubly deceitful intrigue against Clytemnestra.

34 This is a commonplace in tragic texts (as elsewhere): e.g., *Iphigenia in Tauris* 1032; *Medea* 834–35; *Andromache* 85; *Hippolytus* 480–81; *Ion* 483.

35 Even in these plays, masculine honor is protected, as it were, in that each man (Orestes, Menelaus) first proposes force before he accedes to the woman's practical, clever schemes (Iphigenia, Helen), and each, just before the end, is permitted a display of manly strength against the forces of the barbarian king in question.

36 The one exception that comes to mind is Euripides' strange play, *Andromache*, where Orestes, not a major character, successfully plots to have Neoptolemus killed at Delphi so as to reclaim the latter's wife, Hermione, for his own.

37 "The covert theme of all drama," Michael Goldman suggests, "is identification, the establishment of a self that in some way transcends the confusions of self"; *The Actor's Freedom: Toward a Theory of Drama* (New York, 1975), 123. In general, I have learned much from this stimulating study of the workings of theater.

38 Odysseus is the exemplar in the masculine sphere, but he neither generically represents "the race of men" nor, let me repeat, is this adaptable survivor (with strong affinities, in fact, to the feminine) a candidate for tragedy in the dramatic milieu.

39 Earlier I alluded to the creation of Pandora as exemplifying the physical, "creaturely" side of life. I emphasize now the other aspect of woman's creation as an object cunningly wrought; she is a deceptive gift in return for Prometheus' deception of Zeus, herself endowed with a crafty intelligence. Woman therefore embodies both extremes of nature and culture

that together conspire to waste a man's substance and dry him up before his time.

40 For a similar idea, see Ann Bergren, "Language and the Female in Early Greek Thought," *Arethusa* 16 (1983): 74, 77.

41 This is a combined quote and paraphrase (with one small alteration) of Bamber, *Comic Women, Tragic Men*, 15.

42 In this respect, there are strong continuities with the earlier epic tradition. See the interesting conclusions of Hélène Monsacré's fine, nuanced study, *Les Larmes d'Achille: Le Héros, la femme et la souffrance dans la poésie d'Homère* (Paris, 1984), 199–204.

43 We might note that initiation into the "real" Eleusinian mysteries involved some forms of imitating the specifically feminine experiences of Demeter and Kore.

44 More accurately, it is one of the very last, produced posthumously in Athens as was the *Iphigenia in Aulis*.

45 For the interplay of illusion and reality, see Friedrich Solmsen, "*Onoma* and *Pragma* in Euripides' *Helen*," *Classical Review* 48 (1934): 119–21; Ann Pippin (Burnett), "Euripides' *Helen*: A Comedy of Ideas," *Classical Philology* 55 (1960): 151–63; Charles Segal, "The Two Worlds of Euripides' *Helen*," *Transactions of the American Philological Association* 102 (1971): 553–614; and see now George Walsh, *The Varieties of Enchantment: Early Greek Views on the Nature and Function of Poetry* (Chapel Hill, N.C., 1984), 96–106. On the connections with theater and femininity in the context of comic parody, see Zeitlin, "Gender and Genre," 186–89.

46 I simplify here the terms of the debate. Both sides are thoroughly satirized in this brilliant parody. For an excellent discussion, see Walsh, *Varieties of Enchantment*, 80–97.

47 See especially *Republic* 595c, 598d, 605c–d, 607a, 602b.

48 *Republic* 2.366a–b; cf. 361b–c. Strictly speaking, the Aeschylean quotes precede the discussion of the mimetic arts in book 3, but their misuse may not be fortuitous.

49 I include in the discussion the relevant portions of *Republic, Gorgias*, and *Laws*, to be followed by the *Symposium*.

50 This issue deserves far more attention than space permits here.

51 Tragedy is the real target, despite the remarks about epic poetry and comedy. See especially *Laws* 816d–e, 935d–936b for comedy, and 817a–d for tragedy, where Plato expressly sets up the legislators as authors of their own true tragedies as "rivals ... artists and actors of the fairest drama."

52 One single exception is the woman (wife and mother) as instigating in her son the slide toward timocratic behavior by her nagging and greed (*Republic* 549c–e). We will take up the function in the *Symposium* of the priestess, Diotima, in the appropriate context.

53 The ostensible motive for banning poets in book 3 is the education of the young guardians to protect the city. Courage in battle is the model for

control over warring forces within the self, as is emphasized in the second discussion of imitation in book 10. Cowardice is the radically feminine trait, despite Plato's willingness to train selected women as guardians. (The *locus classicus* is *Timaeus* 90e–91a, in which Plato describes the first creation of women as due to "creatures generated as men who proved themselves cowardly and spent their lives in wrongdoing and were transformed at their second incarnation into women.") I simplify Plato's intricate argument, as he further sees this lack of control over the emotions, engendered by tragedy, as leading to an unruliness and violence he does not specify as feminine. Yet the tyrannical man, the most "theatrical" in Plato's view, whose exterior pomp and costume does not at all match his inner self (*Republic* 577b), is seen ultimately as a slave to his passions who becomes so fearful that he "lives for the most part cowering in the house like a woman" (*Republic* 579b–c).

54 In particular, the discussion would benefit from including the important contribution made by Alcibiades, the disruptive latecomer and party crasher, but it would not in any case substantially alter my argument.

55 In this comedy, which satirizes Euripidean tragedy through the women's indignation at the poet for his unflattering (and oversexed) portraits of them, Agathon comes off as the truly effeminate male by contrast to the trickster but more manly figure of Euripides. Agathon appears in feminine accessories, claiming that to write female parts for the theater one must dress as a woman. He refuses to infiltrate the women's festival on the grounds that he would provide unfair competition for the "real" women, and finally supplies the feminine costume for Euripides' kinsman, who has been persuaded to go instead.

56 Aristophanes presents the famous myth of the spherical human beings who, separated by Zeus for their hybris toward the gods, are forever searching for reunion with their other halves. These may be of the same or opposite sex, depending on the original composition of each.

Sources

_____

Sophocles

Composed by the Athenian tragic playwright Sophocles (born c. 490 BCE), *Women of Trachis* concerns the return of the hero Heracles after the completion of his labors. He brings with him a concubine, captured in a recent military campaign. Fearing the loss of his affections, his wife Deianeira secretly rubs a salve into a newly woven cloak in an attempt to regain his love. But the magic potion tragically brings about Heracles' death rather than restores his love.

Sophocles, *Women of Trachis* 531–87

DEIANEIRA:
>   Friends, while the stranger is speaking inside
>   to the captive girls before he takes his leave,
>
>   I have come outside in secret,
>   partly to tell you what I have been contriving,
>   and partly to bewail with you what I suffer.
>   I have received a girl – yet I think she is a virgin no longer,
>   but an experienced woman – as a ship's captain takes on cargo,
>   a deadly merchandise fatal to my wits.
>   And now the two of us wait, a single object of embrace,
>   under one blanket; such is the compensation Heracles –
>   he who is called loyal and good – has sent me
>   for maintaining his house during his long absence.

But I do not know how to be angry at him,
afflicted as he often is with this disease.
And yet as to living with her in the same household,
what woman could do it, who could share the same man in marriage?
For I see her youth advancing, as mine recedes;
men's eyes love to cull the flower of youth,
while they flee older women.
So I fear that Heracles, my husband,
might be called the younger woman's man.
And yet it is disgraceful, as I said, for a woman of sense
to be angry. But I will tell you what means
I have of remedying this pain.

Long ago a centaur gave me an ancient gift,
one hidden in a bronze vessel.
I received it when I was still a girl
from the shaggy-breasted Nessus at his death;
for a fee he carried mortals across the deep-swirling river
Evenus, not plying the water with oars or
with a ship's sails, but with the strength of his arms.
When first I accompanied Heracles as his bride,
a journey undertaken at my father's bidding,
the centaur carried me on his shoulders, and then, mid-stream,
placed his wanton hands upon me. I cried out
and right away the son of Zeus turned around
and launched a feathered arrow. It hissed as it pierced
his chest and his lungs. As the beast lay dying,
he spoke as follows, "Child of aged Oeneus,
if you obey, you will profit from my portage,
because you were the last of my passengers.
If you take the coagulated blood
from my wound, in which the Hydra dipped
his arrows so as to make them poisonous,
you will then have the means to charm

Heracles' heart. Then, even if he looks at another woman,
he will not love her more than you."
Ever since he died, my friends, the charm
has been locked away securely in the house. Remembering it,
I dyed this tunic, applying everything as the centaur instructed
while he was still alive. And this has been accomplished.

May I neither become expert in deeds of wicked daring
nor learn anything about them – and I hate women who attempt them.

If I should overcome this girl
with love charms and spells cast on Heracles ...
but the deed has been done, unless perhaps you think
I am doing something rash. If so, I shall abandon it.

Sophocles, *Women of Trachis* 1046–84

HERACLES:
    Many the labors I have accomplished, perilous and
cruel to relate, with my hands and my back;
And never yet has Hera, bedfellow of Zeus,
nor my enemy Eurystheus imposed such a thing upon me
as the woven net of the Erinyes which the daughter of Oeneus
with beguiling face has put upon my shoulders,
and by which I am perishing.
Clinging to my sides, it has eaten away
at my inmost flesh, and dwells there,
devouring the channels of my lungs.
Already it has drunk my fresh blood,
and my whole body is ruined,
subdued by this unspeakable bondage.
Not the spear on the plain, nor the earth-born
host of the Giants, nor the bestial violence of monsters,
neither Greek nor barbarian, nor any land I visited
in my labors, ever did this to me.
But a woman, a mere female, not male in nature,
alone destroyed me, without a sword.

    Son, show yourself to be my true-born son indeed,
and do not honor the name of your mother any longer.
Take your mother out of the house with your own hands
and give her to mine, that I may clearly know
whether you feel more pain at seeing my injured body
or that of your mother justly maltreated.

    Come, my child, dare to do this thing. Take pity on me,
who am piteous in the eyes of many, I who am howling,
crying like a young girl. No one could ever say
he has seen this man do such a thing before,
rather, I always endured my troubles without lament.
Now, wretched me, from such a thing I am found to be a woman.

And now, come forward and stand near your father,
consider what sort of misfortune I have suffered.
For I will reveal my body to you without the coverings.
Look, all of you, behold this wretched body,
see the unhappy creature, how pitiable I am.
Alas, miserable me,
alas,
again, just now, a spasm of pain has stung me,
it has darted through my ribs, nor will the wretched,
consuming disease leave me undisturbed.

Euripides

Euripides' *Bacchae* was produced at Athens between 408 and 406 BCE, probably after the poet's death. It portrays the return of the god Dionysus to his
birthplace Thebes, where he has introduced his cult, driving the women mad
and causing them to abandon their homes and families. When the city's
tyrant, Pentheus, refuses to acknowledge his power, the god plots revenge.
In this passage, Dionysus prepares the hallucinating king, now dressed in
women's clothes, to witness the women's rites that will ultimately bring about
his death.

Euripides, *Bacchae* 912–44

DIONYSUS:
> You there, since you are eager to see what you should not see,
> hurry up and don't dawdle, I mean you, Pentheus,
> come out before the palace and let me see you,
> dressed as a woman, a maenad and follower of Dionysus,
> a spy on your mother and her band.
> You seem like one of the daughters of Cadmus in your appearance.

PENTHEUS:
> I seem to see two suns,
> a double Thebes and seven-gated city,
> and you seem to walk before me as a bull;
> your head seems horned now.
> Were you perhaps an animal all the time?
> For certainly now you are changed into a bull.

DIONYSUS:

> The god attacks, and while formerly hostile,
> now he is our ally. Now you see what you should see.

PENTHEUS:

> Well, then, how do I look? Do I not have
> the posture of Ino or Agave, my mother?

DIONYSUS:

> When I look at you I seem to see the very women!
> Wait, this lock of hair has come loose from its position,
> It is not how I fixed it under your snood.

PENTHEUS:

> Inside, tossing my hair up and down
> under the spell of Dionysus, I dislodged it from its seat.

DIONYSUS:

> Never mind, since it is my job to wait on you,
> I will put it back in order; but hold your head up straight.

PENTHEUS:

> Go head, dress me, since I am wholly dependent on you now.

DIONYSUS:

> And your hip-band is slack and the folds of your gown
> stretch in disarray below your ankles.

PENTHEUS:

> It seems correct by my right foot at least.
> On that side the gown falls properly next to my ankle.

DIONYSUS:

> Can it be that you believe me to be the best of your friends,
> whenever you see the maenads behave with self-control
> contrary to your previous assumptions?

PENTHEUS:

> Do I look more like a maenad holding
> the thyrsus in my right hand or in my left?

PART II
ROME

Figure 5 *Grave Relief for Lysandra*. First century CE. Collection of the Getty Museum, Malibu, California, no. 75.AA.49 This stele for a Greek woman living in the Roman Empire shows a man and a woman at a funerary banquet; two smaller figures appear at each lower corner, a girl holding a wool basket and a boy extending his right arm across his body in a mourning gesture. The inscription reads: "Lysandra, [wife or daughter] of Dolon, farewell!"

5

THE SILENT WOMEN OF ROME

M. I. Finley

The most famous woman in Roman history was not even a Roman –
Cleopatra was queen of Egypt, the last ruler of a Macedonian dynasty that
had been established on the Nile three centuries earlier by Ptolemy, one
of the generals of Alexander the Great. Otherwise what names come to
mind? A few flamboyant, ruthless and vicious women of the imperial
family, such as Messalina, great-grandniece of Augustus and wife of her
cousin once removed, the emperor Claudius; or the latter's next wife, his
niece Agrippina, who was Nero's mother and, contemporary tradition
insists, also for a time his mistress. One or two names in love poetry, like
the Lesbia of Catullus. And some legendary women from Rome's earliest
days, such as Lucretia, who gained immortality by being raped. Even in
legend the greatest of them was likewise not a Roman but Dido, queen of
Carthage, who loved and failed to hold Aeneas.

Such a short and one-sided list can be very misleading. The Roman
world was not the only one in history in which women remained in
the background in politics and business, or in which catching the eye
and the pen of the scandalmonger was the most likely way to achieve
notice and perhaps lasting fame. However, it is not easy to think of
another great civilized state without a single really important woman
writer or poet, with no truly regal queen, no Deborah, no Joan of Arc,
no Florence Nightingale, no patron of the arts. The women of mid-
Victorian England were equally rightless, equally victims of a double
standard of sexual morality, equally exposed to risk and ruin when they
stepped outside the home and the church. Yet the profound difference
is obvious.

More correctly, it would be obvious if we could be sure what we may legitimately believe about women in Rome. Legend apart, they speak to us in five ways: through the erotic and satirical poetry of the late Republic and early Empire, all written by men; through the historians and biographers, all men and most of them unable to resist the salacious and the scandalous; through the letter writers and philosophers, all men; through painting and sculpture, chiefly portrait statues, inscribed tombstones, and religious monuments of all kinds; and through innumerable legal texts. These different voices naturally talk at cross-purposes. (One would hardly expect to find quotations from Ovid's *Art of Love* or the pornographic frescoes from the brothel in Pompeii on funeral monuments.) Each tells its portion of a complicated, ambiguous story. One ought to be able to add the pieces together, but unfortunately there will always be one vital piece missing – what the women would have said had they been allowed to speak for themselves.

> Friend, I have not much to say; stop and read it. This tomb, which is not fair, is for a fair woman. Her parents gave her the name Claudia. She loved her husband in her heart. She bore two sons, one of whom she left on earth, the other beneath it. She was pleasant to talk with, and she walked with grace. She kept the house and worked in wool. That is all. You may go.

Of course it wasn't Claudia who selected and set up this verse epitaph (the translation is Richmond Lattimore's) in the city of Rome in the second century B.C., but her husband or some other kinsman. And it is easy to make cynical remarks not only in this particular instance but in the hundreds of others recording domestic devotion, commonly including the phrase in one variation or another that husband and wife lived together X number of years *sine ulla querella*, "without a single quarrel". Yet there is much to be learned from the very monotony with which such sentiments are repeated century after century, at least about the ideal woman – an ideal formulated and imposed by middle-and upper-class Roman males.

To begin with, until fairly late in Roman history, women lacked individual names in the proper sense. Claudia, Julia, Cornelia, Lucretia, are merely family names with a feminine ending. Sisters had the same name and could be distinguished only by the addition of 'the elder' or 'the younger', 'the first' or 'the second', and so on. In the not uncommon case of marriage between paternal cousins, mother and daughter would have the same name, too. No doubt this was very confusing: a welcome confusion, one is tempted to suggest, since nothing could have been easier to eliminate. No great genius was needed to think up the idea of giving every girl a personal name, as was done with boys. It is as if the Romans wished to suggest very pointedly that women were not, or ought not to be, genuine individuals but only fractions of a family. Anonymous and passive fractions at that, for the virtues which were stressed were decorum, chastity, gracefulness, even temper and childbearing. They loved their husbands, to be sure – though we need not believe everything that husbands said when their wives were dead – but as one loves an overlord who is free to seek his pleasures elsewhere and to put an end to the relationship altogether when and if he so chooses.

'Family' comes from the Latin, but the Romans actually had no word for 'family' in our commonest sense, as in the sentence, 'I am taking my family to the seashore for the summer.' In different contexts *familia* meant all persons under the authority of the head of a household, or all the descendants from a common ancestor, or all one's property, or merely all one's servants – never our intimate family. This does not mean that the latter did not exist in Rome, but that the stress was on a power structure rather than on biology or intimacy. A Roman *paterfamilias* need not even be a father: the term was a legal one and applied to any head of a household. His illegitimate children were often excluded, even when his paternity was openly acknowledged, and at the same time his son and heir could be an outsider whom he had adopted by the correct legal formalities. Theoretically his power – over his wife, over his sons and daughters and his sons' wives and children, over his slaves and his property – was absolute and uncontrolled, ending only with his death or by his voluntary act of 'emancipating' his sons beforehand. As late as the fourth century A.D. an edict of Constantine, the first Christian emperor, still defined that power as the "right of life and death". He was exaggerating, but around a hard core of reality.

Save for relatively minor exceptions, a woman was always in the power of some man – of her *paterfamilias* or of her husband or of a guardian. In early times every marriage involved a formal ceremony in which the bride was surrendered to her husband by the *paterfamilias*: he 'gave her away' in the literal sense. Then, when so-called 'free' marriages became increasingly common – free from the ancient formalities, that is, not free in the sense that the wife or her husband had made a free choice of partner – she remained legally in the power of her *paterfamilias*. Divorce and widowhood and remarriage introduced more complications and required more rules. Where did property rights in dowry and inheritance rest? In the next generation, too, if there were children? The Roman legislators and lawbooks gave much space to these matters. From the state's point of view it was essential to get the power and property relations right, since the *familia* was the basic social unit. But there was more to it than that: marriage meant children, and children were the citizens of the next generation. Not all children by any means, for as Rome extended her empire to the Atlantic and the Middle East, the bulk of the population within her borders were either slaves or free noncitizens. Obviously the political rights and status of the children were the state's concern and could not be left to uncontrolled private decision. So the state laid down strict rules prohibiting certain kinds of marriage: for example, between a Roman citizen and a non-citizen, regardless of rank or wealth; or between a member of the senatorial class and a citizen who had risen from the class of freedmen (ex-slaves). Within the permitted limits, then, the right to choose and decide rested with the heads of families. They negotiated marriages for their children. And they were allowed to proceed, and to have the marriage consummated, as soon as a girl reached the age of twelve.

The story is told that at a male dinner-party early in the second century B.C., the general Scipio Africanus agreed to marry his daughter Cornelia to his friend Tiberius Gracchus, and that his wife was very angry that he should have done so without having consulted her. The story is probably untrue; at least it is very suspicious because it is repeated about Tiberius's son, the famous agrarian reformer of the same name, and the daughter of Appius Claudius. But true or not, the stories are right in essence, for though the mothers may have been angry, they were powerless, and it is noteworthy that the more 'liberal' and enlightened wing of the senatorial aristocracy was involved. Presumably the wife of the fiercely traditional Cato the Censor would have kept her anger to herself in a similar situation; she would not have expected to be asked anyway. Surely the first of the Roman emperors, Augustus, consulted neither his wife nor any of the interested parties when he ordered members of his family and various close associates to marry and divorce and remarry whenever he thought (as he did frequently) that reasons of state or dynastic considerations would be furthered by a particular arrangement.

Augustus and his family personify most of the complexities, difficulties, and apparent contradictions inherent in the Roman relations between the sexes. He was first married at the age of twenty-three and divorced his wife two years later, after the birth of their daughter Julia, in order to marry Livia three days after she had given birth to a son. At the second ceremony Livia's ex-husband acted as *paterfamilias* and gave her to Augustus. Fifty-one years later, in A.D. 14, Augustus was said to have addressed his last words to Livia: "As long as you live, remember our marriage. Farewell." Livia had had two sons by her previous husband; gossip inevitably suggested that Augustus was actually the father of the second, and the first son, Tiberius, was in 12 B.C. compelled by Augustus to divorce his wife and marry the recently widowed Julia, daughter of Augustus by his first wife. Tiberius was eventually adopted by Augustus and succeeded him to the throne. Long before that, in 2 B.C., Julia was banished by the emperor for sexual depravity, and ten years later the same punishment was meted out to her daughter, also named Julia. That does not end the story, but it should be enough except for two further details: first, one reason for Augustus's getting rid of his first wife was apparently her peculiar unwillingness to put up with one of his mistresses; second, Augustus was the author of a long series of laws designed to strengthen the family and to put a brake on licentiousness and general moral depravity in the upper classes.

Augustus was no Nero. There is no reason to think that he was not a reasonably moral man by contemporary standards (granted that his position as emperor created abnormal conditions). Ancient and modern moralists have a habit of decrying the decline in Roman moral standards from the old days. Talk of 'the good old days' is always suspect, but it may well be that while Rome was still an agricultural community on the Tiber with little power abroad, little luxury, and little urban development, life was simpler and standards stricter. However, the submissive and passive role of women was very ancient, and certainly by the time Rome emerged as a historic and powerful state, say after the defeat of Hannibal late in the third century B.C., all the elements were already there of the social and moral situation which Augustus both represented and tried in some ways to control. Nor is there any justification for speaking of hypocrisy. No one believed or even pretended to believe that monogamous marriage, which was strictly enforced, was incompatible with polygamous sexual activity by the male half of the population. Augustus was concerned with the social consequences of an apparent unwillingness on the part of the aristocracy to produce legitimate children in sufficient numbers, with the social consequences of extravagant and wasteful living, of *public* licentiousness, and in the upper classes, of *female* licentiousness (which may have been on the increase with the breakdown of political morality in the last century of the Roman Republic). It never entered his mind that moral regeneration might include the abolition of concubines, mistresses and brothels, the end of sleeping with one's female slaves, or a redefinition of adultery to extend it to extramarital intercourse by a married man.

There was no puritanism in the Roman concept of morality. Marriage was a central institution but it had nothing sacramental about it. It was central because the whole structure of property rested on it and because both the indispensable family cult and the institution of citizenship required the orderly, regular succession of legitimate children in one generation after another. There were neither spinsters nor confirmed bachelors in this world. It was assumed that if one reached the right age – and many of course did not, given the enormously high rate of infant mortality – one would marry. Society could not pursue its normal course otherwise. But the stress was always on the rightness of the marriage from a social and economic point of view, and on its legitimacy (and therefore also on the legitimacy of the offspring) from the political and legal point of view. If the relationship turned out also to be pleasant and affectionate, so much the better. It was taken for granted, however, that men would find comradeship and sexual satisfaction from others as well, and often only or chiefly from others. They were expected to behave with good taste in this respect, but no more.

Standards, whether of taste or of law, were profoundly influenced by class. Men like Sulla and Cicero openly enjoyed the company of actors and actresses, but by a law of Augustus and before that by custom, no member of the senatorial class could contract a legal marriage with any woman who was, or ever had been, an actress, whereas other Roman citizens were free to do so. Soldiers in the legions, unlike their officers, were not allowed to marry during their period of service, which was twenty years under Augustus and was raised to twenty-five later on. The reasons for this law were rather complicated, the consequences even more so (until the law was finally repealed in A.D. 197). Soldiers, of course, went on marrying and raising families all the time, and their tombstones are as full of references to loving wives and children as those of any other class. Nor, obviously, could they have acted in this way clandestinely. The law and its agents were not so stupid as not to know what was going on. They merely insisted on the formal unlawfulness of the relationship, and then proceeded to make and constantly to revise regulations for the inevitable confusion: confusion about inheritance, about the status of the children, about the rights of all the parties involved following honourable discharge.

Soldiers apart, we know very little about how these matters worked for the lower classes of Roman society. They were all subject to the same set of laws, but law codes are never automatic guides to the actual behaviour of a society, and neither poets nor historians nor philosophers often concerned themselves in a concrete and reliable way with the poorer peasantry or with the tens of thousands crowded together in the urban rabbit warrens which the Romans called *insulae*. Obviously among these people dowries, property settlements, family alliances for political purposes, and the like did not really enter the picture, either in the establishment of a marriage or in its dissolution. Neither could they so lightly dispense with a wife's labour service, whether on the farm or in a market stall, an inn, or a workshop. It was one thing to "work in wool", as did the Claudia whose epitaph I quoted earlier; it was something quite different to work in wool in earnest.

It would probably be a safe guess that women of the lower classes were therefore more 'emancipated', more equal *de facto* if not in strict law, more widely accepted as persons in their own right than their richer, more bourgeois, or more aristocratic sisters. This is a common enough phenomenon everywhere. No doubt they were freer in all senses – far less inhibited by legal definitions of marriage or legitimacy, less bound by the double standard of sexual morality. For one thing, the rapid development of large-scale slavery after the wars with Hannibal and the Carthaginians, combined with the frequent practice of manumitting slaves, meant that a large proportion of the free population, even of the citizen class, was increasingly drawn from ex-slaves and the children of slaves. This alone – and specifically their experience, as females, while they were slaves – would have been enough to give them, and their men, a somewhat different attitude towards the accepted, traditional, upper-class values. Add economic necessity, slum conditions, the fact that their work was serious and not a pastime, and the rest follows.

In all classes there was one inescapable condition, and that was the high probability of early death. On a rough calculation, of the population of the Roman Empire which succeeded in reaching the age of fifteen (that is, which survived the heavy mortality of infancy and childhood), more than half of the women were dead before forty, and in some classes and areas, even before thirty-five. Women were very much worse off than men in this respect, partly because of the perils of childbirth, partly, in the lower classes, because of the risk of sheer exhaustion. Thus, in one family tomb in regular use in the second and third centuries, sixty-eight wives were buried by their husbands and only forty-one husbands by their wives. A consequence, intensified by the ease of divorce, was the frequency of second and third marriages for both sexes, especially among men. This in turn complicated both personal and family relationships, economically as well as psychologically, and the prospect, even before the event, must have introduced a considerable element of tension in many women. Many, too, must have been sexually frustrated and unsatisfied.

None of this necessarily implies that women did not passively accept their position, at least on the surface. It would be a bad mistake to read our own notions and values into the picture, or even those of a century or two ago. The women of French provincial society portrayed by Balzac seem to have been more suppressed and beaten down than their Roman counterparts. The latter at least found their men much more open-handed with money and luxuries, and they shared in a fairly active dinner-party kind of social life and in the massive public entertainments. The evidence suggests that Balzac's women somehow made their peace with the world, even if often an unhappy and tragic peace, and presumably so did the women of Rome. We are told by Roman writers of the educated conversation of women in mixed company. Ovid in *The Art of Love* urged even his kind of woman not only to dress and primp properly, to sweeten her breath, to learn to walk gracefully and dance well, but also to cultivate the best Greek and Latin poetry. It is a pity we cannot eavesdrop on some of these conversations, but there is no Roman Balzac or Stendhal, no Jane Austen or Thackeray or Hardy, to give us the opportunity.

This brings us back to the silence of the women of Rome, which in one way speaks loudly, if curiously. Where were the rebels among the women, real or fictitious – the George Sand or Harriet Beecher Stowe, the Hester Prynne or Tess of the D'Urbervilles? How, in other words, did 'respectable' women of breeding, education and leisure find outlets for their repressed energies and talents? The answers seem to lie within a very restricted range of activities. One was religion. It is a commonplace in our own civilization that, at least in Latin countries, women are much more occupied with their religion than are men. But it would be wrong to generalize too quickly: the same has not been true for most of Jewish history nor for most of antiquity. Much depends on the content and orientation of doctrine and ritual. Traditional Roman religion was centred on the household (the hearth and the ancestors) and on the state cults, and the male played the predominant part in both – as *paterfamilias* and as citizen, respectively – notwithstanding that the hearth was protected by a goddess, Vesta, and not by a god. To be sure, the public hearth, with its sacred fire which must never be allowed to go out, was in the charge of six women, the Vestal Virgins. Other rituals were reserved for women, too, such as the cult of *Bona Dea*, the 'good goddess', or such exceptional ones as the formal reception at the harbour, towards the end of the war with Hannibal, of the statue of *Mater Idaea* brought from Asia Minor in response to a Sibylline prophecy which guaranted victory if that were done. However, the procession was led by a man, "the noblest in the state", as required by the same prophecy. And the Vestal Virgins were subject to the authority of a man, the Pontifex Maximus.

For most of Roman history, then, to the end of the Republic in fact, women were not very prominent even in religion. The change came under the Empire and with the great influx into the Roman world of various eastern mystery cults, carrying their new element of personal communion and salvation. Some of these cults – notably that of Mithras, the soldier's god *par excellence* – were closed to women. Others, however, offered them hope, ultimate release, and immediate status unlike anything they had experienced before – above all, the worship of the Hellenized Egyptian goddess Isis. She became (to men as well as women) Isis of the Myriad Names, Lady of All, Queen of the Inhabited World, Star of the Sea, identifiable with nearly every goddess of the known world. "You gave women equal power with men," says one of her hymns. In another she herself speaks: "I am she whom women call goddess. I ordained that women shall be loved by men; I brought wife and husband together, and invented the marriage-contract."

It was no wonder, therefore, that of all the pagan cults Isis-worship was the most tenacious in its resistance when Christianity ascended to a position first of dominance in the Roman world and then of near monopoly. Christianity itself was soon in some difficulty over the question of women. On the one hand, there was the unmistakably elevated, and for the time untypical, position of women in the life of Christ, and in many of the early Christian communities. Women of all classes were drawn to the new creed. There were women martyrs, too. But on the other hand, there was the view expressed in, for example, I Corinthians 14: "Let your women keep silence in the churches: for it is not permitted unto them to speak; but they are commanded to be under obedience as also saith the law." Women were not allowed to forget that Eve was created from Adam's rib, and not the other way round. Neither in this respect nor in any other did the early church seek or bring about a social revolution. Both the ritual of the church and its administration remained firmly in the hands of men, as did the care of souls, and this included the souls of the women.

Where Christianity differed most radically from many (though not all) of the other mystery religions of the time was in its extension of the central idea of purification and purity beyond chastity to celibacy. For many women this attitude offered release through sublimation. That the traditional pagan world failed to understand, or even to believe, this was possible is comprehensible enough. The Roman aristocracy had long

been suspicious of the various new cults. A great wave of orgiastic Dionysiac religion had spread in Italy after the wars with Hannibal, soon to be
suppressed by the Senate in 186 B.C. Even Isis-worship had a long struggle
with the state before achieving official recognition. Anyone who reads the
hymns or the detailed accounts of the cult in Apuleius or Plutarch may well
find that hard to understand, but the fact is that Isis, though she attracted
all classes, was particularly popular in the *demi-monde*.

Sublimation through religion was not the only outlet for pent-up
female energies and female rebelliousness. There was another in quite
the opposite direction. In the amphitheatres, among the spectators,
the women achieved equality with their men: they relished the horrible
brutality of the gladiatorial shows (and of the martyrdoms) with the same
fierce joy. Gladiators became the pin-ups for Roman women, especially in
the upper classes. And at the very top, the women became, metaphorically, gladiators themselves. The women of the Roman emperors were not
all monsters, but enough of them throughout the first century of our era,
and again from the latter part of the second century on, revealed a
ferocity and sadism in the backstairs struggles for power that were not
often surpassed – though they were perhaps matched in the contemporary court of the Idumaean dynasty founded by Herod the Great in
Judaea. They were not struggling for the throne for themselves – that
was unthinkable – but for their sons, brothers and lovers. Their energy
and, in a curious sense, their ability are beyond argument. The outlets
they found and the goals they sought are, equally, beyond all human
dignity, decency, or compassion.

Obviously Roman women are not to be judged by their worst representatives. On the other hand, there must be something significant, even
though twisted, in that small group of ferocious and licentious royal
females. Under the prevailing value-system, women were expected to
be content with vicarious satisfactions. It was their role to be happy
in the happiness and success of their men, and of the state for which
they bore and nurtured the next generation of men. "She loved her
husband.... She bore two sons.... She kept the house and worked in
wool." That was the highest praise, not only in Rome but in much
of human history. What went on behind the accepted façade, what
Claudia thought or said to herself, we can never know. But when
the silence breaks, the sounds which come forth – in the royal family
at least – are not very pretty. Most of the Claudias no doubt fully accepted
and even defended the values fixed by their men; they knew no other
world. The revealing point is that the occasional rebellion took the
forms it did.

SOURCES

These epitaphs commemorate actual women, most of whom lived during the first century BCE in Rome. While many inscriptions give only the barest of information about their subjects – some contain only a name – some of the examples given below are quite elaborate. The funeral elegy for Murdia may have been delivered by her son from her first marriage at her funeral and then later inscribed on marble.

Latin inscriptions were taken from H. Dessau (ed.), *Inscriptiones Latinae Selectae* (Berlin, 1892–1916 = ILS); F. Buecheler (ed.), *Carmina Latina Epigraphica*, vols. 1–2 (Leipzig, 1895–7 = CE); E. Washington, *Remains of Old Latin* vols. 1–4 (Cambridge, MA, 1935–40 = ROL); and *Corpus Inscriptionum Latinarum* (Berlin, 1862–1959 = CIL).

Funerary Inscriptions

Excerpts

O how great the devotion in this young life,
faithfulness, love, common sense, modesty, and chastity.

(CE no. 81, 1–2, Rome, Augustan)

To a woman faithful, sincere, reverent, and devoted.

(CE no. 158, 2, Uccula, Africa)

Here lies a woman chaste, modest, proper, wise, generous, and virtuous.

(CE no. 843, Turin)

Noble Euphrosyne, an affable, pretty girl,
learned, wealthy, devout, chaste, modest, virtuous.

(CE no. 1136, 3–4)

Complete Inscriptions

Amymone. First century BCE, Rome

Here lies Amymone, wife of Marcus, best and most beautiful,
a worker in wool, devoted, modest, frugal, chaste, one who stayed at home.

(ILS no. 8402)

Claudia. Tablet or pillar found at Rome, now lost; c.135–20 BCE

Stranger, what I have to say is brief: Stand near and read it through.
Here is the unlovely tomb of a lovely woman.
Her parents gave her the name of Claudia.
She loved her husband with all her heart.
She brought forth two sons; one of these
she leaves above the earth; the other she has placed beneath it.
Charming in her conversation, pleasant in her manner,
she kept house, worked in wool. I have spoken. Now go!

(CIL vol. 1, no. 1211; ROL vol. 4, no. 18)

Lucius Aurelius and his wife, Aurelia. Stone slab in the British Museum. c.80 BCE or later

(a) Lucius Aurelius Hermia, freedman of Lucius, a butcher
This woman, who died before me, my only wife,
chaste in body, loving, intelligent,
lived faithful to her faithful husband; equally in her devotion
she never abandoned her duties in times of bitterness.
Aurelia, freedwoman of Lucius.

(b) Aurelia Philematium, freedwoman of Lucius
In life I was called Aurelia Philematium,
a chaste and modest woman, ignorant of public life, faithful to my husband.
He was a freed slave, that man whom I lost, alas;

he was also in truth more than a father to me:
he himself took me to his breast when I was but seven years old.
Now forty years old, I am in the hands of death.
That man, with my constant devotion, flourished at all times . . . .

(CIL vol. 1, no. 1221; ROL vol. 4, no. 53)

Posilla Senenia, daughter of Quartus, and Quarta Senenia, freedwoman of Gaius. Found at Trebula Mutussa in Samnium

Stranger, stop and read through what is written here.

A mother was not permitted to enjoy her only daughter,
whom, I believe, a god fixed with the evil eye.
Since she is not permitted to be adorned by her mother in life,
after her death her mother made this fair thing,
and adorned her beloved daughter with this monument.

(CIL vol. 1, no. 1837)

Eucharis of Lucinia, an unmarried girl educated and skilled in the arts, who died at age 14. First century BCE, Rome

You, there, as you look upon the house of death with a wandering eye,
slow your step and carefully read the words inscribed here,
which a father's love gave to his daughter,
to mark the place where the remains of her body are buried.
Just as my young life was blossoming with skills
as I grew and in time was ascending to glory,
so the sad hour of my death rushed upon me
and denied me any further breath of life.
I was educated and trained as if by the hand of the Muses.
I graced the festivals of the nobles with my dancing,
and I first appeared among the common people in a Greek play.
But now in this tomb the hostile Fates
have placed the ashes of my body together with a poem.
Devotion to a patronness, industry, love, praise, beauty
are silenced by my burned body and by my death.
A daughter, I left only weeping for my father,
and I preceded him in the day of my death, although born after him.
Now my fourteenth birthday is observed here
in the shadows, in the ageless house of Death.
I ask that upon departing you ask the earth to lay lightly on me.

(ILS no. 5213)

A portion of a eulogy for Murdia delivered by her son from her first marriage. First century BCE, Rome

In this way it was determined that she should maintain the marriages to worthy men arranged by her parents with obedience and propriety, and as a bride to become more pleasing because of her merits, be considered more beloved because of her faithfulness, to be left more illustrious because of her good judgment, and, after death, to be unanimously praised by her fellow citizens, since the apportionment of her estate showed her grateful and faithful attitude toward her husbands, fairness toward her children and justice in her honesty.

For these reasons, praise for all good women is simple and similar, because their natural goodness, preserved by the proper restraint, does not desire a diversity of words. Rather, it should be enough that all of them have performed the same deeds worthy of a good reputation. And since it is difficult for women to acquire new praise, because they experience fewer vicissitudes, by necessity they ought to be honored as a group, so that nothing lost from their just precepts might defile the rest.

My dearest mother deserved greater praise than all of the others, because in modesty, virtue, modesty, obedience, wool-working, industry and faithfulness she was on an equal level with other virtuous women, nor did she take second place to any women in bravery, hard work or wisdom in times of danger....

(ILS no. 8394; CIL 6. no. 10.230)

Figure 6   *Tarquin and Lucretia*.   Painting by Titian, c.1568–71 CE. Fitz-william Museum, University of Cambridge. The painter shows the lecher-ous prince clothed as a sixteenth-century noble, who looms menacingly over the idealized, nude figure of Lucretia before committing his brutal act.

6

THE BODY FEMALE AND THE BODY POLITIC: LIVY'S LUCRETIA AND VERGINIA

S. R. Joshel

Brutus, while the others were absorbed in grief, drew out the knife from Lucretia's wound, and holding it up, dripping with gore, exclaimed, "By this blood most chaste until a prince wronged it, I swear, and I take you, gods, to witness, that I will pursue Lucius Tarquinius Superbus and his wicked wife and all his children, with sword, with fire, aye with whatsoever violence I may; and that I will suffer neither them nor any other to be king in Rome!"
– Livy 1.59.1, LCL[1]

Reality, robbed of its independent life, is shaped anew, kneaded into large, englobing blocks that will serve as the building material for a larger vista, a monumental world of the future. . . . Empires can be built only on, and out of, dead matter. Destroyed life provides the material for their building blocks.
– Klaus Theweleit, *Male Fantasies*

Pretext: The Conditions of a Reading

I read Livy's history of Rome's origins, its earliest struggles with neighboring states, and the political events that formed the state that conquered an empire. The historian writes within an immediate past he regards as decadent, a fall from the glorious society of ancestors who made empire possible; he stands at a point where his Rome is about to be reinvigorated by a new imperial order. Raped, dead, or disappeared women litter the pages. The priestess Rhea Silvia, raped by the god Mars, gives birth to Rome's founder, Romulus, and leaves the story. The women of the neighboring Sabines are seized as wives by Romulus's wifeless men. When the Sabine soldiers come to do battle with the Romans, the Roman girl Tarpeia betrays her own menfolk by admitting their foes into the citadel. She is slain by the enemy she helped. By contrast, the Sabine women place their bodies between their kin and their husbands, offering to take on the violence the men would do to each other. Later, a young woman, named only as sister, is murdered by her brother Horatius because she mourns the fiancé he killed in single combat. "So perish every Roman woman who mourns a foe!" he declares, and their father agrees that she was justly slain. Lucretia, raped by the king's son, calls on her menfolk to avenge her and commits suicide. The men overthrow the monarchy. Verginia, threatened with rape by a tyrannical magistrate, is killed by her father to prevent her violation. The citizen body ousts the magistrate and his colleagues. In these stories of early Rome, the death and disappearance of women recur periodically; the rape of women becomes the history of the state.[2]

I read Klaus Theweleit's study of Freikorps narratives, written by "soldier males" who would become active Nazis. They write of World War I, of battling Reds, of living in a time they experience as chaotic and decadent in a Germany fallen from former greatness. Dead, disappeared, and silent women litter their texts. Sexually active working-class and communist women are slain brutally; chaste wives and sisters are made antiseptic, are killed tragically, or do not speak.

And I read Livy and Theweleit in the United States in the summer of 1987, at a time when the title of a recent Canadian film evokes what is often not explicit – *The Decline of the American Empire*. A time of concern about American power abroad and American life at home. The war against drugs and the battle against uncontrolled sex. Betsy North, Donna Rice, and Vanna White litter the TV screen, newspapers, and magazines. Betsy, silent and composed, sits behind her ramrod-straight husband, stiff and immaculate in his Marine uniform. Donna Rice appears in private, now public, photographs with Gary Hart; she has nothing to say. He gives up his candidacy for the presidency, guilty of extramarital sex. Vanna White turns letters on the popular game show "Wheel of Fortune." She does speak. "I enjoy getting dressed as a Barbie doll," she tells an interviewer. An image on our TV screens gotten up like a doll that simulates a nonexistent woman named Barbie, she is rematerialized by her dress in some sort of fetishistic process: "Speaking of *Vanna White*, a polyster magenta dress, one worn by the celebrated letter-turner, is on display at a Seattle espresso bar, where fans may touch it for 25 cents" (*Boston Globe*, June 9, 1987).

I look here at gender relations and images of women in Livy's history of early Rome, focusing on his tales of Lucretia and Verginia, but I do so within my own present. Freikorps narratives and the current mediascape are the "conditions of my narrative," to borrow a phrase from Christa Wolf. I am not equating Rome, Fascist Germany, and the United States of the 1980s; nor am I making the images of women in their histories and fictions exactly analogous. By juxtaposing images, I raise questions about the representations of gender within visions of building and collapsing empires. As Theweleit suggests of fascism, the Roman fiction should be understood and combated not "because it might 'return again,' but primarily because, as a form of reality production that is constantly present and possible under determinate conditions, *it can, and does, become our production*" (1987: 221). Whether our own fictions include tales similar to Lucretia's and Verginia's with names changed or whether, as academics, we dissect Livy's tales, we retell the stories, bringing their gender images and relations into our present (cf. Theweleit 1987: 265–89, 359).

Livy and the Conditions of His Narrative

Livy (64 B.C.–A.D. 12) lived through the change from aristocratic Republic to Principate, a military dictatorship disguised in republican forms. For more than a century before Livy's birth, Rome's senatorial class had ruled an empire; by the time of his death, Rome, its political elite, and the empire were governed by one man. He grew up during the civil wars that marked the end of the Republic, and his adult years saw the last struggle of military dynasts, Octavian and Antony, and the reign of the first emperor, the victor in that struggle. Raised in a Padua known for its traditional morality, Livy was a provincial; he did not belong to the senatorial class and was uninvolved in politics, although he did have friendly relations with the imperial family (Ogilvie 1965: 1–5; Walsh 1961; Syme 1959; see J. Phillips 1982: 1028, for bibliography).

Livy wrote the early books of his history after Octavian's victory over Antony and during the years in which Octavian became Augustus *princeps* – in effect, emperor (J. Phillips 1982: 1029, for the debate on the precise date). Shortly afterward came Augustus's restoration of the state religion and his program of social and moral reform which included new laws on marriage and adultery aimed primarily at the upper classes. The adultery law made sexual relations between a married woman and a man other than her husband a criminal offense. Ineffective and unpopular, the law nonetheless indicates the regime's concern with regulating sexuality, especially female (see Dixon 1988: 71ff). The program was to return Rome to its ancestral traditions, renew its imperial greatness, and refound the state.

The state to be refounded was a Rome uncorrupted by wealth and luxury, greed and license, the supposed conditions of the late Republic. The stories in which Lucretia and Verginia figure record critical points in that state's formation, marking the origin of political and social forms which, along with the behavior of heroes, account for Rome's greatness and its rise to imperial power. The rape of Lucretia precipitates the fall of the monarchy and establishment of the Republic and the Roman version of liberty. The attempted rape of Verginia belongs to a struggle between privileged and unprivileged groups (patricians and plebeians) known as the Conflict of the Orders; the event resulted in the overthrow of the decemvirs, officials who had abused their original mission of codifying the law, and began a long process of reform that eventually changed the form of Roman political institutions.

To modern historians, Livy's stories of Lucretia and Verginia are myths or, at best, legends that include some memory of actual events. Current historical reconstructions of Rome in the late sixth and mid-fifth centuries B.C., the society in which Lucretia and Verginia are supposed to have lived, depend on archaeology, some early documents, antiquarian notices in later authors (Heurgon 1973; Gjerstad 1973; Bloch 1965; Raaflaub 1986 for historical methodology), and, as has recently been suggested, the "structural facts" obtained when Livy's accounts have been stripped of their "narrative superstructure" (Cornell 1986: 61–76, esp. 73; Raaflaub 1986: 49–50). This evidence usually leaves us without a narrative or the names of agents (see Raaflaub 1986: 13–16). But Livy invented neither the outline of events nor the characters in his stories. First written down in the third and second centuries B.C., the tales were perpetuated as part of a living historical tradition by Roman writers of the early first century B.C. who were the major sources for Livy's retelling (for Livy's use of his sources, see Ogilvie 1965; Walsh 1961; Luce 1977). The history of the roughly contemporary Dionysius of Halicarnassus allows us to see how Livy used the tradition.

This tradition "was neither an authenticated official record nor an objective critical reconstruction, but rather an ideological construct, designed to control, to justify, and to inspire" (Cornell 1986: 58). For historian and audience, the past provided the standards by which to judge the present: the deeds of great ancestors offered models for imitation and supported the claims of the ruling class to political privilege and power. Each historian infused his version of events with his own (and his class's) literary, moral, and political concerns. The past, Cornell notes, "was subject to a process of continuous transformation as each generation reconstructed the past in its own image" (1986: 58). For many modern historians, Livy's account of early Rome better reflects the late Republic than the late sixth and fifth centuries B.C. (Raaflaub 1986: 23).

Even if we view Livy's "description of the monarchy and early Republic as prose epics or historical novels" (Raaflaub 1986: 8), we should not ignore the power of his fictions of Lucretia and Verginia. For Livy, they were history, and, as history, they should inform a way of life in an imperial Rome ripe for refounding. In good Roman fashion, Livy views history as a repository of illustrative behaviors and their results: "What chiefly makes the study of history wholesome and profitable is this, that you behold the lessons of every kind of experience set forth on a conspicuous monument; from these you may choose for yourself and for your state what to imitate, from these mark for avoidance what is shameful in conception and shameful in the result" (*praef.* 10, LCL). Before he begins his historical narrative per se, Livy urges a particular kind of reading. His stories will proffer an array of subject positions, beliefs, and bodily practices. The reader should recognize and identify with them and should understand the consequences of assuming particular subject positions. Bodily practices fit into a vision of building and collapsing empire: some result in imperial power; others bring decadence and destruction. The reader should pay close attention to "what life and morals were like; through what men and by what policies, in peace and in war, empire was established and enlarged; then let him note how, with the gradual relaxation of discipline, morals first gave way, as it were, then sank lower and lower, and finally began the downward plunge which has brought us to the present time, when we can endure neither our vices nor their cure" (*praef.* 9, LCL).

Thus, the question for us is not whether victims, villains, and heroes are fictional, but the way Livy tells their story, offering up a blueprint for his imperial present.

Livy's Stories of Lucretia and Verginia: Rape, Death, and Roman History

Lucretia and the fall of the monarchy (1.57–60)

In 509 B.C., the king of Rome, Lucius Tarquinius Superbus, wages war on Ardea in the hope that the booty will lessen the people's resentment at the labor he has imposed on them. During the siege of the city, at a drinking party, the king's sons and their kinsman Collatinus argue over who has the best wife. On Collatinus's suggestion, they decide to settle the question by seeing what their wives are doing. They find the princes' wives enjoying themselves at a banquet with their friends; Collatinus's wife, Lucretia, surrounded by her maids, spins by lamplight in her front hall. Lucretia makes her husband the victor in the wife contest. One of the princes, Sextus Tarquinius, inflamed by Lucretia's beauty and her proven chastity, is seized by a desire to have her. A few days later, without Collatinus's knowledge, he returns to Collatia, where he is welcomed as a guest. That night when the household is asleep, he draws his sword and wakes the sleeping Lucretia. Neither his declarations of love nor his threats of murder nor his pleas move the chaste Lucretia. She submits only when he threatens to create an appearance of disgraceful behavior: he will kill her and a slave and leave the slave's naked body next to hers, so that it will look as if they had been slain in the act of adultery.[3] After the rape, she sends for her husband and her father, instructing them to come with a trusted friend (Collatinus brings Lucius Junius Brutus). To her husband's question "Is it well with you?" she answers, "What can be well with a woman who has lost her chastity? The mark of another man is in your bed. My body only is violated; my mind is guiltless; death will be my witness. Swear that the adulterer will be punished – he is Sextus Tarquinius." The men swear and try to console her, arguing that the mind sins, not the body. She responds, "You will determine what is due him. As for me, although I acquit myself of fault, I do not free myself from punishment. No unchaste woman will live with Lucretia as a precedent." Then she kills herself with a knife she had hidden beneath her robe. While her husband and father grieve, Brutus draws the weapon from Lucretia's body and swears on her blood to destroy the monarchy. Lucretia's body, taken into the public square of Collatia, stirs the populace; Brutus incites the men to take up arms and overthrow the king. Brutus marches to Rome, and in the Forum the story of Lucretia and Brutus's speech have the same effect. The king is exiled, the monarchy ended; the Republic begins with the election of two consuls, Brutus and Collatinus.

Verginia and the fall of the decemvirate (3.44–58)

In 450 B.C., the decemvirs have taken control of the state. They have displaced the consuls and the tribunes, protectors of the rights of plebeians. The chief decemvir, Appius Claudius, desires the beautiful young

Verginia, daughter of the plebeian centurion Lucius Verginius. When Appius fails to seduce her with money or promises, he arranges to have Marcus Claudius, his *cliens* (a dependent tied to a more powerful man or an ex-master), claim Verginia as his (Marcus's) slave while her father is away at war (apparently the client will give the young woman to his patron Appius). Marcus grabs Verginia as she enters the Forum. When the cries of her nurse draw a crowd, Marcus hauls her before Appius's court. The decemvir postpones his decision until her father arrives but orders Verginia turned over to the man who claims her as his slave until the case can be tried. An impassioned speech by Verginia's fiancés Icilius incites the crowd; Appius rescinds his order. The next day, Verginius leads his daughter into the Forum, seeking support from the crowd. Unmoved by appeals or weeping women, Appius adjudges Verginia a slave, but he grants Verginius's request for a moment to question his daughter's nurse in Verginia's presence. Verginius leads his daughter away. Grabbing a knife from a butcher's shop, he cries, "In the only way I can, my daughter, I claim your freedom," and kills her. Icilius and Publius Numitorius, Verginia's grandfather (?), show the lifeless body to the populace and stir them to action. Verginius escapes to the army, where his bloodstained clothes, the knife, and his speech move his fellow soldiers to revolt. The decemvirate is overthrown, and when the tribunate is restored, Verginia's father, fiancé, and grandfather (?) are elected to office.

Flood: Bodily Desire and Political Catastrophe

Livy's narrative of Rome's political transformation revolves around chaste, innocent women raped and killed for the sake of preserving the virtue of the body female and the body politic; Roman men stirred to action by men who take control; and lustful villains whose desires result in their own destruction. Although the basic elements of Rome's early legends were present in Livy's sources, he could have dispensed with the tales in abbreviated fashion or minimized the role of women in stories of political change. Instead, he carefully constructs tragedies, drawing on all the literary techniques and models so meticulously noted by scholars (Ogilvie 1965: 218–32, 476–88; Phillips 1982: 1036–37 for bibliography). Why *this* writing of Roman history in Livy's present?

Livy's view of the immediate past engages him in Rome's ancient history. He elaborates that history, because he finds pleasure in it and relief from recent civil war, social upheaval, and military disaster:

To most readers the earliest origins and the period immediately succeeding them will give little pleasure, for they will be in haste to reach these modern times, in which the might of a people which has long been very powerful is working its own undoing. I myself, on the contrary, shall seek in this an additional reward for my toil, that I may avert my gaze from the troubles which our age has been witnessing for so many years, so long at least as I am absorbed in the recollection of the brave days of old.   (*praef.* 5, LCL)

"The troubles" haunted male authors of the first century B.C. – Sallust, Cicero, Horace, and Livy himself. As in the imagination of Theweleit's Freikorps writers, political chaos and military failure are associated with immorality. Although this vision is familiar to modern historians of ancient Rome, the strikingly similar images of chaos and men's experience in Weimar Germany compel reconsideration of the Roman images. I attend here only to how two elements, marked in these tales of origin, both deaden and kill: male excess and female unchastity.

Ancient authors attributed the crises of the late Republic to political ambition and to male bodies out of control in the social world, guilty of, in Livy's words, *luxus, avaritia, libido, cupiditas, abundantes voluptates* (luxurious living, avarice, lust, immoderate desire, excessive pleasures). Uncontrolled bodies bring personal ruin and general disaster (*praef.* 11–12). For his contemporary Horace (*Odes* 3.6.19–20; cf. 1.2), disaster floods country and people. The body and its pleasures are present only as excess in this vision. The slightest infraction seems dangerous. A single vice can slip into another or into a host of moral flaws, as in Livy's description of Tarquinius Superbus and his son Sextus (Phillipides 1983: 114, 117). Any desire becomes avarice or lust and must be rooted out.

> The seeds of vicious avarice
>   must be rooted up, and our far too delicate
> characters must be moulded by
>   sterner training.
> – Horace, *Odes* 3.24.51–54 (trans. J. P. Clancy)

Men of the Freikorps feared a "Red" flood affecting the entire society, "piercing through the ancient dam of traditional state authority" (Theweleit 1987: 231; see 385 ff., esp. 392, for Freikorps images of chaos). It "brought all of the worse instincts to the surface, washing them up on the land" (Theweleit 1987: 231). Ultimately, comments Theweleit (231), this flood flows "from inside of those from whom the constraint of the old order has been removed." A man could feel "powerless" and "defenseless" before what flows – fearful yet fascinated. The flood solidi-fies in a morass; men can hardly extract themselves from a mire that softness produces within them (404, 388). Indulgence must be rooted out: "If you want to press on forward, you cannot allow this mire of failure of the will to form inside you. The most humane way is still to go for the beast's throat, to pull the thing out by its roots" (388). The "defense against suffocation in flabby self-indulgence and capricious-ness" (389) lies in toughness and self-control: men should "stand fast ... think of, and believe in, the nation" (405).

Livy focuses on what he imagines to be the ancient and necessary virtue of the soldier: *disciplina*. Roman tradition offered him tales of discipline instilled by floggings, sons executed by fathers to preserve *disciplina* for the state, and men hardened to fight both the enemy without and the weakness within themselves (see Valerius Maximus, 2.7.1–15, esp. 2.7.6, 2.7.9, 2.7.10). Neither exceptional bravery nor victory should be allowed to undermine *disciplina*. When Livy's Manlius Torquatus orders the execution of his own son because, although successful in battle, he had ignored a direct order that no one was to engage the enemy, he makes the execution and the sacrifice of his own feelings a model for future gener-ations of Roman men:

> As you have held in reverence neither consular authority nor a father's dignity, and ... have broken military discipline, whereby the Roman state has stood until this day unshaken, thus compelling me to forget either the Republic or myself, we will sooner endure the punishment of our wrong-doing than suffer the Republic to expiate our sins at a cost so heavy to herself; we will set a stern example, but a salutary one, for the young men of the future. For my own part, I am moved, not only by a man's instinctive love of his children, but by this instance you have given of your bravery. ... But ... the authority of the consuls must either be established by your death, or by your impunity be forever abrogated, and ... I think you yourself, if you have a drop of my blood in you, would not refuse to raise up by your punishment the military discipline which through your misde-meanour has slipped and fallen.   (8.7.15–19, LCL)

Whatever his motives (8.7.4–8), the son had not simply disobeyed his commander and father; implicitly, he had failed to maintain the necessary self-control.

In Livy's view, control must be absolute. A slight crack in the edifice brings down the entire structure. *Disciplina* resulted in conquest; its gradual relaxation precipitated a slide, then collapse (*praef.* 9) – personal, social, political. A man, and Rome, would seem to have a choice between obdurate victor and pusillanimous loser, between fighter and pulp in the Freikorps vision (cf. Valerius Maximus, 2.7.9 and Theweleit 1987: 395).

The heroes of Livy's history, the men who act when women are made dead, are disciplined and unyielding. Noble Brutus chastised men for their tears and idle complaints (1.59.4) when they lamented Lucretia's death and their own miseries. He urged them as men and Romans to take up arms. Later, he would administer as consul and suffer as father the scourging and execution of his own sons as traitors. Founder of the Republic and the consulship, he is a model for future consuls and fathers, like Torquatus, whose defense of the state's tradition and existence will require dead sons and numbed affections. No *luxus* here or in the likes of Cocles, Scaevola, and Cincinnatus. These men are stern and self-controlled, bodies hardened to protect Rome and fight its wars. They must have been to have become the foremost people of the world (*praef.* 3) – the rulers of world empire. Like Virgil's Aeneas, Trojan ancestor of the Romans, conceived within a few years of Livy's heroes, they endure pain and adversity to create a Rome whose imperial power is portrayed as destiny (*Aeneid* 1.261–79): "so great was the effort to found the Roman race" (*Aeneid* 1.33). So disciplined, so self-controlled, so annealed, the body as a living, feeling, perceiving entity almost disappears.

Livy's instructions to imitate virtue and avoid vice invoke the *mos maiorum* – the way of the ancestors as a guide for the present. Bodily excess as manifested in the lust of Tarquin and Appius Claudius brings personal ruin and the collapse of their governments. Not incidentally, at the same time, Rome's wars with its neighbors are waged unsuccessfully. Tarquin desires Lucretia during the inactivity (*otium*) of a long siege which is blamed on the king's extravagance and his consequent need for booty. His avarice and his son's lust become "two sides of the same coin, a metaphor of the City's moral sickness," and explain Rome's military failure (Phillipides 1983: 114–15). For the sake of Rome's martial and moral health, father and son as desiring agents must go (Phillipides 1983: 114). The actions of disciplined men like Brutus result in personal success and Roman power. They set the example for Livy's present: the male body must be indifferent to material and sexual desire.

So Woman poses a particular problem.[4] The Roman discourse on chaos often joins loose women with male failure to control various appetites.[5] Uncontrolled female sexuality was associated with moral decay, and both were seen as the roots of social chaos, civil war, and military failure.

Breeder of vices, our age has polluted
first marriage vows and the children and the home;
from this spring, a river of ruin
    has flooded our country [*patria*, lit. "fatherland"] and our people.
                                   – Horace, *Odes* 3.6.17–20 (trans. J. P. Clancy)

Livy's view of control makes it appropriate that his narrative tends toward a simple dichotomous vision of female sexuality: woman is or is not chaste.

This vision may account for the satisfaction Livy's tales find in the point of the knife. Where he omits words about forced penetration, he offers a precise image of the dagger piercing Lucretia's body and her death (1.58.11; cf. Verginia, 3.48.5). Perhaps that knife is aimed at "any unchaste woman," real or imagined, of Livy's age (cf. Freikorps worship of asexual "high-born" women and attack on sexual "low-born" women; Theweleit 1987: 79ff., 315 ff., esp. 367). In Rome's imagined past, the knife constructs absolute control. It eradicates unchastity and kills any anomaly in female sexuality, such as the contradiction between Lucretia's violated body and her guiltless mind, or the blurring between the "good" and the "evil" woman (see Theweleit 1987: 183).

In Livy, the "good" woman's threatening element is her attractiveness. While Livy never explicitly questions the innocence and chaste spirit of Verginia or Lucretia, the beauty of each woman is marked and explains the rapists' actions. Lust seizes each man, as if desire originated outside him in beauty (1.57.10; 3.44.2). If, as the object of desire, a woman's beauty is the condition of male lust, then good as well as evil men are potentially affected. Her existence threatens men's *disciplina*. "The affective mode of self-defense in which [the annihilation of women] occurs seems to be made up of *fear* and *desire*" (Theweleit 1987: 183). Once Woman has played her role – to attract the villain whose actions set in motion other active males who construct the state, empire, and therefore history in the Roman sense – she must go.

As Theweleit suggests, what is at issue in this construction is male uncontrol. "What really started swimming were the men's boundaries – the boundaries of their perceptions, the boundaries of their bodies" (1987: 427). The dagger stems the flood, at least in the imagination. In effect, the aggression men visit on women is really aimed at their own bodies (note Theweleit 1987: 427, 154–55). Woman must die in order to deaden the male body. Aggression toward Woman and self produces *disciplina* (or is it the other way around?). The pathos of Livy's stories displaces the relief at the removal of the threatening element. "How tragic!" sigh author and reader, finding pleasure in the pain of noble loss. Ultimately, the pleasure of the narrative lies in killing what lives: women, the image of Woman as the object of desire, and male desire itself.

Discipline was necessary not only for the acquisition of empire but also for ruling it. The denial of the body to the self speaks the denial of social power to others; a Roman's rule of his own body provides an image of Roman domination and a model of sovereignty – of Roman over non-Roman, of upper class over lower, of master over slave, of man over woman, and of Princeps over everyone else (note Livy's use of a Greek metaphor likening a disordered body to the plebs' revolt against the *patres*, 2.32.9–12). In particular, the morality of control served Rome's new ruler. Augustus presented the required image of control and sacrifice (*Res Gestae* 4–6, 34; Suetonius *Augustus* 31.5, 33.1, 44–45, 51–58, 64.2–3, 65.3, 72–73, 76–77; cf. 71); denial and the morality of control enabled his authority to be "implanted into subjects' bodies in the form of a lack in overflowing" (Theweleit 1987: 414). In the Princeps' new order, there were to be no more selfish desires like those which had precipitated civil war. Woman was to be returned to her proper place. Marriage was to be regulated by the state; women's sexuality was to form the images and establish the boundaries so necessary to secure Rome's domination of others and Augustus's structuring of power. Harnessed, chaste, and deadened, Woman became the matter of a new order designed to control men and the free movement of all bodies. "Women within the new state once again provide the building blocks for internal boundaries against life" (Theweleit 1987: 366).

Woman as Space: Not a Room of Her Own

Within imperial constructions and the political context of the late first century B.C., Livy's account of early Rome creates Woman and her chastity as space, making her a catalyst for male action. She embodies the space of the home, a boundary, and a buffer zone. She is also a blank space – a void, for Livy effectively eliminates her voice, facilitating the perpetuation of male stories about men.

As is well known, a woman's chastity is associated with the honor of her male kin (Dixon 1982; Ortner 1978). Lucretia's behavior makes her husband the victor (*victor maritus*) in a contest between men (1.57). The praise awarded her is for chastity, measured by conduct outside the bedroom. Lucretia, spinning and alone but for her maids, acts out the traditional virtues of the good wife; the princes' wives, banqueting with friends, presumably display Woman's traditional vice, drinking wine, an offense tantamount to adultery (A. Watson 1975: 36–38; MacCormack 1975: 170–74). Verginia's fiancé Icilius (3.45.6–11) equates an assault on female chastity with violence done to male bodies and accuses Appius Claudius of making the eradication of tribunes (whose bodies were sacrosanct) and the right of appeal, defenses of men's *libertas*, an opportunity for *regnum vestrae libidini* ("a tyranny of your lust").

The association of male honor and female chastity makes a different kind of sense when we observe the narrative role of other women in Livy's early books. Women function as obstacles or embody spaces, often between and separating men. The Sabines put their bodies between their battling fathers and new husbands, offering to take on the anger the men feel toward one another and the violence they would inflict (1.13.1–4). Tarpeia fails to use her body in this way. Bribed by the Sabine king when she fetches water outside the city wall, the girl admits Rome's enemies into the citadel (1.11.6–9). The women whose actions preserve the physical integrity of both husbands and fathers are treasured by both; the girl whose treachery leaves her male kin vulnerable is crushed by the very enemy she aided.

As Natalie Kampen has pointed out, Tarpeia crosses the boundary of the city and appropriate behavior; the Sabines make themselves a boundary between warring men and observe appropriate behavior (1986: 10). If the issue is the control of female sexuality, control means the deployment of the female body in relations between men. Proper deployment founds relations between men, making society possible in Lévi-Strauss's terms (1969; cf. Mitchell 1975: 370–76). Not surprisingly, friezes depicting these tales "appeared at the very heart of the nation in the Forum," thus violating a convention that made women "extremely rare in public state-funded Roman sculpture" (1, 3). Kampen dates the friezes to 14–12 B.C., arguing that these representations served Augustus's moral and social program (5 ff.). In effect, the friezes made visible the narrative role of women in Livy's story of origin: within an emergent imperial order, women are fixed within the frame as boundary and space.

The move from animate life to inanimate matter is repeated in etymology. In each case, the Romans used a story of Woman's body to explain the name of a fixture of Rome: from Tarpeia the name of a place, the Tarpeian rock associated with the punishment of traitors, and from the Sabines the names of political divisions of citizens (the *curiae*). Whether the story follows the naming or vice versa, women's bodies literally become building material – the stuff of physical and political topography. Women who are supposed to have lived are transformed into places and spaces.

The Sabines, *matronae* (respectable married women) who voluntarily take up proper control of their own bodies, are reflected in Lucretia, the noble wife who will herself act and speak the proper use of her body. Tarpeia, *virgo* (unmarried girl) in need of paternal control, finds her counterpart in Verginia, whose father administers the necessary disposal of his daughter's body. Livy's *matrona* and *virgo* become spaces within the husband's or father's home. Unlike Dionysius of Halicarnassus (4.66.1), Livy never moves Lucretia out of Collatinus's house. She appears fixed in every scene – spinning in her hall, sleeping and pinned to the bed by Tarquin, and sitting in her bedroom when her kin come to her after the rape. This fixity in space informs her identity in the narrative and constitutes the grounds for male praise (1.57.9). And Verginius (3.50.9) literally equates his daughter with a place within his home (*locum in domo sua*).

In both narratives, the space that is Woman is equated with a chastity that should render the space of the home or between men impenetrable. Thus, rape or attempted rape appears as the penetration of space. The chastity of both women is described as a state of obstinacy or immobility (1.58.3–4, 5; 3.44.4). However, alone or accompanied only by women, wife and daughter are vulnerable to non-kin males who can use force combined with the threat of shame or the power of the state in order to satisfy their lust. Lucretia is a *place* where Tarquin intends to stick his sword or his penis. She appears as an obstacle to his desire, impenetrable even at the threat of death. When she gives way at the threat of a shame worse than rape, Tarquin conquers (*vicisset, expugnato*) not a person but her chastity (*pudicitiam, decore*). The rape of a Lucretia fixed in and identified with Collatinus's home seems equivalent to a penetration of his private sphere, his territory.

Male heroes, not raped women, carry forward the main trajectory of Livy's work – the history of the Roman state (see de Lauretis 1984: 109–24 on Oedipal narratives). They lead citizen males to overthrow a tyrannical ruler, advancing from the sphere of the home to that of the state, from private vengeance to public action. The transition from domestic to political is represented in a shift in the scene of action from Collatia and the private space of Collatinus's home to Rome and the public space of the Forum. Brutus, not Lucretia (1.59.5; cf. Dionysius 4.66.1), effects the change of scene, just as he transposes her request for the punishment of the rapist to his own demand for the overthrow of the monarchy. His oath of vengeance begins with the determination to avenge Lucretia and finishes not with an oath to dethrone Tarquin's family but with the promise to end the institution of monarchy itself.

The connection between the rape of an individual woman and the overthrow of monarchy and decemvirate finds its model in the Greek stereotype of the tyrant whose part Tarquin and Appius Claudius play (Ogilvie 1965: 195–97, 218–19, 453, 477; Dunkle 1971: 16): they are violent and rape other men's women.[6] Livy's rewriting of the Greek paradigm, however, has a particularly Roman subtext: imperial conquest and its product, large-scale slavery. In both tales, men complain that they, Roman soldiers, are treated as Rome's enemies (1.59.4), the conquered (3.47.2, 3.57.3, 3.61.4), or slaves (1.57.2, 59.4, 59.9, 3.45.8). In effect, king and decemvir behave as if citizen males, like slaves, lacked physical integrity. Very importantly, the "slave" makes possible the victimization of both women. Lucretia gives in when Tarquin threatens to kill her in a simulation of adultery with a slave. Appius Claudius intends to rape Verginia by having her adjudicated a slave, thus legally vulnerable to a master's sexual use (cf. Dionysius 11.29–33, making clear the issue of the slave's lack of physical integrity). Tarquin, his father, and Appius Claudius are made to do to Lucretia, Verginia, and their male kin what Roman "soldier males" do to the conquered. Roman wives and children are assimilated to the conquered and slaves (3.57.4, 61.4), and the physical vulnerability of the latter is unquestioned. This was the empire that needed *disciplina*.

Verginia's story sets out a logic of bodies: between the rape of a woman and direct violence to the bodies of her male kin lies male action. "Vent your rage on our backs and necks: let chastity at least be safe," Icilius exclaims to Appius Claudius early in Livy's account (3.45.9). Verginia's betrothed offers to substitute male for female bodies. Appius's lust, inflicted on wives and children, should be channeled into violence, inflicted on husbands and fathers. The switch never occurs, because male action intervenes and removes the source of lust and violence. At the end, Icilius, Verginius, and Numitorius are alive, well, and sacrosanct tribunes; chastity is safe; Verginia is dead.

But Verginia's father makes clear that her rape poses a direct threat to the male body. After slaying her, he states that there is no longer a *locus* in his home for Appius's lust, and he now intends to defend his own body as he had defended his daughter's (3.50.9). The buffer between himself and Appius is gone.[7] Woman's chastity signifies her, and hence his, imperviousness to assault; her rape endangers his body. Thus, the raped woman becomes a *casus belli*, a catalyst for a male response which stems the threatened violence. Men halt the invasion before it gets to them.

Icilius's speech suggests the nature of the threat to the male body (see Douglas 1984: 133 ff. and Donaldson 1982: 23–25, on the fear of pollution). His words effect a displacement.[8] As "rage" (*saevire*) replaces rape, male necks and backs replace female genitals. Although rage and lust seem interchangeable, Icilius's proffered exchange excludes an assault on the body's most vulnerable place – its orifices (Douglas 1984: 121). The very substitution of necks and backs for orifices masks an apprehension about male vulnerability: invasion of woman as boundary threatens penetration of the male body (see Richlin 1983: 57–63, 98–99).

In Livy's accounts, men experience the offense of rape as tragedy. They grieve and are moved, but they do not directly suffer invasion; they remain intact. Moreover, they can feel like men, because they have taken out their own swords. In a most satisfying way, the invader loses ultimate control of the woman's body. While Appius Claudius and Tarquin wield their penises or try to, the father and, even better, the woman herself wield the knife.

Male action against the tyrant (it should be emphasized) begins not with rape but with the woman's death. Narratively, it appears as if Lucretia and Verginia must die in order for male action to begin and for the story to move on. Three logics seem to account for the slaying of the women and explain why the violence done to woman does not end with rape.

In the first place, a living Lucretia or Verginia would stand as evidence of disorder and chaos (see above on Horace *Odes* 3.6). Livy's Verginius and Icilius speak of the social disorder Appius Claudius's desire introduces for the men of their order and the destruction of the social ties between them. Verginius accuses Appius of instituting an order of nature – rushing into intercourse without distinction in the manner of animals (3.47.7). By killing his daughter, he halts the plunge into animality. Of course, animality and the disorder it signals mean that father and husband no longer control the bodies of "their" women. Appius robs Verginius of the ability to give his daughter in marriage to a man of his choosing (3.47.7). Icilius loses a bride *intacta*, and the bond between Icilius and Verginius would be flawed if Verginius offered him "damaged goods." Icilius asserts that *he* is going to marry Verginia, and *he* intends to have a chaste bride (3.45.6–11). He will not allow his bride to spend a single night outside her father's home (3.45.7).

Appius denies plebeian males membership in a patriarchal order. And where the decemvir offends an already existing patriarchal order, only the political change motivated by his assault on the chastity of a plebeian woman assures paternal power to the men of her social class. In versions of the story earlier than Livy's first-century sources, Verginia was a patrician. By changing her status, Livy's sources invested meanings from current political struggles into the fifth century Conflict of the Orders (Ogilvie 1965: 477). Yet the updated political story is essentially a story about patriarchy, for the political events turn on the control of a daughter's/bride's body.

Second, alive, the raped woman would constitute another sort of threat: once invaded, the buffer zone becomes harmful to what it/she once protected. If women are boundaries, rape, which assaults an orifice, a marginal area of the body, creates a special vulnerability for the "center," that is, men. The danger of a living Verginia is noted above. Her life is dearer than her father's own, but only if she is chaste and "free" (3.50.6), a body intact whose access lies in her father's control. A raped Lucretia, still alive, would display the violation of her husband's home. The mark of another man in Collatinus's bed apparently cannot be erased, at least not without his wife's death. Livy's Lucretia speaks as if she and the marked bed are one: although her mind is guiltless, her body is violated and soiled. Only death, self-inflicted, can display her innocence (1.58.7). Soiled, the body must go (see Douglas 1984: 113, 136, on inadvertent pollution and efforts made to align inward heart and public act).

For history to be a source of models for emulation (*praef.* 10), it must demonstrate an unequivocal pattern. The relation of a moral present to its imagined origins constructs chastity as an absolute quality (see Dixon 1982: 4). The pleas of Lucretia's husband and father that the mind, not the body, sins frame her suicide as a tragic martyrdom. Correcting them, Lucretia makes herself an *exemplum:* "no unchaste woman will live with Lucretia as a precedent" (1.58.10). On the surface, the pleas of father and husband imply that men do not require Lucretia's death: suicide appears as woman's choice. This construction of female choice and agency disguises the male necessity at work in Lucretia's eradication. Alive, even Lucretia would confront a patriarchal order with a model, an excuse, for the woman unchaste *by volition.* Lucretia's statement admits no distinction: her suicide leaves no anomaly for the patriarchal future.

Third, and perhaps most important for the narrative: dead, the female body has other purposes. Dead, the woman whose chastity had been assaulted assumes other values. Dead, her body can be deployed, and the sight of it enjoyed, by all men. Without the stabbing of Lucretia and Verginia, there is no bloodied knife, no blood to swear on, no corpse to display to the masses. Brutus, Icilius, and Numitorius use the dead female body to incite themselves and other men (1.59.3, 3.48.7). The woman's blood enlivens men's determination to overthrow the tyrant. Her raped or almost raped and stabbed body kindles thoughts of men's own sufferings and feeds mass male action (note Theweleit 1987: 34,

105–6); in an almost vampiric relation, the living are enlivened by the dead. He becomes free (i.e., comes alive) when she becomes an inert, unliving object.

Actually, Livy's narrative deadens both women before the knife ever pierces them (Theweleit 1987: 90 ff.). Lucretia is introduced as an object in a male contest, as Verginia is an object of contention, pulled this way and that by the men who would claim her body. In the rape scene, Lucretia is inert; appropriately, she sees death from the moment Tarquin enters her bedroom. The stories "record the living as that which is condemned to death" (Theweleit 1987: 217). Narratively, Lucretia and Verginia become ever more dead, as action moves progressively further from them: from the sight of their deaths to the bloodstained knife to the raped, almost raped dead body to the story of that body told to men not present at the murder. The farther removed from the body, the wider the audience, the more public the action, and ultimately the larger the arena of Roman conquest and rule. Male action secures the form of the Roman state and *libertas*. Most immediately, this results in "soldier males" winning wars that, until these episodes, were stalemated.

The tragic effects and pathos evoked by the woman's death veil the necessary central operation of the narrative: to create a purely public (and male) arena. Although presented as tragedies, Lucretia's suicide and Verginia's slaying remove the women from the scene, from between men. With the buffering space gone, there will now ensue a "real" struggle between men, a struggle that moves forward the central narrative, that of state and empire (on the primacy of public and male concerns, see 3.48.8–9 and Theweleit 1987: 88).

While consulship, tribunate, Senate, and assemblies mark the shape of the state whose development Livy traces, each rape, each body willing to bear the wounds men would inflict on each other, and each dead body sets in place a block of a patriarchal and imperial order. The rape of Rhea Silvia gives the Roman state its *pater* (no room here for a queen mother). The rape of the Sabine women makes possible patriarchy by supplying it with its one necessary component: the women who produce children. Lucretia and Verginia precipitate the overthrow of a tyrant and the confirmation, or indeed establishment, of patriarchy for patricians and then plebeians. Assured at home that their wives and children will not be treated as the conquered, these men can go forth, conquer an empire, and do to other men and women what they would not have done to their own wives and children.

It is in this context that we should see the silence in Livy's narrative, the silence of Lucretia and Verginia, and the dead matter these women become. Verginia never speaks or acts. Livy remarks on her obstinacy in the face of Appius's attempted seduction, although, in fact, he speaks not of her but of her *pudor* (3.44.4). When Appius's client grabs her, her fear silences her; her nurse, not Verginia, cries out for help. The girl is led here and there by kin or grabbed by Appius's client. There is no notice of tears, clinging, or interaction with her father, as in Dionysius's telling (11.31.3, 32.1, 35, 37.4–5). Even the women who surround her are moving by the *silence* of their tears (3.47.4). At the moment she would become a slave, Appius shouts, the crowd parts, the girl stands alone *praeda iniuriae* ("prey to sexual assault," 3.48.3). A moment of silence. Her father takes Verginia's life; he acts and speaks the meaning of her death. Nothing of or from Verginia. "From the start, indeed, she [a Freikorps bride] is no more than a fiction. She never appears in her own right; she is only spoken *about*" (Theweleit 1987: 32).

Throughout the events leading up to and including the rape, Livy's Lucretia is also silent. Although the rape scene is highly dramatic, Livy gives us only Tarquin's actions: he waits until the household is asleep, he draws his sword, he enters Lucretia's bedroom, he holds her down, he speaks, pleads, and threatens. Lucretia is mute. Like Verginia's, her terror eliminates speech, and her chastity makes her obdurate: she is a silent stone.

Silence is what Tarquin demands of her: "*Tace, Lucretia, Sex. Tarquin-ius sum*" ("Be quiet, Lucretia, I am Sextus Tarquinius"). His speech could not connect silence and erasure more directly. The command and direct address (*Tace, Lucretia*) imply "I give the orders," and since he orders Lucretia's silence, the command is almost tautological. Then he asserts his own name (*Sex. Tarquinius*) and existence (*sum*). The insistence on his own existence follows from his demand for her silence. Indicative, statement of fact, replaces imperative, command – here an order that she erase the fact of herself as a speaking subject; his name replaces hers. In effect, he says, "I am; you are not, although since I must order your silence, you are and I shall have to make you not be." Implicitly, his existence as a speaking (here, an ordering) subject with a name depends on her status as an object without speech (see Kappeler 1986: 49). Like Brutus's later deployment of her body in the overthrow of the monarchy, Tarquin's words and act are vampiric: her silence (erasure), his existence.

Her silence constructs a pleasure of terror like that of the horror film, where the audience is held in expectation that what it fears will occur. Certainly, tension and terror cannot exist without Lucretia's silence, without her presence as an actionless body. The description of Tarquin's actions delays what every Roman would know to be the inevitable. Livy's account allows the reader to dwell on the details of power asserted – drawn sword, hand on breast, woman pinned to the bed, woman starting out of sleep to hear "*Tace, Lucretia, Sex. Tarquinius sum.*" The mute, immobile victim sets the escalating movement of violation in high relief. As in the cinema, the construction of powerlessness provides a perverse thrill.

What are the pleasures of this silence for male author and reader? Did Livy, "pen" in hand, identify with Tarquin and his drawn sword, experience the imagined exertion of force, and take pleasure in the prospect of *pen*etration with sword or penis (on pen and penis, see Gilbert and Gubar 1979: 3–16)? Is this the titillation found by the male reader? Or does Lucretia's silence also open a space for the flow of the reader's feelings, permitting his entry into the forbidden pleasure of the penetrated, imagined from the place of one required to be a penetrator (Silverman 1980, and Richlin 1992)?

About the act of penetration itself, no words and a gap filled with the language of chastity conquered. Despite rules of taste or convention, such language erases the moment of Lucretia's violation and silences her experience as a subject of violation. Livy comments only, and only after her violation, that she was *maesta* ("mournful"). The place of Lucretia's pain is absent. Without words about her experience at that moment and without that moment, Lucretia is dead matter – not feeling, not thinking, not perceiving. Present is Lucretia's chastity, but not Lucretia. Livy or convention – it doesn't matter which – creates rape as a male event, and an imperial one. Rape consists of male action and female space, the exertion of force and chastity.

After, and only after, the rape, Lucretia speaks and acts as Verginia does not. Donaldson sees Lucretia's act as a sacrifice of self, contrasting it with Brutus's sacrifice of his feelings and his sons (1982: 12). Brutus achieves political liberty, Lucretia personal liberty (8). Higonnet focuses on Lucretia's speech as an explanatory text for suicide (1986: 69). She argues that Lucretia's use of language is "revolutionary" because she sets her own verbal constructs against those of Collatinus which make her a verbal boast and a sexual object (75). With Donaldson (1982: 103ff.), she views the stress on Brutus's role as the "masculine domestication of an essentially revolutionary heroic instance of female suicide."

This assumes that we can return to some origin where women occupied some other role and misses the male production of origin. The sacrifices of Brutus and Lucretia are "radically different," but not for the reasons noted by Donaldson (12). Brutus's words and actions bring a political order in which men like himself can act; his sacrifice preserves that order.

Lucretia's actions result in her own eradication. She is sacrificed so the men of her class may win their liberty – their ability to act. Her language kills no less than her actions: like the Sabines, she "asks for it." Together, words and actions set an example for the control of female sexual activity; in other words, she founds an order in which her female descendants can only enact their own destruction. As with Rhea Silvia, the Sabines, Tarpeia, Horatia, and Verginia, men's liberation and political advances require the sacrifice of Woman.

Moreover, both Lucretia's words and her act silence any difference that would disturb the structural boundaries of an ideal patriarchal order. I find it difficult to see Lucretia's speech (given her by the male historian, it should be emphasized) as revolutionary, when she is made to speak as well as act the absolute, objective quality of chastity and herself as a space invaded. Soiled is soiled: "No unchaste woman will live with Lucretia as a precedent." To see or hear anything else would make Lucretia anomalous – innocent yet penetrated – and alive. Patriarchy in Livy's good old days apparently cannot tolerate a subject whose speech would evoke the disorder of anomaly; it depends on woman's silence, or at most speech that enunciates the role men set out for her (note Theweleit 1987: 123; Gilbert and Gubar 1979: 14).

Theweleit's analysis of the "mode of production of [his] writers' language" is instructive. Freikorps authors employ the postures of description, narration, representation, and argument "only as empty shells" (1987: 215). Rather, their linguistic process is one of transmutation. The events depicted serve a preconceived idea which is not directly described. The "ideational representation" impresses itself on perceived reality and devours it (87). While every linguistic process "appropriates and transforms reality" (215), Freikorps authors deaden what they depict. Theirs is a "language of occupation: it acts imperialistically against any form of independently moving life" (215). The life that especially draws the onslaught is the "living movement of women" and the whole complex of feelings and experiences, sexual and emotional, associated with women.

The thrust of Livy's narrative kills, but with certain effects. Women are made dead, and men come alive. Women as a presence disappear from the narrative and leave the stage of history to men struggling with one another, winning wars, and building an empire which, of course, means making other women and men physically dead in conquest or socially dead in enslavement. Lucretia and Verginia endure and are removed from the scene by the activities of the conqueror – rape, death, enslavement. In effect, Livy builds Rome's origin and its history with what deadens in the imperial present.

Where it would seem that women in Livy are made dead with the result that the men who make empire come alive, this operation of the narrative veils the deadness of the men who build imperial society. *Disciplina* requires bodies insensible to desire. Brutus holds aloft the bloody knife drawn from Lucretia's body and swears the overthrow of tyranny. He evokes the more recent image of his descendant, beloved by Caesar and one of his assassins. Livy seems simply to have replaced one dead body with another; Lucretia's corpse hides another, not of the past but of Augustus's emerging imperial order – Gaius Julius Caesar, a man who controlled neither his ambition nor his bodily desires.

Epilogue: The News, History, and the Body of Woman

The story of Lucretia, Donaldson says, has disappeared from popular knowledge not on account of "moral disapproval, but neglect: the explanation lies in the modern decline in classical knowledge and classical education" (1982: 168). We are too distant from ancient Rome and the eighteenth century that found meaning in its virtues. Instead, "we celebrate the 'heroes' of the sports field and the world of entertainment more readily than the heroes of the battlefield and the deathbed; the word is drained of its moral sense."

I cannot share Donaldson's perception of distance and difference. The news, that raw material of political history, seems to belong to the "world of entertainment": fiction and fact meld, working on and with the same images. Through them echo the women and gender relations in Livy's stories of early Rome, his narrative of origins constructed in apprehension of decadence and decline. The Iran-Contra hearings slip into the air time of the soap opera. The cases of Bernhard Goetz and Baby M become news and made-for-TV movies. In the newspaper, extramarital sex costs a politician his chance at the presidency; in the cinema, it nearly costs a man his family and his life. In Rambo films and *Fatal Attraction*, "the world of entertainment" does offer us heroes of the battlefield and the deathbed (more precisely, death *and* bed). Daily, images of woman as space and void cross my TV screen. Often, the news seems written on the bodies of women; at least, she is there – a part of the landscape of what becomes history.

This is not a Roman landscape. The women belong to seemingly different narratives: hostages, not raped women, catalyzed action in Reagan's White House. Women are not slain in current political narratives, yet seemingly different stories proffer words flooded with "moral sense," implicitly urging correct bodily behavior, generally the practices of self-control – "just say no." These stories, too, require the bodies of women, made dead by their silence and their allocation to a holding place in stories of men. And when these women speak, they enunciate this place or their pleasure as inanimate matter, like a Barbie doll available for purchase.

The "decline in classical knowledge" has not spelled the disappearance of these features of Roman fictions, however unfamiliar the specific narratives. The deadening or silencing of Woman perpetuates the fictions and history of the bodies politic, female, and male. Since the eighteenth century, when some celebrated Lucretia's story, the commodity has taken the place of honor in systems of value as a bourgeois order replaced an aristocratic one, but the images of Woman have followed the displacement. "Her image sells his products" (Pfohl 1990: 223–24); it "sells" Livy's history, too.

NOTES

1 Translations from ancient sources are the author's own, unless indicated otherwise. LCL refers to the Loeb Classical Library.

2 Lavinia, daughter of King Latinus, married to Aeneas in order to cement an alliance between Latins and Trojans, disappears from the text (1.3.3), as do the politically and/or sexually active Tanaquil and Tullia (exiled 1.59.13). On this and related issues, see now Jed 1989 and Joplin 1990, which unfortunately appeared too late to be considered here.

3 By "submits" (or, later, "gives in"), I do not intend to imply consent on Lucretia's part (*contra* Donaldson 1982: 24 and Bryson 1986: 165–66). To speak of consent in conditions of force and violence is meaningless; in Lucretia's situation, it seems perverse. She can die or live through the rape only to defend her honor by suicide.

4 I distinguish an individual woman or women from Woman, "a fictional construct, a distillate from diverse but congruent discourses dominant in Western cultures" (de Lauretis 1984: 5).

5 Appetites include a decadent concern with food, table servants, and dining accoutrements. For discussion and sources on Roman luxury and decadence, see Earl 1961: 41ff; 1967: 17–20; and Griffin 1976. Uncontrolled sexuality and decadent eating fit Lévi-Strauss's observation of a "very profound analogy which people throughout the world seem to find between copulation and eating" (1966: 105). See Modleski's analysis of the "ambivalence towards femininity" played out in a woman's function "as both edible commodity and inedible pollutant" in Alfred Hitchcock's *Frenzy* (1988: 101–14).

6   It is well known that Livy drew on other paradigms and stereotypes, literary
    genres, and Hellenistic historical practices; however, for my purposes, tracing
    the elements from diverse sources is less important than how they work within
    Livy's historical discourse. As Phillipides (1983: 119 n. 20) points out, "the
    elements taken from a prior sign system acquire a different significance when
    transposed into the new sign system." Following Julia Kristeva, she notes that
    "this process of transformation involves the destruction of the old and the
    formation of a new signification."
7   Ironically, the removal of Woman in both stories returns Roman "soldier
    males" to the conditions of their mythical *patres* Romulus and Remus, two
    men without a woman, not even a mother, between them (1.6.4–7.3). Quite
    literally, the twins try to occupy the same space at the same time and do
    violence to each other. Like the Romans and the Sabines, they cannot coexist
    without the body of woman between them, without the space and place of
    "not us."
8   Tales of male bodies that suffer violence and penetration focus on those who
    occupy the place of the son *in potestate* – sons killed by stern fathers and
    young men raped (often unsuccessfully) by evil army officers and magistrates
    (Valerius Maximus 5.8.1–5, 6.1.5, 7.9–12); see Richlin 1983: 220–26, esp.
    225–26. In effect, Roman patriarchy associates all women with sons in
    paternal power. Apprehension about their vulnerability to aggressive non-
    kin males would seem to stem from the "rightful" power that fathers (and
    husbands) wielded over their bodies.

REFERENCES

Bloch, R. 1965. *Tite-Live et les premiers siècles de Rome*. Paris.
Bryson, N. 1986. "Two Narratives of Rape in the Visual Arts: Lucretia and the
    Sabine Women." In S. Tomaselli and R. Porter (eds.), *Rape*, 152–73. Oxford.
Cornell, T. J. 1986. "The Value of the Literary Tradition Concerning Archaic
    Rome." In K. A. Raaflaub (ed.), *Social Struggles in Archaic Rome*, 52–76.
    Berkeley, CA.
de Lauretis, T. 1984. *Alice Doesn't*. Bloomington, IN.
Dixon, S. 1982. "Women and Rape in Roman Law." *Kønsroller, parforhold og
    Samlivsformer: Arbejdsnotat nr. 3*. Copenhagen.
——. 1988. *The Roman Mother*. Norman, OK.
Donaldson, I. 1982. *The Rapes of Lucretia: A Myth and Its Transformations*.
    Oxford.
Douglas, M. 1984. *Purity and Danger*. London.
Earl, D. 1961. *The Political Thought of Sallust*. Cambridge.
Gilbert, S. M. and S. Gubar. 1979. *The Madwoman in the Attic*. New Haven, CT.
Gjerstad, E. 1973. *Early Rome*. Vols. 5 and 6. Rome.

Griffin, J. 1976. "Augustan Poetry and the Life of Luxury." *Journal of Roman Studies* 66: 87–105. Reprinted with Modifications in J. Griffin, *Latin Poets and Roman Life*, 1–31. Chapel Hill, NC.

Heurgon, J. 1973. *The Rise of Rome*. Trans. J. Willis. Berkeley, CA.

Kappeler, S. 1986. *The Pornography of Representation*. Minneapolis, MN and Cambridge.

Luce, T. J. 1977. *Livy: The Composition of His History*. Princeton, NJ.

MacCormack, G. 1975. "Wine-Drinking and the Romulan Law of Divorce." *Irish Jurist* 10: 170–4.

Mitchell, J. 1975. *Psychoanalysis and Feminism*. New York.

Modleski, T. 1988. *The Women Who Knew Too Much*. New York.

Ogilvie, R. M. 1965. *A Commentary on Livy, Books 1–5*. Oxford.

Ortner, S. B. 1978. "The Virgin and the State." *Feminist Studies* 4.3: 19–35.

Pfohl, S. 1990. "The Terror of the Simulacra: Struggles for Justice and the Postmodern." In S. Pfohl (ed.), *New Directions in the Study of Justice, Law, and Social Control*, 207–63. New York.

Phillipides, S. N. 1983. "Narrative Strategies and Ideology in Livy's 'Rape of Lucretia.'" *Helios* 10: 113–19.

Phillips, J. 1982. "Current Research in Livy's First Decade: 1959–1979." *Aufsteig und Niedergang der Römischer Welt* 30.2: 998–1057.

Raaflaub, K. A. 1986. "The Conflict of the Orders in Archaic Rome: A Comprehensive and Comparative Approach." In K. A. Raaflaub (ed.), *Social Struggles in Archaic Rome*, 1–51. Berkeley, CA.

Richlin, A. 1983. *The Garden of Priapus: Sexuality and Aggression in Roman Humor*. New Haven, CT and Oxford.

——. 1992. "Reading Ovid's Rapes." In A. Richlin, ed., *Pornography and Representation in Greece and Rome*, 158–79. New York and Oxford.

Silverman, K. 1980. "Masochism and Subjectivity." *Frameworks* 12: 2–9.

Syme, R. 1959. "Livy and Augustus." *Harvard Studies in Classical Philology* 64: 27–87.

Theweleit, K. 1987. *Male Fantasies*. Vol. 1. Trans. S. Conway. Minneapolis, MN.

Walsh, P. G. 1961. *Livy: His Historical Aims and Methods*. Cambridge.

Watson, A. 1975. *Rome of the XII Tables*. Princeton, NJ.

SOURCE

The Roman writer Livy (64 BCE–12 CE) began his lengthy chronicle of Roman history during the first years of the Emperor Augustus' new regime. *On the Founding of Rome* described Roman history from the origins of Rome until the rise of Augustus in 142 books. This passage describes a pivotal moment in that history: the fall of the monarchy and the dawn of the Republic. Raped by the corrupt Tarquin, Lucretia commits suicide and thus sparks a movement among the people to destroy the monarchy.

Livy, *On the Founding of Rome* 1.57.6–59.6

By chance the soldiers were drinking one day at the quarters of Sextus Tarquinius – where Collatinus, the son of Egerius, was also dining – when the subject of wives happened to come up. Each man praised his own wife to the skies, but when the debate grew heated, Collatinus asserted that there was no need of argument. In just a few hours they could know the extent to which his wife, Lucretia, surpassed the other women in virtue. "Since we are young and strong, why not mount our horses and see in person the characters of our own wives? Let whatever meets his eyes upon the husband's arrival be the ultimate proof of his wife's character." They were inflamed with wine; "Good idea!" they cried. They hurried to Rome with their horses at full speed. Arriving there at dusk, they then proceeded to Collatia, where they found Lucretia occupied very differently from the wives of the other princes, whom they had seen wasting their time with feasting and amusements, with companions of the same age. But they found Lucretia sitting in the atrium, spinning with the maidservants even though it was late at night. In the contest of wives, the prize belonged to Lucretia. As her husband and the

Tarquins arrived, they were received graciously; her victorious husband kindly invited the royal youths to stay. Thereupon an evil desire to possess Lucretia by force seized Sextus Tarquin; for the sight of both her beauty and her well-regarded chastity spurred him on. And then they returned to the camp from their nocturnal youthful escapade.

A few days later, Sextus Tarquin returned with one companion to Collatia without Collatinus' knowledge, where he was graciously received by a household unaware of his intent and led after dinner to the guestroom. Inflamed with passion, he waited until it seemed that the coast was clear and everyone sound asleep, drew his sword and approached the sleeping Lucretia. With his left hand pressed against her breast, he said, "Be quiet, Lucretia. I am Sextus Tarquin. I have a sword in my hand. If you utter a sound, you will die." Lucretia woke up, terrified; she saw no help in sight and death fast approaching. Then Tarquin confessed his love, begged, mingled entreaties with threats, and tried every way to bend a woman's will. When he found her obdurate and not to be moved even by the fear of death, he added disgrace to fear. He said that he would kill her and then cut the throat of his slave and place his naked body next to hers. People would then say that she had been killed for having a sordid affair with a slave. When his desire, as if victorious, had defeated her resolute modesty by this terrifying threat, thereupon brutal Tarquin departed, exulting in his conquest of a woman's virtue. Lucretia, depressed by her great misfortune, sent the same message to her father in Rome and to her husband at Ardea, that they should each come with a trusted friend, and that they should do so quickly, because a terrible thing had happened. Lucretius came with Publius Valerius, Volesus' son, Collatinus brought Lucius Junius Brutus, with whom he chanced to be returning to Rome when he was met by his wife's messenger. They came upon Lucretia sitting sadly in her chamber. At their arrival, tears welled up in her eyes, and when her husband asked, "Is everything all right?" she answered "Not at all. For what can be well with a woman who has lost her virtue? The imprints of another man are in your bed, Collatinus. But only my body has been violated, my mind remains innocent, as death will be my witness. But give me your hands in pledge that the adulterer will not go unpunished. It is Sextus Tarquin who last night returned hospitality with hostility; armed he took his pleasure with me by force, a pleasure fatal for me and for him, if you are really men."

They gave their pledge each in turn. They consoled her mental anguish by shifting the blame from her, a hapless woman, to Tarquin, the author of the crime. They tell her the sin is of the mind, not of the body, and where purpose is wanting, there is no guilt. "It shall be for you to see what that man deserves," she said. "Even though I absolve myself of sin, I do not free myself from punishment. Not in time to come will any woman use the example of Lucretia to justify her shameless behavior." Then she plunged a knife that had been hidden beneath her dress into her heart, and collapsing over the wound, she died as she fell. Both her husband and father cried out her name in horror.

While the others were absorbed in grief, Brutus removed the knife from Lucretia's wound and, holding it dripping with blood before them, said, "By this girl's blood, the purest until the prince's wrong, I swear – and I take you, gods, as my witnesses – that I will pursue Lucius Tarquinius Superbus, along with his impious wife and his entire progeny, with sword, with fire, with whatever force I am able. Nor will I suffer those men, nor any other person, to be king of Rome!" Then he handed the knife to Collatinus, and from him to Lucretius and Valerius: they were astonished, a miracle had happened, he was a changed man. They swore the oath as it was prescribed; all of them turned from grief to anger; and when Brutus called for them to make war from that very moment on the royal throne, they followed Brutus as their leader when he called for them.

They carried out Lucretia's corpse from the house and brought it to the forum; men crowded around, as it happened, surprised, as ever, by the strange event, but shocked as well. Each man had his own complaint to make about the prince's crime and his violence. The sorrow of the father moved them, while it was Brutus who reproved their tears and their idle complaints and who urged them that it was their duty, as men and Romans, to take up arms against those who dared treat them as enemies. The boldest of the young men volunteered with their arms; and the rest of the youths followed. Once a guard had been left at the gates of Collatia, and sentinels posted so that no one would be able to announce their uprising to the royal family, they set out for Rome, equipped for battle and under the leadership of Brutus.

Figure 7 *Couple at a Roman Banquet.* Wall painting from Hercula-
neum, c.70 CE. Museo Nazionale, Naples. A half-naked young man re-
clines on a couch and holds a drinking horn (*rhyton*) to his lips at a
banquet. In front of him sits a woman, perhaps a courtesan, dressed in a
transparent garment.

7
MISTRESS AND METAPHOR IN AUGUSTAN ELEGY

M. Wyke

I.   Written and Living Women

A pressing problem confronts work on the women of ancient Rome: a need to determine the relation between the realities of women's lives and their representation in literature. Several of the volumes on women in antiquity that have appeared in the 1980s expose the methodological problems associated with any study of women in literary texts,[1] but few of their papers have yet investigated the written women of Rome.[2] In any study of the relations between written and living women, however, the heroines of Augustan elegy deserve particular scrutiny because the discourse in which they appear purports to be an author's personal confession of love for his mistress. The texts of Latin love poetry are frequently constructed as first-person, authorial narratives of desire for women who are individuated by name, physique, and temperament. This poetic technique tempts us to suppose that, in some measure, elegy's female subjects reflect the lives of specific Augustan women.

Moreover, in presenting a first-person narrator who is indifferent to marriage and subject to a mistress, the elegiac texts pose a question of important social dimensions: if Augustan love poetry focuses on a female subject who apparently operates outside the traditional constraints of marriage and motherhood, could it constitute the literary articulation of an unorthodox place for women in the world? This question has generated considerable controversy, as the debate between Judith Hallett and Aya Betensky in *Arethusa* (1973, 1974) reveals.[3]

In particular, the corpus of Propertian poems seems to hold out the hope that we may read *through* the written woman, Cynthia, to a living mistress. Poem 1.3, for example, conjures up before its readers a vision of an autobiographical event. The first-person narrator recalls the night he arrived late and drunk by his mistress's bed. The remembered occasion unfolds through time, from the moment of the lover's arrival to his beloved's awakening. The details of the beloved's sleeping posture, her past cruelty, and her present words of reproach all seem further to authenticate the tale. The portrait of a Cynthia possessed of a beautiful body, a bad temper, and direct speech inclines us to believe that she once lived beyond the poetic world as a flesh and blood mistress of an Augustan poet.[4]

Even the existence of Cynthia within a literary work appears to be explained away. Poem 1.8 creates the illusion that it constitutes a fragment of a real conversation. The persistent employment of the second-person pronoun, the punctuation of the text by questions and wishes that center on "you," turns the poem itself into an event. As we read, Cynthia is being implored to remain at Rome with her poet. Subsequently, we are told that this poetic act of persuasion has been successful:

> hanc ego non auro, non Indis flectere conchis,
>   sed potui blandi carminis obsequio.
> sunt igitur Musae, neque amanti tardus Apollo,
>   quis ego fretus amo: Cynthia rara mea est!

> Her I, not with gold, not with Indian pearls, could
>   turn, but with a caressing song's compliance.
> There are Muses then, and, for a lover, Apollo is not slow:
>   on these I relying love: rare Cynthia is mine! (1.8.39–42)[5]

Writing poetry, on this account, is only the instrument of an act of courtship. The text itself encourages us to overlook its status as an Augustan poetry-book and to search beyond it for the living mistress it seems to woo.

There are, however, some recognized dangers in responding to Propertian poetry in this way, for the apparently personal confession of a poet's love is permeated with literary concerns and expressed in highly stylized and conventional terms. Even the female figures of the elegiac corpus – Propertius's Cynthia, Tibullus's Delia and Nemesis, Ovid's Corinna – display highly artful features.[6] Thus, once we acknowledge that elegy's debt to poetic conventions and Hellenistic writing practices is so extensive as to include in its compass the depiction of elegy's heroines, we are forced to call into question any simple relation between elegiac representations and the realities of women's lives in Augustan Rome. But if the relation between representation and reality is not a simple one, what then is its nature?

In the last few decades one answer to this question has gained particular currency. The extreme biographical methodology of the nineteenth and early twentieth centuries – the search for close correspondences between the individual characters and events of the text and those of its author and his milieu – has long since been abandoned. Nor has the opposite view, that elegy's ladies are entirely artificial constructs, proved satisfactory; for, like the Platonic assessment of literary processes, the theory that Latin erotic discourse is modelled on Hellenistic literature, which is itself modelled on Hellenistic life, leaves Augustan poetry and its female subjects at several removes from reality. Recently, critics have preferred to seek accounts of the relation between representation and reality that accommodate the literariness of elegiac writing and yet keep elegy's written women placed firmly on the map of the Augustan world.

Poets, we are told, deal in "verbal artefacts," yet their poetry "adumbrates," "embodies," or "emblazons" life.[7] Love elegy, it is argued, is neither an open window affording glimpses of individual Roman lives, nor a mirror offering their clear reflection, but a *picture* of Roman realities over which has been painted a dignifying, idealizing veneer of poetic devices.[8] Idioms such as these form the ingredients of a critical discourse that does not treat elegiac poems as accurate, chronological documents of an author's affairs, but still describes their stylized heroines as somehow concealing specific Augustan girlfriends.[9] In the vocabulary of this revised critical language, Cynthia, and possibly Delia, are not the mirror images of living women, but their transposed reflections.

Thus the realism of the elegiac texts continues to tempt us. While reading of women who possess some realistic features, we may think that – once we make some allowances for the distortions that a male lover's perspective and a poet's self-conscious literary concerns may impose – we still have an opportunity to reconstruct the lives of some real Augustan mistresses. Controversy arises, however, when we ask exactly what allowances should be made. Is the process of relating women in poetic texts to women in society simply a matter of removing a veneer of poetic devices to disclose the true picture of living women concealed beneath?

It is precisely because readers of Cynthia have encountered such difficulties as these that I propose to explore aspects of the problematic

relations between women in texts and women in society by focusing on
the Propertian corpus of elegiac poems. My purpose is, first, to survey
approaches to the issue of elegiac realism and by placing renewed emphasis on Cynthia as a *written* woman to argue that she should be related
not to the love life of her poet but to the "grammar" of his poetry;
second, to demonstrate that the poetic discourse of which she forms a
part is firmly engaged with and shaped by the political, moral, and literary
discourses of the Augustan period, and therefore that to deny Cynthia an
existence outside poetry is not to deny her a relation to society; and,
third, to suggest that a study of elegiac metaphors and their application to
elegiac mistresses may provide a fruitful means of reassessing one particular set of relations between written and living women.

II.   Augustan Girl Friends/Elegiac Women

The first-person narratives of the elegiac texts and their partial realism
entice us. They lead us to suppose that these texts form poetic paintings
of reality and their female subjects poetic portraits of real women. Yet
realism itself is a quality of a text, not a direct manifestation of a "real"
world. Analysis of textual realism discloses that it is not natural but
conventional. To create the aesthetic effect of an open window onto a
"reality" lying just beyond, literary works employ a number of formal
strategies that change through time and between discourses.[10]
    As early as the 1950s, Archibald Allen drew attention to this disjunc-
tion between realism and reality in the production of Augustan elegy. He
noted that the realism of the Propertian corpus is partial since, for
example, it does not extend to the provision of a convincing chronology
for a supposedly extratextual affair. And, focusing on the issue of "sincerity," Allen argued that the ancient world was capable of drawing a
distinction that we should continue to observe, between a poet's art
and his life. From Catullus to Apuleius, ancient writers could claim that
poetry was distinct from its poet and ancient readers could construe
"sincere" expressions of personal passion as a function of poetic style.[11]
    More recently, Paul Veyne has pursued the idea that the *I* of ancient
poets belongs to a different order than do later "*Is*" and has suggested
that *ego* confers a naturalness on elegy that ancient readers would have
recognized as spurious. Exploring the quality of *ego* in elegy's narrative,
Veyne further argues that the ancient stylistic rules for "sincerity" observed in the Catullan corpus were scarcely obeyed in Augustan love
elegy. Full of traditional poetic conceits, literary games, mannerisms,

and inconsistencies, the texts themselves raise doubts about their potential as autobiography.[12]

Both these readings of elegiac first-person narratives warn us to be
cautious in equating a stylistic realism with Augustan reality. But what of
the particular realist devices used to depict women? Some modern critics
think, for example, that the elegiac texts do offer sufficient materials from
which to sketch the characteristics and habits of their authors' girlfriends
or, at the very least, contain scattered details that together make up
plausible portraits. From couplets of the Propertian corpus, John Sullivan
assembles a physique for Cynthia:

> She had a milk-and-roses complexion. Her long blonde hair was either
> over-elaborately groomed or else, in less guarded moments, it strayed over
> her forehead in disarray... Those attractive eyes were black. She was tall,
> with long slim fingers.[13]

Oliver Lyne adds credible psychological characteristics:

> We find a woman of fine artistic accomplishments who is also fond of the
> lower sympotic pleasures; superstitious, imperious, wilful, fearsome in
> temper – but plaintive if she chooses, or feels threatened; pleasurably
> passionate – again if she chooses. I could go on: Propertius provides a lot
> of detail, direct and circumstantial. But the point I simply want to make is
> that the figure who emerges is rounded and credible: a compelling "cour-
> tesan" amateur or professional.[14]

An ancient tradition seems to provide some justification for this process
of extracting plausible portraits of Augustan girlfriends out of the features
of elegiac poetry-books. Some two centuries after the production of
elegy's written women, in *Apologia* 10, Apuleius listed the "real"
names that he claimed lay behind the elegiac labels *Cynthia* and *Delia*.
Propertius, we are informed, hid his mistress Hostia behind *Cynthia* and
Tibullus had Plania in mind when he put *Delia* in verse. If we accept these
identifications then, however stylized, idealized, or mythicized the elegiac
women Cynthia and Delia may be, their titles are to be read as pseudonyms and their textual characteristics as reflections of the features of two
extratextual mistresses.[15]

There are, however, a number of problems that attach themselves
to this procedure, for the process of extricating real women from realist
techniques involves methodological inconsistencies. Beginning with
an ancient tradition that does not offer "real" names to substitute
for *Nemesis* or *Corinna*, the procedure is not uniformly applied. The

inappropriateness of attempting to assimilate Ovid's Corinna to a living woman is generally recognized. Because the text in which she appears easily reads as a playful travesty of earlier love elegy, most commentators would agree with the view that Corinna is not a poetic depiction of a particular person, but a generalized figure of the Mistress.[16]

As a poeticized girlfriend, a transposed reflection of reality, the second Tibullan heroine has likewise aroused suspicion. David Bright offers detailed support for an earlier reading of Nemesis "as a shadowy background for conventional motifs."[17] Nor does he find that this fictive Mistress is preceded by at least one poeticized girlfriend in the Tibullan corpus. The first Tibullan heroine, Delia, also seems to be entangled in elegy's literary concerns, as the characteristics of Nemesis in Tibullus's second poetry-book are counterbalanced by the characteristics of Delia in the first to produce a poetic polarity. Delia is goddess of Day, Nemesis daughter of Night.[18] Bright states: "The flexibility of fundamental characteristics and the meaning of the two names, indicates that Delia and Nemesis should be regarded as essentially literary creations."[19] Faced with such readings, we may want to ask whether Propertian realism is anchored any more securely to reality than that of Ovid and Tibullus. Does Cynthia offer a close link with a real woman only to be followed by a series of fictive females?

Realist portraits of a mistress do not seem to have so bold an outline, or so persistent a presence, in Propertian poetry as to guarantee for Cynthia a life beyond the elegiac world, because realism is not consistently employed in the corpus and sometimes is challenged or undermined by other narrative devices. Even in Propertius's first poetry-book the apparent confession of an author's love is not everywhere sustained. Poem 1.16, for example, interrupts the realistic use of a first-person narrative. At this point the narrative *I* ceases to be plausible because it is not identifible with an author and is voiced by a door. Poem 1.20 substitutes for expressions of personal passion the mythic tale of Hercules' tragic love for the boy Hylas. The poetry-book closes with the narrator establishing his identity (*qualis*) in terms not of a mistress but of the site of civil war.

The formal strategies that produce for us the sense of an Augustan reality and an extratextual affair are even less prominent or coherent in Propertius's second poetry-book. The *ego* often speaks without such apparently authenticating details as a location, an occasion, or a named addressee. The object of desire is not always specified and sometimes clearly excludes identification with Cynthia.[20] The margins of the poetry-book and its core are peopled by patrons and poets or take for their landscape the Greek mountains and brooks of poetic inspiration. At these points, the text's evident concern is not to delineate a mistress but to define its author's poetic practice.[21]

By the third and fourth poetry-books a realistically depicted, individuated mistress has ceased to be a narrative focus of Propertian elegy. The third poetry-book claims as its inspiration not a girlfriend but another poet. Callimachus has replaced Cynthia as the motivating force for poetic production. The title *Cynthia* appears only as the text looks back at the initial poems of the corpus and draws Cynthia-centered erotic discourse to an apparent close. Far more frequently the first-person authorial narrator speaks of love without specifying a beloved, and poetic eroticism takes on a less personal mode.

In the fourth book there is not even a consistent lover's perspective. Several poems are concerned with new themes, such as the aetiology of *Roma*, rather than the motivations for *amor*. And the narrative *I* fluctuates between a reassuring authorial viewpoint and the implausible voices of a statue, a solider's wife, and a dead *matrona*. When the more familiar mistress appears, the sequence of poems does not follow a realistic chronology but moves from the stratagems of a dead Cynthia who haunts the underworld (4.7) to those of a living Cynthia who raids a dinner party (4.8).[22]

These inconsistencies and developments in the Propertian mode of incorporating a mistress into elegiac discourse cannot be imputed merely to an author's unhappy experiences in love – to Propertius's progressive disillusionment with a Hostia – for each of the poetry-books and their Cynthias seem to be responding to changes in the public world of writing. The general shift from personal confessions of love toward more impersonal histories of Rome may be determined partially by changes in the material processes of patronage in the Augustan era, from the gradual establishment of Maecenas's circle through to the unmediated patronage of the *princeps*,[23] and the particular character of individual poetry-books by the progressive publication of other poetic discourses such as Tibullan elegy, Horatian lyric, and Virgilian epic.[24] But are the individual, realistically depicted Cynthias of the Propertian corpus then immune from such influences?

Literary concerns permeate even the activities and habits of the Cynthias who appear in the first two books. Poem 1.8, for example, implores its Cynthia not to depart for foreign climes and asks: *tu pedibus teneris positas fulcire pruinas,/ tu potes insolitas, Cynthia, ferre nives?* ("Can you on delicate feet support settled frost? Can you Cynthia, strange, snows endure?" 1.8.7–8) The Gallan character of this, Cynthia, and the trip from which she is dissuaded, is well known. In Virgil's tenth *Eclogue*, attention already had been focused on the laments of the earlier elegiac poet over the absence of another snow-bound elegiac mistress. Propertius caps the Virgilian Gallus, in the field of erotic writing, by contrasting his ultimately loyal Cynthia with the faithless Lycoris.[25] Cynthia's delicate feet both recall and surpass the *teneras plantas* of the wandering Lycoris (*Ecl.* 10.49). Simultaneously, they give her a realizable shape and mark a new place in the Roman tradition for written mistresses.

Similarly, it has been observed that the disturbing narrative techniques of the second book – its discursiveness, parentheses, and abrupt transitions – constitute a response to the publication of Tibullus's first elegiac book.[26] And the process of transforming Propertian elegy in response to another erotic discourse again extends to realist depictions of the elegiac beloved. Poem 2.19 presents a Tibullanized Cynthia, closer in kind to the images of Delia in the countryside than to the first formulation of Cynthia in the *Monobiblos*:

> etsi me inuito discedis, Cynthia, Roma,
>   laetor quod sine me devia rura coles...
> sola eris et solos spectabis, Cynthia, montis
>   et pecus et finis pauperis agricolae.

> Even though against my will you leave, Cynthia, Rome,
> I'm glad that without me you'll cultivate wayward fields...
> Alone you'll be and the lonely mountains, Cynthia, you'll watch
> and the sheep and the borders of the poor farmer. (2.19.1–2, 7–8)

Tibullus began his fanciful sketch of a countrified mistress – the guardian (*custos*) of a country estate – with the words *rura colam* (1.5.21). So here *rura coles* begins Cynthia's departure from the generally urban terrain of Propertian discourse. The apparently realistic reference to Cynthia's country visit contains within its terms a challenge to the textual characteristics of a rustic Delia.

The Cynthias of the third and fourth books also disclose the influence of recently published literary works. The third Propertian poetry-book initiates an occasionally playful accommodation of Horatian lyric within erotic elegy. This literary challenge is articulated not only through the enlargement of poetic themes to include social commentary and the elevation of the poet to the rank of priest,[27] but also through the alteration of the elegiac mistress's physique.

The book opens with an erotic twist to the Horatian claim that poetry is an everlasting monument to the poet. For, at 3.2.17–24, Propertian poetry is said to immortalize female beauty (*forma*).[28] The book closes appropriately with the dissolution of that monument to beauty and the threatened construction of one to ugliness:

> exclusa inque uicem fastus patiare superbos,
>   et quae fecisti facta queraris anus!
> has tibi fatalis cecinit mea pagina diras:
>   euentum formae disce timere tuae!

> Shut out in turn – may you suffer arrogant contempt,
>   and of deeds which you've done may you complain –
>   an old hag!
> These curses deadly for you my page has sung:
>   the outcome of your beauty learn to fear! (3.25.15–18)

The threatened transformation of Cynthia on the page from beauty to hag – the dissolution of the familiar elegiac edifice – mirrors similar predictions made about the Horatian Lydia in *Odes* 1.25.9–10.[29]

The two Cynthias of the fourth book take on Homeric rather than Horatian shapes. Although multiple literary influences on the features of these Cynthias may be noted – such as comedy, aetiology, tragedy, epigram, and mime – their pairing takes up the literary challenge recently issued by Virgil. Just as the Virgilian epic narrative conflates an Odyssean and an Iliadic hero in the character of Aeneas, so the Propertian elegiac narrative constructs a Cynthia who becomes first an Iliadic Patroclus returning from the grave (4.7) and then a vengeful Odysseus returning from the war (4.8).

In the last book of the Propertian corpus, the precarious status of realism is put on display. Whole incidents in the lives of a poet and his mistress now reproduce the plots of the Homeric poems, while their details echo passages of the *Aeneid*. In poem 4.7, the first-person authorial narrator recalls the occasion on which he had a vision of his dead mistress. Her reproaches are replete with apparently authenticating incidentals such as a busy red light district of Rome, worn-down windows, warming cloaks, branded slaves, ex-prostitutes, and wool work. But the ghost's arrival and departure, her appearance, and her reproofs sustain persistent links with the heroic world of *Iliad* 23 and the general conventions of epic discourse on visions of the dead. Similarly, in poem 4.8, the first-person narrator recalls the night when Cynthia caught him in the company of other women. The narrative of that night is also littered with apparently authenticating details such as the setting on the Esquiline, local girls, a dwarf, dice, a slave cowering behind a couch, and orders not to stroll in Pompey's portico. But Cynthia's sudden return finds her playing the role of an Odysseus to her poet's aberrant Penelope. Echoes of *Odyssey* 22 dissolve the poetic edifice of a real Roman event.[30]

When critics attempt to provide a plausible portrait of Cynthia, they must undertake an active process of building a rounded and consistent character out of physical and psychological characteristics that are scattered throughout the corpus and are often fragmentary, sometimes contradictory, and usually entangled in mythological and highly literary lore. But the discovery of Gallan, Tibullan, Horatian, and Virgilian Cynthias in the Propertian corpus argues against the helpfulness of this process. The strategies employed in the construction of a realistic mistress appear to change according to the requirements of a poetic project that commences in rivalry with the elegists Gallus and Tibullus and ends in appropriation of the terms of Horatian lyric and Virgilian epic.

It is misleading, therefore, to disengage the textual features of an elegiac mistress from their context in a poetry-book, so as to reshape them into the plausible portrait of an Augustan girlfriend, for even the physical features, psychological characteristics, direct speeches, and erotic activities with which Cynthia is provided often seem subject to literary concerns. Thus the realist devices of the Propertian corpus map out only a precarious pathway to the realities of women's lives in Augustan society and often direct us instead toward the features and habits of characters in other Augustan texts.

The repetition of the title *Cynthia* through the course of the Propertian poetry-books may still create the impression of a series of poems about one consistent female figure.[31] Does support remain, then, for a direct link between Cynthia and a Roman woman in the ancient tradition that *Cynthia* operates in elegy as a pseudonym for a living mistress Hostia?

On entry into the Propertian corpus, the epithet *Cynthia* brings with it a history as the marker of a poetic programme. Mount Cynthus on Delos had been linked with Apollo as the mouthpiece of a poetic creed by the Hellenistic poet Callimachus. That association was reproduced in Virgil's sixth *Eclogue* where the god directing Virgilian discourse away from epic material was given the cult title *Cynthius*.[32] The Propertian text itself draws attention to that history at, for example, the close of the second poetry-book where in the course of poem 2.34, Callimachus, Virgil, Cynthius, and Cynthia are all associated with writing-styles. First, Callimachean elegy is suggested as a suitable model for poetic production (2.34.31–32); then, in a direct address to Virgil, *Cynthius* is employed as the epithet of a god with whose artistry the works of Virgil are explicitly compared: *tale facis carmen docta testudine quale / Cynthius impositis temperat articulis* ("Such song you make, on the learned lyre, as/ Cynthius with applied fingers controls," 2.34.79–80). Finally, a reference to *Cynthia* closes the poem and its catalogue of the male authors and female subjects of earlier Latin love poetry: *Cynthia quin etiam uersu laudata Properti –/ hos inter si me ponere Fama uolet* ("Cynthia also praised in verse of Propertius –/ if among these men Fame shall wish to place me," 2.34.93–94).

The alignment within a single poem of Callimachus, Virgil, Cynthius, and Cynthia constructs for Propertian elegy and its elegiac mistress a literary ancestry. The title *Cynthia* may be read as a term in the statement of a poetics, as a proper name for the erotic embodiment of a particular poetic creed. In a corpus of poems that frequently voices a preference for elegiac over epic styles of writing that use a critical discourse inherited from Callimachus and developed in Virgil's *Eclogues*,[33] the title *Cynthia* contributes significantly to the expression of literary concerns.[34]

The name of the elegiac mistress does not offer us a route out of a literary world to the realities of women's lives at Rome. But, as with her other apparently plausible features, her name is inextricably entangled in issues of poetic practice. Any attempt to read through the name *Cynthia* to a living mistress, therefore, overlooks its place in the "grammar" of elegiac poetry where *Propertius* and *Cynthia* do not perform the same semantic operations. In the language of elegy, a poet generates a different range and level of connotation than his mistress.

The issue of the elegiac mistress's social status further elucidates the peculiar role women play in the poetic language of Augustan love poetry; for, when attempts have been made to reconstruct a real girlfriend out of Cynthia's features, no clear clues have been found in the poems to the social status of a living mistress and conclusions have ranged from Roman wife[35] to foreign prostitute,[36] or the evident textual ambiguities have been read as reflections of the fluidity of social status to be expected within an Augustan *demi-monde*.[37]

In Propertius 2.7, for example, the narrator describes his mistress as having rejoiced at the removal of a law which would have separated the lovers. He declares that he prefers death to marriage:

> nam citius paterer caput hoc discedere collo
> quam possem nuptae perdere more faces,
> aut ego transirem tua limina clausa maritus,
> respiciens udis prodita luminibus.[38]

> For faster would I suffer this head and neck to part
>   than be able at a bride's humor to squander torches,
> or myself a husband pass your shut doors,
>   looking back at their betrayal with moist eyes. (2.7.7–10)

And he rejects his civic duty to produce children who would then participate in Augustus Caesar's wars: *unde mihi Parthis natos praebere triumphis?/ nullus de nostro sanguine miles erit* ("From what cause for Parthian triumphs to offer my sons?/ None from my blood will be a soldier," 2.7.13–14). Here, if nowhere else in Augustan elegy, we might expect to find a clearly defined social status allocated to the elegiac mistress, because, at this point in the elegiac corpus, the text seems to be directly challenging legal constraints on sexual behaviour.

Nevertheless, even when the elegiac narrative takes as its central focus a legislative issue, no clear social position is allocated to Cynthia. We learn instead that men and women play different semantic roles in this poetic discourse. The female is employed in the text only as a means to defining the male. Her social status is not clearly defined because the dominating perspective is that of the male narrator. What matters is his social and political position as a man who in having a mistress refuses to be a *maritus* or the father of *milites*.[39]

What this analysis of elegiac realism seems to reveal is that the notion of *concealment* – the idea that the stylized heroines of elegy somehow conceal the identities of specific Augustan girlfriends – is not a helpful term in critical discourse on elegiac women. Perhaps Apuleius's identification of Cynthia with a Hostia is suspect, since it forms part of a theatrical self-defence and should be read in the light of a long-standing interest in biographical speculation. (We do not now accept, for example, Apuleius's identification of Corydon with Virgil or of Alexis with a slave boy of Pollio.[40]) But the point is that, whether or not a Hostia existed who was associated with Propertius, the Cynthia of our text is part of no simple act of concealment.

While the combination of realist techniques and parodic strategies in the Ovidian corpus is thought to deny Corinna any reality, the realist strategies of the Propertian corpus have been isolated from other narrative techniques and left largely unexplored in order to secure for Cynthia an existence outside the text in which we meet her. But I have argued that, however, even the realist devices of Propertian elegy can disclose the unreality of elegiac mistresses. Cynthia too is a poetic fiction: a woman in a text, whose physique, temperament, name, and status are all subject to the idiom of that text. So, as part of a poetic language of love, Cynthia should not be related to the love life of her poet but to the "grammar" of his poetry.

The Propertian elegiac narrative does not, then, celebrate a Hostia, but creates a fictive female whose minimally defined status as mistress, physical characteristics, and name are all determined by the grammar of the erotic discourse in which she appears. The employment of terms like "pseudonym" in modern critical discourse overlooks the positive act of creation involved in the depiction of elegy's mistresses.[41] Therefore, when reading Augustan elegy, it seems most appropriate to talk not of pseudonyms and poeticized girlfriends but of poetic or elegiac women.

III. Metaphors

So the bond between elegiac women and particular Augustan girlfriends has proved to be very fragile. The realistic features of elegy's heroines seem to owe a greater debt to poetic programmes than to the realities of female forms. But if we deny to Cynthia an existence outside poetry, are we also denying her any relation to society? If elegiac narratives are concerned with fictive females, how do women enter their discourse? What relation might still hold between women in Augustan society and women in its poetic texts? And what function could a realistically depicted yet fictive mistress serve in elegy's aesthetics?

A possible approach to some of these questions has already been suggested, as I have argued that the characteristics of elegiac women are determined by the general idioms of the elegiac discourse of which they form a part and that Cynthia should be read as firmly shaped by the Propertian poetic project. But elegiac discourses and poetic projects are, in turn, firmly engaged with and shaped by the political, moral, and aesthetic discourses of the Augustan period. And so it is through the relation of elegiac narratives to all the other cultural discourses of the specific period in which they were produced that we can at last see a more secure fit between women in elegiac texts and women in Augustan society.

A. Cultural discourses

The general idioms peculiar to elegiac writing have been as intriguing to the reader as the specific attributes provided for women at various points in the elegiac corpus, for they seem to be offering a challenging new role for the female, a poetic break away from the traditional duties of marriage and motherhood.

First of all, features of the elegiac vocabulary seem to overturn the traditional Roman discourses of sexuality. In the poetic texts the elegiac hero is frequently portrayed as sexually loyal while his mistress is not.[42] The Propertian lover protests: *tu mihi sola places: placeam tibi, Cynthia, solus* ("You alone please me: may I alone please you, Cynthia," 2.7.19). He desires as the wording on his epitaph: *unius hic quondam seruus amoris erat* ("Of a single love this man once was the slave," 2.13.36). Now this elegiac expectation of eternal male faithfulness, according to one analysis, "spurns the double standard characterizing Roman male-female relationships" because traditionally, extramarital sex was acceptable for husbands while their wives were legally required to uphold the principle of *fides marita*.[43] It was the ideal of a woman's faithfulness to one man that was most frequently expressed on Roman epitaphs and, furthermore, it was expressed in the same terms as the elegiac ideal: *solo contenta marito, uno contenta marito* ("content with her husband alone," "content with but one husband").[44]

Another feature commonly cited as evidence for an elegiac transformation of traditional sexual roles is the application of the *seruitium amoris* metaphor to a heterosexual liaison.[45] A parallel for the *topos* of the lover-as-enslaver can be found in Hellenistic erotic writing, but Augustan elegy's casting of the female in the dominant sexual role seems to work against the operations of other Roman sexual discourses. The Propertian narrator asks: *quid mirare, meam si uersat femina uitam/ et trahit addictum sub sua iura uirum?* ("Why are you surprised, if my life a woman directs/ and drags bound under her own laws a man?", 3.11.1–2).

The male narrator is portrayed as enslaved, the female narrative subject as his enslaver. The Tibullan lover, for example, says farewell to his freedom: *hic mihi seruitium uideo dominamque paratam:/ iam mihi, libertas illa paterna, uale* ("Here for me I see slavery and a mistress at the ready:/ now from me, that fathers' freedom, adieu," 2.4.1–2). Thus the control of household slaves, a woman's version of the economic status of a *dominus*, has been transformed figuratively into the erotic condition of control over sexual slaves. The sexual domain of the elegiac *domina* contrasts with that traditionally prescribed for Roman wives, namely, keeping house and working wool.[46]

A third significant feature of this poetic discourse is the declaration that the pursuit of love and poetry is a worthy alternative to more traditional equestrian careers. This elegiac declaration is best known in its formulation as the *militia amoris* metaphor.[47] The elegiac hero is portrayed as already enlisted in a kind of military service, battling with love or his beloved. The Propertian narrator receives the following instructions:

> at tu finge elegos, fallax opus: haec tua castra! –
>   scribat ut exemplo cetera turba tuo.
> militiam Veneris blandis patiere sub armis,
>   et Veneris pueris utilis hostis eris.
> nam tibi uictrices quascumque labore parasti,
>   eludit palmas una puella tuas.

> But you, devise elegies, a tricky task: this is your camp! –
>   That they, the remaining crowd, write at your example.
> The warfare of Venus you'll endure under alluring weapons
>   and to Venus's boys a profitable enemy you'll be.
> Because for you whatever Victorias your effort's procured,
>   escapes your awards one girl. (4.1.135–40)

Similarly an Ovidian poem entirely dedicated to the exploration of the metaphor of *militia* begins: *militat omnis amans, et habet sua castra Cupido* ("Every lover soldiers, and Cupid has his own barracks," *Am.* 1.9.1).

Augustan elegy represents its hero as faithful to his usually disloyal mistress, and as engaged metaphorically in either sexual servitude or erotic battles. But the unconventional sexual role bestowed, through poetic metaphor, on the elegiac male seems to implicate the elegiac female in equally unconventional behaviour: he slights the responsibilities of being citizen and soldier, while she operates outside the conventional roles of wife and mother.

So, if specific features of the elegiac mistresses do not seem to reflect the realities of particular women's lives, might not the general idioms employed about them nevertheless reflect general conditions for the female in Augustan society? Is the elegiac woman unconventional because there are now some unconventional women in the world?

Once again, the elegiac texts tempt us: if, as Georg Luck has argued, "the woman's role in the Roman society of the first century BC explains to a large extent the unique character of the love poetry of that period,"[48] then elegy would be invested with a social dimension of substantial interest to the student of women in antiquity. The mistresses stylized in elegy might then constitute poetic representatives of a whole movement of sexually liberated ladies and may be read as "symbolic of the new freedom for women in Rome's social life in the first century B.C."[49]

To establish such a connection between elegiac mistresses and Augustan women it is first necessary to find parallel portraits of the female outside the poetic sphere. If external evidence can be found for the gradual emergence of a breed of "emancipated" women, then it might be possible to argue that such women *provoked* elegiac production.

Sallust's description of an unconventional Sempronia provides the most frequently cited historical parallel for the elegiac heroines:

> litteris Graecis et Latinis docta, psallere, saltare elegantius quam necesse est probae, multa alia, quae instrumenta luxuriae sunt. Sed ei cariora semper omnia quam decus atque pudicitia fuit;...lubido sic accensa ut saepius peteret uiros quam peteretur.

> Well educated in Greek and Latin literature, she had greater skill in lyre-playing and dancing than there is any need for a respectable woman to acquire, besides many other accomplishments such as minister to dissipation. There was nothing that she set a smaller value on than seemliness and chastity... Her passions were so ardent that she more often made advances to men than they did to her.[50]

Similarly, the Clodia Metelli who appears in Cicero's forensic speech *pro Caelio* is often adduced as an example of the kind of emancipated woman with whom Roman poets fell in love in the first century BC and about whom (thus inspired) they composed erotic verse. The early identification of Clodia Metelli with Catullus's *Lesbia* seems to strengthen such a link between living and written women and to bind the habits of a late Republican noblewoman – as evidenced by Cicero's *pro Caelio* – to poetic depictions of a mistress in the Catullan corpus.[51]

But the process of matching love poetry's heroines with a new breed of "emancipated" women raises methodological problems. Sallust's Sempronia and Cicero's Clodia have often been employed as evidence for the phenomenon of the New Woman – as elegy's historical twin is sometimes called.[52] It is important to observe that, even outside the poetic sphere, our principal evidence for the lives of ancient women is still on the level of representations, not realities. We encounter not real women, but representations shaped by the conventions of wall-paintings, tombstones, and, most frequently, texts. Any comparison between elegiac women and emancipated ladies tends, therefore, to be a comparison between two forms of discourse about the female.

Sempronia and Clodia are both to be found in texts. And as written women, they are – like their elegiac sisters – no accurate reflection of particular female lives. Sallust's Sempronia is written into a particular form of literary discourse, for, in the context of his historical monograph, she is structured as a female counterpart to Catiline.[53] Her features also belong to a larger historiographic tradition in which the decline of Roman *uirtus* and the rise of *luxuria* are commonly associated with aberrant female sexuality. Sempronia's qualities contradict the norms for a *matrona*. She is whorish because a whore embodies degeneracy and thus discredits the Catilinarian conspiracy.[54]

Clodia is also written into a text. The villainous features of this prosecution witness are put together from the stock characteristics of the comic *meretrix* and the tragic Medea. Cicero's Clodia is a *proterua meretrix procaxque* (*pro Cael.* 49) because sexual promiscuity was a long-standing *topos* in the invective tradition against women. As part of a forensic discourse, the sexually active woman is designed to sway a jury. The rapaciousness of this supposedly injured party turns the young, male defendant into a victim and her sexual guilt thus underscores his innocence.[55]

When attempting to reconstruct the lives of ancient women from textual materials, some critics have drawn upon a kind of hierarchy of discourses graded according to their usefulness as evidence. Marilyn Skinner, for example, argues that Cicero's letters offer a less tendentious version of Clodia Metelli than does his oratory. And the Clodia she recuperates from that source is one concerned not with sexual debauchery, but with the political activities of her brother and husband and with property management.[56] Perhaps this picture of a wealthy, public woman is a better guide to the new opportunities of the first century B.C., but it is not the picture of female behavior that Augustan elegy paints. The term *domina* could identify a woman of property, an owner of household slaves. But within the discourse of Augustan elegy, it takes on an erotic, not an economic, significance. The female subject that the poetic narrative constructs is not an independent woman of property but one dependent on men for gifts: *Cynthia non sequitur fascis nec curat honores,/ semper amatorum ponderat una sinus* ("Cynthia doesn't pursue power or care for glory,/ always her lovers' pockets she only weighs," 2.16.11–12). Augustan elegy, then, does not seem to be a response to the lives of particular emancipated women, but another manifestation of a particular patterning of female sexuality to be found in the cultural discourses of Rome.

Now Rome was essentially a patriarchal society sustained by a familial ideology. The basic Roman social unit was the *familia* whose head was the father (*pater*): "a woman, even if legally independent, socially and politically had no function in Roman society in the way that a man, as actual or potential head of a *familia*, did."[57] Consequently, in the

conceptual framework of Roman society, female sexuality takes on positive value only when ordered in terms that will be socially effective for
patriarchy. Sexually unrestrained women are marginalized. Displaced
from a central position in cultural categories, they are associated with
social disruption.

Using the Ciceronian Clodia as her starting-point, Mary Lefkowitz has
documented the prevalence of this way of structuring femininity in
antiquity. Praise or blame of women, Lefkowitz argues, is customarily
articulated with reference to their biological role, assigned according to
their conformity with male norms for female behaviour. The good
woman is lauded for her chastity, her fertility, her loyalty to her husband,
and her selfless concern for others. The bad woman is constantly vilified
for her faithlessness, her inattentiveness to household duties, and her
selfish disregard for others.[58]

A notable example of this polarization of women into the chaste and
the depraved occurs at the beginning of the Principate: "In the propaganda which represented Octavian's war with Antony as a crusade, it was
convenient to depict [Octavia] as a deeply wronged woman, the chaste
Roman foil of the voluptuous foreigner Cleopatra."[59]

This patterning of discourses about the female can be grounded in
history. A figure like Sempronia was not articulated in Roman texts before
the middle of the second century B.C., after Rome's rise to empire –
and its consequent wealth and Hellenization – had brought with it
significant social and cultural change.[60] From this period there began a
proliferation of moral discourses associating female sexual misconduct
with social and political disorder. And by the first century BC childless-
ness, procreation, marriage, and adultery were appearing regularly as
subjects for social concern in the texts of writers such as Cicero, Sallust,
Horace, and Livy.[61]

So persuasive have these discourses on the female been that they have
often been taken for truth. Many of the histories on which elegy's
commentators once relied for reconstructions of Rome's New Woman
invested their accounts of changes in women's social position with elements of moral turpitude transferred wholesale from the writings of the
Roman moralists. For example, the *Cambridge Ancient History* claimed
that "by the last century of the Republic, females had in practice obtained
their independence, and nothing but social convention and a sense of
responsibility barred the way to a dangerous exploitation of their privilege."[62] Similarly, Balsdon's *Roman Women* stated emphatically: "Women
emancipated themselves. They acquired liberty, then with the late Republic and the Empire they enjoyed unrestrained licence."[63] Thus in the

ready association of liberty with licence, the strictures of Roman moralists were turned into the realities of Republican lives.[64]

One particular form of discourse about female sexuality had considerable and significant currency during the period in which elegiac eroticism was produced. From 18 BC on, legislation began to appear that criminalized adultery and offered inducements to reproduce. But the production of elegy's female figures cannot be read as a direct poetic protest against this social legislation, although it appears to be the subject of one Propertian poem:

> gauisa est certe sublatam Cynthia legem,
>   qua quondam edicta flemus uterque diu,
> ni nos diuideret.

> She was delighted for sure at the law's removal – Cynthia –
>   over whose publication once we both cried long,
> in case it should part us. (2.7.1–3)

Since the tradition of erotic writing to which the Propertian Cynthia belongs stretched back at least as far as the Gallan corpus, the earliest examples of the elegiac mistress considerably predate the legislation.[65] But the appearance of the Augustan domestic legislation from 18 BC demonstrates that the discourses about female sexuality with which elegy was already engaged were now being institutionalized. Female sexual practice was now enshrined in law as a problematic issue with which the whole state should be concerned.[66]

Augustan elegy and its mistresses constitute, therefore, a response to, and a part of, a multiplication of discourses about, the female, which occurred in the late Republic and earlier Empire. Similarly, in his first volume on the history of sexuality, Michel Foucault demonstrates that, when "population" emerged as an economic and political problem in the eighteenth century, "between the state and the individual, sex became an issue, and a public issue no less: a whole web of discourses, special knowledges, analyses, and injunctions settled upon it."[67] In the first century BC, at a time when female sexuality was seen as a highly problematic and public concern, the poetic depiction of the elegiac hero's subjection to a mistress would have carried a wide range of social and political connotations. And the elegiac mistress, in particular, would have brought to her poetic discourse a considerable potential as metaphor for danger and social disruption.

B. Metaphoric mistresses

A brief outline of the operations of realism and of metaphor in Augustan elegy discloses that elegy's mistresses do not enter literary language reflecting the realities of women's lives at Rome. An examination of their characteristics reveals that they are fictive females engaged with at least two broad – but not necessarily distinct – categories of discourse. Shaped by developments in the production of literary texts and in the social construction of female sexuality, they possess potential as metaphors for both poetic projects and political order.

The second of these two categories will be further explored in the remainder of this article; for it is the range of connotations that the elegiac mistress gains as a result of her association with the erotic metaphors of *seruitium* and *militia*, rather than those arising from her identification with the Muse and the practice of writing elegy, that may most intrigue the student of women in antiquity.[68] Amy Richlin argues that on entry into a variety of Rome's poetic and prose genres such as invective and satire, the ordering of female sexuality is determined by the central narrative viewpoint which is that of a sexually active, adult male.[69] So, in depicting their hero as subject to and in the service of a sexually unrestrained mistress, do the elegiac texts offer any challenging new role for the female, or for the male alone?

Some critics have made much of the boldness of appropriating the term *laus* for the erotic sphere and *fides* for male sexual behaviour, but their descriptions of such strategies are seriously misleading. The Propertian narrator declares: *laus in amore mori: laus altera, si datur uno/ posse frui: fruar o solus amore meo!* ("Glorious in love to die: glorious again, if granted one love/ to enjoy: o may I enjoy alone my love!", 2.1.47–48). Both Judith Hallett and Margaret Hubbard, for example, frequently refer to such material as involving a bold reversal or inversion of sex roles – the elegiac hero sheds male public virtues and takes on the female domestic virtue of sexual loyalty.[70] Such terminology suggests, erroneously, that in elegiac poetry the female subject gains a position of social responsibility at the same time as it is removed from the male.

But it is not the concern of elegiac poetry to upgrade the political position of women, only to portray the male narrator as alienated from positions of power and to differentiate him from other, socially responsible male types. For example, in the same poem of Propertius's second book, the narrator's erotic battles are contrasted with the activities of the *nauita*, the *arator*, the *miles*, and the *pastor*, without any reference to a female partner:

> nauita de uentis, de tauris narrat arator,
>   enumerat miles uulnera, pastor ouis;
> nos contra angusto uersantes proelia lecto:
>   qua pote quisque, in ea conterat arte diem.

> The sailor tells of winds, of bulls the farmer,
>   numbers the soldier his wounds, the shepherd his flock;
> we instead turning battles on a narrow bed:
>   in what each can, in that art let him wear down the day. (2.1.43–46)

Similarly, in the first poetry-book the Propertian lover expresses, in the abstract terms of an erotic militancy, his difference from the soldier Tullus (1.6.19–36).

Furthermore, the elegiac texts take little interest in elaborating their metaphors in terms of female power but explore, rather, the concept of male dependency. The elegiac mistress may possess a camp in which her lover parades (Prop. 2.7.15–16) or choose her lovers like a general chooses his soldiers (*Am.* 1.9.5–6), but generally the elegiac metaphors are more generally concerned with male servitude not female mastery, and with male military service not female generalship. In *Amores* 1.2 it is Cupid who leads a triumphal procession of captive lovers, not the Ovidian mistress, and in *Amores* 1.9 it is the equation *miles/amans* not *domina/dux* that receives the fullest treatment.

The metaphors of *servitium* and *militia amoris* thus disclose the ideological repercussions for a man of association with a realistically depicted mistress. In a society that depended on a slave mode of production and in which citizenship carried the obligation of military service, these two metaphors define the elegiac male as socially irresponsible. As a slave to love he is precluded from participating in the customary occupations of male citizens. As a soldier of love he is not available to fight military campaigns.

The heterodoxy of the elegiac portrayal of love, therefore, lies in the absence of a political or social role for the male narrator, not in any attempt to provide or demand a political role for the female subject. The temporary alignment with a sexually unrestrained mistress that Augustan elegy depicts does not bestow on the female a new, challenging role but alienates the male from his traditional responsibilities. The elegiac poets exploit the traditional methods of ordering female sexuality which locate the sexually unrestrained and therefore socially ineffective female on the margins of society, in order to portray their first-person heroes as displaced from a central position in the social categories of Augustan Rome. And, moreover, they evaluate that displacement in conventional terms. At the beginning of the second book of the *Amores*, the poet is introduced as *ille ego nequitiae Naso poeta meae* ("I, Naso, that poet of my own depravity," 2.1.2) and in the Propertian corpus the lover and poet of Cynthia is also associated with the scandal of *nequitia* ("vice" or "depravity," 1.6.26 and 2.24.6). Thus, the poetic depiction of subjection to a mistress is aligned, in a conventional moral framework, with depravity.

Finally, despite claims of eternal devotion, none of the elegiac poets maintain this pose consistently or indefinitely. At the end of the third poetry-book, the Propertian lover repudiates his heroine and describes himself as restored to Good Sense (*Mens Bona*). At the end of his first poetry-book, the Tibullan hero finds himself dragged off to war. And, toward the end of the *Amores*, the appearance of a *coniunx* on the elegiac scene disrupts the dramatic pretence that the narrator is a romantic lover involved in an obsessive and exclusive relationship.[71]

IV. Conclusion

The purpose of this article has been to suggest that, when looking at the relations between women in Augustan elegy and women in Augustan society, we should not describe the literary image of a mistress as a kind of poetic painting whose surface we can remove to reveal a real Roman woman hidden underneath. Instead, an exploration of the idioms of realism and metaphor has demonstrated that elegiac mistresses are inextricably entangled in and shaped by a whole range of discourses, which bestow on them a potential as metaphors for the poetic projects and political interests of their authors.

I hope that such an analysis proves not the conclusion of, but only the starting-point for, a critical study of elegy's heroines and their constructive power as metaphors for poetic and political concerns. But one aspect of this analysis may still seem unsatisfactory or unsatisfying, for it seems to offer no adequate place for living Augustan women in the production of elegiac poetry. Further questions confront us. How did women read or even write such male-oriented verse? Would a female reader be drawn into the male narrative perspective? And how did a female writer, such as Sulpicia, construct her *ego* and its male beloved? In such a context, would the erotic metaphors of *seruitium* and *militia* be appropriate or have the same range of connotative power?

NOTES

1 See, for example, the comments of Foley in her preface to *Reflections of Women in Antiquity*(1981), and the articles of Skinner and Culham in *Helios* (1986).
2 The bias in favour of Greek material is observed by Fantham (1986), 5–6.
3 Hallett (1973), 103–24, and (1974), 211–17; Betensky (1973), 267–69, and (1974), 217–19.
4 See Wyke (1987a), 47.
5 Quotations from the elegiac corpus follow the most recent editions of the Oxford Classical Texts.
6 For the problematic artifice of Augustan poetry see Griffin (1985), ix. On the genre of personal love elegy see Du Quesnay (1973), 1–2.
7 Lyne (1980), viii and *passim*.
8 The idiom belongs to Griffin (1985), for example, 105.
9 See, for example, Williams (1968), 542.
10 A classic exposition of the disjunction between textual realism and reality and a detailed exploration of the strategies of nineteenth-century French realist writing can be found in Barthes' *S/Z* (1975). For the importance of this work see Hawkes (1977), 106–22.
11 Allen (1950), 145–60.
12 Veyne (1983).
13 Sullivan (1976), 80.
14 Lyne (1980), 62.
15 For Cynthia and Delia as pseudonyms, see, for example, Williams (1968), 526–42.
16 Bright (1978), 104. Cf. Wyke (1989), but contrast McKeown (1987), 19–24.
17 Williams (1968), 537.
18 Bright (1978), 99–123.
19 Ibid., 123.
20 See Veyne (1983), 67 and 71, and Papanghelis (1987), 93–97.
21 Wyke (1987a).
22 For the narrative techniques of Books 3 and 4 see Wyke (1987b), 153–78.
23 See, for example, Stahl (1985).
24 See, for example, Hubbard (1974).
25 For a convenient summary of views on this literary relationship, see Fedeli (1980), 203–5 and 211.
26 For example, Hubbard (1974), 57–58, and Lyne (1980), 132.
27 See, for example, Nethercut (1970), 385–407.
28 For the comparison with *Odes* 3.30.1–7, see Nethercut (1970), 387, and Fedeli (1985), 90.
29 Fedeli (1985), 674 and 692–93.

30 For references to the extensive literature on these two poems, see Wyke
    (1987b), 168–70, and Papanghelis (1987), 145–98.
31 Cf. Veyne (1983), 60 on *Delia*.
32 See Clausen (1976), 245–47, and Boyancé (1956), 172–75.
33 See, for example, Wimmel (1960).
34 For the intimate association of Cynthia and Callimachus in the Propertian
    corpus, see Wyke (1987a).
35 Williams (1968), 529–35.
36 Cairns (1972), 156–57.
37 Griffin (1985), 27–28.
38 The interpretation of verse 8 is open to much dispute.
39 See especially Veyne (1983), who argues that it is sufficient for elegy's
    purposes to locate its *ego* "chez les marginales."
40 See, for example, Fairweather (1974), 232–36.
41 Bright (1978), 103–04.
42 For references to male faithfulness in the elegiac corpus, see Lilja (1965),
    172–86, and Lyne (1980), 65–67.
43 Hallett (1973), 111; cf. ibid., 106.
44 *Carm. Epigr.* 455 and 643.5, for which see Williams (1958), 23–25.
45 For references to erotic *servitium* in the elegiac corpus, see Lilja (1965),
    76–89; Copley (1947), 285–300; Lyne (1979), 117–30.
46 Hallett (1973), 103, contrasts the epitaph of Claudia (*ILS* 8403): *domum
    seruauit, lanam fecit.*
47 For references to erotic *militia* in the elegiac corpus, see Lilja (1965),
    64–66, and Lyne (1980), 67–78.
48 Luck (1974), 15.
49 King (1976), 70.
50 Sallust, *Cat.* 25.2–4 (Budé edition, ed. A. Ernout 1964). The translation is
    that of Lefkowitz and Fant (1982), 205. For Sempronia's use as part of the
    social backdrop for elegiac production, see Lyne (1980), 14, and King
    (1976), 70 and n. 7.
51 See, for example, Lyne (1980), 8–18, and Griffin (1985), 15–28.
52 Balsdon (1962), 45.
53 Paul (1966), 92.
54 Boyd (1987).
55 Lefkowitz (1981), 32–40, and Skinner (1983), 275–76.
56 Skinner (1983).
57 Gardner (1986), 77.
58 Lefkowitz (1981), 32–40.
59 Balsdon (1962), 69. Griffin (1985), 32–47, also draws attention to corres-
    pondences between representations of Antony and the Propertian narrator.
60 I am indebted to Elizabeth Rawson for this observation.
61 See, for example, Richlin (1981), 379–404.
62 Last (1934), 440.

63   Balsdon (1962), 14–15.
64   Cf. Gardner (1986), 261.
65   For the details of the Augustan legislation see Last (1934), 441–56, and Brunt (1971), 558–66. Badian (1985), 82–98, doubts that even by the time Propertius's second book was published any attempt had yet been made to introduce the legislation concerning marriage. For the relation between Augustan elegy and the moral legislation, see also Wallace-Hadrill (1985), 180–84.
66   I am very grateful to Catherine Edwards for giving me access to an unpublished paper on the subject of adultery and the Augustan legislation.
67   Foucault (1981), 26.
68   For the elegiac mistress as a metaphor for her author's poetics, see, for example, Veyne (1983), and Wyke (1987a), 26.
69   Richlin (1983).
70   Hallett (1973) and Hubbard (1974).
71   Cf. Butrica (1982), 87.

REFERENCES

Quotations from Propertius, Tibullus, and Ovid follow the Oxford Classical Texts of E. A. Barber (1960), J. P. Postgate (1915), and E. J. Kenney (1961), respectively.

Allen, A. "'Sincerity' and the Roman Elegists." *Classical Philology* 45 (1950): 145–60.
Badian, E. "A Phantom Marriage Law." *Philologus* 129 (1985): 82–98.
Balsdon, J. P. V. D. *Roman Women.* London: The Bodley Head, 1962.
Barthes, R. *S/Z.* Trans. R. Miller. London: Jonathan Cape, 1975.
Betensky, A. "Forum." *Arethusa* 6 (1973): 267–69.
——. "A Further Reply." *Arethusa* 7 (1974): 211–17.
Boyancé. P. *L'Influence grecque sur la poésie latine de Catulle à Ovide.* Entretiens Hardt 2. Geneva: Fondation Hardt, 1956.
Boyd, B. "Virtus Effeminata and Sallust's Sempronia." *Transactions of the American Philological Association* 117 (1987): 183–201.
Bright, D. F. *Haec mihi Fingebam: Tibullus in his World.* Leiden: Cincinnati Classical Studies, New Series 3, 1978.
Brunt, P. A. *Italian Manpower.* Oxford: Clarendon Press, 1971.
Butrica, J. "Review Article: the Latin Love Poets." *Echos du monde classique/ Classical Views* n.s. 1 (1982): 82–95.
Cairns, F. *Generic Composition in Greek and Roman Poetry.* Edinburgh: Edinburgh University Press, 1972.
Clausen, W. "Cynthius." *American Journal of Philology* 97 (1976): 245–47.

Copley, F. O. "Servitium Amoris in the Roman Elegists," *Transactions of the American Philological Association* 78 (1947): 285–300.

Culham, P. "Ten Years after Pomeroy: Studies of the Image and Reality of Women in Antiquity." *Helios* 13 (1986): 9–30.

Du Quesnay, I. M. Le M. "The Amores." In *Greek and Latin Studies, Classical Literature and its Influence: Ovid*, ed. J. W. Binns: 1–48. London: Routledge and Kegan Paul, 1973.

Fairweather, J. "Fiction in the Biographies of Ancient Writers." *Ancient Society* 5 (1974): 231–75.

Fantham, E. "Women in Antiquity: A Selective (and Subjective) Survey 1979–84." *Echos du monde classique/Classical Views* 30, n.s. 5 (1986): 1–24.

Fedeli, P. *Sesto Properzio: Il Primo Libro delle Elegie*. Florence: Accademia Toscana Studi 53, 1980.

———. *Properzio: Il Libro Terzo delle Elegie*. Bari: Adriatica Editrice, 1985.

Foley, H. P. *Reflections of Women in Antiquity*, ed. H. P. Foley. New York, London and Paris: Gordon and Breach, 1981.

Foucault, M. *The History of Sexuality*. Volume 1: *An Introduction*. Middlesex: Pelican Books, 1981. Reprint and translation of 1976 edition.

Gardner, J. F. *Women in Roman Law and Society*. London: Croom Helm, 1986.

Griffin, J. *Latin Poetry and Roman Life*. London: Duckworth, 1985.

Hallett, J. P. "The Role of Women in Roman Elegy: Counter-Cultural Feminism." *Arethusa* 6 (1973): 103–24.

———. "Women in Roman Elegy: A Reply." *Arethusa* 7 (1974): 211–17.

Hawkes, T. *Structuralism and Semiotics*. London: Methuen, 1977.

Hubbard, M. *Propertius*. London: Duckworth, 1974.

King, J. K. "Sophistication vs. Chastity in Propertius' Latin Love Elegy." *Helios* 4 (1976): 67–76.

Last, H. "The Social Policy of Augustus." In *Cambridge Ancient History*, vol. 10: 425–64. Cambridge: Cambridge University Press, 1934.

Lefkowitz, M. R. *Heroines and Hysterics*. London: Duckworth, 1981.

Lefkowitz, M. R. and M. B. Fant. (eds.) *Women's Life in Greece and Rome*. London: Duckworth, 1982.

Lilja, S. *The Roman Elegists' Attitude to Women*. Helsinki: Suomalainen Tideakatemia, 1965.

Luck, G. "The Woman's Role in Latin Love Poetry." In *Perspectives of Roman Poetry*, ed. G. K. Galinsky: 15–31. Austin, TX: University of Texas Press, 1974.

Lyne, R. O. A. M. "Servitium Amoris." *Classical Quarterly* 29 (1979): 117–30.

———. *The Latin Love Poets: from Catullus to Horace*. Oxford: Clarendon Press, 1980.

McKeown, J. C. *Ovid: Amores*. Volume 1, *Text and Prolegomena*. Liverpool: Arca Classical and Medieval Texts, Papers and Monographs 20, 1987.

Nethercut, W. R. "The Ironic Priest. Propertius' 'Roman Elegies' iii, 1–5: Imitatiors of Horace and Vergil." *American Journal of Philology* 91 (1970): 385–407.

Papanghelis, T. *Propertius: A Hellenistic Poet on Love and Death.* Cambridge: Cambridge University Press, 1987.

Paul, G. M. "Sallust." In *Latin Historians,* ed. T. A. Dorey: London: Routledge and Kegan Paul, 1966.

Richlin, A. "Approaches to the Sources on Adultery at Rome." In *Reflections of Women in Antiquity,* ed. H. P. Foley: 379–404.

——. *The Garden of Priapus: Sexuality and Aggression in Roman Humor.* New Haven and Oxford: Yale University Press, 1983.

Skinner, M. "Clodia Metelli." *Transactions of the American Philological Association* 113 (1983): 273–87.

——. "Rescuing Creusa: New Approaches to Women in Antiquity." *Helios* 13.2 (1986): 1–8.

Stahl, H. -P. *Propertius: "Love" and "War." Individual and State under Augustus.* Berkeley and Los Angeles: University of California Press, 1985.

Sullivan, J. *Propertius. A Critical Introduction.* Cambridge: Cambridge University Press, 1976.

Veyne, P. *L'Elégie érotique romaine.* Paris: Éditions du Seuil, 1983.

Wallace-Hadrill, A. "Propaganda and Dissent?" *Klio* 67 (1985): 180–84.

Williams, G. "Some Aspects of Marriage Ceremonies and Ideals." *Journal of Roman Studies* 48 (1958): 16–29.

——. *Tradition and Originality in Roman Poetry.* Oxford: Clarendon Press, 1968.

Wimmel, W. *Kallimachos in Rom.* Wiesbaden: Hermes Einzelschriften 16, 1960.

Wyke, M. "Written Women: Propertius' Scripta Puella." *Journal of Roman Studies* 77 (1987a): 47–61.

——. "The Elegiac Woman at Rome." *Proceedings of the Cambridge Philological Society* 213, n.s. 33 (1987b): 153–78.

——. "Reading Female Flesh: *Amores* 3.1." In *History as Text,* ed. Averil Cameron. London: Duckworth, 1989.

SOURCES

Propertius

The love poems of Propertius (born between 54 and 47 BCE) celebrate his devotion to his mistress, Cynthia, whose real name may have been Hostia. Little is known about her life or social status. In many of the poems, the poet claims to be his mistress's slave and to have replaced his military career with the pursuit of love. His frequent allusions to classical myth make his poems quite challenging to modern readers.

Propertius 1.8a

Are you out of your mind? Do no thoughts for me make you stay?
Am I worth less to you than icy Ilyria?
Or do you already rate this man, what's his name, so highly
that you would travel in any wind that blows without me?

Can you hear the roar of the raging sea
without flinching? Can you lie on a hard berth?
Can you press the frost upon the ground with your delicate feet,
Cynthia, or bear the unaccustomed snow?
O may the stormy winter season be doubled in length,
and the lagging Pleiads keep the sailor idle,
that your ship's moorings might not be loosened from the Tuscan shore,
and no hostile breeze disparage my prayers!
And yet I would not then see such breezes sink

when the wave carries away the ships sailing forth with you,
leaving me to stand in grief on the empty shore,
calling you cruel again and again with threatening gestures.
But however badly you have treated me, faithless girl,
may Galataea befriend your journey,
that you may be safely rowed past the Ceraunian cliffs,
and Oricos receive you in the quiet waters of its port.
For never again will anyone else have the power to make me false to you,
or to keep me from complaining at your door, my life.
Nor will I fail to ask sailors moving quickly,
"Tell me, do you know what port encloses my girl?"
And I'll say, "Though she may settle on the Autracian or Elean shores,
she will still be mine."

Propertius 1.8b

She will be here! She has sworn to stay. Let the spiteful burst!
I have won: she could not resist my persistent prayers.
Let greedy envy renounce illusory joys!
My Cynthia has ceased to travel an unknown course.
To her I am *dear* and Rome *most dear* on account of me;
without me she says no kingdom is sweet.
She prefers to rest with me in my humble bed,
and to be mine, whatever our style of life,
than to have as her dowry the ancient kingdom of Hippodamia,
and all the wealth that Elis with its horses has amassed.
Though he offered much, though he would have offered more,
yet avarice has not driven her from my arms.
Not with gold, not with Indian pearls, could I move her,
but with the winning homage of my song.
Then the Muses really do exist, nor is Apollo slow to aid a lover,
in these, as a lover, I have confidence: the perfect Cynthia is mine!
Now I can touch the highest stars with the soles of my feet!
Come day or night, she is mine!
Nor will a rival steal my true love away from me,
that glory shall know my old age!

Propertius 2.5

Is it true, Cynthia? That you are the talk of all Rome,
that you openly lead a scandalous life?

Have I deserved to expect *this*? I will make you pay, faithless girl.
A wind will also lead me to some other port, Cynthia.
Though they are all treacherous, still I will find one girl
who will consent to be made famous by my verse,
nor will she mock me with cruel waywardness like yours,
but make you jealous. Too late you'll weep, you who were loved so long.
Now while your anger is fresh, Propertius, now is the time to leave:
once the pain has gone, trust me, love will return.
Not so lightly do the Carpathian waves shift beneath the north winds,
or the dark clouds come and go with the south-westerly squalls,
as angry lovers relent at a word.
While it is still possible, withdraw your neck from an unjust yoke.
On the first night, you will suffer great pain,
but the pains of love are light, if you surrender to them.
But you, my life, by the sweet sovereignty of the mistress Juno,
stop harming yourself with your arrogance.
Not only does a bull strike an enemy with his curved horns,
but even the injured sheep fights back against an attacker.
Neither will I tear the clothes from your perjured body,
nor will I let my anger shatter your locked door,
nor could I dare to pull your braided hair in a rage,
or strike you with my hard clenched hands.
Let some rustic seek such unsavory quarrels,
whose head a wreath of ivy does not encircle.
I will write what your life cannot erase,
Cynthia, powerful in her beauty, Cynthia, light in her words.
Trust me, however much you despise the murmuring gossip,
this verse, Cynthia, will cause you to become pale.

Cicero

In his speech in defense of Caelius, the Roman orator Cicero (born 106 BCE) uses a real woman, Clodia (born c.95 BCE), to slander his opponent. She had a prolonged affair with the poet Catullus while married to a man named Metellus and appears as Lesbia in his poems. She is later said to have poisoned and killed Metellus in 59 BCE. The invectives hurled against Clodia in this passage contrast the more idealized portrait of the mistress in Latin love elegy.

Cicero, *In Defense of Marcus Caelius* 20.47–21.50

Does not a whiff of anything come from that notorious neighborhood? Does public rumor, does Baiae itself say nothing? Why, Baiae does not simply talk, it fairly screams with the tale that one single woman's lusts have reached such depths, that, far from seeking isolation and darkness and the normal cloaks for depravity, she revels in the most disgraceful behavior, courting the most open publicity and the brightest light of day.

However, if there is anyone who thinks that affairs even with courtesans ought to be taboo for youths, he is certainly very prudish, I cannot deny it. He is not only out of touch with the licentiousness of this time, but even with the habits and concessions of the ancients. For when was this not a common practice? When did this bear a stigma? When was it forbidden? And, finally, when was that which is now allowed not allowed? Here I will narrow my very topic, I will name no woman in particular; I will leave just so much in the open. If a woman without a husband opens her house to the lust of all men and publicly leads the life of a prostitute, if she frequents dinner parties with perfect strangers, if she does this in the city, in her garden, amid the crowds of Baiae, and finally if she behaves in such a way that not only her bearing, her apparel and her circle of friends make her seem to be not just a prostitute, but a lascivious and lewd prostitute, not to mention the ardor of her gaze, the unconstrained nature of her gossip, even her embraces and kisses, and activities, her water parties, and her dinner parties.

But if a young man was with this woman, Lucius Herennius, would he be an adulterer or a lover? Would it seem that he wanted to assault her chastity or to satisfy her lust? I am forgetting all the wrongs you have personally done me, Clodia, I am putting aside the memory of my pain; I pass over the cruel things you did to my family in my absence. Please do not imagine that what I have said was meant against *you*. But I am asking you yourself, since the accusers claim that you are to blame for this crime and that they have you yourself as witness to it. If there is a woman of the sort I painted just a moment ago, one quite unlike you, with the lifestyle and habits of a prostitute, would it seem very shameful or disgraceful to you that a young man should have had some dealings with her? If you are not this woman, as I prefer to think, why should any charge be brought against Caelius? But if by such a person they mean you, why should we fear this crime, if you hate it? In that case, give us our manner and method of defense. For either your sense of decency will uphold the statement that Caelius did not act immorally in any way, or your utter indecency will provide him and all the rest of us with an excellent means of defending their conduct.

Figure 8   *"Bikini Girls."*   Mosaic from the villa at Piazza Armerina, the inner of the two rooms at the southeast corner of the peristyle, c.350 CE, No. 38 in Fig. 42. Young girls, probably professional performers, engage in athletic activities either as a dramatic parody of the Olympian games or in an actual competition.

8
PLINY'S BRASSIERE

A. Richlin

As we try to write the history of Roman sexualities, the sexual experience of women is most difficult to recover, almost unknown at first hand, heavily screened in male-authored erotic and literary texts. The journey you are about to undertake travels through little-known wildernesses of Roman texts in search of the sexual experience of Roman women. These texts are far from erotic, a jumble of encyclopedias and agricultural handbooks. In treating their content as pertinent to women's sexual lives, I have to point out that *Our Bodies, Ourselves* has occasionally been targeted as pornographic and is seen even by its creators as an important step forward in women's sexual freedom.[1] Similarly, the material to be examined here brings us into the everyday world of women's sexual experience, including mundane topics like menstruation, fertility, contraception, abortion, aphrodisiacs, pregnancy, childbirth, and well-baby care. The texts treat having babies as part of having sex, and I will, too; though babies are few and far between in love elegy or invective, in the wholly marriage-centered world of the encyclopedias, babies are everywhere.

The question of women's place in ancient medicine has been the subject of much excellent recent scholarship. Despite this, and somewhat surprisingly, the reader will find most of the Roman material here new. Even so eminent a scholar as Ann Hanson, writing about ancient medical writers, treats Soranus as a Greek along with the Hippocratic writers, and moves to the Middle Ages when she wants to talk about *Gynaikeia* in Latin (1990: 311). The majority of the new feminist work on ancient medicine is Hellenocentric, and many studies are not primarily concerned with rooting the systems they analyze in a broader cultural context.[2] Heinrich von Staden's analysis of Celsus on the female body (1991) is exceptional in its attention to the Roman ideologies behind Celsus's ambivalence. Here I will be relying mainly on the *Natural History* of the elder Pliny (24–79 C.E.), along with the encyclopedist Pompeius Festus (second-century C.E. epitomator of an Augustan work), the agricultural writer Columella (60s C.E.), and other similar writers. Although they often leave us in a murky ancient Mediterranean soup of sources, they can also on occasion tie in their dicta with observed practice in the Italian countryside, or let us know that they are turning to female practitioners or popular belief as their source. These writers are not, properly speaking, medical writers – they have no medical training – but they hold up for our perusal a collage of beliefs from many strata of their society, and they richly repay study.

How were these writers different from medical writers as such? What can they tell us about Roman women that medical writers might not? Again, Pliny himself makes a good starting point. As G. E. R. Lloyd suggests in his brief but pointed overview (1983: 135–49), Pliny has the virtues of his faults. His vast encyclopedia is built along contradictory lines: much of it derives from Pliny's enormous reading, yet he generally recognizes the value of experience, and sometimes turns to his own observations; he often inveighs against magic and superstition, then in the next breath records lists of magical cures, with or without negative comment; sometimes he follows Greek scientific sources almost word-for-word, elsewhere he reports what he has seen in the Italian countryside. Cures using bugs are dubbed almost too disgusting to relate (29.61), while earthworms are acclaimed as so versatile that they are kept in honey for general use (29.91–92). He could never be called a critical reader in any consistent sense; as his nephew innocently remarks of him (*Ep.* 3.5.10), "He read nothing without making excerpts from it; indeed, he used to say that there was no book so bad that some part of it wasn't useful." Although he writes a crabbed and difficult prose, often sounds cantankerous, and was certainly a terrible bigot, the *Natural History* exudes a sort of sweetness, like the monologues of the old codger in *The Wrong Box*. That he was extremely curious is well attested by the manner of his death; the *Natural History* itself shows that he carried this curiosity to the point of gullibility, as for example in his account of the herb doctor he met who told him he could get him a thirty-foot moly root (25.26).

He had the deepest contempt for doctors.[3] In a long tirade (29.1–28) he makes it clear that this contempt is ethnic and class-based. Pliny was a wealthy man, a Roman equestrian, a naval commander, author of a book on cavalry tactics, a book of military history, and a book on rhetoric, as well as a slave-owner, landowner, scientist, encyclopedist, and friend of emperors.[4] For him, doctors and their medicine are Greek and worse than useless to Romans; when he proclaims (29.1) that "the nature of remedies...has been treated by no one in the Latin language before this," he ignores Celsus and Scribonius Largus – perhaps because they counted as "no one" to him. Again and again he reviles doctors for making huge profits; this is the contempt of a Roman equestrian for a tradesman. He compares doctors to actors (29.9), persons whose civil status was diminished due to the dishonor felt to adhere to their occupation (see Edwards [1997]). He associates medicine with the luxury and moral corruption that it was a cliché, in Roman oratory, to associate with the Greek East (29.20, 26–27). He repeats seriously what was a standing joke, for example in the epigrams of Martial: that doctors murder their patients (29.11, 13, 18). The Roman people, he says, did "without doctors but not without medicine" for six hundred years (29.11), and he quotes in its entirety a letter of the elder Cato to his son Marcus dismissing Athens, Greek literature, and Greek medicine with loathing (29.14): "A most worthless and intractable race.... They have sworn to kill all of us, whom they call 'barbarians,' by their medicine.... I prohibit you from all doctors." Cato's authority here is guaranteed, in very Roman terms, by reference to his triumph, censorship, age, public service, and experience (29.13, 15). Pliny goes on to claim that he himself is making use of Cato's own book of home remedies (29.15), and insists that *Romana gravitas* must separate Romans from the practice of medicine, even from the writing of medical books in Latin.

Yet he compiled the *Natural History.* There is thus in his text always a tension between the matter at hand and Pliny's attitude toward it; he writes, not (shudder) as a medical professional, but as a Roman equestrian eager to make useful knowledge available to Romans. (In this he succeeded. Despite its chaotic organization, the *Natural History* proved popular; it was to have a long afterlife, enjoying honor and respect down through the Middle Ages and Renaissance [Chibnall 1975], and it is still in print today after two thousand years.) Pliny's book, despite overlaps, is thus essentially different from the texts produced by Roman medical writers: for example, his coevals Celsus and Scribonius Largus, the second-century doctors Galen and Soranus, and the probably later writer Metrodora.[5]

For one thing, the last three of these writers were Greeks, though Galen and Soranus practiced in Rome; and they wrote in Greek. Soranus looks down on his adopted city: "The women in this city do not possess sufficient devotion to look after everything as the purely Grecian women do" (2.44, trans. Temkin). For another, they are concerned, in their writing, to present a system of health care; a section of Metrodora's work is even arranged by headings in alphabetical order, for ease in consultation. Though Soranus's book is largely concerned with advice to women and midwives, he brings up folk medicine in order to discredit it (1.63, contraceptive amulets; 2.6, why women loosen their clothing and hair during childbirth), or patronizes it: "Even if the amulet has no direct effect, still through hope it will possibly make the patient more cheerful" (3.42, trans. Temkin; but cf. Lloyd [1983: 168–82], who credits Soranus for his willingness to humor his patients). To Pliny, doctors, the Magi, peasants, and his own observations are all grist to the mill; just as Cato wrote a *commentarium* for the use of his wife, son, slaves, and *familiares* (*HN* 29.15), so Pliny is writing one for a larger circle. The medical writers write as outsiders, or from above, as professionals; Pliny writes from inside.

This essay takes its name from a brief remark in the *Natural History* (28.76): "I find that headaches are relieved by tying a woman's brassiere on [my/the] head."[6] The strangeness of this image, outstanding even among Pliny's weird parade, has haunted me since first I read it. Of course it made me laugh; I always think of a man in a toga sitting and working late into the night by lamplight, with a contraption on his head that looks like something Madonna would wear. In fact Roman brassieres probably looked more like Ace bandages; yet the image is still strange, because Pliny does not just mean that a headache is cured by wrapping a stretchy thing around your head. He is talking about the medicinal uses of the female human body, and he seems to believe that something is exuded from women's bodies that would make a brassiere cure a headache. Strange as his belief system may be to us, it seems possible to ask what the experience of it would have been like for women contemporary with Pliny.[7] Moreover, Pliny and his bra may be useful as a symbol embodying the yin and yang of Roman medicine: we can focus on Pliny, and consider what his gynecology, his use of the brassiere, has in common with his status in Roman culture; or we can focus on the woman whose brassiere it was.

Linda Gordon, in an important article (1986), delineated two opposing approaches to the writing of women's history. In one approach, the historian paints women as the victims of an oppressive structure, showing how patriarchy and patriarchs keep women downtrodden. In the other approach, the historian paints women as agents, working out their own strategies to deal with whatever system they find themselves in. This second approach often tries to locate and analyze "women's culture": sets of strategies that women at particular times and places have adopted.[8] Following up on a suggestion I made in an earlier article (1993: 291–92), I will here argue that the episode of Pliny's brassiere can be used as a starting point for both these approaches. And I will begin with Pliny.

Pliny and the Brassiere

> I thought of that old gentleman, who is dead now, but was a bishop, I think, who declared that it was impossible for any woman, past, present, or to come, to have the genius of Shakespeare. He wrote to the papers about it. He also told a lady who applied to him for information that cats do not as a matter of fact go to heaven, though they have, he added, souls of a sort. How much thinking those old gentlemen used to save one! How the borders of ignorance shrank back at their approach! Cats do not go to heaven. Women cannot write the plays of Shakespeare.
>
> (Virginia Woolf, *A Room of One's Own*)

What does it mean when Pliny puts a brassiere on his head? Why do we laugh? Partly, at least, because of who he is. He's a man in a toga; the brassiere doesn't suit his dignity. What's a man like that doing with a bra on his head?

The relation between Pliny the scientist and the brassiere on his head might be taken as a symbol of the way Roman medicine colonizes the female body. Pliny's *Natural History* includes a major section in book 28 on the medical uses of the female human body; this section has a lot to say about menstrual blood, about which there is also a section in book 7.[9] In addition, there are a great many other bits about the female body dotted throughout the text, and other writers, as well, talk about the issue – not medical writers, but agricultural writers like Columella, and encyclopedists like Pompeius Festus.

The point is not only that these writers view the female human body as raw material for medicines, but also why they think this would work. Evidently the female body itself is intrinsically powerful – both harmful and helpful; almost uncanny, evidently due to its special processes, not only menstruation but also childbirth and lactation. Anne Carson (1990) has talked about the symbolic properties attributed to Greek women's bodies in literary texts; in Roman encyclopedic writing we see similar attitudes given practical form. Indeed, the Roman texts provide a perfect example of the kind of ambivalence suggested by Thomas Buckley and Alma Gottlieb as the paradigm for menstrual "taboos."[10] Moreover, as we look at the Roman texts, it is useful to contrast them with studies of attitudes toward the female body in other Mediterranean cultures, especially those influenced by Christianity, Judaism, or Islam. Rome has nothing to compare with the theological basis for menstrual disgust in the Turkish village culture studied by Carol Delaney (1988), nor is there any mention of prohibitions concerned with religious ritual.[11] The beliefs attested in the encyclopedic texts are secular and practical in their area of concern; while they use evaluative language, like *tantum malum* ("so great an evil") or *monstrificum* ("monstrous"), there is apparently no theological or cosmological reason for it.

Sometimes just the female body itself, even the sight of it, can be dangerous. Describing the frankincense trade in Arabia, Pliny notes that those who trade in this precious commodity cannot let themselves "be polluted (*pollui*) by any meeting with women or with funeral processions" (12.54).[12] The appearance of a woman as a bad women or pollutant is not uncommon; Pliny describes what he calls "the rustic law on many Italian farms," whereby care is taken to keep women from walking down the road using a spindle, or even carrying one in the open, since such a sight would "blight all expectations," especially for the crops (28.28). While the ostensible source of the problem here is the spindle, the virtual identity between women and spinning/weaving is surely in play.

Often the power of the female body is associated directly with menstruation. Its powers to help are awesome, almost frightening, and are noted with a certain ambivalence; as Pliny says, "Many say there are remedies, too, in such an evil." Hailstorms and tornados are driven away "by the sight of a naked, menstruating woman" (? *mense nudato*); likewise, storms at sea are turned aside by the sight of a naked woman (?), even without menstruation (*etiam sine menstruis*, 28.77). Menstrual blood has general powers to cure diseases, especially epilepsy (28.44), rabies, fevers (28.82–86) – all illnesses involving loss of bodily control.[13] And it is particularly useful to the farmer. Columella lists a whole series of spells to rid the garden of pests, things like caterpillars (*Rust.* 10.337–68). But the best, he says, is to send a menstruating virgin to walk around the fields (10.357–68):

> But if no medicine [*medicina*] has the power to repel the pests,
> bring on the Dardanian arts, and let a woman with bare feet,
> who, first occupied with the regular laws of a girl,
> drips chastely with her obscene blood,
> with her dress and hair unbound, and serious face,

be led three times around the fields and garden hedge.
And when she has purged them by walking, amazing to see! ...
The caterpillars roll to the ground with twisted bodies.

Columella repeats this advice elsewhere (11.3.64), without specifying that the woman needs to be a virgin, and citing a Greek text, Democritus's *On Antipathies*. Pliny repeats the same advice for getting rid of caterpillars, worms, and beetles, along with other pests (28.78); the woman should be naked. He also there cites a recommendation of Metrodorus of Scepsis, derived from Cappadocia, for getting rid of Cantharides in the fields: he says the woman should go through the middle of the fields with her dress pulled up above her buttocks. (Presumably Columella, with his "Dardanian arts," is also thinking of Metrodorus; Scepsis is in the Troad.) Other possibilities are for her to go barefoot, with her hair hanging down and her dress unfastened; but care should be taken lest she do this at sunrise, for this will dry up the crops. Moreover, if she touches them, young vines will be permanently damaged, and rue and ivy, those "most medicinal things" (*res medicatissimos*), will die on the spot. In a discussion of ridding trees of pests (17.266–67), Pliny repeats that many people say caterpillars (*urucae*) can be killed by having a woman just beginning her period walk around each of the trees, barefoot and with her tunic ungirt (*recincta*). Since both writers cite Greek or Asian sources, we cannot tell to what extent such rituals may have been practiced in the Italian countryside, but we gain the added idea that they may have been practiced throughout the Mediterranean. Moreover, we note that even in Columella's discussion of the useful powers of a menstruating woman, the blood itself is referred to as "obscene blood" (*obsceno cruore*, 10.360). The semantic range of *obscenus/ a/um* in Latin leaves us in no doubt that Columella associates the blood with things both sexual and repulsive, things that should not be seen or spoken about (Richlin 1992a: 9; cf. von Staden 1991: 284–86). The mixed emotions attested here are echoed by Pliny's warning about the danger to crops.

Thus it is no surprise to find that, in Pliny's *materia medica*, menstrual blood can do harm. Pliny introduces both of his discussions of menstrual blood with warnings: "Nothing may easily be found more monstrous than the flux of women" (7.64); and "Indeed, from the menses themselves, elsewhere monstrous, ... they rant dire and unspeakable things" (28.77). Intercourse with menstruating women can be "deadly" for men (28.77–78). Speaking of the *violentia* of menstrual blood, Pliny gives a list of its effects (28.79–80): it can put bees to flight, stain linens black, dull barbers' razors, tarnish bronze and give it a bad smell, cause pregnant mares to abort (even when the women are only seen at a distance, if this is the first menstruation), make she-asses sterile if they eat grain contaminated by menstrual blood, and ruin dyes (cf. 28.78, where purple is said to be "polluted" by menstruating women during the times of especially deadly menstruation). Even women themselves, usually "immune among themselves to their own evil" (*malo suo inter se inmunibus*), can be forced to abort by a smear of menstrual blood, especially if a pregnant woman walks over some (28.80). Pliny cites Bithus of Dyrrachium as the authority for one remedy: mirrors that have been dulled by the glance of a menstruating woman can recover their shine by having the woman look at the back of the mirror; and this whole problem can be averted by having the menstruating woman carry a mullet (fish) with her (28.82).

In another list of the harmful properties of menstrual blood (7.64), Pliny says: contact with it sours new wine; crops become barren when touched by it; grafts die; the seeds are burned up in the gardens; fruit falls off the trees; mirrors are dimmed by menstruating women looking into them; the edge of iron tools is dulled; the shine on ivory is dulled; beehives die; bronze and iron corrode, and bronze smells bad; and dogs who taste it contract rabies and their bites are infected with incurable poison (*venenum*). Even ants, people say, can sense it, and will spit out fruit tainted by it, nor will they go back to it afterwards (7.65). Likewise, bees, who appreciate cleanliness, hate both scurf and women's menstrual blood (11.44). All kitchen plants grow yellow at the approach of a menstruating woman (19.176).

Many of these beliefs have an agricultural context, and, indeed, Columella includes a few remarks on menstrual blood among his most humdrum comments on gardening. Like Pliny, he says that plants will dry up if touched by a menstruating woman (*Rust.* 11.3.38); this passage, like most of Columella, is down-to-earth in its tone, and explicitly takes its authority from peasants (*ut rustici dicunt*, 11.3.43, 12.10.1) and from Columella's own experience (11.3.61). Moreover, no women at all should be allowed near cucumbers (hmm...) and gourds, for "the growth of green things droops at contact with them." This is even worse if the women are menstruating, at which time they will kill the new growth just by looking at it (11.3.50).

These beliefs are in keeping with attitudes expressed toward menstruation in other kinds of Roman texts. Menstruation and menstrual blood are mentioned only a few times in Roman satirical and moralizing literature, uniformly negatively (discussed in Richlin 1992a: 169, 281–82).

Attitudes toward the female genitalia generally in Roman texts are highly negative; descriptions appear only in invective, and invective of a most savage sort.[14] Thus Festus lists the word ANCUNULENTAE, which he says is used to refer to "women . . . at the time of menstruation," and suggests that the Latin word *inquinamentum,* which means "stain," comes from this word (10L). *Inquinamentum* is not a neutral word, and it appears with some frequency in sexual contexts (Richlin 1992a: 27).

It is not just menstrual blood, though, that comes into these medical texts. Another peculiarly female body fluid, breast milk, plays a large part in Pliny's account of the female body. And unlike menstrual blood, breast milk is uniformly helpful. Pliny rates women's milk as one of the most useful remedies (28.123):

> Foremost we will expound the common and particular remedies from animals, for example the uses of milk. Mother's milk is the most useful thing for anybody. . . Moreover, human milk is the most nourishing for any purpose, next goat's milk; the sweetest after human [milk] is camel's, the most effective [after human milk] comes from donkeys.

Again, we might be startled to find women listed here among animals, and take this as similar to the attitudes that link menstruating women with animals, crops, and the monstrous. Still, Pliny has many good things to say about women's milk. It is an antidote to poisons, and cures many illnesses, especially illnesses of the eye. A man anointed with the milk of a mother and daughter at the same time, Pliny says, is freed from all fear for his eyes throughout his life (28.73).[15]

Moreover, it is not just these special body fluids that have medical properties. Other effluvia from women's bodies are also powerful, including urine, hair, and saliva. Pliny says, for example, that the saliva of a fasting woman is good for bloodshot eyes and fluxes; the corners of the eye are to be moistened with the saliva occasionally. This works better if the woman has fasted on the previous day as well (28.76).

With all these recommendations, we find ourselves wondering how often people actually used cures like this. We have one valuable attestation in a story about the father of the emperor Vitellius. Suetonius is not sure he approves of him, and describes the senior Vitellius as "a man harmless and industrious, but thoroughly notorious for his love of a freedwoman. He used to bathe his windpipe and throat as a remedy with a mixture of her saliva with honey, and not secretly or occasionally but daily and right out in the open" (*Vit.* 2.4). Presumably what is disgraceful here is the openness and the breach of class boundaries; Suetonius does not really seem to question the belief that the woman's saliva would have curative powers. And as will be seen, there are several accounts of the use of women's saliva to protect babies from harm.

It seems, overall, that Roman medical uses of the female body tie in with a set of beliefs about the female body that is characterized by a deep ambivalence. The body is powerful, but in a frightening way. There is a familiar division between the lower-body fluids and the upper-body fluids – the fluids from the lower body having the power both to help and to harm, while the fluids from the upper body are just helpful. Menstrual blood protects, or harms, a long list of products of culture – crops, metal tools, domesticated animals, dye. So when Pliny puts on that brassiere, he is using the female body to think with in more ways than one.[16]

But who gave him the brassiere? Several of the cures from the female body involve a large degree of cooperation and participation on the part of women themselves: for example, the caterpillar-removal procedure, in which a woman has to walk through the fields barefoot. This certainly implies a scenario with a woman and her powers as the center of attention, and this is not the only such case. One female practitioner whom Pliny quotes, the *obstetrix* Sotira, recommends a cure in which the soles of the patient's feet are smeared with menstrual blood; she notes that this works especially well if done by the woman herself (*HN* 28.83). The saliva to be obtained from a fasting woman implies her cooperation not only in providing the saliva but in fasting as well. We might guess that the elder Vitellius got the saliva from his mistress with her knowledge. And likewise for the other cures and harms. We might indeed extrapolate that this body of medical knowledge implies a great deal about women's experience of themselves in the world. We might further expect that women's beliefs about their bodies might vary according to class, or urban/rural divisions; in any case, we might well turn our attention from the man wearing the brassiere to the woman he got it from.

The Woman Behind the Brassiere

I did not spend the next two weeks worrying about my period. If it did not show up, there was no question in my mind that I would force it to do so. I knew how to do this. Without telling me exactly how I might miss a menstrual cycle, my mother had shown me which herbs to pick and boil, and what time of day to drink the potion they produced, to bring on a reluctant period. She had presented the whole idea to me as a way to strengthen the womb, but underneath we both knew that a weak womb was not the cause of a missed period. She knew that I knew, but we presented to each other a face of innocence and politeness and even went so far as to curtsy to each other at the end.

(Jamaica Kincaid, *Lucy*)

Feminist historians of medicine have made us familiar with the idea that women played an important part in "folk" medicine in western Europe.[17] In the Roman period, the divisions among different kinds of medicine were much blurrier than they are today. There evidently were such divisions; Pliny spends a lot of time complaining about the kinds of medicine he disapproves of, especially "magical" cures – that is, the cures of the Magi, practitioners from Asia Minor (cf. Lloyd 1979: 13 n. 20; 1983: 140–41). But for us, it is very hard to tell the difference between the Roman forms of what we would call folk medicine, scientific medicine, and magic. This section looks at how women themselves might have taken an active role in their cures. And these cures definitely sound folksy. But the reader should be aware that they do not sound more folksy than the general run of cures in Pliny's *Natural History*.

Pliny certainly does not cite many female medical authorities as sources. His sources are most often male, when he cites them, and it is always a question how much descriptive validity we can ascribe to his recommendations. Still, what I will try to do is to recover from Pliny's *Natural History* some idea of women's own health practices in first-century C.E. Rome.

How might we imagine women involving themselves in medical practice? The epigraph to this section comes from the Antiguan writer Jamaica Kincaid; her protagonist is living in contemporary New York. This young woman and her mother are both active and knowledgeable, and the sort of medicine they practice is immediately recognizable in the pages of Pliny's *Natural History*.

If we look long enough, we find that some of Pliny's recipes do involve action by the woman herself. For pains in the *muliebria loca*, women are to wear "constantly" a bracelet containing the first tooth of their child to fall out, which should never have fallen on the ground (28.41). So we can imagine women saving, in their medicine boxes, their children's first baby teeth. To stop menstruation, Pliny recommends catching a spider spinning a thread as it ascends again, crushing it, and applying it (30.129). For a variety of ills, Pliny recommends calf's gall sprinkled on the genitals during menstruation, just before intercourse (28.253); so we have to imagine a woman saying, "Excuse me, dear, while I just sprinkle on some of this calf's gall." Taking a purge could apparently be a complex and drawn-out process: women are to take a decoction of linozostis in food on the second day of menstruation (*purgatio*) for three further days; on the fourth day, after a bath, they are to have sex (25.40). In a rare ethnographic description of actual female practice, Pliny says that the *agrestes feminae*, "peasant women," in Transpadane Gaul wear amber necklaces, mostly as ornaments, but also as *medicina*, to ward off throat problems (37.44).

Another branch of ancient *medicina* that demands active involvement of its consumers is love medicine. Despite disclaimers, Pliny describes more than sixty different aphrodisiacs and more than twenty-nine different antaphrodisiacs. He even has several lists of such materials (26.94–99; 32.139), including one from the Magi (30.141–43), and credits a range of sources, all male.[18] These are mostly given without comment, though Pliny chides Theophrastus for his description of a plant that produces the lust to have sex seventy times (26.99). Considering the common Roman idea that women specialize in potions (see below), this all-male cast is surprising; Metrodora does include a number of aphrodisiacs in her book (1.26, 1.38, 1.39, 4.20–23).[19]

The market for these products seems to be mixed. Some are listed specifically as "for men" (a total of twelve) or "for women" (a total of seven); scandix is for those "exhausted by sex or shriveled from old age" (22.80).[20] Rarely are circumstances specified; Pliny does not tell us of limits on use for self as opposed to use on others. Hyena genitals in honey are said to stimulate desire, "even when men hate intercourse with women"; and so (what's a wife to do?) "the harmony of the whole house is preserved by keeping these genitals, along with a vertebra with some of the skin attached" (28.99).[21] For antaphrodisiacs, several motives seem to be in play. Repeatedly these drugs are said to stop wet dreams (*libidinum imaginationes in somno*, literally "imaginings of lusts in sleep") or sex dreams (*somnia veneris*) (20.68, 20.142–43, 20.146, 26.94, 34.166). Some aphrodisiacs are clearly aimed at influencing an object's desires without his/her knowledge – sprinkling seeds on a woman to agument her eagerness (20.227), placing a southernwood sprig under the pillow (21.162). Others would be harder to miss: putting hyena muzzle hairs on a woman's lips (aphrodisiac, 28.101) or rubbing her groin with blood from a tick or giving her he-goat's urine to drink (antaphrodisiac, 28.256). Erynge root (22.20) is said to make a man who gets hold of it *amabilis*; this, Pliny says, is how Phaon of Lesbos made himself beloved by Sappho. The Magi, among many other powers they attribute to the hyena (including a cure for *probrosa mollitia*, "disgraceful effeminacy"), claim that a hyena anus worn on a man's left arm will make any woman follow him the minute he looks at her (28.106). By way of comparison, Metrodora seems equally to be writing for a mixed audience; five of her eight aphrodisiacs are "for erection" (4.20–23), while one is headed "So that she will howl and make all kinds of sounds" (1.39, Parker trans.). A remedy entitled "For a woman, so she will not be promiscuous" (1.36) requires the man to rub medicine on his penis; another charm promises "to make her confess her lovers" (1.37).[22]

Nowadays we expect that abortion would be something with which women would concern themselves. Roman culture, though, set a high value on women's fertility, and Pliny's text reflects that attitude. His expressed attitude toward abortion is negative, and he mostly gives recommendations for ways to increase fertility and to promote successful delivery of a child. However, he does in fact give formulas for abortifacients, as well as for emmenagogues. (These remedies are referred to by Pliny as "calling forth the menses," much like the cures described by Jamaica Kincaid's narrator; the distinction between such a medicine and an abortifacient is obviously a fine one.[23]) In this context, it seems significant that Pliny attributes the invention of abortion to women; he exclaims (10.172), "Males have figured out all the back alleyways of sex, crimes against nature; but women figured out abortions." This despite evident ideological disincentives.

Pliny himself connects abortion not only with "unnatural" sex, as here, but with magical potions leading to insanity and/or love and lust (25.25):

> But what excuse could there be for showing how minds could be unhinged, fetuses squeezed out, and many similar things? I do not discuss abortifacients (*abortiva*), nor even love potions … nor other magic portents, unless when they are to be warned against or refuted, especially when confidence in them has been undermined.

One such refutation concerns two female practitioners, Lais and Elephantis. In his summary of their accounts of the abortifacient powers of menstrual blood, he faults them for contradicting each other, and concludes (28.81): "When the latter says that fertility is brought about by the same methods by which the former pronounces barrenness [is], it is better not to believe [them]." This tells us a good deal. On the one hand, Pliny's attitude is quite negative: he sums up their accounts as *monstrifica*, in keeping with the general tone of his remarks on menstrual blood. And he is hardly deferential to them as female authorities on abortion. On the other hand, we know through him that these female medical writers talked both about abortion and about fertility. He reproduces

their lists of *abortiva*, along with a warning that barley tainted by menstrual blood will block conception in she-asses.

Furthermore, Pliny himself tells us some things about women's practice. A section headed "Wine, too, has its amazing qualities" moves from
fertility to poisons, taking in abortion along the way. Wine flavored with
hellebore, cucumber, or scammony, he notes (14.110), is called *phthor-
ium* ("destructive") because it produces abortions (*phthorios pessos* is the
term for "abortifacient" in the Hippocratic Oath). One wine from Arcadia produces *fecunditas* in women and madness (*rabies*) in men (14.116),
but in Achaia, there is a wine reported to expel the fetus (*abigi partum*),
"even if pregnant women eat one of the grapes." An Egyptian wine has
the nickname *ecbolada* (Gk. "throw-out"), because it brings on an abortion (14.118). Similarly, ground pine has the Latin name *abiga* ("push-
out"), "because of abortions" (24.29). These descriptive names may
possibly be folk terms; in a discussion of the properties of the willow
tree, Pliny notes (16.110) that Homer calls the willow *frugiperda*, "des-
troys-fruit" (*olesikarpon, Od.* 10.510); he comments, "Later ages have
interpreted this conceit according to their own wickedness, since it is
known that the seed of the willow is a *medicamentum* of barrenness for a
woman." The reported accounts in Lais and Elephantis may have been
part of a how-to guide; similarly, in a discussion of the gynecological
properties of mallow, Pliny notes that another female practitioner, Olym-
pias of Thebes, says that mallows with goose grease bring on abortion
(20.226). That a woman might not wish to conceive is recognized by
another recipe, directed at a male market: a woman unwilling to conceive
is forced to, by means of hairs taken from the tail of a she-mule, pulled
out while the animals are mating, and woven together when the man and
woman are (30.142).[24]

Pliny's connection between female practitioners, abortificaients, and
love potions is common in literary and legal texts. Apart from whatever
doctors may have done, Roman writers portray a market of female consumers whose needs are met by women who concoct potions. Thus Juvenal,
writing fifty years after Pliny, in his sixth satire, against women (6.594–98):

> Hardly ever do you find a woman giving birth in a gilded bed. So great is
> the power of the arts and medicines of that woman who makes women
> sterile, and contracts to kill human beings in the womb. Rejoice, unfortu-
> nate man, and yourself give her whatever it is she has to drink.

The point is that wealthy women, who can afford the cost, would
rather pay for an abortion than bear a child; (cuckolded) husbands are

Juvenal's intended audience. Similarly, at least one legal text envisions the makers of potions as female; the jurist Marcian, writing in the early third century C.E. on serious crimes on a level with murder, writes: "But by law that woman is ordered to be relegated who, even if not with malice aforethought, but setting a bad example, has given any medicine to promote conception by which the woman who took it died" (*Dig.* 48.8.3). Here the line between the practice of doctors and of other practitioners grows particularly blurry. Pliny disapproves, but provides a list that seems to reflect folk practice as much as "medicine"; and at least by the early third century C.E., abortion was considered a serious crime, when self-inflicted (*Dig.* 48.8.8) or performed by others by means of "potions" (*Dig.* 48.19.38.5). Yet it is not clear that abortion itself, when brought about by a doctor, was illegal, or that this female market was ever rigorously controlled.[25]

Pliny devotes much more attention to the methods by which women may cure barrenness and promote conception. He recommends a wide variety of substances, from cow's milk to partridge eggs, and he strongly implies an active female market for these medicines.[26] He even cites from one of his sources a text unfortunately lost: a poem by a woman crediting a gemstone with helping her to conceive (37.178): "What paneros is like is not told us by Metrodorus, but he quotes a not-inelegant poem by Queen Timaris on it, dedicated to Venus, in which it is understood that the stone aided her fertility."

A picture begins to emerge of activities undertaken, mostly by women, in order to ensure the fertility that was so essential to them. The waters of Sinuessa are said to cure barrenness in women (31.8); a spring at Thespiae and the river Elatum in Arcadia help women conceive, while the spring Linus in Arcadia prevents miscarriage. We might imagine women making pilgrimages to these rivers in order to attain their goals, much like the well-attested fourth-century B.C.E. pilgrimages to the temple of Asclepius at Epidaurus, where women sought help toward conception, among other cures, via incubation (Lefkowitz and Fant 1992: 285–87). "Some people," says Pliny, "out of superstition, believe that mistletoe works more effect-ively if it is gathered from an oak at the new moon without iron or touching the ground, and that it cures epilepsy and helps women to conceive if they just keep it with them" (24.12). Women are also advised to keep cucumber seeds fastened to the body, without letting them touch the ground (20.6); thus we imagine the hopeful mother bedecked with seeds and plants. Another recommendation (*tradunt*) is to smell the plant ami during sex (20.164); so we might imagine rituals of the bedroom. (Compare Serenus Sammonicus's recommendation that a woman and her husband pluck the "herb of Mercury" together when they are hurrying to bed at night, *Liber medicinalis* 32.13–14.) Various medicines are said to foster conception, and some of them are not so appealing: the Magi promise that a barren woman will conceive in three days if she takes a hyena eye in her food with licorice and dill (*HN* 28.97); small worms taken in drink promote conception (30.125), as do snails applied with saffron (30.126); likewise hawk's dung in honey wine (30.130).

We might pause here to notice how awful some of the medicines sound. A lot of Pliny's recipes suggest how different the experience of medicine would have been for a Roman than for a modern patient. For the breasts, Pliny recommends crabs applied locally (*inliti*, 32.129); this sounds impossible, but elsewhere he recommends tying frogs backwards onto a baby's head for siriasis (literally "dog-star-itis," a name for infant sunstroke, 32.138); the skull has to be moistened, he notes soberly. Other recommendations for women include the use of beaver testicles, scrapings from the gymnasium, chewed-up anise, earthworms taken in sweet wine, beetles, and a wide variety of kinds of animal dung. There are recommendations for tying on fish, and for fumigation with a dead snake, or with lobsters. The example of the frogs on the baby shows that it is not just women who get stuck with this kind of medicine; however, there does seem to have been an association between disgusting ingredients and women patients. Heinrich von Staden, in a recent study (1992), has pointed out how overwhelmingly such cures are reserved for women, especially the use of dung.

So far we have seen women actively engaged in medical treatments affecting menstruation, abortion, and conception. Once conception was achieved, expectant mothers ran tests to determine the child's sex. For example, Pliny (10.154) says that, as a young woman, Livia, wife of Augustus, was eager to have a boy, and, when she was pregnant with Tiberius, used a special way, "common among girls" (*boc usa est puellari augurio*), to tell the sex of her baby. Suetonius (*Tib.* 14.2) gives a more detailed description:

> Livia, when pregnant with [Tiberius], wanted to know whether she would give birth to a male [child], and tried to find out by various omens; she took an egg stolen from a setting hen and cherished it continually, sometimes in her own hand, sometimes in her maidservants', taking turns (*nunc sua nunc ministrarum manu per vices…fovit*), until a chick was hatched, with a marked crest.

Here this procedure is made into a joint effort by mistress and slaves, all participating together, though the practice is focused on the body of the dominant woman.

Pliny also lists recommendations for materials that will affect the sex of the baby, not just tell the mother what it is. And many of these aim at helping to conceive a male child. Some involve activities by father and mother together (for example, taking crataegonos in wine before supper for forty days before conception, 27.63); often the recommendations are for special additions to the mother's diet.[27] Once in a while, the properties of substances to produce either a girl or a boy are listed; so maybe some people were trying for girls (compare the short list of such medicines in Metrodora, "for the birth of a boy or the birth of a girl," 1.33). On the other hand, there are hints here and there that boy babies are better, and a complete absence of recommendations aimed solely at conceiving a girl baby. So though there is nothing here to indicate any widespread gynecide, there does seem to be an assumption that women will be trying to have male children.[28]

By far the bulk of Pliny's material on fertility has to do with pregnancy, and especially with childbirth. It is ironic that one of the very few reported sayings we have from Roman women has to do with a subversion of what seems to be the norm expected by Pliny. A joke attributed to Julia, daughter of Augustus, has her claiming to use her pregnancies to enable her to have sex with men other than her husband (Macrob. *Sat.* 2.5.9): "And when those who knew of her sins used to marvel at how she gave birth to sons resembling Agrippa, when she made such public property of her body, she said, 'Why, I never take on a passenger until the ship is full.'" Julia, in contemporary histories, has the character of a renegade, a woman who goes against what is expected of women (Richlin 1992b). Certainly, if the list of remedies in Pliny is anything to go by, we would expect that many Roman women were deeply concerned about carrying a baby to term.

Pliny's encyclopedia contains more than 140 remedies concerned with pregnancy and childbirth. A significant category contains substances that help hold off miscarriage or are to be avoided because they will cause miscarriage. Pliny includes miscarriage among the hazards of sexuality, saying that "a yawn indeed is fatal [to a woman] in labor, just as sneezing during sex causes miscarriage" (7.42). Some substances are to be avoided by pregnant women as dangerous, even by proximity; sometimes miscarriage is a risk or side effect. Thus the cases in which activity by the women is demanded include many aimed at staving off miscarriage. Most interesting is a group that involves things women should not step over: these include menstrual blood (28.80); a viper or a dead amphisbaena (30.128); a raven's egg, which will cause a woman to miscarry through the mouth (30.130); and beaver oil, or a beaver (32.133). These are among the most hallucinatory episodes in the *Natural History*. How is it imagined that a woman might accidentally step over a beaver? Did anyone really believe in oral miscarriage? Additional information only raises further questions. Pliny (30.128) offers two remedies for stepping over a dead amphisbaena – a snake with a head at each end of its body. One was to carry a live amphisbaena on your person in a box; the other was to step immediately over a preserved amphisbaena. So we have to imagine the household in an uproar, and somebody yelling, "Marcus! Quick, run down to the drug-store and get a preserved amphisbaena!" The dangers of raven's eggs are clarified by Pliny's notes on the raven (10.32); he says it is a popular belief (*vulgus arbitratur*) that ravens lay eggs or mate through their beaks, and hence a pregnant woman, if she eats a raven's egg, will bear her child through her mouth, and will have a difficult labor if a raven's egg is brought into the house. Though Aristotle is cited for a counteropinion, it seems at least possible that Pliny is preserving a folk belief here – though one that can hardly have had much in women's experience to support it.

Most of the miscarriage insurance is less exotic, and involves amulets, like this one (36.151):

> Eagle stones, wrapped in skins of sacrifical animals, are worn as amulets by women or quadrupeds (*mulieribus vel quadripedibus*) while pregnant to hold back the birth (*continent partus*); these are not to be removed until they give birth, otherwise the vulva will prolapse. But if the amulet is not taken away while they are in labor, they cannot give birth at all.

This kind of recommendation is found for other amulets as well, so when we think of amulets, we also should imagine that each one carries with it its proper procedure.

Indeed, the recommendations here imply women's activities and involvement with the medical care of their own bodies. A woman might experiment with a range of pessaries, ointments, and potions. Pliny recommends tying thirty grains of grit to the body with linen to aid in removing the afterbirth (20.183). A woman might also use a hare-rennet ointment, unless she had bathed the day before (28.248); if she takes sow-thistle potion, she must then go for a walk (22.89). Substances or objects she might keep with her or carry include not only the preserved amphisbaena but a stick with which a frog has been shaken from a snake (30.129); a vulture's feather under the feet (30.130); a torpedo fish, brought into the room (32.133); and a "round ball of blackish tufa" taken from the second stomach of a heifer and not allowed to touch the ground (11.203). Amulets to aid labor include those made from plants sprouting inside a sieve thrown away on a cross-path (24.171); a stone eaten by a pregnant doe, found in her excrement or womb (28.246); and chameleon tongue (28.114). Some amulets or substances have to be placed on certain parts of the woman's body: the afterbirth of a bitch (30.123) and the snakeskin (30.129) have to be put on the woman's groin; the stingray-sting amulet is to be worn on the navel (32.133); the stone voided by a bladder victim is to be tied over the groin (28.42). And some procedures are very elaborate indeed, involving the central participation of other people. To hasten birth, the father of the baby is to untie his belt and put it around the woman's waist, and then untie it, saying the *precatio*, "I bound you, and I will set you free"; he then leaves the room (28.42). Another remedy involves someone throwing over the house where the woman is in labor one of two things: a missile that has killed with one stroke each a human being, a boar, and a bear; or a light-cavalry spear pulled from a human body without touching the ground (28.33–34). Or someone might just bring the spear into the house.

Pliny also lists some medicines that counteract the effects of witchcraft against conception, pregnancy, and childbirth. Some of these indicate women's concern to protect themselves against witchcraft, a sense of the vulnerability of a pregnant woman. The stone called aetites, found in eagle's nests, is also said to protect the fetus "against all plots to cause abortion" (*contra omnes abortuum insidias*, 30.130). Eating wolf meat is recommended for women about to give birth, or else having someone who has eaten wolf meat sit next to them as they go into labor; this prevails even against *inlatas noxias*, "harmful things carried in" (28.247–48). The idea that it is harmful specifically to bring certain things into the house where a woman is in labor recurs in several cases, and the implication is that ill-wishers might do this on purpose. The same may be true of the objects not to be stepped over; perhaps these should be thought of as placed in the woman's path – like the beaver, for example. These all seem to be actions it would be hard to do unintentionally, and so are to be understood as malicious; likewise, Pliny notes that hanging the left foot of a hyena above a woman in labor is fatal (28.103). So we should imagine pregnant women as on their guard, having to be vigilant to make sure nobody is surrounding them with beavers and hyena feet.

Similarly, women are vigilant in protecting the babies once they are born. A fascinating set of texts talks about the use of amulets and other medicines by mothers or *nutrices* to protect young babies.[29] Baby amulets cited by Pliny include branches of coral (32.24); amber (37.50); gold (*ut minus noceant quae inferantur veneficia*, 33.84); malachite (37.114); galactitis (37.162); beetles (11.97); a dolphin's tooth, for children's "sudden terrors" (*pavores repentinos*, 32.137); similarly a wolf's tooth or wolf's skin (28.257); a horse's baby teeth (28.258); and bones from dogs' dung, for siriasis (30.135). One cure especially for girl babies is an amulet of goat's dung in cloth (28.259), recalling von Staden's association of dung therapy with women. The use of protective medicine could continue past baby-hood; Suetonius says that Nero continued to wear on his right arm the cast-off skin of a snake, enclosed in a gold bracelet, "at his mother's wish" (*ex voluntate matris, Ner.* 6.4). This suggests to us (1) that the amulets do not just appear in some Greek medical sources collected by Pliny, but reflect actual Roman practice, (2) that they were used and controlled by concerned mothers, and (3) that they were worn by children as a sign of their mothers' protection.[30] Moreover, David Soren's excavation of an infant cemetery from the late ancient period in the Italian countryside suggests that animals like those recommended in Pliny were indeed fastened onto ailing children.[31]

The classic baby amulet is the *fascinum*, a phallic amulet of which many exemplars survive today. The paramount example of a *male* body part with beneficial properties, the phallus has powers to counteract witchcraft and the evil eye, as has been widely discussed.[32] But Pliny introduces his account of the *fascinum* – protector, he remarks, of babies and generals alike – in the context of women's pediatric practice. Dismissing some practitioners' claims about the use of saliva, he remarks, scornfully, "If we believe those things are done aright, we must think likewise of these, too: that the wet nurse (*nutrix*), at the approach of a stranger (*extraneus*), or if the infant is looked at while sleeping, spits [*adspui*, on the baby? at the onlooker?] three times" (28.39). Here, as elsewhere, the *nutrix* is the protector of the baby, and her saliva has a protective force against the evil eye.[33]

The satirist Persius, Pliny's contemporary, describes the same practice. He is talking about what is best to pray for, and he uses as a negative illustration a picture of a baby and the women who are taking care of him (*Satire* 2.31–40):

> Behold, a grandmother or gods-fearing mother's sister (*matertera*)
> has taken the boy from his cradle and averts evil (*expiat*) from
>   his forehead and wet lips
> with her middle finger (*infami digito*) and her purifying (*lustralibus*) saliva,
> skilled at holding back burning (*urentis*) eyes;
> then with shaking hands and suppliant prayer she sends her hungry hope,
> now toward the fields of Licinius, now toward the house of Crassus:
> "May king and queen choose him for son-in-law, may girls

fight over him; whatever he steps on, let it turn into a rose."
But I don't trust my prayers to a wet nurse (*nutrici*). Deny,
Jupiter, these things to her, though she ask you clad in white (*albata*).

Persius, perhaps the most uninterested in women of all Roman satirists, here affords the reader a sidewise glance at women's folk practice. He lists as possible baby-minders not only the *nutrix*, but two important female kin: the grandmother and the mother's sister, the *matertera* – a family member who shows up elsewhere as important in a child's life (Hallett 1984: 151, 183–86; Richlin 1997). He depicts these women as actively concerned to protect the baby, and using their saliva as an important means of protection against the evil eye. These women pray for riches for the baby, for a good marriage, and for love; and they get dressed up to pray. They have health care down to a system.

Beyond Lingerie

And so we leave Pliny, sitting up late at night, laboring away at the *Natural History*, with a bra on his head. This is surely a case where the cup, so to speak, is both half empty and half full. What Pliny tells us certainly gives us information about Roman women's lives that is both new and disturbing. If we want to view Rome as an oppressive patriarchy, we can carry with us the image of Pliny's recommendation that a menstruating woman should carry a mullet with her so as not to dull the shine on mirrors (28.82). Pliny and the other encyclopedic sources provide a rich supply of fears about the female body – but also show beliefs about its powers. We might compare this ambivalence with Judith Hallett's model (1989) of "woman as same and other" in day-to-day relationships in the Roman elite; or with the perilously permeable boundaries so characteristic of Roman culture, where slave could become freed, Greek could come to Rome, and Pliny could write the *Natural History* and loathe doctors at the same time. The picture of the female body in Pliny also sheds further light on what Roman men feared when they accused each other of effeminacy, as they so frequently did (Richlin 1992a: passim). On the other hand, thanks to Pliny, we are able to fill in a picture of women's lives otherwise only known from material remains and from the somewhat more one-sided view of medical writers. Archaeology can give us votive offerings, dedications, and burials; Pliny and his friends can give us more of a context for them – can help us connect the dots. Pliny and his bra bring us just a little closer to Roman women themselves.

NOTES

1 See Boston Women's Health Book Collective 1992: 15, 205. The current edition of this basic women-centered women's health book contains an eighty-page section on sexuality, along with sections on birth control and abortion, pregnancy, childbirth, and menopause, among others. On attacks on *Our Bodies, Ourselves*, see Hunter 1986: 28 (entries for 1977, 1981), apparently using the BWHBC's own "file on backlash."

2 For studies that link medical theories with their cultural context, see Dean-Jones 1992, on the social function of Hippocratic theories of women's sexual pleasure; and, on Rome, French 1986 (on Pliny and Soranus); Gourevitch 1984 (largely a sourcebook); Hanson 1990: 330–31 (Soranus and Roman culture); Pinault 1992 (Soranus and the rise of asceticism).

3 For discussion of Pliny on doctors, see Nutton 1986, who argues that Pliny overstates his case.

4 On the remarkable life of the elder Pliny, see the younger Pliny, *Ep.* 3.5, 6.16. The extant fragment of Suetonius's *Life* of the elder Pliny may conveniently be found in Rolfe 1914, 2:505. On Pliny's thought generally, see Beagon 1992; French and Greenaway 1986.

5 So also French 1986: 69. The text of Metrodora will someday be available in a new authoritative version (Parker, n.d.).

6 G.E.R. Lloyd points out (1983: 137) that, when Pliny says *invenio* ("I find"), he often seems to be reporting on what he has read in the course of his research, rather than on his personal experience. My imaginings about Pliny, then, must be taken more for their symbolic value than as an idea of Pliny's actual practice.

7 This question has not been the primary focus of work on Greek and Roman gynecology, due to the nature of the extant sources, which are written from the doctor's point of view. For discussion, see Hanson 1990: 309–11 (with bibliography); 1992; 47–48; Dean-Jones 1994: 26–40, 247–48; King 1993: 105, 109–10; and especially King 1995 and Lloyd 1983: 62–79 (on the Hippocratic corpus), 181–82 (on Soranus). Riddle 1992 treats the history of birth control as a slow erosion of women's rights over their bodies; see esp. 165.

8 For women's-culture approaches to antiquity, see Hallett 1989; Skinner 1993; Zweig 1993. Buckley and Gottlieb (1988: 12–15, 31–34) argue vigorously for women's agency within menstrual symbolic systems.

9 The major discussion is at 28.70–86, and note the apology at 28.87. Book 28 begins a long section on remedies from animals, which goes on through book 30. Remedies from human beings begin at 28.4, and include a discussion of verbal charms and superstition, the use of human saliva (28.35–39), human hair (28.41), and other body parts (28.41–44), gymnasium scrapings (28.50–52), and urine (28.65–69). The discussion of the female body follows, and from there Pliny proceeds directly to elephants, apologizing for telling the reader so many disgusting things. The discussion in book 7 comes in a book-long general

discussion of the properties of human beings, and commences with the statement *solum autem animal menstruale mulier est* (7.63). Then Pliny labels the *profluvium* as *monstrificum*, and gives a concise but full list of its properties.

10   Buckley and Gottlieb 1988: 7–8, 35–38; they are among the few writers to discuss Pliny in this context, basing their remarks on a 1916 article in the *Johns Hopkins Hospital Bulletin*. They point to Pliny as an example of a positive attitude toward menstrual blood; as will be seen, this is only half the picture. For brief discussion, see Dean-Jones 1994: 248–49.

11   Thus also Cohen 1991: 287. Cole (1992, esp. 109–11) discusses various conditions in which women were considered polluting in Greek sanctuaries, among them post-childbirth and miscarriage, and during menstruation; cf. Dean-Jones 1994: 223–53 on Greek attitudes toward menstruation. On the application of biblical law on menstruation in ancient and medieval Judaism and in ancient Christianity, see Cohen 1991. On menstruation in rabbinic literature, see Wegner 1991: 77–78, 82. On the increase in misogyny in attitudes toward menstruation from the classical rabbinic period through the Middle Ages, see Boyarin 1993: 90–97. On the meaning of menstruation in the medieval church, see Bynum 1987: 122–23 (holy women's bodies as sources of food), 211, 214, 239. On early Islamic attitudes, see Wegner 1991: 91 n. 28. For a women's-culture approach (early modern Jewish women's own prayers, including those concerning menstrual purity), see Weissler 1991, esp. 165–66.

12   It is enticing to speculate that this prohibition, more severe than any attested for Italy, may reflect a pre-Islamic Arab system underlying beliefs like those examined in Delaney 1988.

13   Other powers are listed at *HN* 28.80–86: menses act as a solvent on bitumen (also at 7.65); menses cure gout, and menstruating women can cure by their touch scrofula, parotid tumors, abscesses, erysipelas, boils, and runny eyes. Lais and Salpe, as well as a male source, recommend menstrual blood for relief of the bites of rabid dogs and of fevers. The *obstetrix* Sotira recommends relieving fevers and epilepsy by smearing the soles of the patient's feet with menstrual blood. Icatidas *medicus* says fevers are ended by intercourse when the menses are just beginning. A menstrual cloth can counteract the effects of rabies, due to the fact that rabies is caused by dogs tasting menstrual blood. The blood is also good for ulcers of draught animals, women's headaches, and protecting the house from the arts of the Magi. Cf. Serenus Sammonicus (*Liber medicinalis* 12.163), who recommends the "obscene dews" of a virgin as a cure for pains in the ears.

14   See Richlin 1992a: 67–69, 115–16; Richlin 1984. Cf. von Staden 1991: 277–80 on Celsus's analogies between womb and anus, labia and wound.

15   On the meaning of the eye in Roman culture, see Barton 1993: 91–98.

16   On the female body in symbolic systems, see Buckley and Gottlieb 1988: 26–30, including discussion of Mary Douglas and the concept of pollution; on the upper body vs. lower body, see Bakhtin 1984.

17   This model, which has gained great popular currency (e.g., students' com-
     ments in class), is well exemplified by Ehrenreich and English 1973. The
     model is somewhat contemptuously dismissed by Green (1989), who
     produces a set of sophisticated and historically informed questions concerning
     women practitioners and women patients in the medieval and early modern
     periods. For a brief but compelling account of the historical vicissitudes of
     knowledge of herbal contraceptives, see Riddle, Estes, and Russell 1994.
18   Sources are given at 20.19, 20.28, 20.32, 20.34, 20.227, 26.99, 28.256.
19   For some examples of texts featuring women who use aphrodisiacs on their
     husbands, see Faraone 1992: 98–99; add Juvenal 6.133–35, 610–26.
20   For men: *HN* 8.91, 10.182, 22.20, 26.96, 26.98, 27.65, 28.99, 30.141
     (four), 30.143. For women: 20.227, 22.87, 28.101, 28.106, 28.256,
     30.143 (two).
21   A cure of the Magi. The text says lust is stimulated *ad sexus suos*, "for their
     own sex"; this does not make much sense with the following clause, and so
     Mayhoff conjectured *ab sexu suo*, "away from their own sex," i.e., the wife
     lures the husband away from his desire for other males.
22   The aphrodisiacs in Pliny and Metrodora would then not support the
     argument made by Faraone for Greek aphrodisiacs (1992): that they tend
     to aim at controlling the ardent male but arousing the passive female. For
     more on the gender politics of Greek love-charms, see Winkler 1990: 90–
     91, 95–98.
23   On emmenagogues, see Riddle 1992: 27 and passim.
24   On abortion and contraception in antiquity, see Riddle 1992; Riddle, Estes,
     and Russell 1994. On abortion in Pliny, see Beagon 1992: 216–20. On
     abortion in the Hippocratic Oath, see Riddle 1992: 7–10.
25   *Dig.* 48.8.8 (Ulp.): "If it is proved that a woman has brought force to bear
     on her own innards in order to avoid giving birth, the provincial governor
     should send her into exile"; *Dig.* 48.19.38.5 (Paulus): "Those who make
     potions, either to cause abortions or love, even if they do not do this
     fraudulently, still, because it sets a bad example, those of the lower class
     are sent to the mines, while those of the upper class are relegated to an island
     and fined part of their property. But if they have caused a woman or man to
     die, they must undergo the supreme punishment." Gardner (1986: 158–
     59) is of the opinion that it is the drugs, rather than abortion, itself, that are
     prohibited here. See further, on the availability and legality of abortion,
     Riddle 1992: 7–10, 109–12; Hopkins 1965, on Roman contraception
     generally; Gamel 1989, on abortion in Ovid's poetry.
26   For conception aids, see *HN* 20.51, 22.83, 23.53, 27.63, 28.52, 28.249,
     28.253, 28.255, 30.131. Serenus Sammonicus devotes section 32 of the
     Liber medicinalis to *Conceptio et partus*; he cites Lucretius as his authority
     on the mysteries of conception, and goes on to offer several cures for
     barrenness (32.607–14).
27   See *HN* 20.263, 25.97, 28.254, 28.254, 30.123.

28 Gender-selective infanticide in antiquity has been the subject of extensive scholarly debate. See discussion in Golden 1992: 225–30, with bibliography; also Boswell 1990: 54 n. 2 (bibliography), 100–103 (primary sources), and in general 53–137; Dixon 1988; Riddle 1992. For reports on the current practice of infanticide in India and on women's statements about the practice, see Dahlburg 1994.

29 On the care of young children by mothers and/or *nutrices*, see Dixon 1988, esp. 120–33.

30 The persistence of some of these amulets is remarkable. Klapisch-Zuber (1985: 149–50, with plate 7.1) publishes a detail of a sixteenth-century Italian painting showing a coral branch and a wolf's-tooth amulet for teething, and discusses the wet nurse's responsibility for the child's health (also at 105 n. 25, on protection from the *maldocchio*). She notes that "dog teeth or wolf teeth" figure in the lists of possessions of four fifteenth-century male babies (149 n. 64). An eighteenth-century American representation of the "coral and bells" may be seen in the Henry Huntington Library and Art Gallery, San Marino, California, in the "Portrait of Mrs. Elijah Boardman and Her Son William Whiting Boardman," by Ralph Earl (c. 1798), displayed alongside a contemporary English specimen.

31 See Soren 1999; Soren, Fenton, Birkby, and Jensen 1997. Soren found puppy bones in with the baby bones; as well as recommending frogs for siriasis (above), Pliny recommends puppies applied to the painful parts of patients for the transfer of the illness, after which the puppies are to be buried (30.42, 30.64).

32 On the phallus and the evil eye, see Barton 1993: 95–98, 171, 189 and fig. 2; Johns 1982; color plate 10 (phallic amulets), 68 fig. 51 (phalluses sawing an eye in half), and in general 62–75.

33 For other examples of apotropaic spitting in Roman belief, see *HN* 28.35–39; the nurse as protector of the baby can be attested in Greek culture at least as early as the seventh century B.C.E. (*Hymn. Hom. Cer.* 228–30). Johnston 1995 provides full treatment and excellent analysis of ancient Greek and Near Eastern beliefs about harm to babies from demons and witchcraft, including discussion of apotropaic spitting. For similar beliefs in Jewish folk culture, see Trachtenberg [1939] 1961: 121 ("threefold expectoration"), 159, 162; my own grandmother, born in Lithuania in the late nineteenth century, practiced the same behavior described by Pliny.

REFERENCES

Bakhtin, M. 1984. *Rabelais and His World*. Trans. H. Iswolsky. Bloomington, IN.

Barton, C. A. 1993. *The Sorrows of the Ancient Romans: The Gladiator and the Monster*. Princeton, NJ.

Beagon, M. 1992. *Roman Nature: The Thought of Pliny the Elder.* Oxford.

Boston Women's Health Book Collective. 1992. *The New Our Bodies, Ourselves.* New York.

Boswell, J. 1990. *The Kindness of Strangers.* New York.

Boyarin, D. 1993. *Carnal Israel: Reading Sex in Talmudic Culture.* Berkeley, CA.

Buckley, T., and A. Gottlieb. 1988. "A Critical Appraisal of Theories of Menstrual Symbolism." In T. Buckley and A. Gottlieb (eds.), *Blood and Magic,* 3–50. Berkeley, CA.

Bynum, C. W. 1987. *Holy Feast and Holy Fast.* Berkeley, CA.

Carson, A. 1990. "Putting Her in Her Place: Woman, Dirt, and Desire." In D. M. Halperin, J. J. Winkler, and F. I. Zeitlin (eds.), *Before Sexuality: The Construction of Erotic Experience in the Ancient Greek World,* 309–38. Princeton, NJ.

Chibnall, M. 1975. "Pliny's Natural History and the Middle Ages." In T. A. Dorey (ed.), *Empire and Aftermath: Silver Latin II,* 57–78. London.

Cohen, S. J. D. 1991. "Menstruants and the Sacred in Judaism and Christianity." In S. B. Pomeroy (ed.), *Women's History and Ancient History,* 273–99. Chapel Hill, NC.

Cole, S. G. 1992. "*Gunaiki ou Themis:* Gender Difference in the Greek *Leges Sacrae.*" *Helios* 19: 104–22.

Dahlburg, J.-T. 1994. "The Fight to Save India's Baby Girls." *Los Angeles Times,* Feb. 22: A1, A14.

Dean-Jones, L. 1992. "The Politics of Pleasure: Female Sexual Appetite in the Hippocratic Corpus." *Helios* 19: 72–91.

———. 1994. *Women's Bodies in Classical Greek Science.* Oxford.

Delaney, C. 1988. "Mortal Flow: Menstruation in Turkish Village Society." In T. Buckley and A. Gottlieb (eds.), *Blood Magic,* 75–93. Berkeley, CA.

Dixon, S. 1988. *The Roman Mother.* Norman, OK.

Ehrenreich, B. and D. English. 1973. *Witches, Midwives, and Nurses: A History of Women Healers.* New York.

Faraone, C. A. 1992. "Sex and Power: Male-Targetting Aphrodisiacs in the Greek Magical Tradition." *Helios* 19: 92–103.

French, R., and F. Greenaway (eds.). 1986. *Science in the Early Roman Empire: Pliny the Elder, His Sources and Influence.* London and Sydney.

French, V. 1986. "Midwives and Maternity Care in the Greco-Roman World." *Helios* 13.2: 69–84.

Gamel, M.-K. 1989. "*Non sine caede:* Abortion Politics and Poetics in Ovid's *Amores. Helios* 16: 183–206.

Gardner, J. F. 1986. *Women in Roman Law and Society.* Bloomington and Indianapolis, IN and London.

Golden, M. 1992. "The Uses of Cross-Cultural Comparison in Ancient Social History." *Echos du monde classique/Classical Views* 36: 309–31.

Gordon, L. 1986. "What's New in Women's History?" In T. de Lauretis (ed.), *Feminist Studies/Critical Studies,* 20–30. Bloomington, IN.

Gourevitch, D. 1984. *Le Mal d'être femme: La Femme et la médecine dans la Rome antique.* Paris.

Green, M. 1989. "Women's Medical Practice and Health Care in Medieval Europe." *Signs* 14: 434–73.

Hallett, J. P. 1984. *Fathers and Daughters in Roman Society.* Princeton, NJ.

——. 1989. "Woman as *Same* and *Other* in Classical Roman Elite." *Helios* 16: 59–78.

Hanson, A. E. 1990. "The Medical Writers' Woman." In D. M. Halperin, J. J. Winkler, and F. I. Zeitlin (eds.)., *Before Sexuality: The Construction of Erotic Experience in the Ancient Greek World,* 309–38. Princeton, NJ.

——. 1992. "Conception, Gestation, and the Origin of Female Nature in the *corpus Hippocraticum.*" *Helios* 19: 31–71.

Hopkins, M. K. 1965. "Contraception in the Roman Empire." *Comparative Studies in Society and History* 8: 124–51.

Hunter, N. D. 1986. "The Pornography Debate in Context: A Chronology." In FACT Book Committee, *Caught Looking,* 26–29. New York.

Johnston, S. I. 1995. "Defining the Dreadful: Remarks on the Child-Killing Demon." In M. Meyer and P. Mirecki (eds.), *Ancient Magic and Ritual Power,* 361–89. Leiden.

Kincaid, J. 1990. *Lucy.* Harmondsworth.

King, H. 1993. "Producing Woman: Hippocratic Gynaecology." In L. Archer, S. Fischler, and M. Wyke (eds.), *Women in Ancient Societies,* 102–14. London.

——. 1995. "Self-Help, Self-Knowledge: In Search of the Patient in Hippocratic Gynaecology." In R. Hawley and B. Levick (eds.), *Women in Antiquity: New Assessments,* 135–48. New York and London.

Klapisch-Zuber, C. 1985. *Women, Family, and Ritual in Renaissance Italy.* Trans. L. G. Cochrane, Chicago.

Lefkowitz, M., and M. B. Fant (eds.). 1992. *Women's Life in Greece and Rome.* 2nd ed. Baltimore, MD.

Lloyd, G. E. R. 1979. *Magic, Reason and Experience.* Cambridge.

——. 1983. *Science, Folklore and Ideology.* Cambridge.

Nutton, V. 1986. "The Perils of Patriotism: Pliny and Roman Medicine." In R. French and F. Greenaway (eds.), *Science in the Early Roman Empire: Pliny the Elder, His Sources and Influence,* 30–58. London and Sydney.

Parker, H. (n. d.). "Metrodora: The Earliest Surviving Work by a Woman Doctor." Unpublished manuscript.

Pinault, J. R. 1992. "The Medical Case for Virginity in the Early Second Century CE.: Soranus of Ephesus, *Gynecology* 1.32." *Helios* 19: 123–39.

Rackham, H., Jones, W. H. S., and D. E. Eichholz (eds. and trans.). 1938–63. *Pliny: Natural History.* 10 vols. Loeb Classical Library. Cambridge, MA.

Richlin, A. 1984. "Invective Against Women in Roman Satire." *Arethusa* 17: 67–80.

——. 1992a. *The Garden of Priapus: Sexuality and Aggression in Roman Humor.* Rev. ed. New York.

Richlin, A. 1992b. "Julia's Jokes, Galla Placidia, and the Roman Use of Women as Political Icons." In B. Garlick, S. Dixon, and P. Allen (eds.), *Stereotypes of Women in Power*, 63–91. New York.

——. 1993. "The Ethnographer's Dilemma and the Dream of a Lost Golden Age." In N. Rabinowitz and A. Richlin (eds.), *Feminist Theory and the Classics*, 272–303. New York and London.

——. 1997. "Carrying Water in a Sieve: Class and the Body in Roman Women's Religion." In K. King, ed., *Women and Goddess Traditions*, 330–74. Philadelphia, PA.

Riddle, J. M. 1992. *Contraception and Abortion from the Ancient World to the Renaissance*. Cambridge.

Riddle, J. M., Estes, J. W., and J. C. Russell. 1994. "Birth Control in the Ancient World." *Archaeology* Mar./Apr.: 29–35.

Rolfe, J. C. 1914. *Suetonius*. 2 vols. Loeb Classical Library. Cambridge, MA.

Skinner, M. 1993. "Woman and Language in Archaic Greece, or, Why Is Sappho a Woman?" In N. Rabinowitz and A. Richlin (eds.), *Feminist Theory and the Classics*, 125–44. New York and London.

Soren, D. 1999. "Hecate and the Infant Cemetery at Poggio Gramignano." In D. Soren and N. Soren (eds.), *A Roman Villa and Late Roman Infant Cemetery: Excavation at Paggio Gramignans (Lugnano in Teverina)*, 619–31. Rome.

Soren, D., Fenton, T., Birkby, W., and R. Jensen. 1999. "The Infant Cemetery at Poggio Gramignano: Description and Analysis." In D. Soren and N. Soren (eds.), *A Roman Villa and Late Roman Infant Cemetery: Excavation at Poggio Gramignans (Lugnano in Teverina)*, 477–530 Rome.

Temkin, O. (trans.), [1956] 1991. *Soranus' Gynecology*. Baltimore, MD and London.

Trachtenberg, J. [1939] 1961. *Jewish Magic and Superstition*. Cleveland, OH.

von Staden, H. 1991. "*Apud nos foediora verba*: Celsus' Reluctant Construction of the Female Body." In G. Sabbagh (ed.), *Le Latin médical: La Constitution d'un language Scientifique*, Mémoirs du Centre Jean Palerne, 10, 271–96. Saint-Étienne.

——. 1992. "Women and Dirt." *Helios* 19: 7–30.

Wegner, J. R. 1991. "The Image and Status of Women in Classical Rabbinic Judaism." In J. R. Baskin (ed.), *Jewish Women in Historical Perspective*, 94–114. Detroit, MI.

Weissler, C. 1991. "Prayers in Yiddish and the Religious World of Ashkenazic Women." In J. R. Baskin, ed., *Jewish Women in Historical Perspective*, 159–81. Detroit, MI.

Winkler, J. J. 1990. *The Constraints of Desire: The Anthropology of Sex and Gender in Ancient Greece*. New York and London.

Woolf, V. [1929] 1957. *A Room of One's Own*. New York.

Zweig, B. 1993. "The Primal Mind: Using Native American Models for the Study of Women in Ancient Greece." In N. S. Rabinowitz and A. Richlin (eds.), *Feminist Theory and the Classics*, 145–80. New York and London.

SOURCE

Pliny the Elder (23/4–79 CE) is primarily known as the author of the 37-book *Natural History*, an encyclopedia of all contemporary knowledge regarding the natural world, including animals, plants, and minerals, as well as ancient technology. This section belongs to a larger discussion of folk medicine and concerns the destructive or curative effects of the products of women's bodies.

The text consulted is that of A. Ernout (ed.), *Pline l'ancien, Histoire naturelle livre xxvii* (Paris, 1962).

Pliny the Elder, *Natural History* 28.70–82

The products of women's bodies approach the level of the miraculous, to say nothing of the criminal practice of tearing apart the limbs of stillborn babies, or the powers of the menstrual fluid, and the other stories told not only by midwives, but even by courtesans themselves. For instance, they say the smell of a woman's burning hair keeps away serpents, while its smoke causes women suffocating from hysteria to breathe easily. Indeed this same ash – if the hair is burnt in a jar or used with a tincture of silver – cures scabrous or itching eyes, likewise warts and the sores of babies. Mixed with honey, it heals head wounds and the cavities formed by all ulcers. When honey is added along with frankincense, it cures abscesses and gout; mixed with lard, it arrests the skin inflammations accompanied by fever, known as "sacred fire," the hemorrhaging of the blood, and likewise the numbness of the body.

As to the use of breast milk, it is considered to be the sweetest and most delicate of all female products; it is most useful in cases of prolonged fever and intestinal disease, especially the milk of a woman who has recently weaned her baby. And it is particularly efficacious for nausea, fevers, and cramps; when mixed with frankincense, for abscesses on the breasts; and also for an eye bloodied by a blow. It provides the maximum benefit for a painful or inflamed eye if it is milked right into it; even more so if it is mixed with honey and with the sap of the narcissus flower or with powdered incense. Above all, for every use, a woman's milk is more effective if she has given birth to a boy, and most effective of all if she has given birth to twin boys and if she herself abstains from wine and very acidic foods. Mixed, moreover, with the liquid whites of eggs and applied to the temples on a piece of damp wool, it reduces the swelling of the eyes. But if a frog has squirted the eye with its fluids, it is an excellent remedy; drunk or poured into the wound by drops, this fluid also counteracts the effect of a frog's bite. They also assert that the man who is rubbed with the milk of a mother and daughter at the same time will be free from the fear of eye trouble for the rest of his life.

In addition, afflictions of the ears are healed by breast milk mixed with a little oil, or, if they are sore from a blow, warmed with goose fat. If there is a very unpleasant smell from the ears, as often happens during a long illness, wool moistened with milk onto which a little honey has been dissolved is put into them. And to counteract the traces of jaundice left in the eyes, droplets of milk with elaterium, a purgative, are used. A drink of milk is peculiarly strong against the poison of the sea slug, also of the buprestis, a kind of poisonous beetle, or as Aristotle maintains, of the plant dorycinium, a species of nightshade, and against the madness induced by drinking henbane. They also prescribe smearing it on with hemlock for gout; others say to apply it with offscourings of wool and goose fat, just as is used for uterine cramps. A drink of breast milk also helps the bowels, as Rabirius writes, and induces menstruation. The milk of a woman who has given birth to a girl has superior power for curing facial blemishes. Woman's milk also cures lung problems. If the urine of a pre-pubescent boy and Attic honey are mixed with this milk, each measured from a single spoon, I find that worms too are driven from the ears. They say that dogs that have tasted the milk of a woman who has given birth to a boy do not become rabid.

As for other bodily fluids, some think the saliva of a fasting woman is a potent remedy for bloodshot and inflamed eyes, if the swollen corners of the eyes are intermittently moistened with it. This remedy works better if the woman has abstained from food and wine on the day before. And I find that a woman's breast-band relieves headaches when tied around the head.

Beyond this, there is no limit. First of all, hailstorms and whirlwinds are driven away when menstrual fluid itself is exposed directly to lightning; it also deters stormy skies. In navigation at sea it prevents hurricanes even without the presence of menstruating women. Dreadful and shocking things are divined about the remarkable power of the menstrual blood itself, as I have already discussed elsewhere, of which I may say the following without embarrassment.

If the power of the menstrual flow coincides with a lunar or solar eclipse, it will cause irremediable damage; nor is this power lessened even at the dark of the moon. Sexual intercourse at such times is fatal for men and induces illness. Then also purple cloth is contaminated by menstruating women, so much the greater is their power. But during any other time, if women walk around a cornfield naked, caterpillars, works, beetles, and other pests fall down. Metrodorus of Scepsis says that this discovery was made in Cappodocia during a cantharid infestation, when women walked through the middle of the fields with their skirts hitched up above their buttocks. Elsewhere it is the custom for them to walk with bare feet, with their hair and clothing unbound. Care ought to be taken that they not do this at sunrise, for the seeds will dry up; likewise young plants are henceforth harmed by the touch; and the medicinal plants rue and ivy die instantly.

I have said many things about the destructive power of the menses, but in addition it is true that when menstruating women touch their hives, bees fly away. When menstruating women boil linen, it turns black, the edges of razors become blunt, upon contact bronze takes on a foul smell and begins to rust, more so if the moon happens to be on the wane. Horses, if pregnant, suffer miscarriages when touched by a menstruating woman. Indeed, these effects may be worked with only a glance, even from a long way off, even if the first menstrual cycle follows the loss of virginity or if it occurs spontaneously while she is still a virgin. For I have already shown that even when touched by the thread of an infected dress, bitumen that comes from Judea can be overcome by this power alone. Not even fire, which conquers everything, can master this substance, and even its ash, if someone were to sprinkle it on clothes in the wash, changes the purple dye and removes the brightness from the colors. Women themselves are not even immune to this evil among them: a dab of it causes miscarriage, even if a pregnant woman walks over it. What the courtesans Lais and Elephantis say concerning abortifacients is contradictory. They prescribe the smoldering root of cabbage, myrtle or tamarisk extinguished by menstrual blood to induce abortion, and likewise assert that donkeys do not conceive for as many years as they have consumed grains of barley infected with this fluid. They also make other remarkable and opposing proclamations, one saying that fertility, the other that sterility, comes about by the same measures. It is better not to believe them. Bithus of Dyrrachium says that a mirror dulled by the glance of a menstruating woman becomes bright again when the same woman looks at its obverse side. He also says that all this power is removed if a woman carries on her person the type of fish called a red mullet.

PART III
CLASSICAL TRADITION

———————

Figure 9 *Procne and Philomela Prepare to Kill Itys.* Attic red figure kylix, c.490 BCE. Musée du Louvre, Paris, G 147. Created several hundred years before Ovid's version, this vase attests to the widespread popularity of the Procne and Philomela story among the ancient Athenians.

9
THE VOICE OF THE SHUTTLE IS OURS

P. K. Joplin

Aristotle, in the *Poetics* (16.4), records a striking phrase from a play by Sophocles, since lost, on the theme of Tereus and Philomela. As you know, Tereus, having raped Philomela, cut out her tongue to prevent discovery. But she weaves a tell-tale account of her violation into a tapestry (or robe) which Sophocles calls 'the voice of the shuttle.' If metaphors as well as plots or myths could be archetypal, I would nominate Sophocles' voice of the shuttle for that distinction. (Geoffrey Hartman, "The Voice of the Shuttle: Language from the Point of View of Literature")[1]

> Why do you [trouble] me, Pandion's
> daughter, swallow out of heaven? (Sappho)[2]

> I do not want them to turn
> my little girl into a swallow.
> She would fly far away into the sky
> and never fly again to my straw bed,
> or she would nest in the eaves
> where I could not comb her hair.
> I do not want them to turn
> my little girl into a swallow.
> (Gabriela Mistral, "Miedo"/"Fear")[3]

In returning to the ancient myths and opening them from within to the woman's body, the woman's mind, and the woman's voice, contemporary women have felt like thieves of language[4] staging a raid on the treasured icons of a tradition that has required woman's silence for centuries. When Geoffrey Hartman asks of Sophocles' metaphor 'the voice of the shuttle': "What gives these words the power to speak to us even without the play?" (p. 337), he celebrates Language and not the violated woman's emergence from silence. He celebrates Literature and the male poet's trope, not the woman's elevation of her safe, feminine, domestic craft – weaving – into art as a new means of resistance. The feminist receiving the story of Philomela via Sophocles' metaphor, preserved for us by Aristotle, asks the same question but arrives at a different answer. She begins further back, with Sappho, for whom Philomela transformed into a wordless swallow is the sign of what threatens the woman's voiced existence in culture.

When Hartman exuberantly analyses the structure of the trope for voice, he makes an all too familiar elision of gender. When he addresses himself to the story or *context* that makes the metaphor for regained speech a powerful *text*, the story is no longer about the woman's silence or the male violence (rape and mutilation) that robs her of speech. Instead, it is about Fate. Hartman assumes the posture of a privileged "I" addressing a known "you" who shares his point of view: "You and I, who know the story, appreciate the cause winning through, and Philomela's 'voice' being restored but by itself the phrase simply disturbs our sense of causality and guides us, if it guides us at all, to a hint of supernatural rather than human agency (p. 338). In the moment she reclaims a voice Philomela is said to partake of the divine; her utterance "skirts the oracular" (p. 347). Noting how Philomela's woven text becomes a link in the chain of violence, Hartman locates behind the woman weaver the figure of Fate, who "looms" like the dark figure of myth, spinning the threads from which the fabric of our lives is woven in intricate design. But if Hartman is right to locate the problem or mystery in the mechanism of revenge, and right to suggest that Philomela's resistance has something of the oracular in it, he nonetheless misses his own part in the mystification of violence.

How curiously the critic remains unconscious of the implications of his own movement away from Philomela, the virgin raped, mutilated, and imprisoned by Tereus, and toward the mythical figure of Fate, the dangerous, mysterious, and enormously powerful "woman." Why is the figure of a depersonalized and distant Fate preferable for this critic? Perhaps because he cannot see in Philomela the violated woman musing over her loom until she discovers its hidden power. Perhaps because he cannot see the active, the empowered, the resistant in Philomela, he cannot see that the *woman* makes her loom do what she once hoped her voice/tongue could do. In Book Six of Ovid's *Metamorphoses*, the most famous version of the tale,

after Tereus rapes her, Philomela overcomes her training to submission
and vows to tell her story to anyone who will listen:

> What punishment you will pay me, late or soon!
> Now that I have no shame, I will proclaim it.
> Given the chance, I will go where people are,
> Tell everybody; if you shut me here,
> I will move the very woods and rocks to pity.
> The air of Heaven will hear, and any god,
> If there is any god in Heaven, will hear me.[5]

For Philomela, rape initiates something like the "profound upheaval"
Lévi-Strauss describes as the experience of "backward subjects" when
they make "the sudden discovery of the function of language."[6] For
Philomela, ordinary private speech is powerless. No matter how many
times she says "No," Tereus will not listen to her. Paradoxically, it is
this *failure* of language that wakes in Philomela "the conception of the
spoken word as communication, as power, as action" (p. 494). If this
concept of speech as powerful action is one essential or "universal" aspect
of human thought that both Lévi-Strauss and Hartman celebrate, neither
addresses the conflictual nature of the discovery of language. No sooner
do structure, difference, and language become visible in Lévi-Strauss'
system, than violence is present. No sooner does Philomela uncover the
power of her own voice, than Tereus cuts out her tongue.

But Tereus' plot is mysterious in its beginning and in its end. What initially
motivates him to violate Philomela? And why, having raped and silenced her,
does he preserve the evidence against himself by concealing rather than
killing her? What is "the cause" that wins through when Philomela's tapestry is received and read, and why is her moment of triumph overcome by an
act of revenge that only silences her more completely? To reconsider these
questions is to reappropriate the metaphor of weaving and to redefine both
the locus of its power and the crisis that gives rise to it. As Hartman suggests,
the tension in the linguistic figure "the voice of the shuttle" is like "the
tension of poetics" (p. 338). But for the feminist attending to the less
obvious details of both text and context, the story of Philomela's emergence
from silence is filled with the tension of *feminist* poetics.

Prior Violence and Feminist Poetics: The Difference
a Tale Makes

In *A Room of One's Own*, Virginia Woolf provides us with a comic metaphor for feminist poetics in the tailless Manx cat, unfortunate inhabitant of

the Isle of Man. Woolf's narrator, moving to the window after luncheon at Oxbridge, suddenly sees the Manx cat crossing the lawn. She notes the cat's apparent "lack" but wonders if its condition is not primarily only a "difference" from cats with tails. Is the cat with no tail a freak of nature, a mutation? Or is it a product of culture, a survivor of some lost moment of amputation, mutilation? The cat, lacking its tail, of course cannot tell her. The figure is mute but pregnant with suggestion. While testifying to a real sense of difference, and a gender-specific one at that, the lost tail as *tale* craftily resists the violence inherent in Freud's reductive theory of women's castration as the explanation for our silence in culture. The narrator perceives a difference so radical that the tailless cat seems to "question the universe" and its Author, simply by being there.[7] This question echoes Woolf's rejection of Milton's bogey, his borrowing of religious authority to explain women's silence in terms of our original fall.[8] For Woolf, the lost tail signifies a present absence: X marks the spot where something apparently unrecoverable occurred; the extra letter signals a broken-off story. It designates mystery, it designates violence.

The lost tail, made known by its stumpy remnant, not only represents our broken tradition, the buried or stolen tales of women who lie behind us in history. It also signifies the cut-off voice or amputated tongue: what we still find it hard to recover and to say in ourselves. We are not castrated. We are not less, lack, loss. Yet we feel like thieves and criminals when we speak,[9] because we know that something originally ours has been stolen from us, and that the force used to take it away still threatens us as we struggle to win it back. Woolf meets this threat with her own carefully fabricated tale. Employing old literary strategy to her new feminist ends, Woolf counters the violence implicit in Freud's and Milton's fictions with her own resisting, subversive fictions, which ask similar questions but refuse the old answers. Woolf's metaphor for muteness, the Manx cat, presses the ambiguities in Freud's and Milton's fictions which, like the myth of Philomela, conceal and reveal at once. For all posit an original moment in which an act of violence (the transgression of a boundary, the violation of a taboo) explains how difference became hierarchy, why women were forbidden to speak.[10]

In the myth of Philomela we can begin to recover the prior violence Woolf ironized in the punning metaphor of the tailless cat. Our muteness is our mutilation; not a natural loss but a cultural one, resisted as we move into language. Woolf has taught us to see the obstacles, and to see that chief among them is internalization of the deadly images of women created in art. Any writer's desire to come into language is a burden. Why have so few women who have carried the burden before us been heard? Like men, women feel the keen anxiety of the writer's approach to the furthest reach of language, the limit or boundary where expression fails, and intimate the moment when death alone will speak. But for the woman writer coming into language, especially language about her body, has entailed the risk of a hidden but felt sexual anxiety, a premonition of violence. When Hartman ends his essay by noting that "There is always *something* that violates us, deprives our voice, and compels art toward an aesthetics of silence" (p. 353, my emphasis), the specific nature of the woman's double violation disappears behind the apparently genderless (but actually male) language of "us," the "I" and the "you" who agree to attest to that which violates, deprives, silences only as a mysterious, unnamed "something." For the feminist unwilling to let Philomela become universal before she has been met as female, this is the primary evasion. Our history teaches us that it is naive to trust that "the truth will out" without a struggle – including a struggle with those who claim to be telling us the truth. It may be that great art always carries within it an anxious memory of an original moment of rupture or violence in coming into being, but the woman writer, and with her the feminist critic, must also ask why art has been so particularly violent towards women, why the greatest of our writers, like Shakespeare, represent their own language anxiety in terms of sexual violation of the woman's body. It is the poet's struggle with words we hear speaking when Shakespeare, depicting the raped Lucrece pacing her bedchamber in grief and rage, says:

> And that deep torture may be called a hell,
> When more is felt than one has power to tell.[11]

What in the text "the voice of the shuttle" feels archetypal for the feminist? The image of the woman artist as a weaver. And what, in the context, feels archetypal? That behind the woman's silence is the incomplete plot of male dominance which fails no matter how extreme it becomes. When Philomela imagines herself free to tell her own tale to anyone who will listen, Tereus realizes for the first time what would come to light, should the woman's voice become public. In private, force is sufficient. In public, however, Philomela's voice, if heard, would make them equal. Enforced silence and imprisonment are the means Tereus chooses to protect himself from discovery. But as the mythic tale, Tereus' plot, and Ovid's own text make clear, dominance can only contain, but never successfully destroy, the woman's voice.

Unravelling the Mythic Plot: Boundaries, Exchange, Sacrifice

> ... but Athens was in trouble
> With war at her gates, barbarian invasion
> From over the seas, and could not send a mission –
> Who would believe it? – so great was her own sorrow.
> But Tereus, king of Thrace, had sent an army
> To bring the town relief, to lift the siege,
> And Tereus' name was famous, a great conqueror,
> And he was rich, and strong in men, descended
> From Mars, so Pandion, king of Athens
> Made him a son as well as ally, joining
> His daughter Procne to Tereus in Marriage.
>
> (Ovid, *Metamorphoses* VI, 319–424)

> Terminus himself, at the meeting of the bounds,
> is sprinkled with the blood of a slaughtered lamb ...
> The simple neighbors meet and hold a feast, and sing
> thy praises holy Terminus: thou dost set bounds
> to people and cities and vast kingdoms; without
> thee every field would be a root of wrangling.
>
> (Ovid, *Fasti*)[12]

In most versions of the myth, including Ovid's, Tereus is said to be smitten with an immediate passion for the beautiful virgin Philomela, younger daughter of Athen's King Pandion.[13] What is usually not observed is that both Philomela and her sister Procne serve as objects of exchange between these two kings: Pandion of Athens and Tereus of Thrace, Greek and barbarian. For the old king to give his elder daughter to Tereus is for Greece to make an alliance with barbarism itself, for the myth takes as its unspoken pretext a proverbial distinction between "Hellenes, Greek speakers, and barbaroi, babblers."[14] In the myth, the political distinction between Athens and Thrace recedes. As the beginning of the mythic tale suggests, Athens was in trouble, but the invasion of the gates by barbarians that brings Tereus into alliance with the city initiates a new crisis of invasion, one that removes the violence from Athens' walls to the home of the barbarian himself: Thrace.

Philomela is the marriageable female Tereus seizes to challenge the primacy of Pandion and the power of Athens. His mythic passion is a cover story for the violent rivalry between the two kings. Apparently, the tragic sequence gets its start not from Tereus' desires, but from Procne's.

After five years of married life in Thrace, she becomes lonely for her sister and asks Tereus to go to Pandion to ask that Philomela be allowed to visit her. When Tereus sees Philomela with Pandion, his desire becomes uncontrollable, and he will brook no frustration of his plan to take her for himself.[15] First, the political anxieties that fuel the myth are transformed into erotic conflicts; then the responsibility for Tereus' lust is displaced onto Philomela herself: as Ovid has it, the chaste woman's body is fatally seductive.[16] We are asked to believe that Philomela unwittingly and passively invites Tereus' desire by being what she is: pure. But if it is Philomela's purity that makes her so desirable, it is not because purity is beautiful. Tereus' desire is aroused not by beauty but by power: Pandion holds the right to offer Philomela to another man in a political bargain because Philomela is a virgin and therefore unexchanged. Tereus is a barbarian, and the giving of the first daughter as gift only incites him to steal the withheld daughter. But both barbarian and virgin daughter are proverbial figures of the Greek imagination. They are actors in a drama depicting the necessity for establishing and keeping secure the boundaries that protect the power of the key figure, that of Pandion, the sympathetic king who disappears from the tale as soon as he gives up both his daughters.[17] The exchange of women is the structure the myth conceals incompletely. What the myth reveals is how the political hierarchy built upon male sexual dominance requires the violent appropriation of the woman's power to speak.

This violence is implicit in Lévi-Strauss' idea that "marriage is the archetype of exchange" (p. 483) and that women are exchange objects, gifts, or "valuables *par excellence*," whose transfer between groups of men "provides the means of binding men together" (pp. 481, 480). In Lévi-Strauss' view, women are not only objects, but also words: "The emergence of symbolic thought must have required that women, like words, should be things that were exchanged" (p. 496). But this discovery began with a connection between prohibitions against "*misuses* of language" and the incest taboo, which made Lévi-Strauss ask, "What does this mean except that women are treated as signs, which are *misused* when not put to the use reserved for signs, which is to be communicated?" (pp. 495–96, emphasis in original). In this light, Tereus' rape of Philomela constitutes a crisis in language – the barbarian refuses to use the women/signs as they are offered him by the Greek – and a violation of the structure of exogamous exchange – the barbarian does not exchange, he steals and keeps all to himself. But nothing in Lévi-Strauss prepares us for the effects of this transgression upon the woman. Though he minimally recognizes that "a woman can never be merely a sign but must also be recognized as a generator of signs," Lévi-Strauss can still envision only women speaking in a "duet": monogamous marriage or right exchange (p. 496). Since marriage is the proper use of woman as sign, it is therefore *the* place where she has the power to speak. But is this pure description? Or does the modern anthropologist share a bias with his male informant, both satisfied that the male point of view constitutes culture? In effect, women are silenced partly by being envisioned as silent. The inability to question (on Lévi-Strauss' part), like the unwillingness to acknowledge (on the men's part) any articulated bonds between women, suggests how tenuous the bonds between men may be. That the bonding of men requires the silencing of women points to an unstated male dread: for women to define themselves as a group would mean the unraveling of established and recognized cultural bonds. Lévi-Strauss acknowledges the ambiguous status of women: woman is both sign (word) and value (person). That is, she is both spoken and speaker. However, he does not perceive either the violational or the potentially subversive aspects of women's position within the system of exchange.

Rather, for Lévi-Strauss, the contradictory status of woman as both insider and outsider in culture provides for "that affective richness, that ardour and mystery" (p. 496) coloring relations between the sexes. Like Ovid, Lévi-Strauss would preserve the "sacred mystery" (p. 489) marriage signifies, preferring the myth of passion to any serious investigation of the implications of the exchange of women for those cultures that practice it.

In the work of René Girard, who refuses to respect mythic passion, the origin of symbolic thought and language is linked not to the exchange of *women*, but to the exchange of *violence*: "The origin of symbolic thought lies in the mechanism of the surrogate victim."[18] For Girard, the mechanism by which the community expels its own violence by sacrificing a surrogate victim, someone marginal to the culture, is linked to the *arbitrary* nature of signs (p. 236). In Girard's revision of Lévi-Strauss, we come closer to a view of exchange that sheds light on some of the paradoxes in the Greek myth:

> The ritual violence that accompanies the exchange of women serves a sacrificial purpose for each group. In sum, the groups agree never to be completely at peace, so that their members may find it easier to be at peace among themselves.   (p. 249)

For Girard, as for Mary Douglas, the aura of the sacred and the mysterious that envelops married sexual relations is a sign of the human need for clear boundaries to contain violence. But while both Douglas and Girard make extremely interesting connections between ritual pollution, violence, and the prohibitions focused on female sexuality in particular (especially on menstrual blood), neither presses these observations far enough.[19] Girard argues that "exchange ritualized into warfare and . . . warfare ritualized into exchange are both variants of the same sacrificial shift from the interior of the community to the exterior."[20] But Girard, too, tends to equate the male point of view with culture, so that he does not pause to see how the woman, in exchange, becomes the surrogate victim for the group. Her body represents the body politic.

When we address the question of the body of the king's daughter, we approach the structure Mary Douglas sees as a dialectical interaction of the "two bodies," the actual physical body and the socially defined body generated by metaphor:

> . . . the human body is always treated as an image of society . . . Interests in apertures depends on the preoccupation with social exits and entrances, escape routes and invasions. If there is no concern to preserve social boundaries, I would not expect to find concern with bodily boundaries. The relation of head to feet, of brain and sexual organs, of mouth and anus are commonly treated so that they express *the relevant patterns of hierarchy.*[21]

The exchange of women articulates the culture's boundaries, the woman's hymen serving as the physical or sexual sign for the limen or wall defining the city's limits. Like the ground beneath the walls of Athens (or Rome),[22] the woman's chastity is surrounded by prohibitions and precautions. Both are protected by political and ritual sanctions; both are sacred. But female chastity is not sacred out of respect for the integrity of the woman as person; rather, it is sacred out of respect for violence. Because her sexual body is the ground of the culture's system of differences, the woman's hymen is also the ground of contention. The virgin's hymen must not be ruptured except in some manner that reflects and ensures the health of the existing political hierarchy. The father king regulates both the literal and metaphorical "gates" to the city's power: the actual gates in the city's wall or the hymen as the gateway to his daughter's body. The first rupture of the hymen is always a transgression, but culture articulates the difference between the opened gate and the beseiged fortress:[23] Pandion will give Tereus free entry to Procne's body if he will agree not to use his force against Athens. Exchange of the king's daughter is nothing less than the articulation of his power and the reassertion of his city's sovereignty.

In the marriage rite the king's daughter is led to the altar as victim and offering, but instead of being killed, she is given in marriage to the rival king. War is averted. But in a crisis, the woman can become identified with the very violence the exchange of her body was meant to hold in check.

The violence implicit in the exchange of women is central not only to Philomela's tale, but to one of Greek drama's great tragedies. The sacrificial nature of the exchange of women is terrifyingly clear in Euripides' *Iphigenia in Aulis*, in which the king's daughter is literally led to the altar as sacrifice under the ruse of wedding her to Achilles.[24] And as the play reveals, the king's daughter is finally a surrogate victim for the king himself: it is Agamemnon the mob of armed and restive Hellenes would kill, were Iphigenia not sacrificed.[25] The threat, as Achilles makes clear, is "stoning."[26] Like the myth of Philomela, the story of Iphigenia reaches back to Greek prehistory (Pandion's boundary dispute was said to have been with Labdacus, of a generation before Laius, Oedipus' father).[27] But both stories were retold in Athens during the years of the Peloponnesian War, when it became clear to the Greek dramatist's mind that the differences that give rise to human sacrifice were located within the city itself.[28]

In Euripides' tragedy it is peace (the stillness or quiet when the wind will not move the ships toward Troy) that makes discord among brother Greeks visible. Euripides interprets the current Greek crisis, imperial Athens' engagement in a protracted war, in terms of the distant past, Homer's tales of the Trojan War. Both are seen in antiheroic terms. The unmaking of Homeric heroes is also the unmasking of the cultural fictions that veil the sacrificial violence at the basis of political domination. As rivalry between brothers threatens to explode into internecine war instead of war against the common enemy, the culture represented by the amassed armies is reunited under Agamemnon's authority only through a ritual sacrifice. And Agamemnon knows that *he* weaves the plot that determines his daughter's destiny.[29]

Two things must happen in order for Iphigenia to undergo her startling transformation into a willing sacrificial victim who forbids her mother from exacting revenge and absolves her father of all responsibility for her death. First, Iphigenia must hear from Achilles that the mob is calling for her and that even if she resists she will be dragged by her hair, screaming, to the altar.[30] And second, Iphigenia must begin to speak the language of the victim: she blames Helen, she sees the Trojan War as an erotic conflict, and she echoes the men who arranged her sacrifice by finally displacing responsibility for her death onto the goddess Artemis.[31]

The myth of Philomela insists upon the difference between legitimate exchange, marriage, and the violent theft, rape. But this difference almost dissolves in Euripides' tragedy not only in Iphigenia's sacrifice, but in Clytemnestra's accusation against Agamemnon. It seems he is guilty of the same crime as Paris; if he is different from Paris, it is only because his later crime was worse:

CLYTEMNESTRA:
Hear me now –
For I shall give you open speech and no
Dark saying or parable any more.
And this reproach I first hurl in your teeth,
That I married you against my will, after
You murdered Tantalus, my first husband,
And dashed my living babe upon the earth,
Brutally tearing him from my breasts.
And then, the two sons of Zeus, my brothers,
On horseback came and in white armor made
War upon you. Till you got upon your knees
To my old father, Tyndareus, and he
Rescued you. So you kept me for your bed. (ll. 1146–58)

In the ambiguities of his final plays, Euripides comes as close as anyone to suggesting that Helen always was a pretext, and that the women who are violated (or, like Clytemnestra, who become violent) in exchanges between men are victims of the polis itself. In the myth of Philomela the fact that both acts are performed by the same man, Tereus, and that both daughters are taken from the same man, Pandion, suggests that the difference between the generative rite (marriage) and the dangerous transgression (rape) is collapsing within the Greek imagination. The myth records, but tries to efface, the political nature of the crisis of distinctions: the trouble at Athens' gates, or the fear that the most crucial distinction of all is about to give way, the identity of the city itself. The first exchange was meant to resolve the threat to Athens but instead brought on the invasion of the virginal daughter's body.

The relationship between the cure (marriage) and the cause (rape) of violence relies upon the assent of the males involved, who must agree to operate on the basis of a shared fiction. We can recover what the Greeks of fifth-century Athens feared by viewing barbarian invasion/rape as an unwilling recognition that fictions of difference are arbitrary, yet absolutely necessary. The effects of invasion we can see symbolized in Philomela's suffering once she is raped. The transgression of all bonds, oaths,

and unstated but firmly believed rules initiates a radical loss of identity, a
terrible confusion of roles:

> Were my father's orders
> Nothing to you, his tears, my sister's love,
> My own virginity, the bonds of marriage:
> Now it is all confused, mixed up; I am
> My sister's rival, a second-class wife, and you,
> For better and worse, the husband of two women,
> Procne my enemy now, at least she should be. (ll. 533–39)

Philomela experiences rape as a form of contagious pollution because it is
both adultery and incest, the two cardinal transgressions of the rule of
exogamy. Should the rule collapse altogether, chaos would ensue. Then
fathers (Pandion instead of Tereus) could have intercourse with daughters
and brothers (Tereus as brother rather than brother-in-law) with sisters.

As the sign and currency of exchange, the invaded woman's body bears
the full burden of ritual pollution. Philomela experiences *herself* as the
source of dangerous contagion[32] because once violated she is both rival
and monstrous double of her own sister. If marriage uses the woman's
body as good money and unequivocal speech, rape transforms her into a
counterfeit coin, a contradictory word that threatens the whole system.
This paradox, the raped virgin as redundant or equivocal sign, is the dark
side of Philomela's later, positive discovery about language: once she can
no longer function as sign, she wrests free her own power to speak. To tell
the tale of her rape is to hope for justice. But justice would endanger not
only Tereus, but Pandion himself. For once raped, Philomela stands
radically outside all boundaries: she is exiled to the realm of "nature"
or what Girard calls undifferentiated violence; she is imprisoned in the
woods. There, she may see just how arbitrary cultural boundaries truly
are; she may see what fictions prepared the way for her suffering. The rape
of the king's daughter is like the sacrifice of Iphigenia. Both threaten to
make fully visible the basis of structure by bringing to light the violence
implicit in culture's inscription of its vulnerable exits and entries on the
silenced woman's body.

Clytemnestra does not remind Agamemnon what the history of their
own union is until the fiction of Iphigenia's marriage gives way to the
reality of her sacrifice. This is precisely the paradoxical nature of domination: authority founded upon the suppression of knowledge and free
speech relegates both the silenced people and the unsayable things to the
interstices of culture. It is only a matter of time before all that has been

driven from the center to the margins takes on a force of its own. Then the center is threatened with collapse. The system of differences the powerful had to create to define themselves as the center of culture or the top of the hierarchy turns against them. To the Greek imagination, this moment of transition was terrifying and in both Euripides' drama and the mythic tale the dread of anarchic violence is obvious. As effectively and as ambiguously as Agamemnon in the act of sacrificing his own daughter, Greek culture uses the myth of Tereus' rape of Philomela on Thracian soil to avoid the knowledge that the violence originated within Athens, with the father/king himself. But like Agamemnon, who begins to see the truth only to turn his back on it, the myth preserves but transforms essential elements in the actual story.[33] The invasion of Athens/Philomela by Thrace/Tereus/barbarism collapses the sacrificial crisis into an isolated moment when the kinship system turns back upon itself. Memory of the chaos that follows unbridled rivalry between brothers is condensed into the moment when Philomela sees Procne as "the enemy." This confusion is part of the face-to-face confrontation with violence itself.

For Agamemnon to refuse to sacrifice his virgin daughter, he would have to relinquish his authority. For Philomela to refuse her status as mute victim, she must seize authority. When Philomela transforms her suffering, captivity, and silence into the occasion for art, the text she weaves is overburdened with a desire to tell. Her tapestry not only seeks to redress a private wrong, but should it become public (and she began to see the connection between the private and the political before her tongue was cut out), it threatens to retrieve from obscurity all that her culture defines as outside the bounds of allowable discourse, whether sexual, spiritual, or literary.

Art and Resistance: Listening for the Voice of the Shuttle

Arachne also
Worked in the gods, and their deceitful business
With mortal girls . . . To them all Arachne
Gave their own features and a proper background.
Neither Minerva, no, nor even Envy
Could find a flaw in the work; the fair-haired goddess
Was angry now, indeed, and tore the web
That showed the crimes of the gods, and with her shuttle
Struck at Arachne's head, and kept on striking,

> Until the daughter of Idmon could not bear it,
> *Noosed her own neck, and hung herself.*
>   (Ovid, *Metamorphoses*, VI, 79–84, my emphasis)

> The explicit message of the myth can still be questioned and criticized from
> a standpoint that has never been tried and that should be the first to be
> tried since it is suggested by the myth itself ... All we have to do to account
> for everything is to assume that *the lynching is represented from the stand-*
> *point of the lynchers themselves.*   (René Girard)[34]

Once Procne receives Philomela's text, reads it, interprets it, and acts upon
it by rescuing her, myth creates a dead end for both the production and the
reception of the woman's text. The movement of violence is swift and sure:
there is hardly any pause between Procne's hatching of a plot and its
execution.[35] Nor is there any hesitation between Tereus' recognition
that he has devoured his own child and his choice to rise up to kill the
bloody sisters. The space most severely threatened with collapse is that
between Tereus and the sisters themselves. Here, the gods intervene: the
three are turned into birds. But paradoxically, this change changes nothing.
Metamorphosis preserves the distance necessary to the structure of dominance and submission: in the final tableau all movement is frozen. Tereus
will never catch the sisters, but neither will the women ever cease their
flight. Distance may neither collapse nor expand. In such stasis, both order
and conflict are preserved, but there is no hope of change.

Metamorphosis and Ovid's *Metamorphoses* fix in eternity the pattern of
violation-revenge-violation. Myth, like literature and ritual, abets structure by giving the tale a dead and deadly end. The women, in yielding
to violence, become just like the man who first moved against them. The
sisters are said to trade murder and dismemberment of the child for rape
and mutilation of the woman. The sacrifice of the innocent victim, Itys,
continues, without altering it, the motion of reciprocal violence. And as
literary tradition shows, the end of the story overtakes all that preceded it;
the women are remembered as *more* violent than the man.[36] This is done
by suppressing a tale: the sacrifice of an actual woman, or the long history
of scapegoating women. The social end toward which fictional closure
reaches in this myth is the maintenance of structure. But narrative, like
myth and ritual (like culture or consciousness), also preserves the contradictory middle. Because the end of the tale fixes itself against the middle
so strenuously, we come to see it as false. It is the middle that we recover:
the moment of the loom, the point of departure for the woman's story,
which might have given rise to an unexpected ending.

Imprisoned in the plot, just as Philomela is imprisoned by Tereus, is the anti-plot. Just as Philomela is not killed but only hidden away, the possibility of anti-structure is never destroyed by structure; it is only contained or controlled until structure becomes deadened or extreme in its hierarchical rigidity by virtue of all that it has sought to expel from itself. Then anti-structure, what Victor Turner calls *communitas*, may erupt. And it may be peaceful, or it may be violent.[37] The violence that ensues when Philomela is rescued and she brings back into culture the power she discovered in exile inheres not in her text, but in structure itself.[38] The end of the tale represents an attempt to forestall or foreclose a moment of radical transition when dominance and hierarchy might have begun to change or to give way. Culture hides from its own sacrificial violence. The Greek imagination uses the mythic end to expel its own violence and to avoid any knowledge of the process. Patriarchal culture feels, as Tereus does, that it is asked to incorporate something monstrous when the woman returns from exile to tell her own story.

But myth seeks to blame the women for the inability of the culture to allow the raped, mutilated, but newly resisting woman to return: the sisters must become force-feeders, they must turn out to be blood thirsty. Supposedly, the sisters quickly forget their long-delayed desire to be together in giving way to the wish for revenge. But the tale can reach this end only by leaving out the loom. There are, after all, two women, and peace (making) and violence (unmaking) are divided between them. Over against Procne's rending of her child and the cooking of the wrong thing which culminates in an inverted family meal – Tereus' cannibalism – myth preserves but effaces the hidden work of Philomela at her loom. Revenge, or dismembering, is quick. Art, or the resistance to violence and disorder, inherent in the very process of weaving, is slow.

Philomela's weaving is the new, third term in what Greek culture often presents us as two models of the woman weaver, the false twins: virtuous Penelope, continually weaving and unraveling a shroud, and vicious Helen, weaving a tapestry depicting the heroics of the men engaged in the war they claim to fight over her body. But in either case the woman's weaving serves as sign for the male poet's prestigious activity of spinning his yarns, of weaving the text of the Trojan War. For their weaving to end, Homer's text/song must end. Both women weave because the structure of marriage is suspended. They will stop weaving when they are reunited with their proper spouses, when the war ends.

To this pair of weavers, Euripides and Aristophanes, writing when Athens was in extreme crisis, add metaphors of *un*weaving. In *The Bacchae*, the metaphor for violent anti-structure is the bacchante, the woman "*driven* from loom and shuttle" by the god Dionysus. And the image Pentheus uses for the reimposition of structure is the bacchantes as women "sold as slaves or put to work at my looms" where they will be *silenced*.[39] But these are also false twins: both represent forms of violence between men worked through the "freeing" of Theban women from their looms (Dionysus' revenge) or the enslaving of the Asian bacchae to the Theban loom (Pentheus' threat).

In Aristophanes' *Lysistrata*, the crisis in Athens is not depicted as women fleeing to the hills to celebrate the rites of Dionysus, but as women occupying the Acropolis in an attempt to restore a true sense of differences among Greeks. To remind the men who their common enemy is will apparently stop their in-fighting. This requires the reassertion of gender as the primary difference, which makes marriage a comic replacement for war. In *Lysistrata*, the men try to lure their wives home by bringing them their babies and by telling them that the chickens have gotten into the work on their looms.[40] In both the tragic and comic representation of disorder as the abandonment of the loom, a return to order, or weaving, is a return to the gender status quo, to the rigid hierarchical roles that gave rise to the crisis at the beginning.

There is another kind of weaving: Arachne's tapestry at the opening of Book Six of the *Metamorphoses* and Philomela's at the close. For these two women, weaving represents the unmasking of "sacred mystery" and the unmaking of the violence of rape. Before the angry goddess Athene (Minerva) tore Arachne's cloth, the mortal woman weaver told a very specific tale: women raped by gods metamorphosed into beasts. Before the advent of the jealous goddess, Arachne was the center of a community of women. Unsurpassed in her art, Arachne was so graceful that women everywhere came to watch her card, spin, thread her loom, and weave. Gathered around her are other women watching, talking, resting. Here, the loom represents the occasion for communitas, or peace, a context in which it is possible for pleasure to be nonappropriative and nonviolent. In this, Arachne suggests Sappho, who was also the center of a community of women and who also, in Ovid, meets a deadly end. Ovid codified the tradition of slander that followed Sappho's death and passed on in his own work the fiction that she died a suicide, killing herself out of desire for a man who did not want her.[41] Sappho's surviving work and the testimony of others enable scholars to reject Ovid's fictional end as false. But only by an act of interpretation can we suggest that Arachne, the woman artist, did not hang herself but was lynched. Suicide is substituted for murder. Arachne is destroyed by her own instrument in the hands of an angry goddess. But who is Athene? She is no real female but sprang,

motherless, from her father's head, an enfleshed fantasy. She is the virgin
daughter whose aegis is the head of that other woman victim, Medusa.
Athene is like the murderous angel in Virginia Woolf's house, a male
fantasy of what a woman ought to be, who strangles the real woman
writer's voice.

Athene is the pseudo-woman who tells the tale of right order. Central
to her tapestry are the gods in all their glory. In the four corners, just
inside the border of olive branches, Athene weaves a warning to the
woman artist that resistance to hierarchy and authority is futile:

> The work has Victory's ultimatum in it,
> But that her challenger may have full warning
> What her reward will be for her daring rashness,
> In the four corners the goddess weaves four pictures,
> Bright in their color, each one saying *Danger*!
> In miniature design.   (ll. 81–86)

Arachne's daring rashness is only apparently her pride in her own artistry
(which is justified: she wins the contest). In truth, she is in danger because
she tells a threatening story. Among the women represented with "their
own features and a proper background" in Arachne's tapestry is Medusa
herself. To tell the tale of Poseidon's rape of Medusa is to suggest what the
myth of the woman who turns men to stone conceals. The locus of that
crime was an altar in the temple of Athene. The background of the crime
was the city's need to choose what god to name itself for, or what is usually
represented as a rivalry between Poseidon and Athene for the honor. Was
Medusa raped or was she sacrificed on the altar to Athene? Was the woman
"punished" by Athene or was she killed during a crisis as an offering to the
"angry" goddess by the city of Athens, much as Iphigenia was said to be
sacrificed to a bloodthirsty Artemis?

Medusa does not become a beautiful human virgin in Greek myth until
very late. Behind the decapitated woman's head Perseus uses to turn men
to stone lies the ancient gorgon. The gorgon or Medusa head was also
used as an apotropaic ritual mask, and is sometimes found marking the
chimney corners in Athenian homes.[42] The mythical Medusa may recall a
real sacrificial victim. The violence is transformed into rape, but the locus
of the act – the altar – is preserved, and responsibility for the crime is
projected onto the gods. But even there, it must finally come to rest upon
another "woman," Athene. Behind the victim's head that turns men to
stone may lie the victim stoned to death by men. Perhaps it is the staring
recognition of human responsibility for ritual murder that is symbolized

in the gaze that turns us to stone. The story is eroticized to locate the violence between men and women, and Freud, in his equation "decapitation = castration" continues the development of mythological and sacrificial thinking inherent in misogyny. If Medusa has become a central figure for the woman artist to struggle with, it is because, herself a silenced woman, she has been used to silence other women.[43]

For Arachne to tell the most famous tales of women raped by the gods is for her to begin to demystify the gods (the sacred) as the beasts (the violent). But it is also for Arachne to make Ovid's text unnecessary: he can spin his version of *Metamorphoses* only because the woman's version of the story has been torn to pieces and the woman weaver driven back into nature. Just as Freud, terrified of the woman-as-mother and the woman weaver, uses psychoanalysis to drive women's weaving back into nature, so myth uses Athene to transform Arachne into the repellent spider who can weave only literal webs, sticky, incomprehensible designs. Metamorphosis (like psychoanalysis in Freud's hands) reverses the direction of violence: Medusa, like Arachne, threatens men. The spider traps and devours the males who mate with her. But Athene, who punished both Medusa and Arachne, does not threaten the male artist. The weaver's instrument, a shuttle, is used to silence her. But it is not used to silence the male artist who appropriates the woman's skill as a metaphor for his own artistry. As an instrument of violence, Athene is an extension of Zeus. However, revenge on the woman artist who uses her loom to tell stories we are never allowed to hear unless they are mediated by men is not the vengeance of the god, but of the culture itself.

When Philomela begins to weave over the long year of her imprisonment, it is not only her suffering but a specific motive that gives rise to her new use of the loom: to speak to and be heard by her sister. As an instrument that binds and connects, the loom, or its part, the shuttle, re-members or mends what violence tears apart: the bond between the sisters, the woman's power to speak, a form of community and communication. War and weaving are antithetical not because when women are weaving we are in our right place, but because all of the truly generative activities of human life are born of order and give rise to order. But just as Philomela can weave any number of patterns on her loom, culture need not retain one fixed structure.

The myth would have us think that after all her long patience and endurance, Philomela would be willing to turn from the labor of the loom to instant revenge. We are asked to believe that the weaver's supple and stubborn transformation of the prison into the workshop, the transfer of the old discipline of feminine domestic work into one year of struggle, would leave her unchanged; that Philomela's discovery would not have the power to change her sister or their situation. For the myth would also have us think that after grieving and mourning over her sister's grave for a year, Procne would make way for a rite not of reunion, but of murder. The one most important alternative suggested by Philomela's tapestry is the one never tried: the power of the text to teach the man to know himself. Is it the barbarian, Tereus, or the Greek male citizen who would respond to the woman's story with violence? Within the Greek tradition, the myth was used to teach women the danger of our capacity for revenge. But if the myth instructs, so does Philomela's tapestry, and we can choose to teach ourselves instead the power of art as a form of resistance. It is the attempt to deny that Philomela's weaving could have any end apart from revenge that makes the myth so dangerous, for myth persuades us that violence is inevitable and art is weak.

But the myth, like Ovid's text, testifies against its own ends: for if Arachne's and Philomela's art is truly weak it would not be repressed with such extreme violence. Why does "the voice of the shuttle" have the power to speak to us even without the *woman's* text? Because we have now begun to recover, to preserve, and to interpret our own tales. And our weaving has not unraveled culture, though we do seek to unravel many insidious cultural fictions. Women's texts of great vision, like Maxine Hong Kingston's *Woman Warrior*, ask us to remember against all odds what we have been required and trained to forget. Philomela and her loom speak to us because together they represent an assertion of the will to survive despite everything that threatens to silence us, including the male literary tradition and its critics who have preserved Philomela's "voice" without knowing what it says. Philomela speaks to us and speaks in us because, as the woman warrior knows when she puts down her sword and takes up her pen, her body was the original page on which a tale was written in blood. Kingston's tale, like Arachne's and Philomela's weaving, represents a moment of choice, the *refusal* to return violence for violence:

> What we have in common are the words at our backs. The idioms for revenge are 'report a crime' and 'report to five families.' The reporting is the vengeance – not the beheading, not the gutting, but the words. And I have so many words – 'chink' words and 'gook' words too – that they do not fit on my skin.[44]

But the writer's act of renunciation and writing as the healing of what is torn in herself and in her community requires that she be *heard*.

The work of modern women writers speaks of the need for a communal, collective act of remembering. Like Gabriela Mistral, some women writers offer their words as food to feed other women. In "El Reparto" ("Distribution"), Mistral offers her poem not as a dismembered body but as a sacramental text:

> If I am put beside
> the born blind,
> I will tell her softly, so softly,
> with my voice of dust,
> "Sister, take my eyes."
> . . . . . .
> Let another take my arms
> if hers have been sundered
> And others take my senses
> with their thirst and hunger.[45]

For us, both the female sexual body and the female text must be rescued from oblivion. We rouse ourselves from culturally induced amnesia to resist the quiet but steady dismemberment of our tales by misogynist criticism. We remember and then hope to forget. Amnesia is repetition; it is being haunted by and continually reliving the pain and rage of each moment we have yielded to the pressure on us to not-see, to not-know, and to not-name what is true for us.

If women have served as a scapegoat for male violence, if the silenced woman artist serves as a sacrificial offering to the male artistic imagination (Philomela as the nightingale leaning on her thorn – *choosing* it – to inspire the male poet who then translates her song into poetry), the woman writer and the feminist critic seek to remember the embodied, resisting woman. Each time we do, we resist our status as privileged victim; we interrupt the structure of reciprocal violence.

If the voice of the shuttle is oracular it tells us Fate never was a woman looming darkly over frightened men; she was a male fantasy of female reprisal. But in celebrating the voice of the shuttle as ours, we celebrate not Philomela the vitim *or* Philomela waving Itys' bloody head at Tereus. Rather we celebrate Philomela weaving, the woman artist who in recovering her own voice uncovers not only its power, but its potential to transform revenge (violence) into resistance (peace). In freeing our own voices, we need not silence anyone else's or remain trapped by the mythic end. In undoing the mythical plot that makes men and women brutally vindictive enemies, we are refusing to let violence overtake the work of our looms again.

NOTES

1   *Beyond Formalism, Literary Essays 1958–1970* (New Haven: Yale Univ. Press, 1970), p. 337. Further citations will appear below.

2   LP 135. See also Fragment #197 in *Greek Lyric Poetry, Including the Complete Poetry of Sappho*, trans. Willis Barnstone (New York: Schocken, 1972), p. 83.

3   *Selected Poems*, trans. and ed. Doris Dana (Baltimore: Johns Hopkins Univ. Press, 1961), p. 68.

4   The phrase is taken from the title of Claudine Harrmann's *Les Voleuses de langue* (Paris: des Femmes, 1979). Alicia Ostriker uses it as the title of her important essay about the ways American women poets have transformed received mythical images. See Ostriker, "The Thieves of Language: Women Poets and Revisionist Mythmaking," *Signs*, 8 (Autumn, 1982), 69–80. My essay began as a commentary on Ostriker's paper, delivered at the Stanford University Conference on Women Writing Poetry in America, April, 1982.

5   Ovid, *Metamorphoses*, trans. Rolfe Humphries (Bloomington: Indiana Univ. Press, 1955), p. 147. All further references to the text will appear above. The reader should note that Humphries' line count at the head of each page in his text is only an approximate guide to the number of each line.

6   Claude Lévi-Strauss, *The Elementary Structures of Kinship*, trans. James Harle Bell, John Richard von Sturmer, and Rodney Needham; ed. Rodney Needham; rev. ed. (Boston: Beacon, 1969), p. 494. Further citations will appear below.

7   *A Room of One's Own* (New York: Harcourt, Brace and World, 1929), pp. 11ff.

8   Hartman discusses the line "O Eve in evil hour..." (*Paradise Lost*, IX. 1067) in "The Voice of the Shuttle" without discussing the "reader insult" or "language injury" Milton works here.

9   For Woolf's own account of her struggle not to be silenced or to feel that she should be punished for speaking/writing with authority, see "Professions for Women," *The Death of the Moth and Other Essays* (New York: Harcourt Brace Jovanovich, 1942, rpt. 1970), pp. 235–42, and the earlier, angrier version of the same essay, "Speech of January 21, 1931," in Mitchell A. Leaska, ed. *The Pargiters: The Novel-Essay Portion of The Years* (New York: Harcourt Brace Jovanovich, 1977), pp. xxvii–xliv.

10 For Milton, the prohibition is God-given, and the transgression is the distance/difference between the mortal and the divine. Why this had to become the difference between male and female is, of course, the obvious question. For Freud, the problem of origins does not begin in relation to the sacred but in relation to violence: that which men most fear happening to themselves has always already happened to women: castration. But as his brooding and strange thoughts on "Medusa's Head" indicate, the prior violence he refuses to name as that which gives rise to Medusa's power to turn men to stone is rape. For his absurd but telling attempt to repress

women's weaving back into Nature (our nature – they are the same), see also "The Psychology of Women," *New Introductory Lectures*, XXXIII. For the short piece on Medusa, see "Medusa's Head," *Sexuality and the Psychology of Love*, ed. Philip Rieff (New York: Collier, 1963), pp. 212–13.

11   William Shakespeare, *The Rape of Lucrece*, ll. 1287–88. Philomela plays an important role as icon in the dramatic poem. By imitating not Philomela the weaver, but Philomela the nightingale leaning on a thorn, Lucrece is shown learning how to complete the cycle of violence by taking revenge on herself: she chooses a weapon like the sword Tarquin held to her throat and kills herself (see ll. 1128–48). This essay is part of a longer study of the iconography of rape, which includes Lucrece and her later Roman counterpart, Virginia, and others who were written about and painted in very different ways to varying ideological ends over the centuries.

12   *Fasti*, trans. Sir James George Frazer (Cambridge: Harvard Univ. Press, 1931; rpt. 1959), pp. 105, 107. There is no room to explore the connections here, but three entries in the *Fasti* which follow each other without commentary or transition first made me study rape as a crisis of boundaries and as sacrifice: the sacrifice to Terminus, the rape of Lucrece, and the perpetual flight of Procne from Tereus. Note that Roman tradition reverses the sisters, Procne becoming the swallow and Philomela the nightingale, taken up in the English tradition as the bird pressing her breast to a thorn to make herself sing.

13   Frazer, in his edition of Apollodorus' *Library*, which also records the myth of Philomela, notes that Sophocles' lost play *Tereus* is the text "from which most of the extant versions of the story are believed to be derived." See Apollodorus, *The Library*, trans. Sir James George Frazer (New York: G. P. Putnam's Sons, 1921), II, 98. The myth was so well known in fifth-century Athens that Aristophanes could use it to make a lewd joke about the lust of women in his comic account of Athens in crisis, *Lysistrata*, trans. Douglass Parker (New York: New American Library, 1964), p. 74.

14   Page du Bois, *Centaurs and Amazons, Women and the Pre-History of the Great Chain of Being* (Ann Arbor: Univ. of Michigan Press: 1982), p. 78. See also Herodotus' interesting description of Thrace and Thracians at the opening of Book v of his *History*. In the Thracians, the Greek historian imagines the inverse of the virtues most highly valued among Hellenes.

15
> ... And Tereus, watching,
> Sees beyond what he sees: she is in his arms,
> That is not her father whom her arms go around,
> Not her father she is kissing. Everything
> Is fuel to his fire. He would like to be
> Her father, at that moment; and if he were
> He would be as wicked a father as he is husband. (ll. 478–84)

Ovid's choice to elaborate on the erotic theme of incest is not merely an element of his voyeurism; it is the sign of mimetic desire/rivalry: Tereus wants to become Pandion, not primarily to have full control over Philomela's body, but to control Athens. This is all, of course, seen from the point of view of the Greek imagination, first, then mediated by the Roman poet's perspective.

16 As Ovid does in his description of Tereus looking at Philomela, Shakespeare implicates himself in the very violence he is depicting in the curiously energetic verses about the sleeping Lucrece. The very bed she lies in is male and angry that she cheats it of a kiss. The chaste woman is a tease even in her sleep:

> Her lily hand her rosy cheeks lies under
> Coz'ning the pillow of a lawful kiss;
> Who, therefore angry, seems to part in sunder,
> Swelling on either side to want his bliss;
> Between whose hills her head entombed is;
>> Where like a virtuous monument she lies,
>> To be admired of lewd unhallowed eyes. (ll.386–92)

The poet's eyes are hardly less lewd than the rapist Tarquin's in the lines that follow (393–420). Implicit in Shakespeare's description of Lucrece asleep is the violence of the male eye. Here, the woman does not turn the man to stone. Rather, the desiring gaze transforms her into a dead object: she is both "entombed" and as reified as a "monument."

17 Ovid, following others, briefly mentions Pandion at the close of the tale as having been ravaged by grief at the loss of both daughters which shortened his reign (ll. 673–75). After his death, the exchange of women and violence between Athens and Thrace continues (ll. 675–721).

18 René Girard, *Violence and the Sacred*, trans. Patrick Gregory (Baltimore: Johns Hopkins Univ. Press, 1977), p. 235. Further citations will appear below.

19 See ch. 9 in Mary Douglas, *Purity and Danger: An Analysis of the Concepts of Pollution and Taboo* (London: Routledge and Kegan Paul, 1966, rpt. 1980); also ch. 1 of Girard's *Violence and the Sacred*.

20 When Girard says, "For me, prohibitions come first. Positive exchanges are merely the reverse of avoidance taboos designed to ward off outbreaks of rivalry among males" (p. 239), he assumes a hierarchical structure within culture in which men vie with each other for possession of the dominated group, women. He does not address the question of how gender difference becomes hierarchy any more effectively than does Lévi-Strauss. Both treat hierarchy as a given; both also assume that the male point of view constitutes culture. They work with male texts and male informants, with almost no recognition that the other part of the story – the woman's point of view – is not there. When Girard speaks momentarily of "a father and son – that is, a family" (p. 217), he is representing the most important weakness in his own approach: another person necessary to the birth of the son is left out, the mother. There is no serious discussion of women or of the role of the mother in Girard. I have also found that the denial or erasure of the mother

or any articulated community of women is a crucial aspect of the myths I am studying. Unlike Philomela who has a sister, Lucrece and Virginia have neither mother, sister, nor daughter.

21 *Natural Symbols, Explorations in Cosmology* (New York: Pantheon, 1970, rpt. 1982), p. 70. Douglas does not pursue the question in feminist terms when she argues "There is a continual exchange of meanings between the two kinds of bodily experiences so that each reinforces the categories of the others" (p. 65). Feminist literary and art criticism demonstrates that this exchange of meanings becomes conflictual the moment the woman decides to reshape the reigning metaphors, whether in language or in the plastic arts. Then her art threatens the other "body" and does, indeed, represent a problem. By its implicit violence, literary criticism that resolves women's artworks back into known categories of bodily images helped give rise to feminist literary criticism: the recovery of a vocabulary to discuss the oppressive as well as the liberating dialectical exchange of meanings for the female body and the body politic.

For a brilliant discussion of one woman painter's use of a received image to represent her suffering when she was raped by her art teacher and then tortured with thumb screws during her suit against the rapist, see Mary Garrard's essay on Artemisia Gentileschi, "Artemisia and Susanna," in *Feminism and Art History: Questioning the Litany*, ed. Norma Broude and Mary D. Garrard (New York: Harper and Row, 1982), pp. 147–72. The raped woman artist who repaints "Susanna and the Elders" reproduces the sacrificial crisis from the point of view of the falsely accused woman. In doing so, Artemisia takes over the role of Daniel and for the first time the woman can speak and free herself – in art – if not yet in law and the culture at large.

Ostriker (see note 4) has demonstrated how women poets first imitate, then deconstruct, and finally refashion the mythical images of their bodies.

22 See Thucydides, *The Peloponnesian War*, trans. Rex Warner (New York: Penguin, 1954), Bk. II, ch. 2, pp. 107–08. Thucydides notes that the population had to crowd into Athens, within the Long Walls, so that some had to settle on what was believed to be the sacred ground abutting the wall itself. Some believed that this transgression brought war and plague to Athens. Though skeptical himself, Thucydides carefully records both the mythic interpretation of violence and his own reading of events:

> It appears to me that the oracle came true in a way that was opposite to what people expected. It was not because of unlawful settlement in this place that misfortune came to Athens, but it was because of the war that the settlement had to be made. The war was not mentioned by the oracle, though it was foreseen that if this place was settled, it would be at a time when Athens was in difficulties.

The echo of the phrase "Athens was in trouble" is noteworthy, as is Thucydides' description of the plague within Athens' walls following the settlement on sacred ground: it has all the elements of the sacrificial crisis – the collapse of all order and differences, legal and religious. See ch. 5 of *The Peloponnesian War.*

For a similar crisis in Rome that ends in rape and not war, see Livy's *Early History of Rome*, Bk. 1. There, he describes Servius' wall and the Tarquins' dangerous extension of both the city's wall and the monarch's power which give rise to the rape of Lucrece. As Livy's *History* and Ovid's *Fasti* suggest, the rape of Lucrece is a crisis of boundaries. The unsuccessful siege of Ardea's walls by Romans gives way to an assault within Rome: or, as Shakespeare puts it, Lucrece becomes the "sweet city" the king's son takes instead (see *Lucrece*, l. 469). In Rome, the women victims, Lucrece and Virginia, are not the daughters of kings, but of the leaders of the republican rebellions.

23 See Freud's essay "The Taboo of Virginity" (1918), in which he addresses the question of why so many cultures have generated rituals surrounding the first penetration of the hymen. Freud does not see the same implications that I argue for in this essay.

24 Agamemnon tells the Old Man, "Not in fact but in name only / Is there a marriage with Achilles" (ll. 127–28), and the Old Man replies, "To bring her here a victim then – a death offering – you promised her to the son of the goddess!" (ll. 134–35).

25 Menelaus chides Agamemnon, "You are wrong / To fear the mob so desperately" (l. 518).

26 See ll. 1345–50.

27 See Apollodorus, *The Library*, II, 98: "But war having broken out with Labdacus on a question of boundaries, he [Pandion] called in the help of Tereus, son of Ares, from Thrace, and having with his help brought the war to a successful close, he gave Tereus his own daughter Procne in marriage."

28 "Difference is represented by Euripides as *internal* rather than external, omnipresent in the body of the Greeks. In the *Bacchae*, Euripides' greatest masterpiece, the tragedian collapses all boundaries, fuses male and female, human being and animal, Greek and barbarian ... The Peloponnesian War, which set Greek against Greek in *polemos*, war, which was also *stasis*, civil war, precipitated the crisis of language, of categories of difference." Du Bois, pp. 118, 119, 120; emphasis in original.

29 Euripides, *Iphigenia in Aulis*, " ... I a conspirator / Against my best beloved and weaving plots / Against her" (ll. 743–45).

30 CLYTEMNESTRA: Will he, if she resists, drag her away?
    ACHILLES: There is no doubt – and by her golden hair! (ll. 1365–66)

The suggestion of a rape in the woman dragged by her hair and screaming is unmistakable.

31 See ll. 1379–1400. Iphigenia offers herself as willing, sacred victim, as "savior of Greece," to uphold the critical difference as her father offers it

to her. After Agamemnon later presents her with an image of Greek women raped by barbarians, Iphigenia says, "It is / A right thing that Greeks rule barbarians, / Not barbarians Greeks." Agamemnon knows, however, that the real conflict is "between brothers" (l. 507).

32 In this, as in many other details, Lucrece is described in terms that recall Philomela. Once raped, Lucrece, too, feels that she is polluted. Her body is her soul's "sacred temple spotted, spoiled, corrupted" (l. 1172). But it is a temple built to male honor. Though Lucrece decides that only the spilling of her own blood can purge her of pollution, for one moment it is suggested that tears and the telling of her own tale might have served equally well:

> My tongue shall utter all; mine eyes, like sluices,
> As from a mountain spring that feeds a date,
> Shall gush pure streams to purge my impure tale. (ll. 1976–78)

But it is the poet, of course, who tells the tale, and not Lucrece. She feels like a sacked city, like Troy; and like Iphigenia, she moves toward death by learning to speak the language of the victim: she blames Helen for Tarquin's violence.

33 "It is the knowledge of violence, along with the violence itself, that the act of expulsion succeeds in shunting outside the realm of consciousness" (Girard, p. 135).

34 *To Double Business Bound: Essays on Literature, Mimesis, and Anthropology* (Baltimore: Johns Hopkins Univ. Press, 1978), p. 188. Though Girard refers to the lynching of blacks in America in this chapter, "Violence and Representation in the Mythical Text," he does not go on to discuss that particular historical example of persecution. Had he done so, he would have had to discuss the rape charge as the excuse commonly used to lynch black men. A double process of scapegoating goes on in racist violence, with tragic results for both categories of victim: the black person, male or female, and the white female. As Ida Wells-Barnett, a militant and peaceful civil rights leader said in a speech to the 1909 National Negro Conference, "Lynching is color-line murder," and "Crimes against women is the excuse, not the cause." See *The Voice of Black America*, ed. Philip S. Foner, Vol. 2, pp. 71–75. Wells-Barnett's brief speech contains a superb example of a persecution myth generated by a white male racist who uses the image of the "mob" to his own ends. It has taken us a long time to see that actual rapes as well as the exchange of accusations of rape across the color line make use of the gender line within both groups; the line that precedes and also appears finally more intractable than the color line.

35 Frazer records, in a note to Apollodorus' text, that "Ovid . . . appears to have associated the murder of Itys with the frenzied rites of the Bacchanals, for he says that the crime was perpetrated at the time when the Thracian women were celebrating the bienniel festival . . . of Dionysus, and that the two women disguised themselves as Bacchanals" (*The Library*, II, 99). See

Humphries' edition of the *Metamorphoses*, ll. 585–607. To frame the rescue of Philomela and the murder of Itys with details of the Bacchanal is to suggest a likeness between Procne as unnatural mother and Agave, her counterpart in Euripides' *Bacchae*, who rends her son, the king Pentheus, under the spell of the bacchic rites. Ovid presents the rites as degenerate: a festival that turns back into bloody and monstrous violence. He also trades on misogynist lore by making it clear that his Procne only pretends to be a bacchante, suggesting that the rites are or were only a cover for the unleashing of female revenge against men. But Ovid cannot draw on *The Bacchae* or other bacchic stories without drawing out the ambiguities within the whole tradition surrounding Dionysus. Greeks believed Dionysus' home was Thrace. The women in the myth are Greeks transported to Thrace. Among the reversals in the myth is this movement away from Athens, an actual center of Dionysian rites, back to the god's home to represent the crisis in Greek culture when invaded by foreign religion.

Girard is shrewd in his analysis of the predominance of women in the Dionysiac cult. For his discussion of the displacement of responsibility for the sacrificial crisis and the ritual murder of the king onto women, see ch. 5, "Dionysus," in *Violence and the Sacred*, especially pp. 139–42.

36 See, for example, Achilles Tatius' novel *Leukippe and Kleitophon*: "Prokne, learning the rape from the robe, exacted an exorbitant revenge: the conspiracy of two women and two passions, jealousy and outrage, plan a feast far worse than his weddings. The meal was Tereus' son, whose mother *had* been Prokne before her fury was roused and she forgot that older anguish. For the pains of present jealousy are stronger than the womb's remembrance. Only passionate women making a man pay for a sexual affront, even if they must endure as much harm as they impose, count the pain of their affliction a small price for the pleasure of the infliction."

I would like to thank John Winkler for pointing out this passage to me and for providing me with his own translation in manuscript. His translation is forthcoming in *The Ancient Greek Novels in Translation*, ed. Bryan P. Reardon (Berkeley: Univ. of California Press); emphasis in original.

37 See Victor Turner, ch. 3, 4 in *The Ritual Process: Structure and Anti-Structure* (Ithaca: Cornell Univ. Press, 1969), and ch. 1, 6, 7 in *Dramas, Fields, and Metaphors: Symbolic Action in Human Society* (Ithaca: Cornell Univ. Press, 1974). Turner says, "In human history, I see a continuous tension between structure and communitas, at all levels of scale and complexity. Structure, or all that which holds people apart, defines their differences, and constrains their actions, is one pole in a charged field, for which the opposite pole is communitas, or anti-structure . . . Communitas does not merge identities; it liberates them from conformity to general norms, though this is necessarily a transient condition if society is to continue to operate in an orderly fashion" ("Metaphors of Anti-Structure," in *Dramas*, p. 274). Structure is coercive, but anti-structure can be crisis *or* peace. If

Turner tends to spend more time looking at the peaceful dimensions of communitas and Girard attends more to the violent, it is nevertheless possible to find in the work of both the ground for symbolic or unbloody sacrifice in art. Or, as Turner suggests, "Metaphor is, in fact, metamorphic, transformative" (*Dramas*, p. 25). The loom as instrument of transformation, and wool as the hair of the sacrificial beast which women, by a long and careful process, transform into clothing suggest why weaving skirts the sacred and the violent. It also suggests why women's power at the loom is both derided and dreaded, transformed, like giving birth, into a sign of weakness by patriarchal uses of language and symbol. I am arguing that Philomela, and with her, feminist theorists and artists, use an old instrument/metaphor to new, positive ends. I am also arguing that this process need not reproduce violence.

38 See Mary Douglas, ch. 6, "Powers and Dangers," in *Purity and Danger*.

39 *The Bacchae*, ll. 118, 512–15.

40 See the exchange between Myrrhine and her husband, Kinesias.

41 Ovid, *Heroides*, 1. 15.

42 See Hazel E. Barnes, "The Myth of Medusa," in *The Meddling Gods: Four Essays on Classical Themes* (Lincoln: Univ. of Nebraska Press, 1974), p. 6; and Jane Ellen Harrison, *Prolegomena to the Study of Greek Religion* (Cambridge: Cambridge Univ. Press, 1903), pp. 187–96. Douglas notes that in some cultures strict taboo regulates when a woman can work with fire. Girard notes that Hestia may be the locus of the early sacrificial rites, but he does not ask why the common hearth should be given a female identity and be identified with virginity. See ch. 9 of *Purity and Danger*, and *Violence and the Sacred*, pp. 166–67 (on masks) and pp. 305, 314–15 (on Hestia). If the common hearth was in fact the locus of ritual sacrifice, it is all the more important that in myth Procne turns back to the hearth to cook her own child as she undoes all of her female roles in culture.

43 Freud's formula can be found in "Medusa's Head," where it becomes clear that his greatest dread is the woman as mother: Medusa's snaky head is the sign of the mother's monstrous genitals. For a list of modern women's poems about Medusa and their intense struggle to free themselves from the mythic uses of her, see Ostriker.

44 Maxine Hong Kingston, *The Woman Warrior: Memoirs of a Girlhood among Ghosts* (New York: Vintage/Random House, 1977), pp. 62–63.

45 *Selected Poems*, p. 204. This is not a new idea, nor is it exclusively a feminist idea. See, for example, "*Revelation*: The Text as Acceptable Sacrifice," in Dennis J. Costa, *Irenic Apocalypse: Some Uses of Apocalyptic in Dante, Petrarch, and Rabelais*, Stanford French and Italian Studies, 21 (Saratoga, Calif.: Anma Libri, 1981), 22–39. See also Costa's "Stuck Sow or Broken Heart: Pico's *Oratio* as Ritual Sacrifice," *JMRS*, 12 (Fall 1982), 221–35.

SOURCE

The Roman poet Ovid (43 BCE–17 CE) provides the fullest account of the story of Procne, Philomela, and Tereus in his epic *Metamorphoses* ("Transformations"), composed in 8 CE. He draws on Sophocles' *Tereus*, a tragedy produced in Athens during the fifth century BCE that now survives only in fragments. The myth tells the story of a woman's rape by a brutal king, her sister's husband, that results in a horrific act of female revenge, the murder of his son, Itys.

The translation refers to the text of W. S. Anderson (ed.), *P. Ovidii Nasonis Metamorphoses* (Berlin, 1977).

Ovid, *Metamorphoses* 6. 424–623

The Thracian king Tereus had conquered these with the aid of his troops,
and through his victory earned a great name for himself.
Because he was strong in wealth and men
and traced his descent perhaps from the great Mars,
Pandion joined him in marriage to his daughter Procne.
Neither Juno, goddess of marriage, nor Hymenaeus, god of weddings,
nor the Graces attended the ceremony.
Instead, the Furies carried torches stolen from a funeral,
the Furies spread the coverings on the nuptial bed,
while an owl of ill omen settled on the house,
and sitting on the rooftop of the bedchamber.
Under this omen Procne and Tereus joined in marriage,

under this omen they became parents. The Thracian people rejoiced with them;
they gave thanks to the very gods and ordered that the anniversary
of Tereus' marriage to Procne, daughter of the tyrant Pandion,
and the birthday of their son Itys be called a public holiday,
completely unaware of the omen's true meaning!

Now the Titan had led the seasons five times from autumn to autumn,
when Procne coaxingly addressed her husband,
"If I am at all dear to you, please let me visit my sister,
or let my sister come here. You will promise my father
that she will return after a little while. If you give me a chance
to see my sister, you will confer upon me a great gift."
Her husband ordered his ships to the sea; with oars and a fair wind,
he entered the port of Cecrops and the shores of the Piraeus.
When the meeting took place, the kings joined right hands in pledge,
and began their conversation with that favorable omen.
Tereus told him about his wife's request, the reason for his journey,
and then promised a speedy return for her sister.

All of sudden Philomela entered, attired in sumptuous clothing,
but even more sumptuous her beauty, moving, so we often hear,
like the water nymphs and wood nymphs in the depths of the forest,
if only one should give them manners and clothing like hers.
Tereus became inflamed at the sight of the maiden,
just as if someone were to set fire to dry grain
or leaves, or burn grass stored up in a hayloft.
Although her beauty deserved this response, his lecherous nature
spurred him on too. And because the Thracians are predisposed to
lust, he burned not only with his own crime but that of his own people.
His impulse was to corrupt her attendants' care and
the loyalty of her nurse, and even by magnificent gifts
to rape the girl and defend the rape with cruel war.
There was nothing he would not dare, overcome by mad lust,
nor could his breast subdue the flames residing there.

Now impatient of delay, he eagerly begged to accomplish
Procne's injunctions, pleading his own cause under her name.
Love made him eloquent, and as often as he asked,
more insistently than was right, he maintained that Procne would also want it.
To words he added tears, as if she had ordered them herself.
By the gods, what blind nights hold mortal breasts!
Tereus appeared pious in his criminal endeavor, receiving praise
instead of blame for his crime – the more so as Philomela had the same wish.
Throwing her arms around her father's neck, she begged to see her sister;

for her own sanity – and against it too – she entreated him.
Tereus gazed at her and in looking seemed to feel her already in his arms,
watching her little kisses, and her arms wrapped around her father's neck,
all this worked like a stimulus on him, as fire or food for his madness.
As many times as the girl embraced her father, Tereus wished to be him;
indeed, even if he were, his intentions would be no less impious.
The father yielded to their prayers; the girl rejoiced and thanked him
and, unfortunate creature, thought it a blessing for both her and her sister.

Now Phoebus' work was almost done and his horses
struck the road to Olympus with down-turned hooves.
A royal banquet was placed on the tables and wine poured into golden cups;
after that the bodies of the celebrants surrendered to peaceful sleep.
But the Thracian king, although he had retired to his chambers,
grew inflamed with thoughts of the girl; recalling her face,
her movements and her hands, he imagined what he wished,
what he had not yet seen. He fanned the flames of his passion,
while his fantasies disturbed his sleep.

At dawn, Pandion clasped his son-in-law's right hand as he departed,
and with tears welling up in his eyes entrusted his daughter to him,
"I give this girl to you, dear son, because a pious cause has compelled me,
both my daughters wished it, and you also wished it, Tereus.
By fidelity, family and the gods, I beg you as your suppliant
to guard her with a father's love and return her –
a sweet solace to my anxious old age – as swiftly as possible,
for it will seem a long time to me already. And you, too, Philomela,
return to me as quickly as possible, if you have any piety at all;
it is enough that your sister is so far away."
As he commanded them, he gave his daughter kisses
and gentle tears fell as he spoke.
He asked for both of their right hands as a pledge of faith,
and he joined their hands together, and entreated them
to remember to greet for him his absent daughter and grandson.
He could scarcely say goodbye, his voice was so choked with sobs,
and he feared the ominous forebodings of his mind.

As soon as Philomela was placed on the painted ship,
once the oars hit the water and the land had receded,
Tereus shouted, "I have won! My prayers are coming with me!"
The barbarian exulted, scarcely able to postpone his pleasure,
never once turning his eyes from her.
Just as one of Jove's predatory birds with his hooked talons
deposited a hare into his high nest,

so the captor looked over his prize, his captive, unable to escape.
Now the journey was over, now they left the tired ships
and set foot on their own shores, when the king dragged Pandion's daughter
into a secret hut deep in an ancient forest,
and there he imprisoned her, pale, trembling and fearing the worst,
and now with tears asking where her sister was.
Then acknowledging his criminal intentions, he raped the virgin, all alone,
as she called in vain on her father, on her sister, and above all the gods.
The girl trembled like a frightened lamb wounded and cast aside
by a grey wolf, and does not yet think itself safe;
or like a dove, its feathers dripping with its own blood,
that still bristles with fright, still fears the greedy claws of its captor
Soon, when her reason returned, tearing her loosened hair,
like one in mourning, her arms bruised with blows,
she cried with outstretched hands, "What terrible deeds you have done,
barbarous, cruel! Did not the injunctions of my father and his pious tears,
my virginity, or the conjugal rights of my sister move you?
You have confused everything; I am now the mistress of my sister's husband,
you, husband to us both! As her enemy I must pay the price.
Why do you not take my life, you traitor, so that no crime remains for you?
I wish you had done this before you committed this outrage.
Then my shade would have been pure of your crime!
But if the gods see these things, indeed, if there are gods at all,
if all things have not perished with me, someday you will pay for this.
I will myself broadcast your crime, setting aside my shame.
If there is an opportunity, I will go to the people; if I am kept
imprisoned in this forest, I will fill the woods with my story
and I will move the stones to witness.

Heaven will hear it, and if there is any god in that place, he will hear it too."
These words aroused the wrath of the savage tyrant,
but his fear matched his anger, and goaded on by both feelings,
he pulled from its sheath his sword, with which he was girded,
and catching her by the hair and twisting her arms behind her back,
he bound them fast. Philomela offered him her throat,
and entertained the hope of her death once she saw the sword:
but he seized her tongue with tongs, and cut it off with his savage sword,
even as it protested against the outrage, ever calling the name of her father,
and struggling to speak. The stump of the tongue quivered,
the severed tongue trembled on the dark earth, faintly murmuring,
and as the tail of a severed snake normally writhes about,
it twitched and dying sought the feet of its mistress.
Even after this outrage – one can scarcely believe it – it is said
his lust drove him on to attack repeatedly her battered body.

After such crimes, he had the gall to return to Procne,
who, when she saw her husband, asked after her sister.
Whereupon Tereus feigned grief and told a fictional account of her death,
his tears lending credibility to his story. Procne ripped off her gown,
gleaming with golden borders, and put on black clothing;
she erected an empty sepulchre, brought offerings to her alleged spirit,
and mourned the fate of her sister, although it did not need mourning.

The god showed through the twelve signs of the zodiac in a year's course.
What will Philomela do? A guard checked her flight,
the walls of the hut built of solid stone stood strong,
its mute mouth did not bear any sign of the deed. But great is
the power of sorrow; ingenuity arises from such sad circumstances.
From her cunning loom hung a warp of Thracian thread;
she wove purple signs into a white background,
the story of the crime. Once completed, she gave it to her one servant,
and with a gesture requested that she carry it to her mistress.
The maid carried it to Procne as requested, not knowing its message.
The wife of the savage tyrant unfurled the cloth
and read of her sister's terrible fate, and said not a word,
a miracle if she could. Grief checked her voice,
her tongue failed to find words commensurate with her outrage.
She did not cry, but right and wrong rushed together
in confusion; revenge was the only thing on her mind.

It was the time when the Thracian matrons used to celebrate
the biannual festival of Bacchus. Night was a witness to their rites:
Mount Rhodope resounded with the shrill clash of their sharp bronze cymbals;
at night the queen left her house, prepared for the rites of the god,
and took up the markers and weapons of frenzy.
Her head was wreathed with vines, a deer skin hung
from her left side, and a light spear rested on her shoulder.
Swiftly through the forest, with a throng of companions,
Procne, dreadful and driven on by the madness of grief,
imitated your madness, Bacchus. She came at last to the secluded hut,
she cried aloud and shrieked "Euhoe!," broke down the doors,
and abducted her sister. She then dressed the abducted girl
with the trappings of Bacchus and hid her face with ivy leaves.
Dragging the astonished girl along she led her within her own walls.

When Philomela perceived that she had reached the impious house,
the unhappy girl bristled with fear and her whole face grew pale;
finding a place Procne removed the trappings of the sacred rites,
uncovered the ashamed face of her sister; and embraced her.

Since she thought of herself as the mistress of her sister's husband
Philomela could not bear to meet her eyes;
instead she turned her gaze to the ground, even though she wanted
to swear by the gods and invoke them as witnesses to the dishonor
that had been forced upon her; instead her hand served as her voice.
But Procne burned and could not control her anger;
rebuking her sister for weeping, she said, "This is no time for tears,
but for the sword, or, if you have it, something stronger than a sword.
I am ready for any crime, sister; I will burn this royal palace with torches,
and send Tereus, the cheat, into the middle of the flames,
or I will cut out his tongue, eyes, and the organs that took away
your virginity, or I will drive his guilty soul out through a thousand wounds.
I am ready to do something great; what that will be, I still do not know."

While Procne was saying these things, Itys came to his mother.
His arrival gave her an idea; looking at him with savage eyes,
she said, "Oh my child, how much you resemble your father!"
Saying no more, she plans the terrible crime and seethes with silent rage.

BIBLIOGRAPHY

Abbott, G. F. 1903. *Macedonian Folklore*. Cambridge.

Allen, A. 1950. "'Sincerity' and the Roman Elegists." *Classical Philology* 45: 145–60.

Archer, L., Fischler, S., and M. Wyke (eds.). 1994. *Women in Ancient Societies: "An Illusion in the Night."* New York and London.

Ardener, E. A. 1975. "Belief and the Problem of Women." In S. Ardener (ed.), *Perceiving Women*, 1–17. London.

Arthur, M. B. 1976. "Review Essay: Classics." *Signs* 2: 382–403.

Austin, N. 1975. *Archery at the Dark of the Moon*. Berkeley, CA.

Bachofen, J. J. 1967. *Myth, Religion, and Mother Right*. Trans. R. Manheim. Princeton, NJ.

Badian, E. 1985. "A Phantom Marriage Law." *Philologus* 129: 82–98.

Bakhtin, M. 1984. *Rabelais and His World*. Trans. H. Iswolsky. Bloomington, IN.

Ballentine, F. G. 1904. "Some Phases of the Cult of the Nymphs." *Harvard Studies in Classical Philology* 15: 97–110.

Balsdon, J. P. V. D. 1962. *Roman Women*. London.

Barnard, M. 1980. "Static." *Woman Poet, I: The West*, 34. Reno, NV.

Barthes, R. 1975. *S/Z*. Trans. R. Miller. London.

Barton, C. A. 1993. *The Sorrows of the Ancient Romans: The Gladiator and the Monster*. Princeton, NJ.

Beagon, M. 1992. *Roman Nature: The Thought of Pliny the Elder*. Oxford.

Benardete, S. 1969. *Herodotean Inquiries*. The Hague.

Benedetto, V. di. 1973. "Il volo di Afrodite in Omero e in Saffo." *Quaderni urbinati di cultura classica* 16: 121–3.

Bernikow, L. 1974. *The World Split Open*. New York.

Betensky, A. 1973. "Forum." *Arethusa* 6: 267–9.

Betensky, A. 1974. "A Further Reply." *Arethusa* 7: 211–17.

Bloch, R. 1965. *Tite-Live et les premiers siècles de Rome.* Paris.

Blok, J. 1987. "Sexual Asymmetry: A Historiographical Essay." In J. Blok and P. Mason (eds.), *Sexual Asymmetry: Studies in Ancient Society,* 1–57. Amsterdam.

Boedeker, D. D. 1979. "Sappho and Acheron." In G. W. Bowersock, W. Burkert, and M. Putnam (eds.), *Arktouros: Hellenic Studies Presented to Bernard W. M. Knox on the Occasion of his 65th birthday,* 40–52. New York.

Bolling, G. 1958. "POIKILOS and THRONA." *American Journal of Philology* 79: 275–82.

———. 1959. "Restoration of Sappho, 98a 1–7." *American Journal of Philology* 80: 276–87.

Bonner, C. 1949. "KESTOS IMAS and the Saltire of Aphrodite." *American Journal of Philology* 70: 1–6.

Boston Women's Health Book Collective. 1992. *The New Our Bodies, Ourselves.* New York.

Boswell, J. 1990. *The Kindness of Strangers.* New York.

Bourdieu, P. 1979. *Algeria 1960.* Cambridge.

Bourgey, L. 1953. *Observation et expérience chez les médécins de la collection hippocratique.* Paris.

Boyancé, P. 1956. *L'Influence grecque sur la poésie latine de Catulle à Ovide.* Entretiens Hardt 2. Geneva.

Boyarin, D. 1993. *Carnal Israel: Reading Sex in Talmudic Culture.* Berkeley, CA.

Boyd, B. 1987. "Virtus Effeminata and Sallust's Sempronia." *Transactions of the American Philological Association* 117: 183–201.

Brashear, W. 1979. "Ein Berliner Zauberpapyrus." *Zeitschrift für Papyrologie und Epigraphik* 33: 261–78.

Brelich, A. 1969. *Paides e Parthenoi.* Rome.

Brendel, O. 1970. "The Scope and Temperament of Erotic Art in the Graeco-Roman World." In T. Bowie et al. (eds.), *Studies in Erotic Art,* 3–107, New York.

Bright, D. F. 1978. *Haec Mihi Fingebam: Tibullus in his World.* Cincinnati Classical Studies n.s. 3, Leiden.

Brunt, P. A. 1971. *Italian Manpower.* Oxford.

Bryson, N. 1986. "Two Narratives of Rape in the Visual Arts: Lucretia and the Sabine Women." In S. Tomaselli and R. Porter (eds.), *Rape,* 152–73. Oxford.

Buckley, T. and A. Gottlieb. 1988. "A Critical Appraisal of Theories of Menstrual Symbolism." In T. Buckley and A. Gottlieb (eds.), *Blood and Magic,* 3–50. Berkeley, CA.

Bulkin, E. and J. Larkin (eds.), 1975. *Amazon Poetry.* New York.

Burkert, W. 1977. *Griechische Religion der archaischen und klassichen Epoche.* Stuttgart.

Butrica, J. 1982. "Review Article: The Latin Love Poets." *Echos du monde classique/Classical Views* n.s. 1: 82–95.

Bynum, C. W. 1987. *Holy Feast and Holy Fast.* Berkeley, CA.

Cahen, E. 1930. *Les Hymnes de Callimaque.* Paris.

Cairns, F. 1972. *Generic Composition in Greek and Roman Poetry.* Edinburgh.

Calame, C. 1997. *Choruses of Young Women in Ancient Greece: Their Morphology, Religious Role and Sexual Functions.* Lanham, MD. [Translation of *Les choeurs de jeunes filles en Grèce archaïque,* Part 1. Rome, 1977.]

Calder, W. M. 1988. "F. G. Welcker's *Sapphobild* and its Reception in Wilamowitz." In W. M. Calder et al. (eds.), *Friedrich Gottlieb Welcker, Werk und Wirkung,* 131–56. Stuttgart.

Cameron, A. 1949. "Sappho's Prayer to Aphrodite." *Harvard Theological Review* 32: 1–17.

——. and A. Kuhrt (eds.). 1993. *Images of Women in Antiquity.* 2nd ed. Detroit, MI.

Campbell, D. A. 1982. *Greek Lyric. I. Sappho, Alcaeus.* Cambridge, MA.

Carlier, J. 1980–1. "Les Amazones font la guerre et l'amour." *L'Ethnographie* 76: 11–33.

Carson, A. 1990. "Putting Her in Her Place: Woman, Dirt, and Desire." In D. M. Halperin, J. J. Winkler, and F. I. Zeitlin (eds.), *Before Sexuality: The Construction of Erotic Experience in the Ancient Greek World,* 309–38. Princeton, NJ.

Cassin, E. 1982. "Le Proche-Orient ancien: virginité et strategie du sexe." In Tordjinian (ed.), *La première fois ou le roman de la virginité perdue,* 241–58. Paris.

Chantraine, P. 1946–7. "Les Noms du mari et de la femme, du père et de la mère en grec." *Revue des études grecques* 59–60: 219–50.

Chibnall, M. 1975. "Pliny's Natural History and the Middle Ages." In T. A. Dorey (ed.), *Empire and Aftermath: Silver Latin II,* 57–78. London.

Chicago, J. 1975. *Through the Flower.* Garden City, NY.

——. 1979. *The Dinner Party.* Garden City, NY.

Clark, G. 1993. *Women in Late Antiquity: Pagan and Christian Lifestyles.* Oxford.

Clark, S. R. L. 1975. *Aristotle's Man.* Oxford.

Clausen, W. 1976. "Cynthius." *American Journal of Philology* 97: 245–47.

Clay, J. S. 1980. "Sappho's Hesperus and Hesiod's Dawn." *Philologus* 124: 302–5.

Cohen, B. 2000. *Not the Classical Ideal: Athens and the Construction of the Other in Greek Art.* Leiden.

Cohen, D. 1991. *Law, Sexuality, and Society: The Enforcement of Morals in Classical Athens.* Cambridge.

——. 1992. "Review Article: Sex, Gender and Sexuality in Ancient Greece." *Classical Philology* 87: 145–67.

—— and R. Saller. 1994. "Foucault on Sexuality in Greco-Roman Antiquity." In J. Goldstein (ed.), *Foucault and the Writing of History,* 35–59. Oxford.

Cohen, S. J. D. 1991. "Menstruants and the Sacred in Judaism and Christianity." In S. B. Pomeroy (ed.), *Women's History and Ancient History,* 273–99. Chapel Hill, NC.

Cole, S. G. 1992. "*Gunaiki ou Themis*: Gender Difference in the Greek *Leges Sacrae*." *Helios* 19: 104–22.

Conze, A. 1893–1922. *Die attischen Grabreliefs*. Berlin.

Cook, B. W. 1979. "'Women Alone Stir my Imagination': Lesbianism and the Cultural Tradition." *Signs* 4: 718–39.

Copley, F. O. 1947. "Servitium Amoris in the Roman Elegists." *Transactions of the American Philological Association* 78: 285–300.

Cornell, T. J. 1986. "The Value of the Literary Tradition Concerning Archaic Rome." In K. A. Raaflaub (ed.), *Social Struggles in Archaic Rome*, 52–76. Berkeley, CA.

Culham, P. 1986. "Ten Years after Pomeroy: Studies of the Image and Reality of Women in Antiquity." *Helios* 13: 9–30.

Dahlburg, J.-T. 1994. "The Fight to Save India's Baby Girls." *Los Angeles Times*, Feb. 22: A1, A14.

Daremberg, C. and E. Saglio. 1877–1919. *Dictionnaire des antiquités*. Paris.

Dean-Jones, L. 1992. "The Politics of Pleasure: Female Sexual Appetite in the Hippocratic Corpus." *Helios* 19: 72–91.

——. 1994. *Women's Bodies in Classical Greek Science*. Oxford.

DeJean, J. 1989. *Fictions of Sappho, 1546–1937*. Chicago.

Delaney, C. 1988. "Mortal Flow: Menstruation in Turkish Village Society." In T. Buckley and A. Gottlieb (eds.), *Blood Magic*, 75–93. Berkeley, CA.

de Lauretis, T. 1984. *Alice Doesn't*. Bloomington, IN.

del Grande, C. 1959. "Saffo, Ode *phainetai moi kênos isos*." *Euphrosyne* 2: 181–8.

Detienne, M. 1972. *Les Jardins d'Adonis*. Paris.

——.1976. "Protagenie de femme, ou comment engendrer seule." *Traverses* 5–6: 75–81.

——. 1977. *Dionysos mis à mort*. Paris.

——. 1979. "Violentes 'eugénies'." In M. Detienne and J.-P. Vernant, *La cuisine du sacrifice en pays grec*. Paris.

Diepgen, P. 1937. *Die Frauenheilkunde der alten Welt*. Munich (W. Stoekel (ed.), *Handbuch der Gynäkologie* XII/1).

Dixon, S. 1982. "Women and Rape in Roman Law." *Kønsroller, parforhold og Samlivsformer: Arbejdsnotat nr. 3*. Copenhagen.

——. 1988. *The Roman Mother*. Norman, OK.

Dodson, B. n.d. *Liberating Masturbation*. B. Dodson, Box 1933, New York, NY 10001.

Donaldson, I. 1982. *The Rapes of Lucretia: A Myth and Its Transformations*. Oxford.

Douglas, M. 1984. *Purity and Danger*. London.

Dover, K. J. 1989. *Greek Homosexuality: Updated and with a New Postscript*. Cambridge, MA.

DuBois, P. 1978. "Sappho and Helen." *Arethusa* 11: 88–99.

Dunkle, J. R. 1971. "The Rhetorical Tyrant in Roman Historiography: Sallust, Livy and Tacitus." *Classical World* 65: 12–20.

Du Quesnay, I. M. Le M. 1973. "The Amores." In J. W. Binns (ed.), *Greek and Latin Studies, Classical Literature and its Influence:Ovid*, 1–48. London.

Earl, D. 1961. *The Political Thought of Sallust*. Cambridge.

Edwards, C. 1997. "Unspeakable Professions: Public Performance and Prostitution in Ancient Rome." In J. Hallett and M. Skinner (eds.), *Roman Sexualities*, 66–98. Princeton, NJ.

Ehrenreich, B. and D. English. 1973. *Witches, Midwives, and Nurses: A History of Women Healers*. New York.

———. 1979. *For Her Own Good*. London.

Fairweather, J. 1974. "Fiction in the Biographies of Ancient Writers." *Ancient Society* 5: 231–75.

Fantham, E. 1986. "Women in Antiquity: A Selective (and Subjective) Survey 1979–84." *Echos du monde classique/Classical Views* 30, n.s. 5: 1–24.

———, Foley, H., Kampen, N., Pomeroy, S., and H. Shapiro (eds.). 1994. *Women in the Classical World*. New York.

Faraone, C. A. 1992. "Sex and Power: Male-Targetting Aphrodisiacs in the Greek Magical Tradition." *Helios* 19: 92–103.

Farnell, L. R. 1896–1909. *Cults of the Greek States*. 5 vols. Oxford.

Fasbender, H. 1897. *Entwicklungslehre, Geburtshülfe und Gynäkologie in den hippokratischen Schriften*. Stuttgart.

Fedeli, P. 1980. *Sesto Properzio: Il Primo Libro delle Elegie*. Accademia Toscana Studi 53, Florence.

———. 1985. *Properzio: Il Libro Terzo delle Elegie*. Bari.

Fehrle, E. 1910. *Die kultische Keuschheit im Altertum. Religionsgeschichtliche Versuche und Vorarbeiten 6.6*. Giessen.

Foley, H. P. (ed.). 1981. *Reflections of Women in Antiquity*. New York, London, and Paris.

———. 1981. "The Conception of Women in Athenian Drama." In H. P. Foley (ed.), *Reflections of Women in Antiquity*, 127–68.

Foster, B. O. 1899. "Notes on the Symbolism of the Apple in Classical Antiquity." *Harvard Studies in Classical Philology* 10: 39–55.

Foucault, M. 1976. *The History of Sexuality. Vol. 1: An Introduction*. Trans. R. Hurley. New York. (Reprint and translation of 1976 ed. Harmondsworth, 1981).

———. 1988. *The Use of Pleasure: The History of Sexuality Vol. 2*. Trans. R. Hurley. New York.

———. 1988. *The Care of the Self: The History of Sexuality Vol. 3*. Trans. R. Hurley. New York.

Foxhall, L. 1994. "Pandora Unbound: A Feminist Critique of Foucault's *History of Sexuality*." In A. Cornwall and N. Lindisfarne, *Dislocating Masculinity: Comparative Ethnographies*, 133–46. New York and London.

French, R., and F. Greenaway (eds.). 1986. *Science in the Early Roman Empire: Pliny the Elder, His Sources and Influence*. London and Sydney.

French, V. 1986. "Midwives and Maternity Care in the Greco- Roman World." *Helios* 13.2: 69–84.

Gallavotti, C. 1947. *Saffo e Alceo: Testimonianze e frammenti.* Naples.

Gamel, M.-K. 1989. "*Non sine caede*: Abortion Politics and Poetics in Ovid's *Amores.*" *Helios* 16: 183–206.

Gardner, J. F. 1986. *Women in Roman Law and Society.* Bloomington and Indianapolis, IN and London.

Garrison, D. 2000. *Sexual Culture in Ancient Greece.* Norman, OK.

Gentili, B. 1966. "La veneranda Saffo." *Quaderni Urbinati di Cultura Classica* 2: 37–62.

Gilbert, S. M. and S. Gubar. 1979. *The Madwoman in the Attic.* New Haven, CT.

Gjerstad, E. 1973. *Early Rome.* Vols. 5 and 6. Rome.

Golden, M. 1992. "The Uses of Cross-Cultural Comparison in Ancient Social History." *Echos du monde classique/Classical Views* 36: 309–31.

Gordon, L. 1986. "What's New in Women's History?" In T. de Lauretis (ed.), *Feminist Studies/Critical Studies*, 20–30. Bloomington, IN.

Gould, J. P. 1980. "Law, Custom and Myth: Aspects of the Social Position of Women in Classical Athens." *Journal of the Historical Society* 100: 38–59.

Gourevitch, D. 1984. *Le Mal d'être femme: La Femme et la médecine dans la Rome antique.* Paris.

Green, M. 1989. "Women's Medical Practice and Health Care in Medieval Europe." *Signs* 14: 434–73.

Griffin, J. 1976. "Augustan Poetry and the Life of Luxury." *Journal of Roman Studies* 66: 87–105. Reprinted with modifications in J. Griffin, *Latin Poets and Roman Life*, 1–31. Chapel Hill, NC.

——. 1985. *Latin Poetry and Roman Life.* London.

Hallett, J. and M. Skinner (eds.) 1997. *Roman Sexualities.* Princeton, NJ.

Hallett, J. P. 1973. "The Role of Women in Roman Elegy: Counter-Cultural Feminism." *Arethusa* 6: 103–24.

——. 1974. "Women in Roman Elegy: A Reply." *Arethusa* 7: 211–17.

——. 1979. "Sappho and her Social Context." *Signs* 4: 447–64.

——. 1984. *Fathers and Daughters in Roman Society.* Princeton, NJ.

——. 1989. "Woman as *Same* and *Other* in Classical Roman Elite." *Helios* 16: 59–78.

Halperin, D. 1990. *One Hundred Years of Homosexuality.* New York and London.

——, Winkler, J. J., and F. I. Zeitlin (eds.) 1990. *Before Sexuality: The Construction of Erotic Experience in the Ancient Greek World.* Princeton, NJ.

Hanson, A. E. 1990. "The Medical Writers' Woman." In D. M. Halperin, J. J. Winkler, and F. I. Zeitlin (eds.), *Before Sexuality: The Construction of Erotic Experience in the Ancient Greek World*, 309–38. Princeton, NJ.

——. 1992. "Conception, Gestation, and the Origin of Female Nature in the *Corpus Hippocraticum.*" *Helios* 19: 31–71.

Hartog, F. 1980. *Le Miroir d'Hérodote.* Paris.

Hastrup, I. 1978. "The Semantics of Biology: Virginity." In S. Ardener (ed.), *Defining Females*, 49–5. London.

Hawkes, T. 1977. *Structuralism and Semiotics*. London.

Hawley, R. and B. Levick (eds.). 1995. *Women in Antiquity: New Assessments*. New York and London.

Heckenbach, J. 1911. *De nuditate sacra sacrisque vinculis*. Giessen.

Henderson, Jeffrey. [1975] 1991. *The Maculate Muse: Obscene Language in Attic Comedy*. 2nd ed. Oxford.

Henderson, John. 1989. "Satire Writes Woman: Gendersong." *Proceedings of the Cambridge Philological Society* 215: 50–80.

Heurgon, J. 1973. *The Rise of Rome*. Trans. J. Willis. Berkeley, CA.

Higonnet, M. 1986. "Speaking Silences: Women's Suicide." In S. R. Suleiman (ed.), *The Female Body in Western Culture*, 68–83. Cambridge, MA.

Hooker, J. T. 1977. *The Language and Text of the Lesbian Poets*. Innsbruck.

Hopkins, M. K. 1965. "Contraception in the Roman Empire." *Comparative Studies in Society and History* 8: 124–51.

Hubbard, M. 1974. *Propertius*. London.

Hunter, N. D. 1986. "The Pornography Debate in Context: A Chronology." In FACT Book Committee (ed.), *Caught Looking*, 26–9. New York.

Janko, R. 1988. "Berlin Magical Papyrus 21243: A Conjecture." *Zeitschrift für Papyrologie und Epigraphik* 72: 293.

Jed, S. 1989. *Chaste Thinking: The Rape of Lucretia and the Birth of Humanism*. Bloomington, IN.

Johansen, K. F. 1951. *Attic Grave-reliefs*. Copenhagen.

Johns, C. 1982. *Sex or Symbol? Erotic Images of Greece and Rome*. Austin, TX.

Johnston, S. I. 1995. "Defining the Dreadful: Remarks on the Child-Killing Demon." In M. Meyer and P. Mirecki (eds.), *Ancient Magic and Ritual Power*, 361–89. Leiden.

Joplin, P. 1990. "Ritual Work on Human Flesh: Livy's Lucretia and the Rape of the Body Politic." *Helios* 17: 51–70.

Just, R. 1975. "Conceptions of Women in Classical Athens." *Journal of the Anthropological Society of Oxford* 6.3: 153–70.

Kaibel, G. (ed.) 1878. *Epigrammata Graeca*. Berlin.

Kakridis, Ph. I. 1972. "Une Pomme mordue." *Hellenica* 25: 189–92.

Kampen, N. 1986. "Reliefs of the Basilica Aemilia: A Redating." Paper delivered at Brown University Conference, "Roman Women: Critical Approaches."

——.1996. *Sexuality in Ancient Art*. Cambridge.

Kappeler, S. 1986. *The Pornography of Representation*. Minneapolis, MN and Cambridge.

Keuls, E. 1985. *The Reign of the Phallus*. New York.

Killeen, J. F. 1973. "Sappho Fr. 111." *Classical Quarterly* 23: 197.

Kincaid, J. 1990. *Lucy*. Harmondsworth.

King, H. 1993. "Producing Woman: Hippocratic Gynaecology." In L. Archer, S. Fischler, and M. Wyke (eds.), *Women in Ancient Societies*, 102–14. London.

King, H. 1995. "Self-Help, Self-Knowledge: In Search of the Patient in Hippo-cratic Gynaecology." In R. Hawley and B. Levick (eds.), *Women in Antiquity: New Assessments*, 135–48. New York and London.

——. 1998. *Hippocrates' Woman*. New York and London.

King, J. K. 1976. "Sophistication vs. Chastity in Propertius' Latin Love Elegy." *Helios* 4: 67–76.

Kirk, G. S. 1963. "A Fragment of Sappho Reinterpreted." *Classical Quarterly* 13: 51–2.

Klapisch-Zuber, C. 1985. *Women, Family, and Ritual in Renaissance Italy.* Trans. L. G. Cochrane. Chicago.

Koloski-Ostrow, A. and C. Lyons (eds.). 1997. *Naked Truths: Women, Sexuality, and Gender in Classical Art and Archaeology.* New York and London.

Koniaris, G. 1968. "On Sappho fr. 31 (L-P)." *Philologus* 112: 173–86.

Konstan, D. and M. Nussbaum (eds.). 1990. *Sexuality in Greek and Roman Society.* Special Issue of *Differences* 2:1.

Laín Entralgo, P. 1970. *The Therapy of the Word in Classical Antiquity.* New Haven, CT.

Lanata, C. 1966. "Sul linguaggio amoroso di Saffo." *Quaderni Urbinati di Cultura Classica* 2: 63–79.

Larmour, D., Miller, P. A., and C. Platter (eds.). 1998. *Rethinking Sexuality: Foucault and Classical Antiquity.* Princeton, NJ.

Lasserre, F. 1974. "Ornements érotiques dans la poésie lyrique archaïque." In J. L. Heller (ed.), *Serta Turyniana*, 5–33. Urbana, IL.

Last, H. 1934. "The Social Policy of Augustus." *Cambridge Ancient History* 10: 425–64.

Lawler, L. B. 1948. "On Certain Homeric Epithets." *Philological Quarterly* 27: 80–4.

Lefkowitz, M. R. 1973. "Critical Stereotypes and the Poetry of Sappho." *Greek, Roman and Byzantine Studies* 14: 113–23.

——. 1981. *Heroines and Hysterics*. London.

——. and M. B. Fant (eds.). 1992. *Women's Life in Greece and Rome: A Source Book in Translation*. 2nd ed. Baltimore, MD.

Lévi-Strauss, C. 1966. *The Savage Mind*. Chicago.

——. 1969. *The Elementary Structures of Kinship*. Boston.

Lewis, I. M. 1971. *Ecstatic Religion*. Harmondsworth.

Licht, H. 1932. *Sexual Life in Ancient Greece*. London.

Liddell, H. G., Scott, R., and H. S. Jones. 1968. *A Greek–English Lexicon* (with Supplement). Oxford.

Lilja, S. 1965. *The Roman Elegists' Attitude to Women*. Helsinki.

Linton, R. 1942. "Age and Sex Categories." *American Sociological Review* 7: 589–602.

Lippard, L. 1977. "Quite Contrary: Body, Nature, Ritual in Women's Art." *Chrysalis* 2: 30–47.

Littlewood, A. R. 1968. "The Symbolism of the Apple in Greek and Roman Literature." *Harvard Studies in Classical Philology* 72: 147–81.

Littré, E. 1839–61. *Oeuvres complètes d'Hippocrate*. Paris.

Lloyd, G. E. R. 1975. "The Hippocratic Question." *Classical Quarterly* 25: 171–92.

———. 1979. *Magic, Reason and Experience*. Cambridge.

———. 1983. *Science, Folklore and Ideology*. Cambridge.

Lobel, E. and D. Page. 1955. *Poetarum Lesbiorum Fragmenta*. Oxford.

Loraux, N. 1978. "Sur la race des femmes et quelques-unes de ses tribus." *Arethusa* 11: 43–87.

———. 1981. "Le lit, la guerre." *L'Homme* 21: 37–67.

Luce, T. J. 1977. *Livy: The Composition of His History*. Princeton, NJ.

Luck, G. 1974. "The Woman's Role in Latin Love Poetry." In G. K. Galinsky (ed.), *Perspectives of Roman Poetry*. Austin, TX, 15–31.

Lugauer, M. 1967. "Untersuchungen zur Symbolik des Apfels in der Antike." Unpublished dissertation. Erlangen- Nürnburg.

Lyne, R. O. A. M. 1979. "Servitium Amoris." *Classical Quarterly* 29: 117–30.

———. 1980. *The Latin Love Poets: From Catullus to Horace*. Oxford.

MacCormack, G. 1975. "Wine-Drinking and the Romulan Law of Divorce." *Irish Jurist* 10: 170–4.

Maltomini, F. 1988. "P. Berol. 21243 (Formulario Magico): Due Nuove Letture." *Zeitschrift für Papyrologie und Epigraphik* 74: 247–8.

Manuli, P. 1980. "Fisiologia e Patologia del Femminile negli Scritti Ippocratici dell' Antica Ginecologia Greca." In M. D. Grmek (ed.), *Hippocratica. Actes du Colloque hippocratique de Paris*. September 4–9, 1978, 393–408. Paris.

Marry, J. D. 1979. "Sappho and the Heroic Ideal." *Arethusa* 12: 271–92.

McAuslan, I. and P. Walcot (eds.). 1996. *Women in Antiquity*. Oxford.

McCartney, E. S. 1925. "How the Apple Became the Token of Love." *Transactions of the American Philological Association* 56: 70–81.

McKeown, J. C. 1987. *Ovid: Amores*. Volume 1: *Text and Prolegomena*. Arca Classical and Medieval Texts, Papers and Monographs 20, Liverpool.

Merkelbach, R. 1957. "Sappho und ihr Kreis." *Philologus* 101: 1–29.

——— and M. L. West. 1967. *Fragmenta Hesiodea*. Oxford.

Merskey, H. 1979. *The Analysis of Hysteria*. London.

Meuli, K. 1975. *Gesammelte Schriften II*. Basle.

Mitchell, J. 1975. *Psychoanalysis and Feminism*. New York.

Modleski, T. 1988. *The Women Who Knew Too Much*. New York.

Motte, A. 1973. *Prairies et jardins de la Grèce antique*. Brussels.

Nagy, G. 1974. *Comparative Studies in Greek and Indic Meter*. Cambridge, MA.

Nethercut, W. R. 1970. "The Ironic Priest. Propertius' 'Roman Elegies' iii, 1–5: Imitations of Horace and Vergil." *American Journal of Philology* 91: 385–407.

Neuberger-Donath, R. 1969. "Sappho Fr. 1.1: POIKILOTHRON' oder POIKILOPHRON." *Wiener Studien* 82: 15–17.

Nilsson, M. 1961–7. *Geschichte der griechischen Religion.* 2 vols. Munich (I. von Müller (ed.), *Handbuch der Altertumswissenschaft* II, 1–2).

Nutton, V. 1986. "The Perils of Patriotism: Pliny and Roman Medicine." In R. French and F. Greenaway (eds.), *Science in the Early Roman Empire: Pliny the Elder, His Sources and Influence*, 30–58. London and Sydney.

Obbink, D. n.d. "Apples and Eros: Hesiod frag. 72–75 M.- W." Unpublished paper.

Ogilvie, R. M. 1965. *A Commentary on Livy, Books 1–5.* Oxford.

Ortner, S. B. 1978. "The Virgin and the State." *Feminist Studies* 4.3: 19–35.

Padel, R. 1983. "Women: Model for Possession by Greek Daemons." In A. Cameron and A. Kuhrt (eds.), *Images of Women in Antiquity*, 3–19. London. (2nd ed. 1993, Detroit, MI).

Page, D. 1955. *Sappho and Alcaeus.* Oxford.

——. (ed.). 1962. *Poetae Melici Graeci.* Oxford.

Papanghelis, T. 1987. *Propertius: A Hellenistic Poet on Love and Death.* Cambridge.

Parker, H. (n.d.). "Metrodora: The Earliest Surviving Work by a Woman Doctor." Unpublished manuscript.

Paul, G. M. 1966. "Sallust." In T. A. Dorey (ed.), *Latin Historians.* London and New York.

Peradotto, J., and J. P. Sullivan (eds.). 1984. *Women in the Ancient World: The Arethusa Papers.* Buffalo, NY.

Pfeiffer, R. 1968. *History of Classical Scholarship – From the Beginning to the End of the Hellenistic Age.* Oxford.

Pfohl, S. 1990. "The Terror of the Simulacra: Struggles for Justice and the Postmodern." In S. Pfohl (ed.), *New Directions in the Study of Justice, Law, and Social Control*, 207–63. New York.

Phillipides, S. N. 1983. "Narrative Strategies and Ideology in Livy's 'Rape of Lucretia.'" *Helios* 10: 113–19.

Phillips, J. 1982. "Current Research in Livy's First Decade: 1959–1979." *Aufsteig und Niedergang der Römischer Welt* 30.2: 998–1057.

Pinault, J. R. 1992. "The Medical Case for Virginity in the Early Second Century CE: Soranus of Ephesus, *Gynecology* 1.32." *Helios* 19: 123–39.

Pomeroy, S. 1975. *Goddesses, Whores, Wives and Slaves.* New York.

——. 1991. "The Study of Women in Antiquity: Past, Present, and Future." *American Journal of Philology* 112: 263–8.

——. (ed.). 1991. *Women's History and Ancient History.* Chapel Hill, NC.

Porter, J. (ed.). 1999. *Constructions of the Classical Body.* Ann Arbor, MI.

Privitera, G. A. 1969. "Ambiguità antitesi analogia nel fr. 31 L-P di Saffo." *Quaderni Urbinati di Cultura Classica* 8: 37–80.

Pucci, P. 1977. *Hesiod and the Language of Poetry.* Baltimore, MD.

Putnam, M. 1960/1. "*Throna* and Sappho 1.1." *Classical Journal* 56: 79–83.

Raaflaub, K. A. 1986. "The Conflict of the Orders in Archaic Rome: A Comprehensive and Comparative Approach." In K. A. Raaflaub (ed.), *Social Struggles in Archaic Rome*, 1–51. Berkeley, CA.

Rabinowitz, N. and A. Richlin (eds.). 1993. *Feminist Theory and the Classics.* New York and London.

Rackham, H., Jones, W. H. S., and D. E. Eichholz (eds. and trans.). 1938–63. *Pliny: Natural History.* 10 vols. Loeb Classical Library. Cambridge, MA.

Redfield, J. 1977. "The Women of Sparta." *Classical Journal* 73: 141–61.

Richlin, A. 1981. "Approaches to the Sources on Adultery at Rome." In H. P. Foley (ed.), *Reflections of Women in Antiquity,* 379–404.

——. 1984. "Invective Against Women in Roman Satire." *Arethusa* 17: 67–80.

——. 1991. "Zeus and Metis: Foucault, Feminism, Classics." *Helios* 18: 160–79.

——. [1983] 1992. *The Garden of Priapus: Sexuality and Aggression in Roman Humor.* Rev. ed. New York.

——. 1992. "Julia's Jokes, Galla Placidia, and the Roman Use of Women as Political Icons." In B. Garlick, S. Dixon, and P. Allen (eds.), *Stereotypes of Women in Power,* 63–91. New York.

——. (ed.) 1992. *Pornography and Representation in Greece and Rome.* New York and Oxford.

——. 1992. "Reading Ovid's Rapes." In A. Richlin (ed.), *Pornography and Representation in Greece and Rome,* 158–79, Oxford.

——. 1993. "The Ethnographer's Dilemma and the Dream of a Lost Golden Age." In N. Rabinowitz and A. Richlin (eds.), *Feminist Theory and the Classics,* 272–303. New York and London.

——. 1997. "Carrying Water in a Sieve: Class and the Body in Roman Women's Religion." In K. King (ed.), *Women and Goddesses,* 00–00. Philadelphia, PA.

Riddle, J. M. 1992. *Contraception and Abortion from the Ancient World to the Renaissance.* Cambridge.

——, Estes, J. W., and J. C. Russell. 1994. "Birth Control in the Ancient World." *Archaeology* Mar./Apr.: 29–35.

Rissman, L. 1983. *Love as War: Homeric Allusion in the Poetry of Sappho.* Königstein.

Rolfe, J. C. 1914. *Suetonius.* 2 vols. Loeb Classical Library. Cambridge, MA.

Rousselle, A. 1980. "Observation féminine et idéologie masculin: le corps de la femme d'après les médecins grecs." *Annales ESC* 35: 1089–115.

——. 1988. *Porneia: On Desire and the Body in Antiquity.* Trans. F. Pheasant. Oxford.

Rowlandson, J. 1998. *Women and Society in Greek and Roman Egypt.* Cambridge.

Russo, J. 1973–4. "Reading the Greek Lyric Poets (Monodists)." *Arion* 1: 707–30.

Saake, H. 1971. *Zur Kunst Sapphos.* Munich.

Schadewaldt, W. 1936. "Zu Sappho." *Hermes* 71: 363–73.

Schaps, D. 1982. "The Women of Greece in Wartime." *Classical Philology* 77: 193–213.

Schmitt, P. 1977. "Athene Apatouria et la ceinture." *Annales ESC* 32: 1059–73.

Scott, J. 1986. "Gender: A Useful Category of Historical Analysis." *American History Review* 91: 1053–75.

Shaw, M. 1975. "The Female Intruder: Women in Fifth-Century Drama." *Classical Philology* 70: 255–66.

Silverman, K. 1980. "Masochism and Subjectivity." *Frameworks* 12: 2–9.

Simon, B. 1978. *Mind and Madness in Ancient Greece.* Ithaca, NY.

Skinner, M. 1983. "Clodia Metelli." *Transactions of the American Philological Association* 113: 273–87.

——. 1986. "Rescuing Creusa: New Approaches to Women in Antiquity." *Helios* 13:2: 1–8.

——. (ed.). 1986. *Rescuing Creusa: New Methodological Approaches to Women in Antiquity.* Special issue of *Helios* 13.2. Lubbock, TX.

——. 1987. "Classical Studies, Patriarchy and Feminism: The View from 1986." *Women's International Studies Forum* 10.2: 181–6.

——. 1993. "*Ego Mulier*: The Construction of Male Sexuality in Catullus." *Helios* 20: 107–30.

——. 1993. "Woman and Language in Archaic Greece, or, Why Is Sappho a Woman?" In N. Rabinowitz and A. Richlin (eds.), *Feminist Theory and the Classics*, 125–44. New York and London.

——. 1996. "Zeus and Leda: The Sexuality Wars in Contemporary Classical Scholarship." *Thamyris* 3: 103–23.

Slater, P. 1992. *The Glory of Hera: Greek Mythology and the Greek Family.* Princeton, NJ.

Snell, B. 1931. "Sapphos Gedicht *phainetai moi kênos.*" *Hermes* 66: 71–90.

Soren, D. 1999. "Hecate and the Infant Cemetery at Poggio Gramignano." In D. Soren and N. Soren (eds.), *A Roman Villa and Late Roman Infant Cemetery: Excavation at Poggio Gramignano (Lugnano in Teverina)*, 619–31. Rome.

Soren, D., Fenton, T., Birkby, W., and R. Jensen. 1999. "The Infant Cemetery at Poggio Gramignano: Description and Analysis." In D. Soren and N. Soren (eds.), *A Roman Villa and Late Roman Infant Cemetery: Excavation at Poggio Gramignano (Lugnano in Teverina), Italy*, 477–530. Rome.

Stahl, H.-P. 1985. *Propertius: "Love" and "War." Individual and State under Augustus.* Berkeley and Los Angeles, CA.

Stambolian, G. and E. Marks (eds.), 1979. *Homosexualities and French Literature.* Ithaca, NY and London.

Stanley, K. 1976. "The Role of Aphrodite in Sappho Fr. 1." *Greek Roman and Byzantine Studies* 17: 305–21.

Stehle, E. 1977. "Retreat from the Male: Catullus 62 and Sappho's Erotic Flowers." *Ramus* 6: 83–102.

——. 1979. "Romantic Sensuality, Poetic Sense: A Response to Hallett on Sappho." *Signs* 4: 464–71.

Stewart, A. 1997. *Art, Desire and the Body in Ancient Greece.* Cambridge.

Sullivan, J. 1976. *Propertius. A Critical Introduction.* Cambridge.

Svenbro, J. 1975. "Sappho and Diomedes." *Museum Philologum Londoniense* 1: 37–49.

Syme, R. 1959. "Livy and Augustus." *Harvard Studies in Classical Philology* 64: 27–87.

Temkin, O. (trans.) [1956] 1991. *Soranus' Gynecology.* Baltimore, MD and London.

Theweleit, K. 1987. *Male Fantasies.* Vol. 1. Trans. S. Conway. Minneapolis, MN.

Trachtenberg, J. [1939] 1961. *Jewish Magic and Superstition.* Cleveland, OH.

Trumpf, J. 1960. "Kydonische Apfel." *Hermes* 88: 14–22.

Turyn, A. 1942. "The Sapphic Ostracon." *Transactions of the American Philological Association* 73: 308–18.

Van Straten, F. T. 1981. "Gifts for the Gods." In H. Versnel (ed.), *Faith, Hope and Worship*, 65–151. Leiden.

Vatin, C. 1970. *Recherches sur le mariage et la condition de la femme mariée à l' époque hellénistique.* Paris.

Vernant, J.-P. 1968. Introduction to *Problèmes de la guerre en Grèce ancienne.* Paris.

——. 1974. "Le mariage." In *Mythe et société en Grèce ancienne*, 57–81. Paris [*Myth and Society in Ancient Greece*, trans. J. Lloyd, Oxford, 1980].

——. 1979–80. Cours. *Annuaire du Collège de France*, 435–66.

——. 1983. *Myth and Thought among the Greeks.* Boston and London.

Veyne, P. 1983. *L' Elégie érotique romaine.* Paris.

Vidal-Naquet, P. 1986. *The Black Hunter: Forms of Thought and Forms of Society in the Greek World.* Trans. A. Szegedy-Maszak. Baltimore, MD.

von Staden, H. 1991. "*Apud nos foediora verba*: Celsus' Reluctant Construction of the Female Body." In G. Sabbagh (ed.), *Le Latin médical: La Constitution d'un langage Scientifique*, Mémoirs du Centre Jean Palerne, 10, 271–96. Saint-Étienne.

——. 1992. "Women and Dirt." *Helios* 19: 7–30.

Wallace-Hadrill, A. 1985. "Propaganda and Dissent?" *Klio* 67: 180–4.

Walsh, P. G. 1961. *Livy: His Historical Aims and Methods.* Cambridge.

Watson, A. 1975. *Rome of the XII Tables.* Princeton, NJ.

Wegner, J. R. 1991. "The Image and Status of Women in Classical Rabbinic Judaism." In J. R. Baskin (ed.), *Jewish Women in Historical Perspective*, 94–114. Detroit, MI.

Weissler, C. 1991. "Prayers in Yiddish and the Religious World of Ashkenazic Women." In J. R. Baskin (ed.), *Jewish Women in Historical Perspective*, 159–81. Detroit, MI.

West, M. L. 1970. "Burning Sappho." *Maia* 22: 307–30.

Williams, G. 1958. "Some Aspects of Marriage Ceremonies and Ideals." *Journal of Roman Studies* 48: 16–29.

——. 1968. *Tradition and Originality in Roman Poetry.* Oxford.

Wills, G. 1967. "The Sapphic 'Umwertung aller Werte.'" *American Journal of Philology* 88: 434–42.

Wimmel, W. 1960. *Kallimachos in Rom*. Hermes Einzelschriften 16, Wiesbaden.
Winkler, J. J. 1990. *The Constraints of Desire: The Anthropology of Sex and Gender in Ancient Greece*. New York and London.
Wirth, P. 1963. "Neue Spuren eines Sapphobruchstücks." *Hermes* 91: 115–17.
Woolf, V. [1929] 1957. *A Room of One's Own*. New York.
Wyke, M. 1987. "The Elegiac Woman at Rome." *Proceedings of the Cambridge Philological Society* 213, n. s. 33: 153–78.
——. 1987. "Written Women: Propertius' Scripta Puella." *Journal of Roman Studies* 77: 47–61.
——. (ed.) 1998. *Parchments of Gender: Deciphering the Body in Antiquity.* Oxford.
——. 1989. "Reading Female Flesh: *Amores* 3.1." In A. Cameron (ed.), *History as Text: The Writing of Ancient History*, 113–43. London.
Zweig, B. 1993. "The Primal Mind: Using Native American Models for the Study of Women in Ancient Greece." In N. Rabinowitz and A. Richlin (eds.), *Feminist Theory and the Classics*, 145–80. New York and London.

Index